PRESERVED

PRESERVED

A CULTURAL HISTORY OF THE FUNERAL HOME IN AMERICA

DEAN G. LAMPROS

Johns Hopkins University Press | Baltimore

To my parents, who taught me to
love cultural landscapes

To the nation's funeral directors, the unsung heroes
of historic preservation

And to Joe, who dragged me to New Bedford
that autumn day

Johns Hopkins University Press
2715 North Charles Street
Baltimore, Maryland 21218
www.press.jhu.edu

Library of Congress Cataloging-in-Publication Data is available.

A catalog record for this book is available from the British Library.

ISBN 978-1-4214-4840-4 (hardcover)
ISBN 978-1-4214-4841-1 (ebook)

*Special discounts are available for bulk purchases of this book. For more information, please
contact Special Sales at specialsales@jh.edu.*

CONTENTS

ACKNOWLEDGMENTS

This book was more than twenty years in the making and got its start in the autumn of 2003. Back then I was working in alumni relations at Boston University's School of Theology during the day and taking courses in historic preservation at night. I had been a graduate student in Boston University's American and New England Studies Program in the early 1990s but withdrew to study music in Greece. When I returned to Boston, however, I decided not to reenter my doctoral program. I'd been conducting ethnographic research among Greater Boston's Greek and Armenian Protestant communities, but toward the end of my graduate coursework I made the decision to come out. I wasn't sure that being openly gay was a good fit for the evangelical-oriented congregations I'd been studying, and keeping my sexual orientation hidden for the sake of my research was not an option.

In 2003 I decided to use Boston University's generous tuition remission benefit offered to employees and their families to take some courses in the Preservation Studies Program, which shared a suite with American and New England Studies. I was already familiar with the program, because during my first time around as a graduate student I'd taken practically all of my elective courses in what was then called vernacular architecture with Richard Candee, who at the time was the director of Preservation Studies, and Abbott Lowell Cummings, the guru of New England's first-period architecture and timber-framed houses. All of those credits, I learned, were easily transferred into the Preservation Studies Program. I figured that in lieu of a PhD in American studies, I'd get an MA in preservation studies, after which I'd go to work for a nonprofit or perhaps even the Massachusetts Historical Commission.

The introductory seminar I took in the autumn of 2003 was structured around a series of guest speakers. One of them was Tony Souza, the director of the Waterfront Historic Area League (WHALE) of New Bedford, Massachusetts, who spoke to our class about adaptive use. Having grown up north of Boston, I'd never had much reason to visit New Bedford, but after class that night I told my husband, Joe Teja, about WHALE and the exciting things happening along the New Bedford waterfront. A few weeks later he announced one Saturday afternoon that we were going to New Bedford. He had a craving for Cape Verdean food and thought it would be fun for us to explore the downtown and waterfront to see all the things I'd learned about in class.

I'd had a long week and wasn't in the mood to go exploring. I just wanted to stay home and take it easy. I had a few chores around the house and some reading to do, so I suggested that perhaps it would be better if we went the following weekend. Joe wouldn't take no for an answer, however, and soon I found myself in the passenger seat as we sped down Route 24 toward New Bedford. As we entered the city we passed through block after block of triple-deckers, but as we neared the downtown we found ourselves in an area in which Victorian houses and beautiful old churches mixed with filling stations and convenient stores, fast-food restaurants, and parking lots. I felt saddened by the amount of commercial infill in an area that had clearly once been a refined residential district, but then a grand Italianate mansion caught my eye, the best preserved by far of all the structures in the vicinity. On the front lawn stood a sign stating that the structure was a funeral home. That's when the proverbial light bulb above my head turned on.

In that instant, I thought about how for every one historic house museum that might exist in any given city or town, there were likely half a dozen or more funeral homes housed in old mansions. I thought about all the funeral homes I remembered from my childhood and adolescence in Lynn, Massachusetts. I thought about the Landergan Funeral Home, where my maternal grandmother's wake had been held in 1987. Back then the establishment was housed in a beautiful Colonial Revival dwelling situated in Lynn's Diamond District, which even in my grief I was able to admire. As I thought about these structures, I realized that I had no idea how this particular kind of adaptive use had come about. When and why had funeral homes come to occupy vintage dwellings? I understood that this was a story that hadn't been told. And I understood that I would be the one to tell it.

There are many people besides Joe who had a hand in bringing this story to life. I eventually pitched the idea to Claire Dempsey, who took over as the director of the Preservation Studies Program during my second stint as a graduate student. She listened intently to the story of my trip to New Bedford, looked me in the eye, and told me that I needed to transfer my credits back into American studies, petition the university to be readmitted as a doctoral student, and write up my prospectus. Richard Candee, by then emeritus, and William Moore, an associate professor of history and material culture who headed my dissertation committee as first and second readers, were an unending source of wisdom and support. I am proud to have been molded by my time in Boston University's American and New England Studies Program (both times actually) and by the faculty who instructed and guided me; these include Peter Berger, Richard Fox, Marilyn Halter, Keith Morgan, Anita Patterson, Jessica Sewell, Kim Sichel, Nina Silber, and Shirley Wajda. Each of them played a role in shaping me into the scholar and the person I am today. It was a great privilege to be taught by them.

I offer special thanks to Louisa Iarocci at the University of Washington for her interest in my work and for giving me an opportunity to highlight the funeral home as a part of the story of American consumer culture. My exploration of the funeral home as a feature of the nation's decentralized consumer landscape along with my research into its role in the birth of American zoning was presented at several conferences, and I am indebted to the many participants who asked tough questions and offered valuable feedback. I am equally grateful to Laura Davulis and Johns Hopkins University Press for giving me the opportunity to tell this story.

Although my research led me to digital collections of newspapers, out-of-print books, legal documents, and photographs, this book would never have been written without Thomas Parmalee, former executive editor, and Tanya Kenevich, former associate editor of Kates-Boylston Publications, who opened up the company's archives in New Jersey, where I spent hours poring over dozens of bound volumes of *The American Funeral Director*. In those pages, I became acquainted with the first generation of funeral directors who left congested downtowns during the interwar period and boldly pushed into residential neighborhoods, preserving countless Victorian dwellings in the process and creating what would become an iconic feature of the nation's cultural landscape.

Finally, I would like to thank the many generous and hospitable funeral directors who shared historic photographs and stories and opened their beautiful and impressive establishments to me. I have had the pleasure of touring funeral homes in Massachusetts, New Hampshire, Pennsylvania, West Virginia, Maryland, Delaware, and Michigan. The pride and love that these men and women feel for their funeral homes and the hard work and precious resources that go into maintaining these historic structures remind us that cultural landscapes survive because of the people who care for and about them.

THE OTHER PRESERVATION

G ossip spreads the news even before the sign is placed on the manicured lawn of the house that sold last fall on this tree-lined residential street. The Victorian dwellings here are grand but worn. It is 1925. There are newer, more fashionable neighborhoods farther afield and accessible by automobile or streetcar. This one is too close to the edge of the downtown and much too old-fashioned for the smart set, but for the respectable families who call it home, it is the picture of upper-middle-class cozy domesticity, refinement, and gentility even if, they are reluctant to admit to themselves, it has an aura of faded glory.

One of the downtown undertakers—all of the undertaking parlors are downtown—has purchased the house. Everyone knew it had been on the market. The grown children of the previous owners, now deceased, are all established in homes of their own elsewhere, some even in other cities. It was never really expected that they would move back and take over the family home. What was also never expected was that an undertaker would move in; and not just move in but also set up shop there.

Of course, when a neighbor dies, it's perfectly normal for the hearse to show up at the home of the deceased. A casket is carried in and out. The street fills up with the automobiles of mourners. After all, where else would the viewing be held? Downtown funeral chapels are only for out-of-town strangers with no family nearby. Downtown is where one goes to pick out a casket and burial clothes for a loved one, but the body of the deceased is always prepared at home and laid out in the parlor. It's a sad affair but a natural and inevitable part of life and thankfully rare. What is unnatural, unheard of, and intolerable is a funeral parlor on a residential street. Hearses and caskets on a daily basis. The street perpetually choked with traffic. Mournful hymns played morning, noon, and night, a constant reminder of death. Corpses in the basement. Foul odors. Flies.

Around the time of the First World War, enterprising undertakers throughout the United States brazenly began acquiring stately old mansions in aging residential neighborhoods at the edge of downtown business districts. After carrying out a series of interior renovations to outfit their new quarters, undertakers set out their shingles, advertised in the local papers, and held open houses. Soon after, they often found themselves hauled into court facing lawsuits as neighboring homeowners cried foul and argued that an undertaking parlor on a residential street constituted a nuisance. Sometimes their ambitious plans were upended when cities and towns took matters into their own hands, hastily passing ordinances barring mortuaries from residential zones.

What motivated the nation's undertakers to undertake such a costly and often controversial move? For starters, undertakers, already maligned in the popular imagination, recruited mansions to elevate a trade with roots in the livery stable to the status of an exalted profession. For African American undertakers, the stakes were even higher. By moving into homes and neighborhoods that were once the exclusive domain of white elites, they simultaneously uplifted their industry and undermined the landscape of white supremacy. As savvy retailers, undertakers nationwide also saw in mansions the kind of sumptuous shopping environment believed to stimulate consumer desire for luxury burial goods. Additionally, a quiet and spacious homelike atmosphere could help pry the funeral service from the home of the deceased, which would allow undertakers to exercise greater control over the funeralization process and help reduce their overhead. Finally, a residential setting offered far more space for parking than was available in any bustling and congested downtown. In fact, funeral directors were among the nation's earliest merchants to recognize that automobility portended a future for commerce beyond the confines of the downtown. The funeral home was both harbinger and pioneer of the decentralized consumer landscape.

While modern purpose-built mortuaries replaced converted mansions as the dominant trend within the deathcare industry at the end of the twentieth century, many funeral homes continue to occupy grand old structures that began their lives generations ago as single-family dwellings. What is striking about this hidden history is that in virtually every instance the conversion of mansion to funeral home was made without a preservationist intent or consciousness. Even today, mention the word "preservation" to a funeral director, and the conversation will quickly turn to embalming. Remodeling mansions into funeral homes constitutes a kind of inadvertent or accidental preservation, meaning a preservation effect was achieved without a preservation intent. Accidental preservation often includes what preservationists call "adaptive use"; that is, when an existing structure that has outlived its usefulness is redeveloped and repurposed for a new and different use. Long-abandoned mills become artist lofts, churches become luxury condominiums, train stations become art museums, and mansions become funeral homes. Of all the different types of adaptive use projects that have taken place in the United States, the conversion of home to funeral home is one of the most widespread and iconic.

As uses change, structures change with them, and a new use can breathe new life into a tired old structure even if the new use is a funeral home. At its heart, this book is about the intersection of a particular use with a particular type of structure within a particular landscape. Each and every cultural landscape is more than simply an assemblage of man-made structures and natural features. Cultural landscapes are also constellations of changing uses and meanings. This book explores three overlapping and evolving landscapes; namely the landscape of professional deathcare, America's changing residential landscape, and the landscape of mass consumption. During the interwar period, cities and towns witnessed professional deathcare's shift from a largely downtown landscape—even in rural villages, the undertaker was located along Main Street—to a predominantly residential landscape. The residential landscapes in which funeral directors sought new quarters were themselves changing, moreover, as commercial districts spilled over their borders into adjacent neighborhoods. This in turn unleashed a new type of consumer landscape whose principal feature was not proximity to the downtown but rather the availability of parking. Each of these threads is woven into the fabric of the residential funeral home.

I have relied heavily on the fields of vernacular architecture and material culture to shed light on how funeral homes have been consistently used to communicate meaning and construct identity. In other words, funeral directors chose mansions not merely for their utilitarian function but because of the symbolic value they possessed. Funeral homes have functioned in the dimension that Christian Norberg-Shulz calls the social milieu, where "the building 'transcends' the functional frame to materially express such things as economic status, inclusion in or exclusion from a group, [or] a particular role in society."[1] Beyond the specific symbolic qualities possessed by mansions, their residential context was meant to surround the funeral home with an aura of domesticity as a means of setting it apart from its downtown competitors.

Throughout the twentieth century, funeral homes became sites of contested meaning as neighbors, reformers, civic leaders, and judges created their own meanings. Being housed in mansions meant, for example, that funeral homes were, for some consumers at least, less evocative of their living rooms and more reminiscent of the grand and lavish public spaces found in department stores, hotels, restaurants, and cinemas. For many neighbors they were simply a nuisance. Nonetheless, funeral directors knew what they wanted, and by choosing spacious older dwellings, they ended up preserving the structures themselves and something of the residential character of a street in the midst of a transition from residential to commercial. They were also preserving an older—and largely discredited—housing ideal that valued strict spatial boundaries, formality, grace, and grandeur over the simplicity and relaxed informality that had become a national obsession shared by architects, builders, and homeowners alike after the First World War. This was true for converted mansions and purpose-built, residential-style mortuaries too. The spaces chosen and created by funeral directors contrasted sharply with newer residential dwellings in form, size, style, and interior arrangement. They offered a tacit critique of the progressive ideals and values shaping new construction, a set of ideals that for funeral directors was too closely associated with the simplicity championed by the funeral reformers.

During the first half of the twentieth century, funeral directors saw beauty and utility in the Victorian architecture that was reviled by so many, including historic preservationists.[2] Victorian houses were deemed garish and not worth saving and, as a result, were passed over in favor of the architectural heritage of colonial America. By the 1920s when the Society for the Preservation of New England Antiquities was still in its infancy, the number of nineteenth-century mansions that had been converted into funeral homes was likely already in the thousands. The Victorian Society of America wasn't founded until 1966, by which time funeral directors had already been preserving Victorian dwellings, albeit accidentally, through adaptive use for half a century. The decades between 1916 and 1966—the year in which the National Historic Preservation Act was passed by the US Congress and signed into law by Lyndon B. Johnson—witnessed the emergence of numerous preservation societies, the creation of local historic districts, and legislation at both the federal and state levels, all developments recognized by historians of the American preservation movement. If one were to consider the recycling of countless Victorian dwellings by funeral directors during the same time span, it could be argued that the funeral industry had at least as great a preservation impact and in an area largely neglected by mainstream preservationists. American funeral directors truly were—and in many ways still are—the unsung heroes of historic preservation.

Nevertheless, those who study the American preservation movement have been slow to acknowledge the impact of the funeral industry. One possible reason for this is that with the exception of the historic house museum, adaptive use does not occupy a prominent position in the historiography of preservation.[3] Because funeral homes have gone largely unnoticed, the handful of preservationists and field-workers who have begun to take notice of funeral homes deserve some mention. A 2001 article titled "An Unheralded Preservation Influence" in *Cultural Resource Management*, the National Park Service's journal of heritage stewardship, recognizes funeral directors as preservationists and explores "why the adaptive re-use of large vintage properties has been embraced by the modern funeral industry."[4] The authors suggest that issues of size, cost, and declining property values in certain urban neighborhoods during the first half of the twentieth century all played a role in the decision of funeral directors to move to remodeled mansions. The authors' principal concern, however, is with domesticity and the homelike qualities retained by the rehabilitated structures.

Some research has also been done on nineteenth-century purpose-built mortuaries,[5] but even within the sizable body of literature covering the American way of death, the material setting in which funeral directors operate has for the most part been neglected.[6] It is curious that the history of the American funeral industry has been written with hardly a mention of physical space. Over the past three decades, deathcare studies have explored the ceremonies and services offered by the funeral industry and the professionals who have performed them but not the spaces that have accommodated them. Historians have focused on the work of funeral directors and their socioeconomic and cultural contexts—including changing attitudes toward death and the medicalization and commercialization of death and dying—but not on the spatial setting within which practitioners have operated, the significance of that spatial setting for both industry professionals and the public, or the industry's impact on the built environment.

This lack of attention to the funeral industry's material setting is puzzling, given the prominent role of material culture—stuff, in other words—alongside services within professional deathcare. Truly, it is a combination of goods, services, and spaces that has historically defined the transaction between funeral directors and consumers. At least one major element of that transaction has been neglected by historians of the funeral industry. The historiography of the American way of death cannot be considered complete without a broad study of the changing landscape of professional deathcare. Up to now, there has never been a deep exploration of the spaces within which funeral directors have performed their work and interacted with the public. This book is a step in that direction.

What the existing corpus on the American way of death has provided are invaluable narrative elements that allow one to piece together the development of the modern funeral industry: its beginnings during the American Civil War, through the spread of embalming during the late nineteenth century and the subsequent rise of undertaking establishments, usually as a sideline to cabinetmaking or the livery stable, and finally to the middle of the twentieth century, when funeral homes emerged as the principal setting for memorial services.[7]

My goal is neither to rewrite the history of the American funeral industry nor to take sides in the debate over its relative merit or lack thereof. The industry has already been attacked and defended to death (so to speak), and while I attempt to shed some light on the evolution of professional deathcare by looking at its material setting, I also look to the industry itself for clues on the meanings attached to its spaces. Along the way, I offer neither an indictment nor an apology. I do not endeavor to solve the ever-present riddle of friend or fiend when it comes to the industry and its practitioners. Instead, what interests me is how this discourse has shaped the industry's decisions about space.[8] Regardless of which side one takes, what the majority of deathcare historians have in common is that they attempt to address the shift from home funeral to funeral home while saying next to nothing about the industry's shift from downtown to residential neighborhood. There is reasonable consensus that the shift from home funeral to funeral home took place gradually between 1920 and the end of the Second World War. Virtually all agree that prior to 1920, the majority of wakes and funerals took place at the home of the deceased. The existence of funeral homes as an option for the bereaved after 1920 is, however, simply taken for granted, never analyzed.

While various factors have been cited to explain the demise of the home funeral, such as the "privatization of the family,"[9] the "shifting space of dying,"[10] and the medicalization of death,[11] changes to domestic architecture are also frequently discussed, with shrinking living quarters and the disappearance of the parlor being given special prominence. James Farrell argues that "by the time that funeral directors began to build funeral parlors, the domestic parlor was becoming an anachronism,"[12] and Gary Laderman refers specifically to "the disappearance of the parlor."[13] Leroy Bowman is more concerned with size and argues that "parlors or living rooms were too small to accommodate the visitors at the wake and funeral assemblages."[14] Similarly, Robert Habenstein and William Lamers point to "the smallness of the quarters" in apartment houses.[15]

While changes to domestic architecture certainly played a role in the shift from home funeral to funeral home, the precise nature of the changes that most affected families and funeral directors has been little understood. I believe that it was not the disappearance of the parlor but rather the disappearance of the entrance hall that mattered most to funeral directors. Moreover, during the first two decades of the twentieth century, it was the loss of formality, not a loss of square footage, that presented the greatest blow to the home funeral. In other words, smaller accommodations were not the problem; less formal domestic arrangements were.[16]

In examining the dominant middle-class housing types from the 1920s, it quickly becomes apparent that the qualities promoted by architects and homebuilders and most prized by middle-class Americans were absent in the large Victorian mansions so eagerly sought by funeral directors. This is one of the reasons why funeral directors chose them. Similarly, most new houses built after 1915 lacked the spatial features, such as well-articulated partitions between rooms, that helped funeral directors transform home funerals into orderly affairs. Kenneth Ames's research on entrance halls and hall furnishings offers a way of understanding the nature and use of a domestic space that was present in the older houses chosen by funeral directors but largely absent from newly built middle-class dwellings after 1920.[17]

Understanding the rise of the residential funeral home requires an analysis of both push and pull factors. This is true whether one is looking at the shift from downtown to residential neighborhood or the shift from home funeral to funeral home. In other words, there were factors that pushed funeral establishments out of the business district, just as there were factors that pushed the funeral service out of the home of the deceased. Driving both of these developments, however, were also pull factors that drew funeral directors to residential neighborhoods and the public, in the fullness of time, to funeral homes. Those who have touched upon the funeral home write about the importance of domesticity, but the discussion begins and ends with its mere mention. It is not enough—or possibly correct at all—to say that domesticity was the chief draw of the mansions into which funeral directors relocated from their downtown locations. This oversimplification has meant that the shift from downtown to residential district has been virtually ignored. As a result, there has never been an attempt by any historian of American deathcare to explain why mansions in residential neighborhoods were so aggressively sought by funeral directors or why consumers chose to relinquish the custom of the home funeral, as opposed to having their changing living quarters choose for them.

It is here that several narratives converge. The story of the emergence, proliferation, and eventual acceptance by consumers of the residential funeral home as a ritual space offers more than simply a missing chapter within the history of the American funeral industry.[18]

It is also a story deeply rooted in American consumer culture and the recurring tension between democratized luxury and extravagance, on one hand, and simplicity and restraint, on the other. It is a story whose context is a blend of changing ideas about the family home amid an evolving and contested residential landscape. Above all, the story of the residential funeral home demonstrates the cultural power of spaces and landscapes and how they are used to construct identity and convey legitimacy.

By the early twentieth century, funeral directors and consumers alike were well versed in what historian Katherine Grier has described as "the material vocabulary of gentility."[19] Seeking to cast off their lowly origins in the livery stable and cabinetmaking shop and reinforce their professional identity, funeral directors put mansions to work for them. One reason why they chose grand old dwellings long associated with an area's elites was to capitalize on the communicative ability and the symbolic value that mansions were believed to possess. Funeral directors were attempting to convey something about themselves, their work, and the nature of the goods and services they were offering, and they enlisted mansions to accomplish this task.

African American funeral directors also understood the communicative power of spaces and landscapes. Throughout the American South they acquired vintage dwellings once owned by white elites in neighborhoods that were historically segregated. They were concerned, as was every funeral director, with their industry's tarnished public image,[20] and they turned to mansions to uplift what was regarded as a trade to the status of an esteemed profession. African American funeral directors were well aware, however, that by moving into spaces and landscapes once occupied exclusively by whites, they were challenging racial hierarchies and undermining white supremacy. Their funeral homes were a source of great pride within the African American community, for they were physical, tangible monuments to how their community had crossed the color line.

Within the pages of their industry publications, such as the *American Funeral Director, Casket and Sunnyside*, the *Embalmers Monthly*, and the *Colored Embalmer*, funeral directors nationwide regularly discussed the nature of the residential spaces into which they were shifting their operations and the messages they wished to convey to a wary public. Advertising and marketing materials offer important clues as well. Grant McCracken writes at length about the role of advertising in transferring meaning from the culturally constituted world to material objects and consumer goods by bringing the object "and a representation of the culturally constituted world together within the frame of a particular advertisement."[21] Funeral directors were relying on what they felt was the clear, well-established symbolic value that venerable old mansions held in the mind of the general public. Funeral directors hoped, moreover, that the positive qualities associated with mansions—dignity, respectability, prestige, grandeur, comfort, and luxury—would attach to not only their work but also the goods and services they sold.

Situated within the landscape, funeral homes served as three-dimensional advertisements for luxury burial goods. Two-dimensional images of funeral homes in newspaper advertisements displayed what was being offered while simultaneously offering a symbolic representation of luxury. In other words, the structure was both what was being advertised, as a setting for the services, and a marketing tool to sell high-end goods and services to consumers. Images alone were not enough, however. The juxtaposition of architectural renderings and photographs of funeral homes alongside carefully worded text in advertisements helped reinforce the specific messages that funeral directors were trying to convey.[22] Time and again, the message was that funeral directors were not just offering luxury goods but an opulence that was "within the means of all."[23] This was democratized luxury.

It was no accident that the shift from storefront to mansion took place during a period that witnessed an orgy of consumption.[24] Additionally, recent works on the history of department stores and hotels shed new light on the grand public spaces with which funeral homes had something in common.[25] In their own writings, funeral directors displayed a keen awareness of the connection between sumptuous spaces and the marketing of luxury goods. They sought to harness what they saw as increased consumer demand for a wide range of luxury items and take utmost advantage of the link between selling and setting to foster demand for a higher class of funeral goods. To do this, they needed two things. First, they needed retail spaces that would encourage the purchase of an expensive casket. Next, they needed to exert greater control over the funeral than the home of the deceased allowed. Mansions provided both.

Industry publications and advertisements cover only one side of the equation, however. Funeral homes, like virtually every component of the built environment, have been sites of contested meaning. This is also true of sacred spaces, government buildings, schools, prisons, factories, shopping malls, banks, hotels, skyscrapers, private dwellings, apartment houses, housing projects, and highways. Rarely is there consensus about the meaning and value of the various kinds of created spaces that constitute the built environment. Funeral homes are no different. I am interested in the variety of responses to funeral homes, not just the intended meanings constructed by funeral directors.

The numerous court cases that resulted when funeral directors attempted to move their businesses from commercial districts into long-established residential neighborhoods provide an invaluable source of information on the meanings attached to funeral homes by members of the general public. The transition from downtown to mansion was risky and did not go unchallenged. A funeral director who attempted to relocate to a residential district risked conflict with both the neighbors and the municipal government. Zoning ordinances, which began to appear after the First World War, and the common law pertaining to "private nuisances" presented serious obstacles to funeral directors seeking to acquire mansions. The ensuing litigation offers clues into both the types of structures and neighborhoods sought by funeral directors and how neighbors, municipal authorities, and judges viewed funeral homes. It was a rare judge who sided with a funeral director. The image of beauty and professional legitimacy that funeral directors hoped to craft by acquiring mansions contrasted with the surrounding community's perception that the funeral home was an invasion of commerce into the domestic realm and "a constant reminder of death,"[26] which threatened them with contagion, destroyed their quality of life, and lowered their property values. When a fine old dwelling was converted into a funeral home, some observers took it as a sign that the neighborhood had begun to decline. They feared that if it was allowed to remain, it would further accelerate the decay that had already begun. A Black funeral home in a white neighborhood was regarded by white residents as a form of racial contamination as well.

The story of the residential funeral home is a complex one, spread out over many decades, and is ongoing. One reason to tell this story is that the history of adaptive use has much to contribute to the study of America's evolving cultural landscape. Few architectural historians have explored the dramatic changes in meaning wrought by a sudden and abrupt shift in use. As a result, studies in vernacular architecture tell us much about how structures were created and how they have been used but far less about how they get recycled. It is only by looking at changes in usage, in addition to changing users and changing building practices, that one can understand the full range of socioeconomic, cultural, political, and demographic forces that have shaped the built environment.

Including funeral homes within the history of historic preservation in the United States probes the very meaning of preservation and the question of whether it requires any kind of group consciousness. Most funeral directors weren't thinking about saving historic structures, yet their collective actions had a tremendous preservation impact. While historic preservation has often been narrowly construed by historians as a self-conscious movement, it is perhaps best understood more broadly as a land-use phenomenon or series of actions that preserves the built environment regardless of intentions. Finally, when one considers the collective choices made by funeral directors, the natural

affinity that exists between the funeral industry and historic preservation becomes apparent. In many cases, funeral directors took dead and
decaying structures (in decaying neighborhoods) and restored them
to their former grandeur. For their industry, this was familiar work.

Funeral homes have in recent years found a hearty advocate in the
preservation community, at least some of the time. Preservationists
are beginning to understand that funeral directors have saved many
grand old mansions from the wrecking ball. Nonetheless, one of the
most compelling reasons to explore this phenomenon is that many of
these structures are currently in danger of being torn down. While
many vintage dwellings continue to serve as funeral homes, new
conversions are virtually nonexistent today. There are fewer funeral
homes in stately mansions today than there were a generation ago.
Throughout the 1980s and 1990s, funeral industry chains acquired
thousands of family-run funeral homes and began a process of consolidation that resulted in the closing of numerous locations as a result of demographic shifts or because maintenance of such properties
was no longer deemed cost-effective. Mansions that served many
decades as funeral homes have in many cases reverted back to private
ownership as single-family residences or have been converted to condominiums or office space. Some continue to serve as funeral homes
after being reacquired by the family that had initially sold their interest to one of the big funeral corporations. In other cases, however, the
structures sit vacant and neglected and are eventually demolished. I
suspect that more instances of this will occur in the future.

Funeral homes housed in remodeled mansions remain a prominent, if not ubiquitous, feature of cultural landscapes throughout the
United States, but the story of how this came to be has received barely
a mention. A thorough investigation of the rise and spread of the residential funeral home can teach us something about America's changing residential neighborhoods, the impact of automobility and consumer culture on the built environment, and the history of preservation
itself, which, intentional or accidental, has been a powerful force
shaping the cultural landscape. Because of their work during both the

interwar and postwar periods, funeral directors have truly earned the right to be called pioneers of preservation. From the outset, they understood that using these structures to house operations and equipment was only the beginning of what their spaces could do for them. Over the course of many decades, they have displayed a sophisticated and advanced awareness of the communicative power of objects of all kinds, from hearses to houses. Whether they recognized it or not, they were preserving more than just bodies. They were preserving mansions. They were preserving a housing ideal that prized formality and privacy over informality and openness. They were preserving the residential character of neighborhoods on the cusp of commercialization. More recently, they have found themselves preserving the tradition of small, local, family-owned businesses. And in the present postpandemic moment, they are preserving the tradition of brick-and-mortar spaces in a world that is fast becoming more virtual and remote. The residential funeral home continues to speak about the ever-changing, multifaceted work of funeral directors, an increasing number of whom have begun to realize that they are also preservationists and not just because of embalming.

PART ONE

SHIFTING SPACES

CHAPTER ONE

DEATH
DOWNTOWN

The Landscape of Deathcare before
the Residential Funeral Home

In late June 1913, one month after moving into their brand-new quarters in downtown Fort Wayne, Indiana, undertakers Robert Klaehn and Albert Melching placed a full-page pictorial advertisement in two of the city's newspapers, the *Fort Wayne Journal-Gazette* and the *Fort Wayne Daily News*. Doubtless, they were exceedingly proud and eager to publicize their magnificent new structure. Having occupied three prior locations on Main Street, the firm's new purpose-built mortuary was their most elaborate headquarters to date. Built at the staggering cost of $43,000, it stood on East Washington Boulevard in the heart of the downtown. A two-story structure, its facade consisted of white Bedford stone on the ground floor with glazed brick above. The main entrance was surrounded by a Tudor arch flanked by stained glass windows. Two bay windows trimmed in copper projected from the upper story.

The interior rooms were finished in golden oak and consisted of an office, a reception room, a ladies' lounge, a private bedroom for the overnight staff, restrooms, a slumber room, and a showroom featuring over forty-five different casket styles in a range of materials from the less expensive cloth-covered to a solid bronze model valued at $1,000, with a variety of hardwoods in between. "All," the owners assured readers, were "fitted with massive extension handles and upholstered in silks and satins."[1] An additional sales area contained women's burial garments displayed in a manner that the public was told closely resembled "the high-grade dress counter of some immense department store."[2] The embalming room was situated in the basement, while the upper story contained two separate staff apartments. The owners reserved their most effusive boasts, however, for the chapel.

Entered through two sets of massive oak doors, the chapel was adorned with frescoes and stained glass and extended the entire width of the building. It was capable of seating 200 people, "making it amply large enough for any ordinary funeral,"[3] and possessed an indirect lighting system consisting of four large domes near each corner of the room and one immense dome in the center, with eight small ornamental sidelights along the walls. "The chapel is a marvel," the owners declared. "The innovation of having a chapel in connection with an undertaking establishment, it is thought, will prove to be especially well liked by the people of Fort Wayne. Time after time there is a demand for such, and the Klaehn & Melching undertaking establishment is now the only firm in the city that can satisfy this demand."[4]

Whether it was excess pride, a desire to edge out their competition at the expense of their scruples, or simply a lack of knowledge about the facilities possessed by their fellow undertakers, the claim made by Klaehn and Melching was false. Five years earlier, J. C. Peltier's downtown undertaking parlor on West Wayne Street had been described as having "a well appointed chapel for holding funeral services" (fig. 1.1).[5] The parlor had space on its premises for conducting funerals as early as 1883, and by 1913, when Klaehn and Melching advertised theirs as the sole funeral chapel in Fort Wayne, Peltier's was still in business.

Others as well had been advertising space for funeral services in their downtown parlors for years. From its choice location in the Fox Building on Calhoun Street, the firm Getz & Cahill had space for services since at least 1909. The firm Schone & Ankenbruck, situated at the corner of Berry and Barr Streets directly across from city hall,

FIGURE 1.1   J. C. Peltier, Undertaker, Fort Wayne, Indiana, ca. 1900. Allen County Public Library's Community Album.

was offering chapel space as early as 1907, while Scheumann's, also on Berry Street, was doing so by 1902. Klaehn & Melching itself had been able to accommodate funeral services from an earlier location as far back as 1901. Whether these spaces were as elaborate as the chapel housed in their 1913 mortuary is unclear. The ability to hold funeral services from one's premises did not necessarily require a permanent, dedicated chapel, and ad hoc chapels had been in existence for many decades. Still, with what seems to have been a permanent chapel in place at J. C. Peltier's establishment by 1908, it would appear that Robert Klaehn and Albert Melching were not the first to introduce the concept of the funeral chapel to Fort Wayne. They were certainly not the only option for funeral services, despite their bold claims. By the second decade of the twentieth century, downtown Fort Wayne possessed a handful of establishments offering various kinds of cere-monial space for those rare instances when a funeral from the home of the deceased was either not desired or not possible.

For several generations prior to the debut of the residential funeral home on the eve of the First World War, the landscape of professional deathcare was dominated by downtown undertaking parlors ranging from modest storefronts in smaller towns to multiple floors in larger commercial structures and elaborate purpose-built mortuaries, such as J. W. Wagner in Kansas City, Missouri (fig. 1.2). What began during the antebellum period as a sideline to either the cabinetmaker or the livery stable (fig. 1.3) evolved into an independent, professionalized, and self-supporting industry in the years following the Ameri-

FIGURE 1.2   Wagner Funeral Home, Kansas City, Missouri, ca. 1895. Missouri Valley Special Collections, Kansas City Public Library, Kansas City, Missouri.

FIGURE 1.3   Nelson Brothers Livery and Undertaking, Janesville, Wisconsin, ca. 1890. *Janesville Gazette.*

can Civil War with the rise in popularity of arterial embalming.[6] By the 1880s, establishments devoted exclusively to undertaking had sprung up in the business districts of many cities and towns, although establishments that combined undertaking with the livery stable or, more commonly, the sale of furniture and hardware persisted in many places, especially smaller towns, for many decades (fig. 1.4).[7]

Nineteenth-century undertaking parlors possessed a mixture of public and private spaces. Private spaces typically included offices; stockrooms; work rooms for trimming out caskets; staff accommodations, ranging from simple bedrooms to private apartments; and livery stables in which were kept the hearses, carriages, ambulances, and, at least prior to the advent of motorized vehicles, the horses. Some establishments, such as the H. H. Birkenkamp Funeral Home in Toledo, Ohio, also possessed embalming rooms, which became gradually more common during the early years of the twentieth century (fig. 1.5). The public spaces, in which arrangements were made, caskets and other burial merchandise were selected, and, on occasion, funerals were held, consisted of a reception room and a display space for caskets

FIGURE 1.4 Joseph Backs, Furniture Store and Mortuary, Anaheim, California, ca. 1886. Anaheim Public Library.

FIGURE 1.5 Preparation room of the H. H. Birkenkamp Mortuary, Toledo, Ohio, ca. 1900. Toledo Lucas County Public Library.

FIGURE 1.6   Casket display room of the H. H. Birkenkamp Mortuary, Toledo, Ohio, ca. 1900. Toledo Lucas County Public Library.

and other burial goods (fig. 1.6). Some of these also doubled as chapels for funeral services when the need arose. "As early as 1880," recalled deathcare historians Robert Habenstein and William Lamers in 1955, "the choice of . . . the undertaking parlor service was available in some places."[8] What matters is that however small or large, modest or elaborate, and with or without chapel space, establishments were located downtown, which remained the center of the undertaker's trade well past the turn of the century.

PARADING DEATH IN THE PRESENCE OF THE NEIGHBORS

In larger cities and towns, it was not unusual to find groups of three or more undertaking establishments clustered together along a particular corridor or within several square blocks of one another. For example, by 1905 most of the eight downtown undertaking establishments in La Crosse, Wisconsin, were located in two distinct clusters. Four of the eight were within walking distance of one another in the city's bustling commercial district in a single square block area bounded by Main and Pearl Streets to the north and south and by Fourth and Third Streets to the east and west. An additional establishment was situated on Third Street two blocks down. Two others were located a block apart in a secondary business district to the north, along Caledonia Street. Only one, an establishment on Mill Street in neighboring Shelby, existed in isolation. Similarly, of the eight principle undertaking establishments operating in Lowell, Massachusetts, in 1910, seven were located relatively close together. Three were clustered near the busy intersection of Market and Worthen Streets, with an additional establishment a few short blocks farther down on Market Street. Three more were clustered nearby along the Gorham Street–Central Street commercial corridor. Only one was located apart from these larger groupings, on Branch Street.

In some instances, there may have been safety in numbers. In at least two cases from the final quarter of the nineteenth century, undertakers were sued by neighbors seeking to enjoin the operation of their establishments. In 1887 Elenger Westcott, who lived above his offices on Market Street in downtown Camden, New Jersey, petitioned New Jersey's Court of Chancery to shut down the undertaking parlors of Frank Middleton, who had occupied the three-story building next door for the previous eleven years. His rooms were typical of early establishments consisting of a ground-floor office and a storeroom, with no dedicated chapel on the premises. The second and third stories served as his family's residence, while at the "extreme rear end of his lot" was a workshop employed in the construction of coffins. Westcott, who was over seventy at the time, cited offensive sights and odors arising from Middleton's establishment. The court felt, however, that Westcott was of "a most sensitive taste" and that his discomfort arose from "an excited imagination." Accordingly, the judge in *Westcott v. Middleton* declared that businesses conducted in a lawful manner could not be barred "from the populous parts of our cities" and that "the business of an undertaker is not a nuisance *per se.*"[9]

Less than four years later, a much less favorable opinion was handed down by the Superior Court of the City of New York in *Rowland v. Miller*. In that case the court upheld the validity of a restrictive covenant prohibiting things "injurious or offensive to the neighboring inhabitants" after Eliza Rowland sued the Taylor Company in an effort to prevent it from operating an undertaking establishment on the corner of Madison Avenue and Forty-Third Street in New York City in a dwelling it had leased from Charles Miller in December 1890. Rowland, who lived next door, was not required to demonstrate that the defendants were maintaining a nuisance. All she was required to prove, Judge McAdam explained, was that "the use complained of" was "repugnant to the covenant."[10] On this particular issue, he had much to say. From his remarks it also appears that he found the whole idea of a downtown undertaking establishment abhorrent. His understanding of popular opinion, however exaggerated, perhaps points to the underlying discomfort with the numerous undertaking establishments that had become commonplace along busy commercial thoroughfares:

> While every advance in science is hailed with delight, popular opinion has not yet reached the belief that the general good requires that private corporations or individuals shall for gain or from motives of philanthropy open dead-houses in fashionable or thickly populated parts of the city, where autopsies and post mortems are held, or where dead bodies are cut up and stored, or where funerals are furnished.[11]

Undertaking parlors, McAdam argued, "have no place in a city like New York, and, if tolerated, should, for sanitary and other reasons, be permitted only along the river fronts, or in some out-of-the-way place, so far removed from habitations as not to offend the amenities of life, and to be absolutely free from all harmful influences."[12]

Judge McAdam's position was extreme but may have been what many felt deep down. Doubtless, part of his personal aversion to undertaking parlors was his nostalgia for an idealized past when family members cared for their own dead. "Thus," McAdam asserted, if a person is taken sick and dies in his own house, he is entitled to appropriate attendance therein and burial therefrom, and no one will be heard to complain, for the consequences are natural, unavoidable, and such as every neighbor must, in the nature of things, expect and submit to. This is a lawful thing . . . where, as in this case, the occupant of a house advertises for and invites persons in all parts of the country to send dead bodies to his establishment, to be temporarily stored, cut up, artistically coffined, and furnished with elaborate funeral outfits, services, hearses, and carriages, human agency, acting on choice, makes a business of other people's misfortunes and parades death in the presence of the neighbors to their pleasure or discomfort. . . . This is objectionable and illegal.[13]

In expressing his resentment of the increased professionalization of deathcare that had occurred during his lifetime, McAdam revealed his allegiance to widely held and long-standing prejudices against undertakers, who were frequently stereotyped as ghoulishly profiting from death and preying on the vulnerable bereaved.

Further complicating matters in this case was that the structure at the corner of Madison and Forty-Third had previously "been occupied as a dwelling house" and continued to possess the appearance of "an ordinary first-class corner dwelling house in that locality." Once the Taylor Company had obtained the lease from Miller, the parlor floors were "elegantly fitted up for funeral purposes." A room was set up in the front basement for "holding autopsies upon and for the dissection and other post-mortem examination of dead human bodies," with "a marble table for that special purpose." The windows were covered over "in order to prevent observation of idle or curious people, who might otherwise be tempted to congregate about and look into the basement windows while dead human bodies were undergoing such dissection or examination."[14]

In addition to using the space to sell "coffins, caskets, shrouds and other paraphernalia generally used in the final disposition of dead human bodies," the Taylor Company arranged one of the rooms as a chapel, and intended by it for the use of people who desire to conduct or hold funeral services, and not for religious worship or services except so far as such worship or services may be incidental to such funeral ceremonies, which use of said chapel is a part of the business of the said company, and from which it expects and intends to make money.[15]

By all accounts, this appears to have been one of the earliest instances in the United States of a dwelling being converted into an undertaking establishment. While the neighborhood was densely urban and was located downtown, the structure was unmistakably residential in nature. Establishments of this kind likely existed in other large cities and can be considered the forerunner to the residential funeral home.

A key claim for the defendants was that although the structure was formerly a dwelling, the neighborhood was itself no longer residential. They argued that the covenant should not be enforced precisely because the character of the neighborhood had changed from "a locality of first-class residences into a locality of miscellaneous business" and that "most of the lots" on Rowland's block were "no longer occupied for residences," as they were now "devoted to business purposes." This claim was dismissed, and it was pointed out that Rowland continued to occupy her lot as a residence, from which she should not be "daily compelled to witness the arrival and removal of bodies in wagons and hearses, followed by the sorrowing friends and relatives of the departed."[16]

The judgment that an undertaking establishment, "no matter how well conducted, is a source of injury to adjoining property," was not based solely on Rowland's annoyance and discomfort with regularly having to witness funeral corteges and observe mourners coming to and from the neighboring house. The presence of the Taylor Company made the neighborhood less desirable as a place of residence, and this, the court recognized, had financial consequences as well. The Taylor Company depreciated the "selling and rental value" of Rowland's property, as "an ordinary person desiring to rent such a house as plaintiff's would not take her house if he could get one just like it at the same rent at some other suitable and convenient place. Indeed, her house would be shunned by people generally who could afford to live in such an expensive house."[17] The court concluded that "people of ordinary sensibilities would not willingly live next to a lot upon which such a business is carried on."[18] Such arguments would resurface a quarter century later as undertakers began their push into residential areas beyond the downtown.

THE MOST ELABORATE STYLE

By the turn of the century, a widespread campaign to change the public perception of undertaking rooms as somber and dismal was under way, with advertisements seeking to emphasize their cheerfulness, beauty, and elegance. The new undertaking parlors of E. James Finney, which opened in 1905 on Sixteenth Street between San Pablo and Clay in Oakland, California, were described the following year as twelve rooms "suggestive of cheerfulness and brightness" and "appointed in the most elaborate style." Finney, who came from Chicago, sought "to demonstrate that mortuary parlors having cheerful environments and devoid of the semblance of things dismal and gloomy would be appreciated."[19] Similarly, when Otto A. Schroeder of Madison, Wisconsin, remodeled his downtown quarters in 1923, he "took into consideration the fact that most funeral homes are decorated in somber colors. In his new home the decorations and colors are of as light a shade as would be consistent with the purpose of the home and will do much to banish that feeling of depression one feels when entering the ordinary undertaking parlors."[20] In 1904 Elmer E. Freeman and W. A. Marshall's newly constructed undertaking parlors of "white enamel brick and imported white tile" on Main Street in Kansas City, Missouri, were said to be "beautiful," with the inside furnishings "rich and elegant."[21] Such descriptions were not uncommon, and establishments were routinely written up as being elaborately furnished with beautiful and artistic interiors in exquisite or luxurious taste.

African American undertakers, no less than white undertakers, strove to create settings that were beautiful, elegant, and luxurious. In 1905 William Isaac Johnson of Richmond, Virginia, owned a "magnificent brick building, three stories high," at 207 Foushee Street with a "workshop and stables for his horses" in the basement, "office and storeroom for ready-made coffins and trimmings" on the ground floor, and living quarters for his family on the second floor, while the third floor was "divided into lodge-rooms, which are rented to different colored societies that hold monthly meetings there."[22] As was the case throughout the industry, Black undertaking parlors ranged from modest storefront establishments, such as that of C. W. Franklin in Chattanooga, Tennessee (fig. 1.7), to elaborate purpose-built mortuaries. James Jefferson Pipkin, African American history scholar, noted in 1902 that "the demand for pomp and display has compelled these undertakers to equip their establishments unusually well." In cities with sizable African American populations, moreover, large and richly furnished Black funeral establishments were not uncommon. "In

FIGURE 1.7   C. W. Franklin Undertaker, Chattanooga, Tennessee, ca. 1899. Library of Congress.

Philadelphia, Baltimore, Atlanta and other cities," observed Pipkin, "there are Negro undertaking establishments equal in most of their appointments to the best white establishments."[23]

Irrespective of race, undertaking parlors differed little from other kinds of business establishments and public rooms of the same era in their pursuit of elegance. Gilded Age public parlors and lounges of all kinds, department stores, hotel and theater lobbies, banks, saloons, and restaurant dining rooms were elaborately furnished or "fitted up." For example, following some renovations in 1899, the girls' clothing department on the second floor of Boston's Jordan Marsh department store was said to be "fitted up in the same elaborate manner [as the boys' department] and double its former size. Here again is the same lavish expenditure of money for the convenience of patrons."[24] Similarly, the "spacious dining room" of the Exchange Hotel, which opened in New Philadelphia, Ohio, in 1884, was said to be "handsomely decorated and elaborately furnished in every particular, the verigated [sic] light occasioned by different colored globes of the chandeliers adding greatly to enhance and magnify the already beautiful appearance of the room."[25]

The advent of incandescent bulbs offered increased flexibility in creating attractive, well-lit spaces. Like other entrepreneurs, undertakers grasped the importance of effective lighting. This would not only assist in dispelling the notion of somber, gloomy undertaking rooms but was also deemed essential for the effective displaying of merchandise. In addition to adding a "neat and attractive electric sign" to the front of his building, Howard Wolf fitted up the casket display room of his new establishment on South Fourth Street in Coshocton, Ohio, in 1905 with "an elaborate system of electric lights, so arranged in various colors that will match the different kinds of goods that are being exhibited."[26] Systems of indirect lighting, such as inverted sconces, were used alongside more traditional fixtures such as the "pretty electric chandelier . . . in the centre of the ceiling" that adorned the display room of E. B. Waters's establishment in Lock Haven, Pennsylvania, which in 1909 was said to be "without doubt one of the best arranged in this section of the state for the display of caskets." The "artistically papered" room possessed hardwood floors as well as expensive rugs, furniture, and fixtures "of the latest design." Moreover, the room was so arranged that it could "be used as a chapel for holding funeral services when desired."[27]

THE MOST PLEASANT OF GLOOMY PLACES

During the nineteenth century, much attention was focused on the public spaces of undertaking establishments. Because of the prevalence of home funerals, undertaking rooms were regarded chiefly as places in which caskets were displayed and sold, their role as ceremonial spaces being secondary when it was mentioned at all. In an 1879 description of J. C. Peltier's establishment, for example, the *Fort Wayne Daily Gazette* wrote that "one of the most pleasant of gloomy places is the Peltier undertaker's establishment in which is always kept the latest and most beautiful styles of caskets. Some fine styles have just been received."[28] Following an extensive remodeling of Peltier's establishment four years later, a vivid description of the office and showroom appeared in the *Fort Wayne Gazette*:

> His rooms have been newly refitted and an elegant office placed in the front, with the parlors, which are the finest in the state, immediately in the rear, which contain elegant cabinets of French walnut for the reception of caskets. The office which is separated from the parlors by an enameled glass partition with folding doors and finished in walnut, is one of the finest in the city, the work of Mr. L. O. Hull, No. 90 Calhoun Street, who makes a specialty of wall and ceiling decorations, and is conceded to be THE decorator of this city, thoroughly understanding the harmony and contract of colors and personally superintends this class of work.
>
> The paper is of solid gold ground with center piece and corners of ceiling in beautiful designs, the prevailing colors being terra-cotta, peacock blue and old gold, with velvet trimmings and a frieze of old gold with clusters of begonias forming a circle of boquets [sic] around the

entire ceiling. The dado of terra-cotta and old gold flowers entwined in trellis work is exquisite. The decoration is one of Bartholmae's New York designs, and is said to be beyond compare in this city. The ceilings in the parlors that contain the cabinets are decorated with a beautiful gold ground velvet trimmings and gold frieze of water lillies [*sic*]. Mr. Hull has the reputation of doing the finest and the most satisfactory work in this line of any establishment in this city.[29]

Although there was no mention of a chapel, Peltier's was by that time already able to conduct funerals from its premises when called upon to do so. This suggests that a makeshift space, as distinguished from a dedicated, permanent chapel, was available on those rare occasions when on-site funeral services had to be accommodated.

Peltier's ad hoc chapel space was almost certainly the room with the "elegant cabinets" in which the caskets were kept. By the turn of the century, most up-to-date undertaking parlors had a "sample room" in which the caskets were stored upright, hidden behind panels that pivoted downward horizontally for display purposes (fig. 1.8).[30] This replaced the older method of storing caskets on shelves or keeping them "standing on end in a row behind the glass doors of a tall vertical showcase along one side of [the] showroom," explained a Portsmouth, New Hampshire, undertaker in 1906. He noted that one could still "find such a display as this, but not often."[31] More modern methods allowed for caskets to

> be contained in cabinets, or they might be secured, in vertical position, to the backs of panels running continuously along the side of the room, and forming, to the eye, a continuous high panelling. Each of these panels, with a casket attached to it, is so pivoted and balanced that without effort it can be pulled down into a horizontal position for the display of the casket at a convenient height from the floor.[32]

Keeping their merchandise hidden from view ostensibly made for a less gloomy establishment, or so undertakers hoped. The firm Harvey & Sullivan in Saint Albans, Vermont, remodeled its downtown estab-

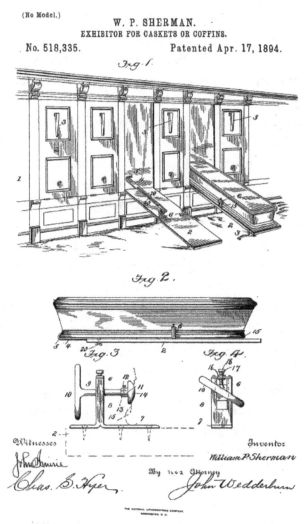

W. P. SHERMAN.
EXHIBITOR FOR CASKETS OR COFFINS.

No. 518,335.   Patented Apr. 17, 1894.

FIGURE 1.8 W. P. Sherman Exhibitor for Caskets or Coffins, US patent US518335A, 1894.

lishment in 1892, creating a reception room that was "handsomely furnished, with upholstered chairs, a fine carpet, an elegant ceiling, wall and window decorations." There was, an advertisement stated, "nothing about the room to suggest the nature of the business done there." This discretion was possible in part because "around two sides [of the room] extend what would at first seem to be a closed bookcase, handsomely finished. Therein are placed the caskets, standing upright and fastened to the doors. By an ingenious device these can be tipped outward into the room, disclosing nearly every style of caskets that the market affords."[33] Such arrangements were common, and Peltier's showroom was very similar. His "caskets—with the exception of a few superb ones in glass cases—were ranged about the room in walnut closets, and it was only necessary to touch a spring in one of the panels to bring into view the dark, upright article it concealed."[34]

While a system such as Peltier's gave his display room an air of discretion, it also made the space more versatile. His caskets being kept hidden from view most likely allowed his showroom to be used for funerals when the need arose. In the case of Roy Lynn of Portsmouth, Ohio, it was actually his "elegant new mortuary chapel" that doubled as his display room. "The chapel is a thing of beauty," declared the *Portsmouth Times* in July 1911. According to the brief article, the chapel was "constructed exclusively of Cypress wood, stained with mission. The walls are of beaver board and doted [*sic*] with attractive Tunsgen [*sic*] lights. The chapel also serves the purpose of a display room."[35] Presumably, the versatility was achieved by means of display cabinets such as those employed by Peltier's. This was certainly true of the showroom set up in 1887 by Trueman & Woodrow in its new headquarters in San Jose's recently constructed Tantau commercial block. Described as "the most convenient, elegant and completely appointed in the State," the establishment possessed two entrances,

> one to the parlor, which is finely carpeted and furnished in the latest style. Around the room appears, what at first glance is supposed to be carved wood-work. By touching a spring-belt, doors fly open a few feet apart, showing samples of the stock of coffins, which comprises every variety, price and style know[n] to the trade. This room, which, when the doors are closed, presents the appearance of an elegant private parlor, can be used when desired, for the purpose of holding funeral services.[36]

In Trueman & Woodrow's case, it was precisely the versatility afforded by the cabinets that allowed the display space to be used for funeral services. With a seating capacity of more than 120 people, the room also possessed "a platform for the officiating clergyman and a handsome oak pedestal for the Bible."[37] The room was said to give the appearance of "an elegant private parlor," reflective of the vast majority of funerals continuing to take place at home in the parlor.[38]

THE REALLY UNIQUE FEATURE

Display rooms that doubled as chapels were widespread. As late as 1920, industry insider Charles Berg reported that "some undertakers have their display room so arranged that it may be converted, temporarily, into a place for holding funeral services."[39] Dedicated chapel space did not initially constitute part of the average establishment's layout, given the long-standing custom being for the funeral to be held at the home of the deceased or a relative. Toward the close of the nineteenth century, more establishments began incorporating permanent chapels, including the chapel of the H. H. Birkenkamp Funeral Home in Toledo, Ohio (fig. 1.9), which boasted a small organ and a raised platform with a lectern. Undertaking establishments of all kinds were becoming more elaborate and complex, and many had evolved to include innovative spaces, such as morgues and slumber rooms, in which the deceased were laid out in beds prior to casketing. In the development of dedicated chapels, however, California and the western states led the way beginning in the 1880s.

One of the earliest dedicated funeral chapels belonged to William T. Hamilton, who opened an elegant new establishment in 1889 on the southwest corner of Geary and Stockton Streets in the heart of downtown San Francisco. "The really unique feature of the institution," declared the *San Francisco Bulletin*,

> and the one on which Mr. Hamilton prides himself most is the large parlor or mortuary chapel on the main floor. No private parlor could be furnished more elegantly and no chapel more appropriately. The windows are of stained glass, the rich chenille portières of a subdued shade

FIGURE 1.9   Chapel of the H. H. Birkenkamp Mortuary, Toledo, Ohio, ca. 1900.
Toledo Lucas County Public Library.

to match the carpet and other furniture. In these spacious rooms services can be held without the least inconvenience or the slightest unpleasant surrounding.[40]

Hamilton's chapel was its own dedicated space, separate from his display room, which was upstairs on the second floor together with the robe and trimming room, the embalming room, and private quarters for the staff.

Within the span of a decade, the concept of a dedicated funeral chapel had spread to the rest of the United States. By 1896, for example, Charles T. Whitsett of Indianapolis, Indiana, possessed an elaborate establishment that occupied "a substantial three-storied brick building" with "a chapel for the holding of funeral services" on the first floor, along with

a handsomely appointed office with walls hung with pictures of appropriate character.... The rear portion of this floor including telephone room, sleeping apartments for assistants, morgue for the reception of remains, and large stable with cedar block flooring, containing three funeral cars and four undertakers' wagons, also other vehicles used in the conduct of the business. Second Floor, department for ordinary caskets of all kinds, and general funeral supplies; the balance of the structure being relegated to the storage and display of the finest class of wooden and metallic caskets, lying-in-state caskets, couch caskets, specialties in ebony, hand carved oak, etc.[41]

Likewise, the firm Dunn & Rice, located in New Castle, Pennsylvania, remodeled its downtown quarters in 1898 with "elegance as the only consideration" to create an "elegant outfit" that included "a chapel for holding funeral services" on the first floor, while the casket display and stockrooms occupied the second floor.[42] N. C. Hiatt & Company's undertaking parlors, which opened its doors on Main Street in Boise, Idaho, in 1906, offered a dedicated chapel for "funeral assemblies" that was "neatly carpeted and furnished with piano and pulpit and pedestal, over which will appear mottoes or the emblems of the different orders."[43] When in 1908, moreover, the Cole-McKay Company of Omaha, Nebraska, announced that the plans for its new two-story brick mortuary included a dedicated "burial chapel," it noted that while the structure was "an innovation for Omaha," it was "not new in the larger cities."[44]

African American undertakers also participated in this trend. By the turn of the century, dedicated chapels could be found in many Black undertaking parlors, such as Preston Taylor's "large two-story brick" quarters at 449 North Cherry Street in Nashville, Tennessee. "The building," wrote G. F. Richings in his 1902 work, *Evidence of Progress among Colored People*, "is 42 × 180 feet and it is divided and furnished in the most convenient style, with reception hall, office, chapel, show rooms, supply rooms, trimming rooms, dry rooms, carpenter shop, paint shop and a morgue."[45] J. Dalton Smith's downtown establishment at the corner of Washington Street and Twenty-Third Avenue in Gary, Indiana, consisted of a two-story brick building 25 feet wide by 125 feet deep, with office, chapel, an embalming room, and various stockrooms occupying the first floor, while the second floor was given over to lodge rooms, where over fifteen lodges held their regular fraternal meetings.[46]

Dedicated chapels could also be found in the undertaking departments of furniture stores, another type of downtown establishment, hearkening back to a time when undertaking existed as a sideline to cabinetmaking. In April 1914, the C. F. Murray-Smith Company opened the doors to its four-story furniture store complete with "undertaking department and Gothic chapel, under one roof," in downtown Wilkes-Barre, Pennsylvania. The brand-new structure was situated "on a newer street," explained an article in the *Grand Rapids Furniture Record*, "where are located . . . department stores and theaters," placing it "into the center of activities" and making it "easy of access to all car lines, inter-urban trolleys, etc." The ground floor housed a

> completely equipped undertaking department, with chapel for funeral services, display-rooms and operating chamber for embalming, post-mortem examinations, etc. The chapel is beautifully finished with a dark wood base under a wall and ceiling of buff, with art stained windows and doors. Immediately adjoining is the chief undertaker's office, which holds the casket display cabinets, etc. At the rear is the operating room, probably the most complete in this part of the country.[47]

Such establishments were not uncommon, and by the second decade of the twentieth century, cities and towns possessed a mixture of storefront parlors equipped with either ad hoc or permanent chapels, furniture stores with undertaking departments and chapels, and elaborate free-standing purpose-built mortuaries, which almost certainly possessed dedicated funeral chapels. These competed with one another for the business of burying the dead until the residential funeral home began to assert its hegemony over the American deathcare industry during the interwar period.

HORSES AND HEARSES

True to their roots, many downtown undertaking establishments possessed a livery stable. The provision of horse-drawn funeral cars of various kinds, ranging from hearses and flower wagons to carriages for the family, not to mention ambulances, was an important component of the services offered by undertakers. As one of the least public and certainly least presentable spaces maintained by an establishment, the livery stable was often tucked away in the rear or located to the side or in the basement, which is where William Isaac Johnson of Richmond kept his horses. Another common arrangement was that of A. Blanchard's firm at the corner of North Delaware and Ohio Streets in downtown Indianapolis. Having started his business on Pennsylvania Street in 1885, in 1889 he moved to his new office, adjoining which was "a neat stable" where he kept "four fine horses, two undertakers' wagons and two handsome hearses."[48] Similarly, in the rear of Preston Taylor's two-story brick building in Nashville stood "a large stable occupied by eighteen horses, seven carriages, hearses and all kinds of vehicles used in the undertaker's business."[49] A generation later in 1910, Frank P. Malloy described the changes to his own livery stable as part of a large remodeling of his quarters in downtown Galveston, Texas:

> The old wooden floor has been removed and a filling of several hundred loads of beach sand has been placed. After this has been tamped a sloping concrete floor will be placed, connected with the city sewer and so arranged that all waste matter will be quickly disposed of. Seventy stalls will be erected for the accommodation of as many horses. These stalls will be built, looking not only to the sanitary condition, but also to the comfort of the animals.[50]

As late as 1912, the firm Dillon & Smith of Cleburne, Texas, was advertising a storeroom in the rear of its building for half a dozen funeral vehicles along with "quarters in the building for a team of horses."[51]

In addition to being integrated into one's structure or located in a separate structure on the same lot, stables might also be situated anywhere from a few doors down to several blocks away. In 1883 the Indianapolis firm Herrmann & Ruschaupt maintained a livery stable on East Pearl Street, which it "fully equipped and stocked with horses, hearses, carriages, phaetons, buggies, etc., for the effective carrying on of a first class livery and boarding stable." Its main headquarters was one block away on South Delaware Street in a "two story brick building 20 × 50 feet in dimensions for office and storage purposes."[52] An 1887 description of M. J. Boylan's undertaking establishment at 494 Grove Street in Jersey City, New Jersey, lists "a neat, well-appointed office 20 × 50 feet in dimensions, and connected with this a stable 75 × 90 feet in dimensions, with accommodation for twenty horses." A few doors down, however, he operated "another stable, two stories high, covering an area of 50 × 100 feet, and having accommodation for twenty-five horses." Half a dozen blocks away on Ninth Street, he had two more "fine stables with accommodation for eighteen to twenty horses and as many carriages." Boylan kept "a fine line of carriages, buggies, coaches, etc. of the first quality, both in make and appearance."[53] His rolling stock and horses were available for not just funeral cortèges but also pleasure riding and weddings.

Adequate vehicle storage remained a concern into the twentieth century, even as more progressive undertakers soon began replacing horse-drawn vehicles with automobiles and the old livery stables were gradually replaced by garages. When it opened in 1911, the rear portion of J. C. Wolford's new two-story structure of gray pressed brick on South Liberty Street in Cumberland, Maryland, contained "ambulance and vehicle rooms for casket wagon and hearses" with "concrete floors and a wide entrance opening upon the alley running into Harrison Street."[54] It is unclear whether Wolford's vehicles were motorized or horse drawn, but two years later the three-story mortuary of "dark red brick, trimmed with terra cotta, ornamental carved panels and granite" constructed by the firm Hileman & Gindt on Mulberry Street in Waterloo, Iowa, possessed "a large garage at the rear of building, of sufficient size to hold four automobiles," including "one of the finest electric ambulances in the country," which was kept "in readiness at all times."[55] Similarly, the largest first-floor room of Klaehn & Melching's new quarters was a back room measuring 40 × 40 feet to be "used for an auto hearse and funeral auto room." In 1913 the room's sole occupant was Mr. Klaehn's automobile, but the firm had plans to purchase "a complete line of auto cars for funeral purposes."[56] Downtown mortuaries were still in operation in many parts of the United States by 1930, when the Groven Memorial Home in Piqua, Ohio, leased a large building with a three-car garage in the back at the corner of Ash and Wayne Streets. In earlier instances, however, when motorized funeral cars were still a novelty, carriages and automobiles sometimes existed alongside one another. For example, in 1913 W. I. Wilder of Gulfport, Mississippi, was leasing the C. H. Williams Building, opposite his parlors, for "a carriage and automobile store room."[57] Likewise, when in 1915 the Schaffner Company of Marion, Ohio, introduced its first motorized vehicle, a combination hearse and ambulance, it made sure to let the public know that it was "still retaining its horse-drawn equipment so that those needing their service [would] have their preference."[58]

AS MUCH PRIVACY AS AT ANY RESIDENCE

Another private space that was becoming increasingly common by the turn of the century was a room for on-site embalming. Although it was customary for embalming, along with the funeral itself, to take place at the home of the deceased, many establishments began incorporating preparation rooms, or morgues, such as the one included in the remodeled quarters of G. S. Harrington & Company beginning in 1900.[59] With these quarters, housed in the Chase block at the corner of North Rose Street and West Michigan Avenue in downtown Kalamazoo, Michigan, the firm introduced to the city the "innovation . . . of a morgue in connection with the other departments." Mr. Harrington, who had taken "a post-graduate course in the latest methods of preparing bodies for interment," also added "another department for the proper disinfecting of bodies after contagious disease, which does not injure the most delicate fabrics or articles in the room."[60] A little over a decade later when J. C. Wolford constructed his new two-story mortuary in Cumberland, Maryland, it had become standard practice to include a morgue, which in his case was "constructed on the latest improved and sanitary design with concrete floor and enameled brick interior."[61]

Whereas elegance, luxury, and good taste mattered in the public spaces of one's undertaking rooms, in the private space of the morgue it was sanitation that took precedence, as emphasized by Frank P. Malloy in 1910 just prior to the renovation of his quarters. The morgue, he announced, "will be wholly in white and so arranged that sanitation and cleanliness will be a noticeable feature. The embalming table will be of white enamel. Entirely new and up-to-date instruments will be purchased, and in the hands of the expert embalmer this room will compare favorably with the best in the country."[62] Morgues were customarily located in either the rear of the establishment or the basement, which was where Klaehn & Melching chose to locate its "postmortem room" so that "the physicians may carry on their work without being interrupted by the many people who gather around an undertaking establishment when anything unusual occurs."[63] In rare cases, however, it was not only professional embalmers, coroners, and physicians who were afforded space in which to carry out their work. In the two-story brick "burial chapel" constructed in 1907 on the north side of Douglas Street between Seventeenth and Eighteenth Streets in the heart of Omaha as a joint venture between the recently merged Cole-McKay Company and the Maul Undertaking Company, there was "a room equipped with special lights and elaborate toilet facilities for friends and relatives wishing to assist in the preparations for burial."[64]

With the spread of preparation rooms, undertakers found that they needed a less clinical space in which the remains could lie in state after embalming. Regardless of whether the body was to be returned home for the actual funeral, which was true in the majority of cases, or the funeral was to take place from the undertaking parlor or funeral chapel, keeping the embalmed body in the preparation room was considered cold and inhumane. The solution was the laying-out or "slumber" room. It offered a setting in which the body could remain while a casket was chosen and in which the family and friends could view the preserved remains and spend some time in private with their deceased loved one in a homelike setting. In 1906, E. James Finney of Oakland claimed to be the first in his area "to introduce the very sensible feature of a laying-out room connected with a guests' chamber."[65] Klaehn & Melching advertised its laying-out room as "a place [for the remains] to rest in as much privacy in this room as at any residence."[66]

A typical slumber room was set up like a bedroom in a private residence. When Otto A. Schroeder's purpose-built mortuary was completed in Madison, Wisconsin, in 1923, it included a "bedroom for the laying out of the bodies so that friends of the deceased may view the body without having that suggestive casket present. Pictures on the walls and the wicker chairs in the room give it a homelike appearance."[67] Other slumber rooms contained couches instead of beds. In 1924, J. J. Moran & Son of Decatur, Illinois, opened the doors to its new purpose-built mortuary, which contained "four pleasantly appointed rooms for bodies to be laid out, where the families can be with their dead before the funeral, and where the friends can gather." Each of the rooms was done "in a different style, with easy chairs, handsomely upholstered couches and divans, lamps and cheerful pictures." The firm went out of its way to emphasize the homelike nature of the spaces:

> The home atmosphere prevails in the warm colors of the upholstery, the soft tints of the walls and the appointments generally. The thought was to make these rooms like living rooms in residences, and it has been accomplished. One of the most attractive of these rooms is done in the early American style, with Windsor chairs, a gateleg table and an old fashioned couch. On the table is a glass lamp from Marshall Field's at Chicago that is perfect to add to the effect. There is nothing doleful about these "slumber rooms." They are pleasant and comfortable—unfunereal in every way.[68]

Creating a "homelike" atmosphere had been a preoccupation of undertakers for well over a decade, but the task acquired special urgency for J. J. Moran & Son. Two years earlier one of its chief competitors, the firm

Dawson & Wikoff, had opened a funeral home seven blocks away in what was "formerly one of Decatur's finest residences," offering "absolute privacy" in a setting that was "comfortable and homey" (fig. 1.10).[69]

In addition to standard adult slumber rooms, nursery slumber rooms were offered by some undertaking parlors as well. In 1921, the Harbach Funeral Parlors in Des Moines, Iowa, installed "a nursery that any little tot would be proud to possess" to be used in when the bodies of infants and toddlers were brought in. "It always seemed a little out of place," explained the manager, Bert L. Zuver, "to put the body of a little child in the regular dressing room used for an adult. So the idea of a room exactly like a nursery in a home came into our minds." Furnished with "a little white crib, playthings, child's chairs and gay paper bedecked with Mother Goose characters and familiar pets," the special room was created to enhance "the home surroundings" that Harbach tried "to reproduce . . . as closely as possible in his funeral rooms."[70]

VERY HOMELIKE

For many early twentieth-century undertakers, a homelike setting was more desirable than a church-like setting. As a result, space for funerals within downtown establishments typically mirrored domestic rather than ecclesiastical spaces. It is no surprise therefore that in 1908 Alonzo M. Ragsdale of Indianapolis chose to advertise his "large double parlors for holding funeral services" as "very homelike."[71] Only later with the shift from incidental to dedicated chapels did church-like become a sought-after quality. Even then, the quest for the homelike was hardly abandoned. On the contrary, many firms such as J. J. Moran & Son sought to evoke both a home and a church. Notwithstanding its efforts in 1924 to create a homelike atmosphere in its slumber rooms, the firm included many church-like details in its chapel, such as a large pipe organ; wooden pews; "large hanging lamps of wrought iron, touched with color"; and a "high-backed bench of good design for the singers."[72] Likewise, the Cole-McKay Company's

FIGURE 1.10 Advertisement for the Dawson & Wikoff Funeral Home, Decatur, Illinois, 1924. *Decatur Review*, November 12, 1924, 11.

burial chapel, begun in 1908, had "the interior appearance of a beautiful small church." When completed, the company advertised, the chapel would possess "stained glass windows, dimly frescoed walls, heavily beamed ceilings, handsome altar, a seating capacity for 150 people, and all of the appointments of a magnificent church." At the same time, Cole-McKay promised a reception room "like the parlor of a fine private residence."[73]

It was not inevitable, moreover, that undertakers would choose ecclesiastical appointments for dedicated chapels. In 1923, Otto Schroeder finished his chapel "completely in gray" with "wicker chairs and settees mak[ing] up the furnishings of the room."[74] "The tendency in recent years," explained California Funeral Directors' Association president Frank Bevan of Marysville, California, in 1921, "seems to be to get away from the idea of a chapel. A funeral parlor furnished with chairs placed at random, flower stands, appropriate pictures and other home-like decorations is quite in vogue today."[75] Firms wrestled with the question of atmosphere precisely because they understood how great a challenge they faced in attempting to change where families held the funerals of their loved ones. Whatever atmosphere an undertaker chose, home funerals remained the norm in most parts of the United States into the 1930s.

Foreshadowing a marketing tactic that would be widely used later on to promote residential funeral homes, downtown undertaking parlors emphasized not only homelike settings but also privacy in their attempt to draw funerals to their chapels. When it opened in 1913 on Sixth Street in downtown Racine, Wisconsin, the Beffel Undertaking Company's new two-story stone and stucco structure featured both a "large funeral parlor" with "leather furniture, . . . massive fireplace and mahogany piano" as well as an adjoining "private funeral parlor, for "those desiring extreme privacy."[76] Many establishments bolstered their claim to privacy, moreover, by carving out semienclosed spaces in which families could see and hear the funeral service unobserved, thus mirroring the custom of having the immediate family of the deceased listen to the funeral service from either an adjoining room or an upper story whenever domestic arrangements allowed this separation to take place during home funerals. Finished in 1907, the new undertaking parlors of Curry & Gripenstraw in the Laine building, "a handsome structure of tiled brick" situated at 48 and 50 North Second Street in San Jose, California, placed to one side of the chapel "a recess for the relatives, who may desire to avoid the gaze of those attending the funeral rites. This room is separated from the main chapel by heavy portieres and connects with a sleeping room provided with every toilet necessary."[77] Likewise, N. C. Hiatt & Company had "a curtained department for the chief mourners and the choir" attached to its chapel.[78] By the 1920s it had become standard practice to afford families greater privacy by means of a screened space, such as the "retiring room behind the organ" in the chapel of J. J. Moran & Son, "where the family and close friends may sit for the service, hearing all without being seen." The firm was very honest about the purpose of the room, which was "to hide grief."[79]

THOSE DYING DISTANT FROM THEIR HOMES

Although the number of chapels attached to downtown undertaking parlors had been on the rise since the turn of the century, there were alternatives to the home funeral besides undertaking rooms. For example, when eighty-year-old Mary Koeninger died in July 1909 at Trenton's Saint Francis Hospital, which "she had made her home . . . for the past six years,"[80] her funeral mass was held from the hospital's chapel. More popular still were cemetery chapels. During the nineteenth century some wealthy families had private burial chapels constructed, such as the one built by the Warren family of Troy, New York, prior to 1878:

> The only private mortuary chapel in the United States is in Oakwood Cemetery, Troy, N.Y. It belongs to the wealthy Warren family. It is built of stone, with a vault underneath, and has handsome appurtenances of Episcopal worship, elaborate adornments, and a stained window of great value. The only services held there are at the burials of members of the family.[81]

FIGURE 1.11   Bigelow Chapel, Newton Cemetery, Newton, Massachusetts, 1888.
Newton Illustrated: Twenty-Eight Illustrations of the Streets, Public Buildings and General View of "The Garden City."

Such luxuries were rare, but many cemeteries possessed burial chapels that could be used by those desiring a graveside ceremony. For example, in 1885 J. S. Farlow, a "wealthy and public-spirited citizens of Newton, [Massachusetts]," commissioned "at his own expense exclusively, an elegant mortuary chapel receiving tomb at the Newton cemetery, the cost being about $25,000," which he "presented as a free-will gift to the Newton Cemetery Corporation for the use of rich and poor alike" (fig. 1.11). The chapel, explained an article in the *Boston Daily Globe*,

> is of pure Gothic architecture, 22 × 44 feet in size and 38 feet high to the roof, the latter being of solid timber style, and is supported by four full and two half trusses of hard pine, with heavy carved brackets. The windows are of beautiful stained glass. Five tablets of Tennessee marble, appropriately inscribed, are cased in a heavy carved screen of oak, and the pulpit, reading desk, chairs and pews are of carved oak. The

chapel at rear part is two stories high, the entrance there being in the basement. In front of the pulpit is a moveable bier, which is operated by machinery to lower the casket to the basement for burial, a fixture peculiar to this chapel. Left of the main chapel entrance is a robeing [sic] room for the minister, and on the right is a ladies' lavatory. The main entrance is through a vestibule $8 \times 4\frac{1}{2}$ feet with terra cotta walls and tile floor. The outside of the building is of Cape Ann granite, of a rusty face, the trimmings being of Nova Scotia freestone. The conservatory is 35×54 feet and will be 23 feet high in the centre of the roof when completed. The sides of the building run up for about ten or twelve feet, from which extends a domed roof, and above this is a pitched root which extends to the centre of the apex. The receiving tomb, a few rods east of the chapel, is finished and in use. It contains thirty-six cells, varying from $3 \times 2^2/_3$ feet to 2 feet $\times$ 20 inches. It is built like the chapel, except that it has granite trimmings.[82]

The construction of burial chapels such as this and others such as the one put up in 1896 by the Brighton Cemetery Association in Atlantic, Iowa, "for the purpose of holding funeral services in" continued into the first quarter of the twentieth century.[83] When the Vale cemetery in Schenectady, New York, built a brick chapel resembling "a church of small design" in 1923, it did so within a context in which the bereaved had several options for the funeral service:

> Hard wood decorations lend considerable color to the chapel proper . . . and in this good sized room, accommodation is so sixty or more persons may take seats and be present at a funeral service, if the family or friends of the deceased should so desire at any time it was not convenient to hold a funeral service at the home of the deceased or in an undertaker's parlor.[84]

By the 1920s cemetery associations, like funeral directors, understood that in spite of the lingering popularity of the home funeral, individuals and families might choose another setting if appropriate alternatives were made available.

Some cemetery burial chapels also included crematorium and co-lumbarium facilities alongside ceremonial space. In other instances, however, cremation societies built their own chapels apart from any cemetery.[85] One observer in 1892 placed the number of cremation societies in the United States at thirty-two, "most of which have a fur-nace and mortuary chapel of their own." According to the article, such operations "are more numerous west than east, and in the north than in the south. In the south there are only three cremation societies, one at Louisville, another at St. Louis and a third at New Orleans, where, on account of the swampiness of the soil, tombs for ordinary burial are built above ground. California alone has three cremation socie-ties."[86] Like cemetery burial chapels, cremation society chapels were located away from the downtown. In 1885 one year after its founding, the Cincinnati Cremation Company acquired "a piece of ground, two and a quarter acres in extent, . . . in the northern part of the city, near the suburban village of Clifton." It took three years to raise the neces-sary funds to complete the edifice, described as

> octagonal in shape, of a composite style of architecture, and has an im-posing entrance and stairways constructed of stone. The foundation is extremely heavy and substantial, and the basement is built of cut lime-stone, while the superstructure comprises alternate series of stone and brick, and almost the entire edifice is covered with a dense growth of Virginia creeper, which gives it, in the proper season, a picturesque and even a romantic appearance. On the first floor will be found the janitor's apartment, a preparing-room, a columbarium, and the rooms contain-ing the sarcophagi or retorts. Above these, on the second floor, is the chapel, which has a seating accommodation for about one hundred and fifty persons, and is provided with an appliance for lowering the body to the incinerating-room.[87]

In a move that seems to have preceded even the earliest residential funeral homes, some cremation societies began looking to residential neighborhoods as possible locations for their facilities. In 1893, for example, some trustees of the newly formed Cleveland Cremation

Company wished to erect a building in the city's Lake View Cemetery, a garden cemetery that had been created in 1869. The majority of trustees rejected the plan, however, and opted instead for a site at the corner of Page Road and prestigious Euclid Avenue, where "many wealthy and influential citizens had their residences." Foreshadowing the numerous battles that would ensue decades later when undertakers attempted to move into residential neighborhoods, area residents protested "when it became known for what purpose the land in question had been secured."[88]

Ignoring the challenge to its plans, the company proceeded to break ground at the site and laid the cornerstone of the proposed structure. In response, neighbors petitioned the state legislature, which subsequently passed an act "prohibiting the erection of a crematorium within 900 feet of the public highway or any dwelling-house." The result was that the project had to be abandoned, the land was sold, and the company dissolved.[89] In 1900, however, a new company was formed under the same name, and its first act was to petition the legislature for a modification of the earlier law. The company succeeded in securing "a reduction of three hundred feet," after which "about two acres of well wooded land were purchased, and contracts for putting up the crematorium awarded."[90] According to John Storer Cobb's 1901 work *A Quarter Century of Cremation in North America*, the company then erected a structure

> composed of brick intermingled with stone, and the main building is of three stories, one of which is mostly below the level of the ground. The first floor, or the middle of these three stories, comprises a vestibule, a reception-hall, and a chapel. Below is a store-room and a room for the furnace, while the upper floor is intended for a columbarium. Adjoining the main building is an extension of one story, containing an incineration-room, an apparatus-room, and a receiving vault. In the fitting up of the chapel and the other rooms upon this floor an endeavor has evidently been made to avoid all sombre and gloomy accessories to a funeral service, and to banish from the minds of attending friends all

melancholy thoughts in relation to the one who has gone forward a little in advance of them.[91]

Like turn-of-the-century undertakers, cremation societies sought to create spaces that were bright, beautiful, and richly finished. "As cremationists gained respectability," explains Stephen Prothero, "they articulated their newfound status in more ornate architecture." Consistent with the aesthetic of the Gilded Age, crematories possessed imposing exteriors, and their opulent interiors included carved oak woodwork, mosaic floors, heavy altars, and stained glass. "Already elegant at the turn of the century," concludes Prothero, they "became only more extravagant over time."[92]

The interior of the Cleveland Cremation Company's chapel exemplifies this love of opulence. Entered through "a pair of heavy antique oak doors," it was sheathed in multicolored marble. "The floor," Cobb explained,

> is also laid in pattern; and, in lieu of the ruddy wainscot of the vestibule, we find one of the purest white just flecked with the darkest blue. It is composed of Georgia marble, and in the upper walls the blue is continued, with a gradually receding depth, to the ceiling, where . . . it shows an almost imperceptible tint. The upper frames of the windows are filled with art glass in designs of wreaths and vases, while the lower sashes are supplied with the clearest plate, through which are obtained glimpses of the trees and the skies outside. The seats remind one somewhat of the modern church pew, although more suggestive of comfort in their use, and are provided in sufficient number to accommodate one hundred and fifty people. A reading-desk and an organ, whose use can be had without any charge at any service, complete the furniture.[93]

It was not uncommon for crematory chapels and burial chapels to be modeled after churches. In spite of attempts to banish gloominess and create elegant and attractive spaces, however, it is not clear how often these facilities were used for actual funeral services.[94] Instead, what is known is that while a lasting preference for home funerals was the main reason funeral chapels were underutilized, undertakers were extremely wary of the competition posed by crematories and were among the most vocal and ardent opponents of cremation.[95] In deciding to venture into residential neighborhoods, moreover, undertakers may well have followed the lead of their competitors, who had attempted that bold move much earlier.

For the most part, nineteenth- and early twentieth-century undertakers appear to have understood that funerals held from a location other than the home of the deceased were the exception rather than the norm. They believed, however, that there were certain classes of people who were more inclined to hold funeral services from undertaking parlors. Those residing in hotels were one such group. "With the growth of our population in hotels and boarding houses, and so situated that home burial services are impossible," explained the Omaha firm Cole-McKay in 1907, "the chapel will especially appeal."[96] When in 1890 one San Francisco undertaker "fitted up a large and handsome funeral parlor" for the purpose of holding funerals, it was intended, one observer noted, "to meet the needs of families who live in hotels."[97] In 1896, Charles Whitsett of Indianapolis stated that his dedicated chapel was designed primarily for "those who have met death suddenly or otherwise in hotels, sanitariums, etc."[98] Of course, even hotel residents did not automatically opt for undertaking rooms in the event of a death. For example, when in January 1895 sixty-nine-year-old Dr. M. Perl was stricken with apoplexy and died after a meal in the dining room of Galveston's Capitol Hotel, "for many years the home of the family,"[99] his surviving loved ones chose to hold the funeral from the hotel's main parlor.

Undertakers concluded that those whose funerals were most likely to be held from undertaking rooms were as a group more transient, possessing fewer family connections than the population at large. This was a commonly held view at the turn of the century. The long-standing custom of the home funeral engendered an assumption that only "the dead stranger" or "those dying distant from their homes" would ever require the use of a funeral chapel.[100] Curts & McBride of Des Moines,

Iowa, advertised that it was "especially equipped to handle out-of-town and hospital cases."[101] Concerning the latter, Curts & McBride was not alone in its belief that an individual who died in a hospital was more likely to end up in an undertaking parlor. However, just as residing in a hotel did not necessarily mean that one's funeral would be held from an undertaker's chapel, neither did dying in a hospital.[102] For the majority of American families, including the families of those whose lives ended in a hospital ward, the ritual of a home funeral with its trappings of domesticity possessed a strong cultural appeal. In spite of a widespread campaign among undertakers to promote funeral chapels as a suitable alternative for funeral services, not to mention all their efforts to transform their downtown undertaking parlors into cheerful homelike spaces, it would take many decades before they were able to wrest this most sacred of rituals from the family home.

THE PURE ATMOSPHERE OF THE HOME

Less than a decade after Klaehn and Melching opened their new mortuary on East Washington Boulevard, their competitors Joseph Getz and James Cahill abandoned their downtown quarters on Calhoun Street. Feeling that "they could not do justice to their patrons or themselves in that busy and congested quarter of the city,"[103] they chose a location several blocks away on West Berry Street in a more residential section of Fort Wayne but still convenient to the downtown. Rather than build new as Klaehn and Melching had done, Getz and Cahill chose instead to convert a structure formerly occupied as a dwelling, the Baltes homestead, to which they relocated in October 1919 after securing a lease with the estate's heirs. With minimal interior alterations, the dwelling offered a layout that easily accommodated Getz and Cahill's needs. On the first floor was a large reception hall, opening off of which were front and back parlors. The rooms could be used singly or as one large room as the occasion demanded and, Getz and Cahill pointed out, provided "an ideal chapel." In addition to a bedroom for the night attendant, there were two offices and multiple showrooms offering "everything in the casket line from the 'cheapest crepe cloth' to 'a bronze.'" In the southwest corner, far removed from the public sections of the funeral home, was the embalming room. The former carriage house in the back was large enough to accommodate eight vehicles, including an ambulance and a fleet of Cadillac hearses and service cars.[104]

Described as "a large commodious two-story structure of brick and stone" with "an outward appearance of quiet elegance," the detached nineteenth-century house with Italianate details was nothing like Getz and Cahill's previous quarters despite being within walking distance. Getz and Cahill sought to make it clear just how different their new quarters were: "The decorations are rich," they wrote, "getting entirely away from the old idea of an undertaking establishment, nothing whatsoever savors of business and commercialism. Instead, there is the pure atmosphere of the home." In this way, they were not only contrasting their new quarters with their former location in the Fox Building on Calhoun Street but also ostensibly offering a critique of all undertaking establishments that remained in the heart of the business district. "A quietness, a richness, a neatness, and above all a sanctity is made possible that another location could not afford," they proclaimed. They also made sure to emphasize the structure's architectural details, such as the "beautiful wall and ceiling decorative designs" and the "large marble fireplace" contained in each of the two parlors.[105]

Three and a half years earlier in Indianapolis, the firm Hisey & Titus had introduced the concept of the residential funeral home to the city, or so the firm claimed,[106] by leasing and remodeling the circa 1869 Bals-Wocher house, a substantial brick mansion "of massive proportions," today considered one of the finest examples of Italianate architecture in Indianapolis (fig. 1.12). "Distinctive in its exterior design and convenient in its interior arrangements,"[107] the dwelling contained fourteen rooms and with minor modifications accommodated a reception hall, a double parlor, an embalming room, a garage, three

FIGURE 1.12   The Bals-Wocher House, 1869 (formerly Hisey & Titus Funeral Home), Indianapolis, Indiana, 2010.

display rooms, a guest room, an office, and staff quarters, along with a trimming room and a stockroom in the basement. It is likely that Getz and Cahill knew Hisey and Titus personally through the Indiana Funeral Directors Association. After all, Hisey had served as its president in 1909. Moreover, the decision to abandon the business district for residential quarters would surely have been a much-discussed topic of conversation at the organization's annual meeting.

Business districts throughout the United States had experienced significant growth since the debut of the earliest downtown undertaking parlors during the last quarter of the nineteenth century.[108] On one hand, the "patterns of commercial development that were established by the mid-19th century," points out Richard Longstreth, "remained dominant for another hundred years, despite the spiraling growth of concentrated settlements, an ever more complex infrastructure of retail and service-oriented businesses and new forms of transportation—first the electric streetcar, then the automobile."[109] While the basic forms, elements, and settlement patterns that made up American business districts remained relatively unchanged, they had grown dramatically during the late nineteenth and early twentieth centuries. "Myriad changes did, of course, occur," Longstreth explains,

> in the size and extent of commercial districts between the mid-19th and mid-20th centuries. What may have seemed like a large core area for a city of 1850 would have been considered modest 40 years later. The advent of tall buildings—skyscrapers—not long after the Civil War radically altered the complexion of the metropolis and, after 1900, of many smaller communities as well. Isolated clusters of stores serving new residential areas in 1870 often led to a continuous linear development by 1900 and, at strategic points, were by 1930 transformed into major shopping districts, equivalent to the downtown of a modest city.[110]

With expansion came congestion, and downtown undertakers such as Hisey & Titus took note. Increased automobile use was creating traffic, parking, and noise problems for cities and towns nationwide.[111] As municipalities scrambled to solve parking shortages along their principal commercial thoroughfares, undertakers began to abandon their old quarters for locations that offered ample parking and relief "from the hurry and noise and dust of the downtown district."[112] Most were initially reluctant to move too far afield and sought a location "near enough to the business district to be convenient, and yet far enough removed from the center of activity to be possessed of the quiet and dignity necessary for a funeral home."[113] In practice, this often meant a change of address only a few blocks distant from the downtown.

Klaehn & Sons was not far behind its competitors. Not to be outdone, in 1926 the firm purchased a Romanesque-style mansion formerly belonging to the late Robert C. Bell, a prominent Fort Wayne resident who had served as an attorney, a state senator, and a former US court commissioner (fig. 1.13). Designed by Fort Wayne architects John F. Wing and Marshall S. Mahurin and built between 1893 and 1895, the grand stone dwelling stood on West Wayne Street, a short five blocks from Klaehn & Sons' former mortuary on East

FIGURE 1.13   Klaehn, Fahl & Melton Funeral Home (Residence of R. C. Bell, ca. 1893–95), Fort Wayne, Indiana. Allen County Public Library's Community Album.

Washington Boulevard. Less than a decade and a half had elapsed since the firm had invested a small fortune to build that structure, but with both Robert Klaehn and Albert Melching deceased and Klaehn's sons in charge of the business, they recognized and chose to follow the new direction that progressive funeral directors were taking in Fort Wayne and throughout the United States.

CHAPTER TWO

A NEW DEPARTURE

From Downtown to Residential Neighborhood

In 1923 the undertaking firm M. H. McDonough Sons changed the landscape of professional deathcare in the city of Lowell, Massachusetts, by following a trend that had already begun a decade or so earlier in other parts of the United States. The firm had converted "a fine old stately mansion" into a funeral home, which it officially opened to the public in October.[1] The large Italianate dwelling stood at 14 Highland Street, only two short blocks from the firm's old downtown quarters on Gorham Street and directly across from the South Common in what the local newspaper called "one of the finest residential sections of Lowell." The rest of Lowell's roughly two dozen undertaking firms remained situated throughout the central downtown or along secondary commercial thoroughfares, with several clusters along Merrimack, Market, and Gorham Streets. The move to residential quarters was, in the words of the pictorial spread that ran in the *Lowell Sun* to announce the funeral home's grand opening, "a new departure."[2] Although the concept of the residential funeral home had not been invented by McDonough and Sons, it was still a novel idea in 1923 for both Lowell and much of the nation. Within a few years, however, the funeral industry's shift from the downtown to a predominantly residential landscape was apparent in every part of the United States.

RESIDENTIAL FUNERAL PARLORS IN VOGUE

"Residential funeral parlors are in vogue," declared the *American Funeral Director* in June 1921. "Many places," the article explained, "have adopted the plan of transforming fine residences to the purpose of the profession."[3] By the 1920s a small but growing number of pioneering undertakers were exchanging their downtown quarters for domestic quarters, though the trend had begun earlier in some places.[4] When the Indianapolis firm Hisey & Titus opened its new residential funeral home in 1916, Edwin Hisey claimed that "the idea of a home, in place of an 'establishment,' took hold some time ago in other cities, and now a number of places have their funeral homes." Elaborating further, he singled out Aurora, Illinois; Battle Creek, Michigan; Brooklyn, New York; East Orange, New Jersey; and Vincennes, Indiana, as being among the cities already featuring residential funeral homes. "The idea," he explained, "is not new."[5]

Indeed, the idea was not new. There is evidence that in a handful of locations, the move to residential quarters began during the first decade of the twentieth century and as early as the last decade of the nineteenth century in Indianapolis, the very city in which Hisey & Titus was located. In early 1893 the Indianapolis firm Flanner & Buchanan was advertising that it had moved to new and commodious quarters. This referred to a two-and-a-half-story brick dwelling located at 172 North Illinois Street along a leafy section at the edge of the downtown. Twenty years later, however, in 1913, Flanner & Buchanan was back downtown, this time in an elaborate purpose-built mortuary, which the firm shared with the YMCA. On the ground floor of the structure, which cost $160,000 to build, the firm had its offices, while the upper three stories served as dormitories. In a world in which automobile ownership had not yet been democratized, a residential location made little sense. Indeed, it may have been more of a liability in that it was farther from the downtown and the city's churches and hospitals.

In 1909 at the far northern end of the state in Elkhart, the firm Stephens & Heltsmith moved into the H. C. Dodge residence (fig. 2.1), an ornate, turreted brick dwelling built during the last quarter of the nineteenth century and considered one of the finest houses in the city at the time.[6] A front-page article in the *Elkhart Daily Review* noted that the firm had "plenty of room" in its new quarters, which accommodated both a chapel and a reception room. The article also mentioned that one of the most comfortable rooms in the house was set aside for Stephens's widowed mother. More importantly, the move was considered innovative. "Their removal from the business district to a residence portion of the city," the newspaper acknowledged, "is an innovation in this part of the country, although common in eastern cities and large western cities."[7]

It should also be pointed out that early residential-style funeral homes were not confined to converted dwellings. In 1906 Thomas Mooney moved his operations from the business district of Rochester, New York, to the "commodious colonial mansion" that he had erected

FIGURE 2.1   Stephens & Heltsmith, Elkhart, Indiana, ca. 1910. Elkhart County Historical Society.

in a residential section across from the downtown on the opposite shore of the Genesee River. The structure possessed "a reception hall of spacious proportions" along with a reading room, office, and chapel on the ground floor, while the upper story contained the casket display room and the embalming room. When interviewed by the *Catholic Journal*, Mooney boasted that his rooms were "airy and cheerful. All gloomy features formerly found in undertaking establishments," he claimed, "have been toned downs so that my rooms resemble a beautiful dwelling more than anything else." Moreover, the article asserted that holding funerals from establishments "equipped with all the paraphernalia of a private home" had become "a custom rather than an innovation."[8] Although there is ample evidence that home funerals were still the dominant custom during the first decade of the twentieth century, it is true that even downtown establishments touted their homelike touches. However, it is important to point out that the article wasn't arguing that residential funeral homes were common in 1906; rather, it was arguing that holding funeral services at the funeral parlor had become common, notwithstanding evidence to the contrary. Well into the 1930s, funeral directors were running advertisements that attempted to persuade the public to give up the custom of the home funeral. Setting aside the exaggerated claims made by early twentieth-century funeral directors and newspapers alike about the preponderance of both home funerals and residential-style funeral homes, there is no question that in some parts of the United States, residential-style funeral homes had begun to appear during the first decade of the twentieth century.

Precisely how many funeral directors ventured into residential neighborhoods during the first decade and a half of the twentieth century varied from place to place, and in no place was the number large, the vast majority continuing to operate from downtown establishments. As early as 1912, however, Chicago modified its municipal code, making it

unlawful for any person to establish or maintain a morgue or to carry on the business of an undertaker as defined in this article who, in connection with such business, receives at his place of business the body of any dead person for embalming or other purposes on or along any street in any block in which two-thirds of the buildings on both sides of the street are used exclusively for residence purposes without the written consent of a majority of the property owners.[9]

Something had prompted Chicago lawmakers to act. The most likely scenario is that undertakers had begun to relocate to predominantly residential districts or were attempting to do so at the time the law was passed.

Even before the First World War had ended, moreover, undertakers challenged injunctions barring them from residential neighborhoods by arguing that residential funeral homes existed in other locales. For example, in 1917 W. H. Joy, an undertaker based in Lansing, Michigan, testified before the Michigan Supreme Court that establishments fully equipped to embalm bodies and perform funerals could be found in the residential areas of some of Michigan's other cities. The court was not convinced, however, and questioned the strictly residential character of the neighborhoods in question.[10] Pointing out that residential funeral homes had become established fixtures in many cities and towns became a common strategy employed by undertakers hauled into court by aggrieved neighbors. In 1918 Roy Osborn of Shreveport, Louisiana, claimed that funeral homes were "permitted on residential streets in New Orleans, Denver, St. Louis, Cleveland, Dallas, and many other cities in the United States."[11] Although attorneys for Willis Crosby of Omaha acknowledged in the brief they filed with the Nebraska Supreme Court in 1920 that the funeral home was "a comparatively new institution," they expressed their confidence that the members of the court would be familiar with the increasingly popular trend. "In recent years," the brief explained, "there has been a marked change in the manner of conducting funerals, including occupancy of old residences in residential neighborhoods with which this Court is so familiar that it needs no evidence on the subject."[12] On the other hand, a 1920 article in the *American Funeral Director* contained an article highlighting the purpose-built, residential-style funeral home of the Dodds-Dumanois Company in Flint, Michigan, and referred to the "new idea of conducting an undertaking business far removed from the commercial centers of a city."[13] Yet another article on a proposed zoning ordinance in Portland, Oregon, focused on whether undertaking parlors would be able to continue operating in business districts.[14]

Issues of the *American Funeral Director* from the earliest years of the 1920s often included collages featuring half a dozen or more different undertaking establishments from various cities and towns throughout the United States and Canada. For example, a 1920 a pictorial spread showcasing "Modern Funeral Homes" included a mixture of downtown mortuaries and converted dwellings (fig. 2.2).[15] While such collages typically included a couple of elaborate downtown mortuaries, they tended to be dominated by new residential funeral homes, either converted mansions or purpose-built mortuaries that looked like mansions. With their mixture of older downtown funeral parlors and newer residential funeral homes, the collages in the *American Funeral Director* and other industry publications reflected the varied landscape of professional deathcare that survived into the 1930s and beyond in many locations. "In some places," explained Curtis Frederick Callaway in his 1928 handbook *The Art of Funeral Directing: A Practical Manual on Modern Funeral Directing Methods*, "the funeral home is easily the most popular. In other cities the funeral home seems unpopular. In some places the trend is easily toward the mortuary or semi-business place. In other places we find the most popular establishments occupying business blocks."[16] Clearly, downtown funeral parlors did not disappear. In many big cities large downtown mortuaries continued to operate, as did smaller establishments serving dense urban neighborhoods. Medium-sized towns often employed a dozen or more professional undertakers, and not every practitioner chose to make the move to residential quarters. Those who did relocate did not leave the downtown en masse. Rather, the industry's shift from business district to residential district occurred gradually over several decades.

Modern Funeral Homes: From left to right—W. H. Sutch, Los Angeles; A. E. Howe, Boulder, Colo.; N. A. Stevens, Altoona, Pa.; Myers & Owens, Columbus, O.; Ruhl & Ebert, Davenport, Iowa; F. L. Wallace & Sons, Manchester, N. H.

FIGURE 2.2   Modern Funeral Homes, 1920. Note the mixture of downtown mortuaries and converted residential dwellings. *American Funeral Director.*

Lowell, Massachusetts, offers an interesting case in point. In 1920 on the eve of M. H. McDonough Sons' removal to its new Highland Street quarters, twenty-four undertaking firms operated in downtown Lowell, whose population was just over 112,000. Ten years later the number of establishments had grown to thirty, and while only seven firms had left the downtown, the exodus had begun. That number continued to increase, and by 1940 twelve out of the city's twenty-eight funeral establishments were housed in remodeled dwellings. By 1950 residential funeral homes had finally topped just over half the total number of establishments, at sixteen out of thirty. The peak seems to have been reached by the mid-1960s, when residential funeral homes accounted for 85 percent of Lowell's funeral establishments. For the next several decades, residential funeral homes hovered at around 80 percent of the total number of firms active in the city.

Tracking the progress of the residential funeral home in any given location requires using a combination of city directories, maps, architectural inventories, historic photographs, digital mapping technology, and data collected from the field. Census data offers few clues. Prior to 1930 the US Census did not include figures for undertaking establishments, opting to record the number of professional undertakers instead. By 1930, establishments selling funeral supplies were being categorized under "miscellaneous" in the figures for retail distribution. While funeral establishments were separated out in the figures for Massachusetts, Connecticut, and Ohio, there was no effort to distinguish between downtown establishments and residential funeral homes. By 1940 "funeral directors, embalmers, and cemeteries" were considered "service establishments," as opposed to entities engaged in retail distribution, but were treated as a uniform group, with no attempt made to separate out residential funeral homes.

One important bit of information buried in historical census data pertains to old-style combination undertaking and furniture establishments. Combination establishments were a holdover from the antebellum period when undertaking had developed as a sideline to cabinetmaking. Such establishments survived into the twentieth century as part of the landscape of professional deathcare but were typically found only in smaller towns and rural communities. One such establishment was Albert Buenneke's furniture and undertaking business in Oelwein, Iowa. "The Buenneke store," noted a 1921 advertisement, "carries a most comprehensive line of furniture, rugs and linoleums, a line of electrical merchandise, features the Hoover suction sweeper, does picture framing and furniture repairing, and operates an undertaking parlor in connection."[17] A. F. Koller Furniture and Undertaking in East Berlin, Pennsylvania, was advertising its home-like chapel as late as 1931. "All the comforts of one's own home," the advertisement promised, "plus every facility that is needed to perform the service with the utmost satisfaction to his patrons, will be found in his funeral home. It is a beautiful, quiet, restful place, affording all the privacy, comforts and conveniences of a private residence."[18]

In 1930 3,590 combination furniture and undertaking establishments operated in the United States. In Connecticut, 35 out of 126 (27 percent) were combination businesses. For Massachusetts and Ohio the numbers were 21 out of 499 (4 percent) and 201 out of 628(32 percent), respectively. Thus, in some places relatively few such establishments remained, while in other locations they constituted almost one-third of the total number of funeral establishments. Although no actual figures for combination establishments were recorded by the 1940 census, it has been noted that in rural areas undertaking establishments were frequently operated in connection with retail furniture establishments.[19]

Within the pages of industry publications, a spotlight was clearly being shone on developments understood to be new and innovative within the industry, and dozens of articles were devoted to funeral homes in remodeled mansions each year. "The Funeral Home idea is growing rapidly all over this country among funeral directors and morticians," declared a 1921 article in the *American Funeral Director* featuring the newly established Johnson & Wilkins Funeral Home in Buffalo, New York.[20] The "beautiful old mansion" chosen was a two-story Gothic Revival brick dwelling on a quiet, tree-lined residential street. The funeral home was formerly in "a location more given over to business," the article explained, but its "well merited reputation" gave the owners the confidence they needed to make the move, capitalizing "upon the success of those in other cities who broke away from business marts and went into quieter ways."[21]

Highlighting what was quickly becoming a new trend brought a growing awareness of regional differences within the landscape of professional deathcare as well. Some observed that residential funeral homes were initially more common in the western states than they were in the more conservative East. One commentator from Lowell, Massachusetts, posited in 1929 that "the movement toward the establishment of funeral homes was initiated in the west and was in full swing there 10 or more years ago."[22] Indeed, one of the earliest residential funeral homes in the nation was established in 1910 by Burton L. Ward of San Jose, California. "Like all progressive men who have ideals and ideas of their business," explained the newspaper article announcing the formal opening, Ward "leased the old Sexton residence at No. 408 North First Street, its beautiful grounds and garden and its spacious rooms being particularly adapted for his purpose."[23] Many considered the western states "the leader in this form of progress,"[24] while the Northeast was generally seen as lagging behind. "It is true," argued one industry expert in 1920, "that the middle and far west, and some sections of the south, provide more 'funeral homes' of elegance than the older sections of the east."[25] However, as other regions caught up during the late 1920s with "fine modern establishments," some noted that those other parts of the country "profited by the experience of the western men in this line."[26]

GETTING AWAY FROM THE OLD IDEA

Despite the sincere attempts of turn-of-the-century undertakers to take the gloom out of the downtown funeral parlor, a growing number of funeral directors deemed those efforts a failure. "When we look back a few years and take a survey of the way in which many funeral directors conducted their establishments, and then turn our faces in the direction of the modern funeral home," noted industry insider Warfield Webb in 1920,

> we are likely to marvel at the wonderful changes that have taken place in that short period. . . . The old idea of a funeral parlor, as it is still called by some, was anything but a place that would appeal to the bereaved family. The casual passerby was loath to enter such a place, and there was a feeling of dread, a desire to hasten away from an abode that smacked of a morgue.[27]

A new generation of funeral directors had come to regard the downtown funeral parlor with its somber appearance and "staid solemnity" as old-fashioned, unappealing, forbidding, and even gruesome.[28] "The bare office or reception room, with only a limited amount of furniture, . . . and its solemnity, its coldness, its repugnance," Webb continued, "gave one a chill, and there was a desire to seek more agreeable quarters."[29] More agreeable quarters, the industry claimed, could be had in the form of residential funeral homes such as the Ford & Douglas Funeral Home, which opened its doors in Gastonia, North Carolina, in May 1926. "From cellar to garret," its owners promised, "an air of refinement and homelikeness . . . takes away much of the cold and forbidding atmosphere that hovers about the average undertaking establishment."[30]

There were "many reasons," industry experts such as Callaway pointed out, why the funeral home "must be considered rather than the old style business place location."[31] Many funeral directors were looking for ways to counter what one described as "that creepy feeling which so many persons have before they enter the doors of a funeral directing concern."[32] Others shared the opinion of George H. Burnett of Batavia, New York, who felt that "conducting the profession of the funeral director from a store room pertained too much of commercialism."[33] A steady increase in automobile usage also meant a downtown that was crowded, congested, busy, loud, and dirty, and many within the industry had begun to feel that it was no longer a suitable environment in which to serve bereaved individuals and families.[34] As it was, downtown undertakers had good reason to feel this way. Their chapels and service parlors stood empty and were rarely used. Long-reigning custom placed the funeral at the home of the deceased or of a family member. Most clients went to the downtown parlor merely to make arrangements and purchase a casket from the undertaker's well-stocked display room.[35]

Given their failure to wrest the funeral from the home of the deceased, it made sense that many undertakers sought a change of scenery. "Funeral parlors in congested business districts are but poor substitutes for home surroundings," industry insider Charles Berg declared unapologetically in his popular 1920 exposé *The Confessions of an Undertaker*. The solution lay beyond the downtown. "Ideal homes for the modern undertaking establishment," he observed, "are those remodeled from large residences, or constructed after the style of residential architecture."[36] A residential location presented a marked and marketable contrast to the downtown undertaking parlor. "Many funeral directors in all parts of the country," explained a short piece in the February 1921 edition of the *America Funeral Director*, "have left their former places in the business section of their town or city and have moved into elegant residence sections or have built new places in such localities."[37] The article, titled "Beautiful Funeral Home in the North-West," featured the Davies Mortuary in Minneapolis, which the previous year had moved into "the old mansion in Harmon Place, formerly owned by Mrs. H. Alden Smith, one of the most beautiful private homes in that northern city" (fig. 2.3). Davies had operated a downtown mortuary until he decided that "his business in the busy section of the city savored too much of commercialism." He moved not once but twice "that he might be further away from the busy hum of industry." Finally, in 1920 he set his sights on Harmon Place. "As a residence," the article explained, "it was known as one of the most beautiful in the city, and as a funeral home there are but few, if any such places in the United States, that excel it." According to the article, the dwelling was well suited for use as a funeral home and "required

A MAGNIFICENT FUNERAL HOME
No. 1—Beautiful Davies Mortuary of Minneapolis. No. 2—View Through Several of the Parlors. No. 3—One of the Parlors. No. 4—Exterior View of Mortuary. No. 5—The Office. No. 6—The Hall.

FIGURE 2.3   The Davies Mortuary, Minneapolis, Minnesota, 1921. *American Funeral Director.*

but little change from the arrangements left by its former inhabitant."
The mahogany woodwork and paneling along with the rugs and tapestries chosen by Davies made the place "one of unusual richness and
beauty." More importantly, there was, the article argued, "nothing
about the place suggestive of a funeral place, until one gets into the
show rooms."[38] Some firms, such as J. J. Sullivan & Co. of Cincinnati,
Ohio, linked the move to boosting the practice of holding funerals at
the funeral home. "There is the idea, too," the firm offered, "of holding
more funerals at the director's chapel, because of the convenience
that this affords, due to much of our modern home life."[39] The firm
were seeking "to make the surroundings inviting, pleasant, convenient,
and, at least, are robbing it of that cold and lonely place that we have
known for many years."[40] While it is unlikely that J. J. Sullivan & Co.
saw a dramatic overnight rise in the number of funerals held from
their premises, the firm clearly hoped that the move would result in
more families choosing that option.

The critique of downtown parlors within the pages of funeral industry publications naturally carried over into funeral home advertising
as well. In a 1916 advertisement for its new residential funeral home,
the firm Hisey & Titus struck a blow at its downtown competitors by
charging that there was "a want of privacy and homelike atmosphere in
an undertaker's parlor in the congested business district." The residential funeral home, posited Edwin Hisey, was "as different from the
earlier undertaker's office in the business district as a man's desk space
in his residence is different from his office in a skyscraper."[41] This was
an important point, because establishments in the heart of the downtown had been advertising homelike rooms since at least the turn of
the century.[42] The new residential funeral homes offered stiff competition to downtown undertakers, whose ability to lay claim to a homelike atmosphere was steadily being undermined. Those who had
made the move to residential quarters strove to let prospective clientele know not simply that they had a new address but that their new
quarters offered a fundamentally different setting from the conditions
that characterized their former downtown location. The "quiet spot

away from heavy traffic and business activities" advertised in 1924 by the Griesmer-Grim Funeral Home in Hamilton, Ohio, was something that no downtown funeral parlor could provide.[43] "Located away from the congested district, quiet is assured," promised the Robert H. Kroos Funeral Home in Sheboygan, Wisconsin, in 1933.[44]

Of course, firms also sought to reassure customers that they hadn't moved too far away from the city center and were still conveniently located. "Experience and experiment within the profession," explained a 1929 advertisement for the Griesmer-Grim Funeral Home, "have proved exclusively that the best location for a funeral home is a quiet and attractive residential district, yet fairly close to the business district."[45] Similarly, the Logansport, Indiana, firm Peirce & Easterday advertised "a residence with large, homelike rooms . . . convenient to [the] business district,"[46] while the Ehlers Funeral Home in Dunkirk, New York, pointed out that it was situated "away from the noise of the business district, yet within a few minutes walk of it."[47] C. E. Curtis Co. Funeral Directors of Marion, Ohio, promised a funeral home that was "very centrally located so as to be of most convenience to the majority of their patrons, yet far enough away from the 'city noises' and traffic to give it that quiet dignity and reserve."[48]

It was generally understood within the industry that "the funeral home should be in a section not too far removed from the business center," for even residential establishments had to be near churches, many of which were centrally located downtown, and also "within easy access of the hospitals." Funeral directors were also keenly aware of being "on a street where there was enough travel to keep his name before the passerby."[49] Residential streets that had in recent years become major thoroughfares to and from the downtown as well as roadways possessing streetcar lines were all considered desirable locations. Mack Johnson of Cincinnati, Ohio, chose a boulevard "with a number of well patronized electric [street]cars passing all the time." At the same time, he was careful to point out that the house itself was "located on a rolling knoll . . . sufficiently removed from the street to make it an abode of quiet."[50] Remarkably similar language was used to describe the location of Vonderhaar, Stetter & Erschall in Newport, Kentucky, featured in the March 1921 edition of the *American Funeral Director*. "The location is ideal," extolled the article, "for the house is located on a prominent street, at the intersection of a thoroughfare that is largely traversed by auto traffic, as well as one of the main arteries traversed by the electric [street]cars. There are still the outstanding marks of the mansion noted in this old home, and the building is situated on a rolling knoll, and attracts by its very setting."[51] Busy streets, it seems, were not a problem as long as the property was set far enough back and maintained some semblance of its former grandeur.

The ideal location often meant proximity to other funeral homes. Groups of anywhere from two to half a dozen funeral homes located within one or two blocks or in some cases a few doors apart from one another were not uncommon. Clusters emerged somewhat organically because funeral directors sought out not only similar structures but also similar locations in older residential neighborhoods close to the downtown. Nonetheless, there was also a strategic advantage to clustering. Funeral directors nationwide were aware that their presence amid residential dwellings often aroused suspicion and even hostility among neighboring homeowners and municipal authorities seeking to keep residential districts free from commerce. A funeral director who successfully set up shop in a converted mansion or built a new mortuary in a residential area without conflict or litigation was often followed by others, in part because the location was considered a safe bet. Indeed, many funeral directors were accustomed to being near to one another, having been clustered together in their former downtown locations.

Although no undertakers followed M. H. McDonough Sons to Highland Street, by the mid-1930s several clusters of residential funeral homes had emerged in other Lowell neighborhoods. For example, along a five-block stretch of Pawtucket Street there were four funeral homes, three of which were within a block of one another. Archambault's Funeral Home was the first to set up shop there in the mid-1920s. About five years later James F. O'Donnell & Sons opened its doors across the street (fig. 2.4). Two others, the Savage Funeral Home and the M. R. Laurin Funeral Home, followed in 1935. However, if Savage and Laurin were under the impression that they would have an easier time because the area was already home to two other funeral homes, they were mistaken. Both were forced to overcome neighborhood opposition stemming largely from fears that additional funeral homes would result in increased traffic along Pawtucket Street.

While area homeowners and planning departments worried about congestion on residential streets, funeral directors saw an opportunity to remedy their parking woes. Downtown undertaking parlors doubtless felt the same parking crunch encountered by all downtown businesses, whose customers were increasingly using automobiles as a means of transportation.[52] As downtown merchants of all kinds wrestled with parking shortages in congested city centers, a residential location afforded funeral directors more room for parking, which

FIGURE 2.4   The James F. O'Donnell Funeral Home, Lowell, Massachusetts, 2010. Photograph by the author.

gave them a significant advantage in the local deathcare marketplace. When R. G. Roberts and Glen A. Blue of the Roberts-Blue Funeral Service in Emporia, Kansas, announced their purchase in April 1938 of a large Colonial Revival brick dwelling a short three blocks away from their old downtown location, they left no room for doubt as to their chief motivation. "Mr. Roberts and Mr. Blue said that the primary reason for changing their location," recounted the notice that ran in the local newspaper, "was the traffic problem, which is increasing on Merchant Street. Lack of congestion and more parking space, they said, made the residence location more desirable." Their plans for the new property included a driveway with space for more than twenty-five cars.[53]

In countless advertisements that appeared throughout the interwar period, residential funeral homes across the United States promised ample parking in locations away from crowded downtowns. The Daehler Mortuary in Portsmouth, Ohio, noted their "private driveways for the comfort and privacy of relatives and friends" when it announced its formal opening in 1925.[54] Likewise, the Thorpe J. Gordon Funeral Service in Jefferson City, Missouri, boasted room for twenty cars in its own lot, "eliminating any parking problems of those who come to pay their respects."[55] In addition to shortening the walk from patrons' automobiles to the funeral home, a long driveway allowed the funeral cortege to form in an orderly fashion,[56] a process that had become very difficult for downtown parlors to orchestrate in congested city centers.

A residential location also gave funeral directors more room for their own vehicles (fig. 2.5). Motorized hearses and ambulances had been in service since before the First World War and were often housed in specialized garages opening onto alleyways in the rear of downtown establishments.[57] Space, however, was limited in such cramped quarters, and the move to a residential location allowed for long driveways and large garages to accommodate growing fleets of motorized funeral cars. For both patrons and owners, the residential funeral home with its promise of space and quiet must have seemed

FIGURE 2.5   J. L. Reed & Son Funeral Home, Tampa, Florida, 1932. Courtesy,
Tampa-Hillsborough County Public Library System.

like a world away from cramped and congested downtown streetscapes
that for more than half a century had been the sole home of professional undertaking establishments.

FOR THE SERVICE OF THE RACE

Some undertakers fled more than simply noise, dust, and traffic. In
many American cities the influx of African Americans into previously
white areas during the interwar years left white business owners and
residents feeling estranged and resentful. Around 1911, undertaker
E. C. Marshall of Detroit began noticing changes on Beaubien Street,
where his undertaking establishment had been situated since 1883,
when it was founded by his father. "When the surroundings of the old
office where we were located for twenty-eight years underwent the

changes characteristic of old quarters in big cities," he recounted, "it naturally had a pronounced effect on the inside of our offices. Garages on each side made our rooms dingy, and a colored element moving into buildings around meant that we would either cater to that trade or move out. For a long time we had felt that we wanted a change not only of location but of business methods as well."[58] Marshall decided to move out. As he explained, the move was not solely the result of African American businessmen moving into that section of Detroit's downtown. He had for some time wanted "something new" and different "in place of undertaking offices," he mused, "to have an undertaking home." Marshall, like many others in his field, struggled to balance the business side of his work with the service component and had come to feel that an undertaking parlor in the middle of a busy downtown missed the mark. He wanted an establishment where "burial services could be kept apart from the unavoidable commercial side. In other words," he explained, he wanted "to offer our patrons the sympathy of home surroundings, and the only way to do that, of course, was to get away from office buildings."[59] When Black businesses began moving into the area, Marshall saw this as the final nail in the coffin. The demographic shifts that were transforming his street only strengthened his resolve to leave his downtown quarters once and for all. Marshall opened a funeral home in a large Colonial Revival brick dwelling that was "one of the oldest in Detroit." It was situated on Jefferson Avenue "in a large yard apart from other buildings."[60] Not every white undertaker succumbed to white flight, however, and some remained in their old quarters in spite of the changes taking place around them. "I've been here for over fifty years," explained a white Chicago-based undertaker in the early 1940s, "and have seen this area change from all white to all black. However, I've never catered to the Negro business and at no time conducted a Negro funeral."[61]

The same demographic shifts that drove away some white business owners and residents opened up opportunities for Black entrepreneurs. Shortly after its completion in 1888, the palatial Chateauesque mansion (fig. 2.6), built by circus entrepreneur James A. Bailey on the

FIGURE 2.6   James Bailey House, ca. 1886–1888 (formerly M. Marshall Blake Funeral Home), New York, New York, 2010. Photograph by the author.

corner of St. Nicholas Place and 150th Street in Harlem, had already begun to lose some of its luster when, instead of other mansions being constructed on neighboring streets, apartment houses went up during the 1890s. Bailey eventually sold the house in 1904, two years before his death. The colossal dwelling, which was designed by Samuel Burrage Reed and Joseph Burr Tiffany, was later owned by Franz Koempel, a Bavarian-born doctor whose family lived there until 1951, though the area, later known as Sugar Hill, had decades earlier become a predominantly African American neighborhood.

During the 1930s, a young Marguerite Marshall used to pass the house on the way from her home on West 153rd Street to the Wadleigh High School for Girls on West 114th Street. She dreamed of owning it and, as she was fond of telling in later years, rang the doorbell one day and asked Dr. Koempel and his wife, Bertha, if she could have the first right of refusal if and when the house was sold. The Koempels, in a good-natured but condescending fashion, agreed, undoubtedly wondering to themselves how the Black teenager, whose mother was a dancer at the Cotton Club, would ever be able to afford the thirty-room limestone mansion. In 1951 the widowed Bertha Koempel finally put the house on the market, and Marguerite Marshall Blake fulfilled her dream. With help from her husband and family, she cobbled together the funds to purchase the dwelling and four years later in 1955 opened the M. Marshall Blake Funeral Home, which operated from the premises until a fire on the upper floors forced Blake and her husband to close in 2001. During the almost half century that it functioned, the M. Marshall Blake Funeral Home was housed in what was arguably one of the most opulent settings of any funeral home in America.[62]

Not every Black undertaker moved to residential quarters. Field-workers for the Works Project Administration noted that in Chicago in the late 1930s, many Black funeral establishments continued to be located in business centers along main thoroughfares, and while some were "mere deserted stores with a chapel in the front and an embalming room in the rear," others were "very elaborate."[63] In an essay titled "Monopoly in Death," which appeared in the March 1947 volume of Negro Digest, Allan Morrison wrote that "most colored morticians operate on a small scale, frequently from store-front premises." He also acknowledged, however, that "they build elaborate funeral homes."[64] For example, in 1941 J. Walter Wills Sr. of Cleveland, Ohio, purchased a turn-of-the-century forty-two-room freestanding Jacobean-style theater formerly owned by a German American social club and transformed it into the House of Wills, one of the largest and most successful Black funeral homes in the nation.

Black funeral directors also converted existing dwellings, and in this they were not unlike their white counterparts. Those who exchanged their downtown offices for residential quarters sought older, larger dwellings situated in neighborhoods once home to wealthy and influential families. Consequently, it was practically inevitable that Black funeral directors would end up occupying spaces vacated by white elites. In 1933, for example, S. W. Qualls of Memphis, Tennessee, opened a casket showroom in a large stone dwelling situated on a street occupied by white families,[65] while A. G. Gaston of Birmingham, Alabama, moved his undertaking business into a somewhat dilapidated neoclassical mansion (fig. 2.7) opposite the city's Kelly Ingram Park in 1938. Following his purchase of the structure, Gaston embarked on an extensive restoration of the majestic dwelling, once home to a coal baron but more recently a boarding house for elderly white schoolteachers. By the early 1950s there were approximately 3,000 Black mortuary establishments in the United States. What percentage of these were residential funeral homes is unclear; however, one observer noted in 1953 that "mortuaries have become among the most attractive Negro-owned buildings in most cities."[66] For example, after relocating to the Porter mansion in 1908, funeral director Andrew N. Johnson took out a full-page advertisement in the *Nashville Globe* boasting of the "magic touch" with which he had returned "an ancient landmark of Nashville . . . to its ancient splendor for the service of the race." The structure had been "beautifully decorated as

FIGURE 2.7   Postcard showing Smith and Gaston Funeral Home, Birmingham, Alabama, ca 1945. Troy University Library, Special Collections.

in antebellum days" prior to opening in 1909 and could, Johnson declared, "plainly and appropriately be termed 'The Restoration.'"[67]

In addition to being attractive, African American funeral homes also served a vital social function by helping members of the Black community navigate the segregated terrain they inhabited. They "provided a safe place to meet in cities and towns where Jim Crow restrictions sharply circumscribed blacks' ability to gather or to be treated with respect in public places,"[68] writes Suzanne Smith in her history of the African American way of death, *To Serve the Living*. Johnson converted one of his downstairs rooms into "a Ladies Parlor and Resting Room" and invited the female members of Nashville's Black middle-class to use his quarters as a resting place while on shopping excursions, during which they were likely to suffer discriminatory treatment at the hands of white business owners. "Here," he explained, "the tired shopper can come and rest and be free from offense as at those places where our women are not wanted longer than they have made settlement for their purchases."[69] Throughout the era of Jim Crow, Black funeral directors also made their rooms available to Black fraternal organizations and secret societies. Later during the second half of the twentieth century, Black funeral homes frequently offered covert meeting space and sanctuary to embattled activists during the African American struggle for civil rights.[70]

While many of the neighborhoods in which Black funeral homes opened would eventually come to reflect the segregated landscape of twentieth-century American cities, the situation was in reality far more complex. For starters, the structures remodeled into Black funeral homes often housed white families just prior to their acquisition. Many of the neighborhoods in which the dwellings stood were still home to white residents, not all of whom were happy about a funeral home moving in, let alone a Black funeral home. When S. W. Qualls first attempted to establish a funeral home in a predominantly white neighborhood of Memphis, the city's building commissioner denied him the necessary permits. The area, however, had become increasingly commercialized in the years prior to Qualls' purchase of the structure, and this metamorphosis fit the pattern observed by contemporary sociologists who analyzed both the socioeconomic and demographic shifts that were transforming the landscape and human geography of American cities during the interwar period.

Writing in 1926, sociologist Jerome Dowd pointed out that an influx of African American residents to a previously white neighborhood was often preceded, not followed, by a decline, which was caused by "the invasion of a white residence district by apartment houses, theaters, garages, and a boarding population, causing the general flight of the home-owners to a new residence center."[71] In other words, many white elites fled their homes in older residential neighborhoods in the face of expanding business districts and the emergence of higher-density housing in the form of apartment buildings. This wealth flight paved the way for a lower-income "rooming and boarding population of whites" to move in.[72] It was often in these declining neighborhoods filled with old houses and working-class white residents that Black funeral directors found dwellings that satisfied their need for bigger, grander spaces, even ones that had fallen into disrepair such as A. G. Gaston's mansion across from Kelly Ingram Park.

OF THE HIGH TYPE

By the 1930s, remodeled mansions located in older residential districts had become the setting of choice for funeral directors and formed a key component of the industry's signature brand. "The home itself," wrote one industry expert in 1920, "should be of the high type. The building must be imposing, and the grounds of an inviting kind."[73] Converting a mansion—or constructing a new one to be used as a funeral home—in a residential neighborhood offered certain advantages but also required funeral directors to take risks. The more elite and exclusively residential the neighborhood was, for example, the greater the likelihood of offending one's neighbors or running afoul of zoning laws. Nonetheless, the lure of the mansion proved too powerful to resist among enterprising funeral directors who saw in the grand and opulent dwellings not merely an antidote to the cold and businesslike downtown parlor but an opportunity to legitimate their claim to the professional status they had long coveted while simultaneously creating the kind of opulent shopping space believed to stimulate consumer demand for higher-quality and more expensive goods.

"If [the funeral director] was to get away from the idea of a funeral parlor, and still maintain the ideals that were vital, the house should be architecturally attractive," stated one industry expert in 1920.[74] Beauty was a key consideration when selecting a dwelling to remodel or constructing a new mortuary. The "emotional effect of attractive surroundings" was highly prized by funeral directors.[75] The psychological comforts offered by beautiful surroundings were believed to benefit not just the patrons but the funeral director as well. "Spacious lawns, the smooth driveways, the wide stairways and spotless verandas," explained a 1922 advertisement for the Welch & Sovern Funeral Home in Modesto, California, "give it an inviting air—homelike. These environments are associated with the modern funeral director, for they, sub-consciously, tend to lighten the sorrow attendant in the performance of his service."[76] In addition to softening grief, "the beauty and homelike appointments of the funeral home," argued one practitioner, "drive away many of the false impressions, the fear and distrust which so many harbor."[77]

There is no doubt that funeral directors who selected vintage mansions found them beautiful. "The modern funeral home," wrote one funeral director, "is usually a distinct ornament to the neighborhood in which it is situated. Whether built new or remodeled, it is usually far superior in architectural design to the homes around it, and in many cities the mortuaries are among the show places."[78] That they considered so many nineteenth-century mansions to be beautiful suggests that funeral directors were driven by a more conservative aesthetic than those who eschewed what they considered excessively ornate and gaudy Victorians. By the interwar period, tastes in domestic architecture had changed. Many looked back with scorn and dismay on the Victorian era when, according to one critic in 1920, "beauty was apparently taboo and all that was ugly in houses and furniture and so-called art was allowed full development."[79] Imagining what in the late nineteenth century would have been esteemed "a very fine house," with its shingled upper story stained red and its clapboarded lower story painted brown, "jig-saw ornaments" embellishing the cornice and piazza, and the front door "bristling with mouldings," one art historian wrote in 1917 that he had always found it "difficult to understand the artistic (or inartistic) madness that fell upon us during the greater part of the nineteenth century, during the period commonly spoken of as the Victorian Era."[80] For their part, funeral directors saw potential and beauty in structures that the general public was ready to cast off. In 1920 Chester Mullen, a Cincinnati funeral director, chose "an old family residence of the antiquated type" that, in the eyes of others, had "outlived its usefulness to a great extent as a place of residence. . . . To the casual onlooker," he noted, "it was of little value for anything save as a first class job for the wrecker."[81]

It was not uncommon for funeral directors to conclude that old mansions required few if any changes in order for them to serve as funeral homes. Many possessed layouts that readily lent themselves with minimal modifications to the needs of funeral directors. "Very little changes will have to made," stated the notice announcing the Ford Undertaking Company's conversion of the old Sloan mansion in Gastonia, North Carolina. An electric elevator was installed in the rear portion of the structure, but "no changes visible from the outside will be made," promised the announcement.[82] When Cincinnati's J. J. Sullivan & Co. found the fifteen-room mansion that was to be its new funeral home, the firm discovered that "on account of the ideal arrangement of the structure," it needed only "a very limited number of changes to make it a very complete funeral home." The firm noted, in fact, that it did "not need any interior changes" and that the alterations consisted merely of two posts flanking the driveway entrance.[83] In reality there may have been additional modifications, at the very least to construct a proper embalming room, as was the case one block away at the W. Mack Johnson Funeral Home, located at the intersection of McMillan Street and Upland Place. "With some additions," explained a September 1920 article in the *American Funeral Director* featuring Johnson's establishment, the former dwelling "could be made the ideal for its purpose." Specifically, the additions included the construction of a porte cochere at the main entrance. In addition, the basement embalming room was "fitted up with the most modern devices."[84] The second floor was likely modified to accommodate the family's living quarters.

The amount of remodeling needed varied. The Dunbar Funeral Home in Columbia, South Carolina, required a bit of work before it opened its doors in January 1925. "Painters, carpenters, decorators, and landscape gardeners were put to work," recalled an article in the *American Funeral Director* celebrating the firm's first year in its new quarters, "and, as time passed, the house that had served for a number of years as a residence began to take on a more colorful and artistic coat. It took several months for the establishment to be put into shape, but when once completed it looked out upon Gervais Street with an aspect of 'something nice'—cozy, inviting and beautiful."[85] Some dwellings were run-down, and more substantial repairs were required. In 1919 an undertaker in Port Townsend, Washington, selected a dwelling that needed a significant amount of work. "The house," according to one account, "was somewhat out of repair, one of the windows was entirely gone, and others had in them broken panes of glass, all were without fly screens, or screens of any sort, save for some sash curtains of a flimsy nature, and there were no proper sewer connections."[86] It was not unusual for large sums of money to be invested in transforming old, often historic mansions into modern funeral homes, and funeral directors were not shy about letting the public know exactly how much was spent. "Thousands of dollars were expended in converting this structure into a funeral home which is second to none in this section of the state," proclaimed the Heinrichs Funeral Home in Jefferson City, Missouri, in 1932. "Improvements have been made both on the exterior and interior," the firm continued, "an addition has been erected in the rear, and the yards surrounding the home now are being landscaped and made more beautiful."[87]

When additions were made, great care was often taken to ensure that they conformed to the scale and style of the original structure. When in 1926 the Dallas, Texas, firm Loudermilk-Sparkman Co. obtained a fifty-year lease on the "fine old colonial mansion" formerly home to the late Colonel A. H. Belo and his family, the firm immediately added a two-story chapel "conforming to the architecture of the main structure."[88] It was advertised that Loudermilk-Sparkman spent $25,000 in the process, an enormous sum at the time.[89] Other firms pointed out that funds spent modernizing an old residence constituted a direct stimulus to the local economy. After converting a dwelling in Sheboygan in 1929, A. W. Ramm made sure to remind the public in the publicity announcing his formal opening that "all of the construction work was done by local workmen."[90]

Some funeral directors demonstrated a keen awareness that eyebrows were often raised when cherished local landmarks were converted to funeral homes. When, for example, residents of Frederick, Maryland, learned in 1939 that the beloved Trail Mansion (fig. 2.8) had been sold to funeral director A. Hart Etchison, "apprehensive questions arose in the community." Having been owned by the family of Colonel Charles E. Trail since its construction in 1852, the three-story brick Italianate mansion, "with its lovely big trees, its fountain and its air of tranquility reminiscent of a bygone day," seemed to have "become public property in the minds of many people." Etchison and his wife understood this and reassured Frederick residents that it would not "be defaced in any way or have a single partition torn out. Everything is to be restored," Etchison explained,

> in so far as possible, to its former state. The first floor is to be refinished, decorated in Victorian style and used entirely for business purposes. However everything will be arranged to appear just as a normal home. The two rooms on the right of the house as one faces it which were formerly the drawing rooms have had the old tapestry wallpaper removed.

FIGURE 2.8   Keeney and Basford Funeral Home (Trail Mansion, ca. 1854), Frederick, Maryland, 2011. Photograph by the author.

This was done only because the paper was past repair. The gold leaf on the ceilings will be cleaned and kept intact wherever it is at all possible throughout the house. . . . No outer changes are contemplated other than the cleaning of the brownstone and marble front, the painting of the stucco on the rest of the building to match, and lightening of the woodwork.[91]

The popularity of the Trail Mansion together with Etchison's unapologetic decorating decisions challenged the notion that the self-appointed arbiters of good taste who reviled all things Victorian held universal sway over public opinion. Although the Victorian Society would not make its debut for more than a quarter of a century, nineteenth-century landmarks often had hearty advocates at the local level.

In general, funeral directors were eager to put any fears to rest and proudly advertised the care they put into restoring historic properties to their former glory. The "artisans' and decorators' touch" employed by Lowell's M. H. McDonough Sons, for example, was not so heavy-handed as to destroy the historic interior of the mansion the brothers chose for their new headquarters in 1923. Among the features left untouched was "much of the original fresco work." Their interest in the house's history was demonstrated in the advertisement announcing the funeral home's formal opening, which mentioned the original owner, Benjamin Webber. The firm drew attention to the house's "solid construction," which was clearly visible in the heavy timbers held together with the "old fashioned wooden pegs, a relic of [the] substantial carpentry of other days." It is not difficult to imagine, however, that saving original details was purely incidental and had more to do with their utility than with any moral imperative to preserve a piece of Lowell's history. "The embellishment of the interior has been carried out," they explained, "with a view to preserving much of its original capacious layout and hence, one is impressed indeed with the cozy, homelike atmosphere within."[92]

More than a few within the industry wanted homelike surroundings and a residential location but chose to build new rather than remodel an existing dwelling. During the interwar period many of the newly constructed mortuaries in the United States were sited in residential neighborhoods and were built to look like mansions. This trend continued up to the Second World War, after which mortuary design began to feel the impact of architectural modernism and veered away from the residential model. During the 1920s and 1930s, however, funeral directors who built new frequently took the residential route, and the results were at times indistinguishable from converted mansions. Although newly built in 1925, the two-story Colonial Revival structure housing the Robert H. Kroos Funeral Home in Sheboygan,

Wisconsin, gave the appearance of large well-to-do, albeit somewhat old-fashioned, residential dwelling. It was "planned to represent a palatial residence,"[93] pointed out the firm's advertisements, which promised patrons "a beautiful, quiet, restful place affording all the privacy, comfort and convenience of a private residence," not unlike the claims made by funeral directors in converted mansions.[94] Similar pledges were made by the Malloy & Son Funeral Home in Galveston, Texas, when it opened in 1930. "A far cry from the gloomy, drab 'undertaking parlors' of former days," the "stately colonial mansion" constructed by Frank P. Malloy and his son offered "all the conveniences and comforts of a home, together with a home-like atmosphere."[95] Just as those converting existing dwellings strove to maintain the outward appearance of a home, those erecting new structures sought to fit in with their residential surroundings. For both groups, conformity was the key to not only creating a homelike atmosphere but also building good relationships and avoiding conflicts with one's neighbors. No funeral director wanted to stand out or become an eyesore.

Vernacular traditions also impacted mortuary design. "Spanish architecture," noted Callaway, "prevails and is proper in some sections of the country," clearly referring to California and parts of the Southwest, where the Spanish Mission style was frequently employed by funeral directors who opted for new construction. "The type and style of architecture suitable for the modern funeral home," he argued, "must depend upon several factors. . . . It must depend on the community in which we are situated."[96] In the end, regional style traditions were likely less of a constraint on funeral directors who chose to build new than available inventory was for those looking to convert an existing dwelling. Nonetheless, both groups of funeral directors found room to exercise individual stylistic preferences, just as both were bound by budgetary and legal constraints. No funeral director could build whatever he wanted wherever he wanted, and many a funeral director who had his heart set on converting a grand and venerable dwelling was thwarted by neighbors who were opposed to having a funeral home move in next door. Both groups of funeral directors were driven by a similar vision. Both strove to create beautiful, comfortable, homelike, and luxurious settings as they competed with not only each other but also the family home, which remained the setting of choice for funeral services well into the interwar period.

A SPIRIT OF REFINEMENT

Notwithstanding efforts to distance themselves both geographically and conceptually from downtown undertaking parlors, residential funeral homes housed many of the same spaces contained by their predecessors, especially the elaborate freestanding downtown mortuaries that had made their appearance toward the end of the nineteenth century. Like their downtown predecessors, residential funeral homes possessed a mixture of public, private, and semiprivate spaces. The public spaces included the entrance hall, reception rooms, the general office, casket display rooms, lounges, restrooms, service parlors, and chapels. The chief private spaces of the funeral home consisted of the embalming room, trimming and stock rooms, the living quarters for the family and staff members, the crematory if one existed, and the office. Offices could be either private or semiprivate depending on whether they functioned solely as a business office or as a space in which funeral directors met with individuals and families making funeral arrangements. The family room and music room off of the main ceremonial space, the slumber rooms, and the rooms for overnight guests were semiprivate spaces, access to which was restricted to select visitors.

One's first impression of the funeral home was formed no doubt while still standing on the outside. "A spirit of refinement," counseled Callaway, and an air of quietness must pervade the modern establishment. This impression should prevail in the outward appearance and impress itself upon our friends before they enter the place."[97] Funeral directors understood this and paid attention to exterior features, landscaping, and signage, which varied in both size and prominence. Generally speaking, industry experts advised a "less is more" approach regarding exterior signage. "Everything which might indicate a funeral place should be kept hidden away," Callaway instructed. "A modest sign should indicate the firm's name and the business."[98] Many funeral directors followed his advice and kept signage small and inconspicuous. "One would never suspect," wrote Warfield Webb describing the outward appearance of Vonderhaar, Stetter & Erschall in 1921, "that this structure was now the abode where the dead are brought to be prepared for their final resting place. There are no outward indications of this change; the only reminder being a small metal sign, on the iron fence at the stairway leading from the street."[99] The Ford & Douglas Funeral Home was marked "only by a handsome sign at the entrance to the lawn." Landscaping mattered too, and funeral directors took care to create neat, well-maintained, and beautiful front yards. At Ford & Douglas "flower boxes filled with the fragrant bloom of petunias" flanked the front steps, "giving a homelike touch to the exterior."[100]

Upon entering a typical funeral home housed in a remodeled residence, one stepped into the entrance hall. Most nineteenth-century and turn-of-the-century upper-class dwellings possessed either a center hall or a side entry hall as part of their layout, and this feature naturally lent itself to the needs of funeral directors wishing to create a lobby. Those coming in to make funeral arrangements were immediately ushered into an adjoining reception room or general office, most likely a space originally designated as a parlor or library. As the impression the funeral director wished to give was of a well-maintained and prosperous residential dwelling, the reception spaces played a crucial role in reinforcing the illusion that one had entered a domestic space rather than a commercial establishment. "Nothing which suggests a funeral should be in evidence in the reception room," Callaway advised. "Nothing but the fine atmosphere of a quiet, homelike, comfortable place," he insisted, "where one may rest and visit, and be forever among friends who are ready at the moment of suggestion to minister to their every need, should ever be the impression gained by any who enter."[101] At Buffalo's Johnson & Wilkins Funeral Home the reception

room was "arranged primarily to give privacy in making funeral arrangements, leaving out as much as possible the suggestion of business."[102]

A brief description of an early reception room was given in a 1928
advertisement for the newly opened Bender Funeral Home in Gettysburg, Pennsylvania. Situated to the left of the entrance hall, the
room was "outfitted similar to the living room of a modern home, with
a fireplace, brighter curtains at the windows than those in the chapel
itself, floor lamps, a heavy carpet, a small writing desk and attractive
furniture."[103] A 1926 article announcing the opening of the Ford &
Douglas Funeral Home offers an even more detailed look at a reception area. In this case, the "reception suite" consisted of the center entrance hall and two front rooms:

> Entering the reception suite on the lower floor, the visitor sees nothing
> of a funereal aspect. Nothing of a depressing atmosphere is found here.
> Spacious and cool, carpeted with soft, luxurious rugs and hung with
> silken draperies in pleasing colors, the three rooms which open to-
> gether here have the appearance of a comfortable living suite in a well-
> ordered home. The furnishings are such as one would find in a home of
> this sort; and the atmosphere is quiet and restful.[104]

Within the context of an advertisement, this description of the reception area sheds as much light on the desired impression that funeral
directors wished to make as on the actual space itself. It reveals the
reception suite as an imagined, idealized space while at the same time
providing information about the kinds of furnishings and finishes
typically employed to create a beautiful, comfortable, and homelike
environment. Photographs of the hall and adjoining rooms show original wainscoting and moldings, a large central staircase, a multiglobed
chandelier, carpets, Windsor chairs, side tables, table lamps, and a deer
head mounted over a columned and mirrored mantelpiece.

Virtually every residential funeral home possessed space of some
kind for the display of caskets and other funeral paraphernalia. While
the industry's need to sell burial goods was hardly diminished by the

departure of funeral directors from the downtown, merchandising itself was problematized by the domesticity of their new residential
quarters. With the change of scenery came a renewed debate about the
nature of funeral directors and their work, a debate reflected in the type,
amount, and precise location of space devoted to selling. At the heart
of the debate was the question of whether the funeral director was
a professional service provider or merely a salesman. Many robustly
embraced their role as businessmen with no qualms whatsoever. In
those funeral homes the display rooms were likely to be prominently
located, well lit, and strategically arranged. In other establishments,
however, display spaces were small, haphazardly organized, and out of
the way. Although a first-floor location suggested the proprietor's comfort with his or her role as a salesman, a second floor or basement
showroom did not necessarily reflect indifference to salesmanship or
modern merchandising.

The Baker Mortuary, which occupied a striking turn-of-the-century
neoclassical mansion in Wisconsin Rapids, Wisconsin, contained a
prominently situated suite of display rooms on the main floor adjacent to the offices and front entrance. The space was big enough to
hold eighteen caskets along with a selection of burial garments.[105]
M. H. McDonough Sons had a large room, twenty by thirty feet, for
the display of "caskets and funeral paraphernalia," situated on the first
floor directly off the central hall but toward the rear of the edifice,
behind the service parlors.[106] The "large, spacious Show-room" at
Andrew N. Johnson's in Nashville was located behind the chapel,
though in 1908 he was still relying upon a method of displaying caskets commonly used by turn-of-the-century undertakers, most of
whom were still located downtown. "All grades of casket from the cheapest to the high prices," explained the newspaper article accompanying
his new establishment's formal opening, "are exhibited in automatic
folding, golden oak cabinets."[107]

More secluded were the display rooms of the Riemann Funeral
Home in Gulfport, Mississippi, which were situated "on the second
floor with the employees' sleeping quarters."[108] Although the display

rooms of Klute & Son's Funeral Home in Richmond, Indiana, were also located upstairs, "the greater part of the second floor of the mortuary," explained an article in the September 1930 issue of the *American Funeral Director*, was set aside for the display of caskets, with "four rooms being devoted to this purpose."[109] The four showrooms on the second floor of the Ford & Douglas Funeral Home were "elegantly appointed throughout, with well-chosen draperies and wall papers," and displayed "everything which is needed in time of bereavement, including caskets ranging from those of moderate cost to the more luxurious and imposing ones." Clearly, the owners did not shun salesmanship, and their decision to put their display rooms on the second floor was driven less by discomfort with merchandising and more by a desire to keep the main floor free from any obvious reminders of death. "All of these reminders of grief," they explained, "are, as has been said, on the second floor, well away from the reception suite downstairs, and thus the first floor is almost entirely free of anything of a funereal appearance."[110] Likewise, the showrooms at Vonderhaar, Stetter & Erschall were on the second floor, accessible by means of "a stairway leading from the front section of the main hall." The carefully arranged rooms were described by one industry observer as being large with high ceilings, offering "quiet and a place wherein a selection can be made for the deceased" as well as "a large number of caskets of varying prices, some being of a very costly type."[111] Wherever a showroom was placed, it was customary for funeral directors to emphasize their varied stock covering a wide range of prices to suit every family's budget. Advertising a "large and varied selection of funeral merchandise in all price groups" became a hallmark of a fine establishment.[112]

Rooms set aside for memorial services were practically guaranteed a first-floor location. Typically branching off the main hall or reception area, these rooms consisted of either a grouping of service parlors or a large funeral chapel. In rarer instances, a funeral home possessed both. Such was the case at Cincinnati's George Rhode Funeral Home, a purpose-built, residential-style mortuary whose layout offered a chapel and three funeral parlors on either side of a large central hall.[113]

In most cases, however, funeral directors chose one or the other, depending on their personal predilection. "The chapel," explained Callaway, "may be equipped similar to a church, or it may be more homelike."[114] Charles Berg elaborated further:

> Some establishments contain a large room arranged and decorated in a manner similar to a church or chapel; it is equipped with an organ, and pews are provided as well as a rostrum from which the minister may speak. Other undertakers provide for this need of a place for holding services by having a suite of rooms furnished similar to a parlor or drawing room. This latter arrangement serves to give a home-like atmosphere to the funeral service.[115]

Instead of pews, the chapel might contain upholstered sofas and chairs, end tables, carpets, and other homelike effects. More than a decade after the residential funeral home made its initial debut, funeral directors were still wrestling with the question of which was a more suitable atmosphere for the funeral home's main ceremonial space, church-like or homelike. "There is a strong difference of opinion among funeral directors," observed one insider in 1931, "as to the relative merits of a chapel, with church-like effects, as compared with a service parlor, where home-like atmosphere is featured. In making a selection between the two, the funeral director must be guided by local demands."[116]

Some funeral homes such as Dawson & Wikoff, which opened in Decatur, Illinois, in September 1922, pursued a more church-like approach. Its chapel contained an Estey pipe organ, and although there were no fixed wooden pews, the chairs were arranged in rows in longitudinal fashion with a center aisle. The same was true of the chapel at the Bender Funeral Home in Gettysburg, which used "comfortable chairs . . . instead of pews" and could accommodate eighty mourners. "The chapel," proclaimed a 1928 announcement,

> takes its place among the most artistically appointed. In the front part of the chapel are four Ionic pillars, and countersunk in the ceiling, back of the pillars, lights are concealed so as to throw a subdued, indirect glow

over the casket and the officiating clergyman. The draperies at the windows in the chapel are a rich wine color, fringed with gold, while the walls are done in dark tan textone, a new process for finishing walls. . . . The floor is laid in mottled black and white linoleum blocks, set in cement.[117]

Even without fixed pews, the effect of such an arrangement was likely more church-like than homelike.

Others, such as Fred G. Marshall Sons of Detroit, rejected the chapel concept. "Chapels," the firm argued, "are cold and unsympathetic, so we have done away with that feature entirely and have substituted parlors."[118] Some expressed ambivalence toward the notion of a chapel even while creating spaces that, from their descriptions, seem to have been church-like in appearance. "Care was taken" at the Ramm Funeral Home in Sheboygan, explained an advertisement, "to avoid any chapel appearance and all plans were concentrated upon providing as nearly as possible a homelike atmosphere and homelike surroundings to the new funeral home." At the same time, the firm freely referred to its principal ceremonial space as a chapel. The large room, which could accommodate one hundred mourners, was adorned with stained glass windows, "diffusing a mellow light throughout the spacious room."[119] East of the chapel was a separate music room containing an organ. Cincinnati's W. Mack Johnson Funeral Home referred to the main ceremonial space off the entrance hall as "the main funeral parlor" in an attempt to distance itself from the concept of a funeral chapel. "No," explained the 1920 article in the *American Funeral Director* on Johnson's establishment, "this is not a chapel. . . . There is not any attempt here to take the place of a place of worship." The room resembled a large living room, although it did possess a lectern. Additionally, the adjoining room had an organ and "a number of chairs with white linen covers," arranged, one suspects, in chapel-like fashion.[120]

In reality, many chapels combined church-like effects with homelike appointments. Pipe organs were relatively common. Some were integrated into the main chapel space or service parlor, while others were housed in a separate music room. Such was the case at the Boland

Mortuary in Peoria, Illinois, whose music room housed a pipe organ that could "fill the entire house with its tones."[121] Other funeral homes, such as the Hege and Flanigan Funeral Home in Columbus, Indiana, kept a small pipe organ in the front hall. Certain ecclesiastical elements, such as fixed pews and vaulted ceilings, were much less common in converted dwellings than they were in purpose-built mortuaries, however. For starters, houses obviously lacked such components, and installing them meant undertaking substantial renovations or constructing an actual chapel addition, such as the two-story chapel added to the rear of the Belo Mansion by Loudermilk-Sparkman in 1926 and the "long, cylindrical roofed addition" housing the chapel at the Moreland Funeral Home (fig. 2.9) in Pittsburgh, Pennsylvania. With its "beamed ceiling and massive pipe organ," it was an impressive sight, though its owners chose to forgo fixed pews.[122]

Lowell's M. H. McDonough Sons opted for multiple service parlors. To the east side of the center hall was a "spacious parlor" fourteen by thirty feet in size. On the opposite side were two additional parlors fifteen by fifteen feet, each separated by a doorway. The two smaller rooms could be used "in conjunction with the larger parlor on the

FIGURE 2.9   Chapel of the Moreland Funeral Home, Pittsburgh, Pennsylvania, 1928.
Courtesy of Kates-Boylston Publications.

other side of the hall" or separately if the occasion arose. "It is possible," McDonough explained, "with the layout of these three rooms and the method of entrance into the hallway and then into the funeral carriages, to conduct three distinct funerals at the same time without the slightest confusion." While funeral services outside of the home of the deceased were still relatively rare in the early 1920s and it seems unlikely that a situation would have arisen in which three funerals would be held simultaneously at his new quarters, McDonough noted that "the need of such an arrangement" had been made manifest at the firm's previous location.[123]

None of M. H. McDonough Sons' service rooms was called a chapel. Instead, the firm was quick to point out, "the furnishings of the room on the first floor, particularly that part of which is to be utilized at funerals, are in keeping with a finely kept home."[124] For M. H. McDonough Sons and many other funeral directors in remodeled mansions, the emphasis fell squarely on homelike and the "convenience, comfort and beauty that would be expected in a finely appointed residence of the better class."[125] The firm preserved and capitalized on the dwelling's residential character and steered away from changes, such as the addition of more church-like features, which risked undermining the atmosphere of "an exquisitely fitted and furnished private residence,"[126] something, they believed, a remodeled mansion effortlessly conveyed.

THE THINGS THAT ARE DESIRED

Both chapels and service parlors almost always included a nearby or adjoining room in which members of the immediate family could be seated in relative isolation during funeral services. A "private room for the sorrowing family,"[127] or "family room" as it came to be called, had been a feature of some downtown funeral parlors, but its popularity increased dramatically with the rise of the residential funeral home. The primary purpose of such rooms was to provide the immediate family their own comfortably furnished space in which they could hear the funeral services without being seen by other mourners. This gave family members an extra measure of privacy by shielding them from "the curious gaze of others."[128] Throughout the 1920s and 1930s, the family room featured prominently in many funeral home advertisements. This room formed a key component of the larger marketing campaign to persuade families to hold the funeral services of their loved ones at the funeral home. With their emphasis on the seclusion afforded by the family room, funeral directors hoped to convince the public that modern funeral homes could offer greater privacy than modern American homes of the period. "Nowhere else," boasted a 1926 advertisement for the Mansfield Funeral Home in Mansfield, Ohio, "could one have the same privacy and comfort and yet see and hear the services as well, save in our beautiful and commodious family room."[129]

Family rooms were often separated from the service parlor or chapel by either a set of French doors or portieres, as was the case at the Croxford Funeral Home in Great Falls, Montana, in the 1930s and is still the case today (figs. 2.10, 2.11). Similarly, at the Klute & Son's Funeral Home in Richmond, Indiana, "a beautiful arched doorway with heavy drapes" separated the family room from the service parlor.[130] Doors and drapes allowed for flexibility and varying degrees of seclusion, depending on whether they were open or closed. The Erwin Funeral Home in Pontiac, Illinois, had a family room that could be "completely shut off to secure any desired privacy" or, when services were being held, "made part of the service room by opening wide French doors" for those desiring less privacy.[131] Mack Johnson of Cincinnati offered members of the immediate family use of a sunny private solarium "just off the funeral parlor on the front," furnished with wicker furniture, ferns, and a bubbling fountain. The family, explained the 1920 article in the *American Funeral Director*,

> can remain here, with the French doors ajar, and see and not be seen, and find comfort in the environment that the scene lends. They will be curtained and made as cozy as artistic taste can make possible. The idea of the solarium is to make possible an abode where one may find rest amid surroundings that will be soothing, and at the same time removed from the immediate vicinity of the service.[132]

FIGURE 2.10 Family room of the Croxford Funeral Home, Great Falls, Montana, ca. 1930. Courtesy of the Croxford Funeral Home and Crematory.

FIGURE 2.11 Family room of the Croxford Funeral Home and Crematory, Great Falls, Montana, 2023. Courtesy of the Croxford Funeral Home and Crematory.

In other establishments the family room was not directly adjacent to the service parlor or chapel but was situated on the opposite side of the entrance hall, as was the case at the Boland Mortuary, whose "cozily furnished" family room was so situated, the owners pointed out, "as to permit the relatives to see and hear funeral services in the chapel without exposing themselves to public view."[133]

Most layouts allowed access to the family room from the entrance hall without forcing the family to pass directly through the main chapel or service parlor. In some instances the family room opened onto a separate hallway or vestibule or had its own private entrance. The family room at the Dunbar Funeral Home was "arranged so as to be free from all disturbances" and was situated so that mourners could "enter from the side door and not come in contact with any other persons."[134] Likewise, at J. Ed. Phillips's establishment in Glendale, California, the cars carrying members of the immediate family pulled up to the rear of the establishment, and the family then entered through a private door that led directly to the family room. "The others who attend," Phillips explained, "come through the reception hall at the front. The family, screened by the portières, hear the service, and remain in the room until the chapel is cleared."[135] In rare instances the family room was located on the second floor. The Fred G. Marshall Sons Funeral Home in Detroit included "a parlor upstairs for the family, as would be the case in a private home."[136] Similarly, the Corken Funeral Home in Cincinnati, Ohio, offered family members desiring greater privacy "a handsomely furnished guest room" on the second floor. "Here," the owners explained, "members of the family may remain in absolute privacy, yet within hearing of the service below."[137]

Another room accessible only to funeral home staff, members of the immediate family of the deceased, and their close friends was the laying-out room, otherwise known as the slumber room. Like the family room, the slumber room traced its roots to the downtown funeral parlor in which it had made its debut around the turn of the century as a semiprivate space for the laying out of the deceased prior to casketing. In spite of these early antecedents, funeral directors in the 1920s routinely spoke as if their generation had invented the concept. Probably the reason for this claim is that prior to the 1920s, the popularity of home funerals meant that few bodies were laid out in downtown undertaking parlors even though comfortable facilities existed for families who preferred that option. "As far as I can discover," stated Glendale's J. Ed. Phillips in 1926, "I am the originator of the idea of a slumber room, though many others have put them in since I started several years ago. In the East it is the general custom to move the bodies home after they are prepared, or to prepare them in the house and leave them."[138] The W. B. Coon Company of Long Beach, California, had multiple slumber rooms, "a chamber each for men, women, and children ... furnished similarly to the bedroom of a home." In fact, it was not unusual for establishments to offer a separate slumber room for children and infants such as the one offered by the Croxford Funeral Home, which featured a child's bed, plush toys, and a mural of a fairytale landscape painted on the walls (fig. 2.12). Often referred to as "the nursery," the space was equipped with either a crib

FIGURE 2.12   Children's slumber room of the Croxford Funeral Home, Great Falls, Montana, ca. 1930. Courtesy of the Croxford Funeral Home and Crematory.

or a cradle, whichever the occasion required. The Malloy & Son Funeral Home in Galveston, Texas, included a "baby room, fitted up with a small baby bed and a cradle as well as other comfortable furniture."[139] The wallpaper and furnishings in the nursery of the Noel Funeral Home in Pekin, Illinois, were chosen to "suggest the very spirit of childhood instead of an unnatural gloom."[140]

"After the body has been prepared," explained a 1926 article in the *American Funeral Director* describing the W. B. Coon Company's funeral home, "it will be removed to one of [the] slumber rooms, where it will appear as though asleep. Thus when the relatives visit the home to select a casket it will to some degree alleviate their sorrow."[141] Funeral directors were confident that the slumber room's homelike appearance would exert a positive and therapeutic psychological effect on the bereaved. "In most rooms where the bodies are laid out," explained one industry insider,

> there is a cheerlessness and discomfort which adds to the grief of the bereaved ones. . . . We have called the room a slumber room, and the word is painted on the doors, as you see; and we provide a bed, with real springs and mattress, for the body. . . . And it is very comforting to them to see the body resting peacefully on a bed, rather than on an unyielding preparation room table.[142]

For most practitioners, a slumber room was considered an indispensable component of the residential funeral home.

"Every funeral director," Callaway taught,

> should have a room so appointed that he can bring the body to this room when embalming is completed. The family will thus find their dead in a quiet, beautiful room, not very unlike the bedroom of their home. This impression, the first time they have seen the deceased since the body was entrusted to you, is an impression that shall never be forgotten. By this you will always be remembered. Make the memory a pleasant one for the family.[143]

Callaway's clear preference was for bedroom furniture, and many funeral directors followed his advice. "The slumber room," he argued, "should be equipped very much like a neat bedroom. As soon as the body is prepared it should be placed in this room for the relatives and friends to visit. To find one's dear one in a room of this kind is a great relief to those who mourn."[144] Slumber rooms furnished like bedrooms were intended to function almost as stage sets and constituted an important part of the funeral director's art. They were homelike but not home, constructing the fragile illusion that the family was with the remains of their loved one in the privacy of their own home. Slumber rooms were carefully crafted to bring to mind a peaceful domestic deathbed scene, a crucial component of what was considered a good death.

While bedroom furniture was commonplace in many slumber rooms prior to the Second World War, some, such as Gettysburg's Bender Funeral Home, included a couch instead of a bed. At the Ford & Douglas Funeral Home the room "arranged for the repose of the body after embalming" contained "a softly draped couch." The room, explained an advertisement, was "furnished in a homelike manner, with nothing in its appearance to jar the sensibilities of bereaved relatives and friends."[145] Regardless of the particular furniture employed as props in re-creating familiar laying-out rituals, it is clear that in the context of the residential funeral home, a comfortable slumber room was one of the key features relied upon by the funeral director to evoke a homelike atmosphere and commodify both privacy and domesticity.

Some funeral directors also offered guest accommodations as part of their funeral homes for either the family, if they wished to stay overnight at the funeral home under the same roof with the remains of their loved one, or for out-of-town family members attending the funeral.[146] "It has been found to be quite practical," explained Berg, "to provide rooms for members of the deceased's family, for there are occasions when the family is summoned from a distant city and it is pleasing for them to be near their dead."[147] The Indianapolis funeral home of Hisey & Titus had "a guest room . . . especially fitted for strangers in the city," the firm explained in an advertisement, "who are here to attend the last rites, or are escorting a body either to or from the city."[148] Johnson & Wilkins offered patrons "a guest room completely furnished, like a hotel," the firm explained, "for use of any who come in from another city, and who shrink from hotel surroundings at such a time."[149] There is little doubt that the "splendid chamber" on the second floor of the M. H. McDonough Sons Funeral Home offered to those who desired "to remain in the home with the bodies of their friends or relatives" was one of the amenities referred to in a 1925 advertisement as "the things that are desired" by grieving families.[150] These things, M. H. McDonough Sons claimed, "are all to be found in our funeral home; nothing has been overlooked or omitted."[151]

Guest rooms were surely appreciated by not only out-of-towners but also more progressive families already committed to the idea of holding the funeral of their loved one at the funeral home. With the remains of their loved one laid out in the slumber room downstairs, some must have taken advantage of accommodations that allowed them to stay in the funeral home overnight, a prospect that seems inconceivable today. Furthermore, the convenience and comfort afforded by guest lodgings was an additional means of reaching the unconverted and dislodging the cherished custom of the home funeral. For those families who were on the fence and willing to consider an alternative, nontraditional setting for the funeral service but disliked the idea of leaving the body of their loved one under a strange roof overnight, the guest room offered a solution and a way of removing what may have been for some the final impediment to services at the funeral home. The guest room was intended to ease the conscience and provide peace of mind.

BEHIND THE SCENES

The truly private portions of the funeral home, the areas strictly off limits to all but funeral home staff, consisted of living quarters for the owner or some other staff member, sundry stock rooms and trimming rooms, flower rooms, the embalming room and morgue, the garage, utility rooms, and the crematory if one was included in the arrangement. The location of workspaces within the funeral home was flexible, and they were found on every floor from the basement to the upper stories. The number and type of private rooms varied depending on the size of the funeral home. Large or small, however, virtually every residential funeral home possessed an embalming room and living quarters for the owners or staff. The owner's living quarters were likely to be situated on one of the upper floors, but overnight rooms for the staff sometimes had ground-floor locations. The embalming room in particular was often singled out by industry experts as requiring firm boundaries. "No idle loafers or curiosity seekers," admonished Callaway, "should ever see this room at any time, and no one but a relative or physician or an official who has reason to do so should ever be admitted to the embalming room while a body is within the room."[152] Except in rare instances, no members of the public except perhaps the immediate family of the deceased ever had reason to enter this space.

While layouts differed, there was widespread agreement that the embalming room should be far removed from the display room and reception area as the structure's square footage and interior arrangement would allow. For example, at Klute & Son's the preparation room, which was "fitted with the most modern equipment" and "finished in pea green," was in the very rear of the first floor with no street frontage. In addition, it was separated by the rest of the funeral home by the staff's overnight quarters (fig. 2.13). Because the converted mansion occupied a corner lot, the placement of the preparation room, buried in the innermost portion of the structure, was considered ideal because it was "remote from both streets and completely isolated from the public parts of the building."[153] The preparation room at the Holeton Brothers Funeral Home in Niles, Ohio, was also situated in the back portion of the first floor, "as far away from visitors as possible," with "a doorway connecting [it] with the slumber room,"

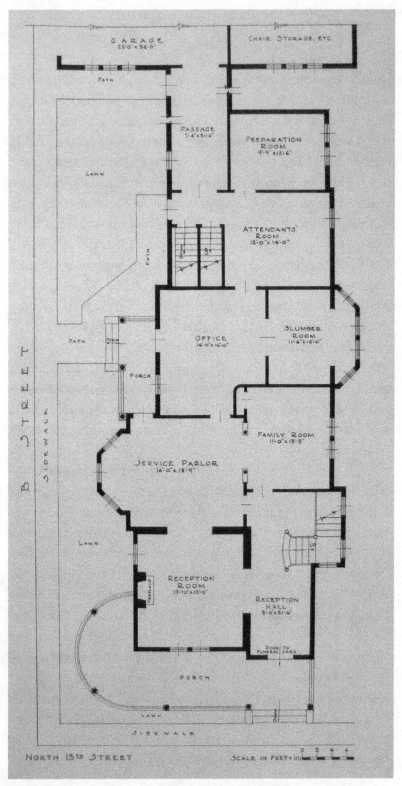

FIGURE 2.13 First-floor plan of the Klute & Son's Funeral Home, Richmond, Indiana, ca. 1930. Courtesy of Kates-Boylston Publications.

most likely for convenience.[154] The preparation room at the Dunbar Funeral Home was also directly adjacent to the slumber room. First-floor locations next to the slumber room were not unusual, but basement embalming rooms were equally common. The Baker Mortuary in Wisconsin Rapids possessed a basement embalming room that was described as being "spotlessly white and clean . . . well lighted and airy."[155] A preparation room on one of the upper floors was not out of the question, however. Frank Cook and Don Wright of Cambridge City, Indiana, had a second-floor "operating room . . . as clean and sanitary as that of any hospital."[156] That Cook and Wright had installed an elevator in the converted dwelling surely helped.

More than any other room in the funeral home, the embalming room required technical, even hazardous, equipment, such as a porcelain or metallic embalming table and special pumps, not to mention chemicals. "No part of the establishment," argued Callaway, "deserves better equipment than the embalming room, for no room is more important. Every instrument, all furniture and the walls and floors should be thoroughly cleaned and sanitized. Strong light and good ventilation are necessary."[157] The first-floor preparation room at the Jones & Jones Mortuary in Wenatchee, Washington, was lit by "four large white overhead lights" in addition to the frosted windows, offering both illumination and privacy. The room was equipped with an exhaust fan "to take out all offensive odors," explained an article in the May 1931 edition of the *American Funeral Director*. "The floor and six feet up on the wall," the piece continued, "is composed of acid proof white tiling. There are three separate drains with tables and two instrument cabinets and a sterilizer for use in the preparation of bodies."[158]

The well-lit embalming room at M. H. McDonough Sons was on the first floor directly off the trimming room, where caskets were fitted up. The embalming room had a "karbolith sanitary floor" with "walls and ceiling done in white enamel." Multiple windows, presumably with frosted glass panes, gave "floods of natural light," making the room, the owners claimed, "one of the finest and brightest rooms of its kind in the state."[159] Similarly, the well-lit embalming room of the

Moreland Funeral Home in Pittsburgh possessed both a tiled floor and tiled walls (fig. 2.14). While some embalming rooms were tiled or enameled, others were merely painted. For example, the ground-floor preparation room of the Sumrall-O'Quinn Funeral Home in Laurel, Mississippi, was "painted in spotless white," giving it "an impression at once of perfect cleanliness and efficiency."[160]

Other private spaces included flower rooms, which often contained cabinets and shelves for the storage of vases, refrigerated storage units, and a lavatory sink; sundry stock rooms; trimming rooms, where caskets were finished and customized with whatever textiles and hardware the family had selected; possibly a crematory, though these were far more common in purpose-built mortuaries;[161] and garages. The garage might be integrated into the main structure or separate. The advantage of an integrated garage was that it allowed funeral directors to load and unload bodies in complete privacy. Garage additions were also common. Callaway believed that remodeled dwellings were especially well suited to receive a garage addition in the rear. "These good homes," he argued,

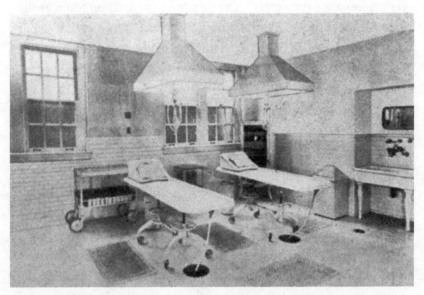

FIGURE 2.14   Embalming room of the Moreland Funeral Home, Pittsburgh, Pennsylvania, 1928. Courtesy of Kates-Boylston Publications.

almost always occupy an estate large enough to admit of the construction of a garage in connection with the rear of the home. This prevents any outward appearance of the funeral. When bodies are brought to the place the car drives inside the garage and the doors are closed before the body is removed. There is a door leading from the garage into the establishment through which the body is conveyed. No one on the outside is ever attracted by anything that is done. After the service in this home, the body is conveyed to the garage through the way constructed for that purpose. When the funeral car drives from the garage it already contains the body.[162]

At M. H. McDonough Sons "the last unit of the first floor organization" was "a garage 20 × 33 feet," so situated that bodies could be "placed in the morgue from the garage without being in full view of passersby."[163] Access to the garage was possible from either the morgue or the trimming room. Nonetheless, separate garages situated away from the street, usually behind the main funeral home, were not unusual. The Thronson Undertaking Co. in Racine, Wisconsin, for example, advertised "an elaborate garage" behind the large Neoclassical mansion that it had converted into a funeral home in 1922,[164] while the "spacious grounds" of the Barlow Funeral Home in Charleston, West Virginia, included a separate six-car garage in addition to the two driveways traversing the property, "affording convenient ingress and egress for those attend[ing] even the largest funerals."[165]

While more than half of the overall square footage of many funeral homes was customarily given over to private "behind the scenes" spaces, one space in particular dominated the private areas of the funeral home: the family living quarters. On the second floor of M. H. McDonough Sons Funeral Home, for example, was "a splendid six room apartment" in which John L. McDonough resided with his family.[166] Similarly, the second floor of the Bender Funeral Home housed "a modern nine-room apartment . . . occupied by the junior member of the firm and his family." Access to the apartment was "through a side entrance separate from the funeral home itself."[167] George Rhode resided with his family on the second floor of his purpose-built funeral home in Cincinnati. "There are two entrances to this part of the building," explained an article in the September 1920 issue of the *American Funeral Director,*

> one from the front hall and the other from the side door, which opens to the driveway. There are on this floor a living room, a dining room, breakfast room, kitchen, two bed rooms and a bath. In addition to this, there is also a sunroom that makes it possible to get a view of four streets, which intersect at this place. The third floor contains three bedrooms and a lavatory. The upper portion of the house is finished for living quarters, and the rooms are light and cozy.[168]

Although family living quarters were, at least in theory, completely private and separate from the public spaces of the funeral home, they were frequently mentioned in advertisements and newspaper articles featuring recently opened or remodeled establishments. Beyond merely housing the owner and his or her family, private staff apartments took on an almost spiritual significance, reminding the public that the funeral home was not simply a place of business but also an actual home. This was to become a key weapon in the arsenal of residential funeral home owners in their campaign to undermine their downtown competitors.

THE TRUE FUNERAL HOME

During the interwar period the funeral industry was enlivened by an often heated debate over nomenclature. Who specifically had the right to designate their establishment a funeral home was a matter of widespread disagreement. While most agreed that a residential location was a key component of a funeral home's identity, some downtown establishments had begun calling themselves funeral homes. For those in remodeled dwellings, only structures that had once housed a family deserved the designation, while those in purpose-built mortuaries fired back, arguing that efficient service could be rendered only in structures specifically designed to care for the dead. Still others argued that what really mattered was whether someone, a family, lived on-site. In this way, the owner's living quarters, though invisible, came to play a symbolic and defining role in making the funeral home its own distinct entity within the crowded field of professional deathcare.

Many felt that the presence of living quarters was the key element that defined the funeral home as such. In 1930 G. R. Lawson of Lawson & Son in Brazil, Indiana, wrote to the editor of the *American Funeral Director* to put the question to its readers. "We claim to have the only funeral home in Clay County," he wrote,

> but one of our competitors (who is also a very good friend of ours) claims that his establishment is also a funeral home. Now, our place was formerly our family abode. It has been remodeled and enlarged to accommodate our business and we continue to live in it. On the other hand, our competitor has his complete establishment—preparation room, casket display, garage and office—in a re-built down-town building, to which he has added a porch. His home is in another section of the city quite some distance from his place of business. No one resides in his place and there are no provisions made for the possibility of any one ever residing there.[169]

Callaway had observed in 1928 that the term "mortuary," which was "quite the rage" not too many years earlier, had by the time he wrote *The Art of Funeral Directing* come "to mean only certain designs, certain characteristics of funeral establishments. We do not find," he observed, "this title attached to the home-like place so much as to the semi-business place." The funeral home, on the other hand, was "thought of as the residence place. In the true funeral home," he argued,

> we expect to find someone living. We expect to find a part of the place occupied by the proprietor or some responsible employee. If this part of

the picture is not carried out we feel that the name is not properly applicable to the place. . . .

To be a Funeral Home the establishment must be a real home. There must be a real living place and a family actually living in the place. Without this we cannot conscientiously call the establishment a Funeral Home and the public will not so accept the name.[170]

For Callaway, the distinction between funeral home and mortuary was clear. It was neither the chapel nor the display room but rather the family's living quarters that were the very essence of the funeral home. Without them, he claimed, there were no funeral homes, only mortuaries.

Having on-site living quarters also meant that a staff member was on call at all times. As a result, an upstairs apartment or, at the very least, staff bedrooms such as the one at the Loudermilk-Sparkman Funeral Home allowed funeral directors to highlight their availability at a moment's notice, especially at night when the offices of a downtown parlor would have been shut up, its proprietors gone home for the evening. This distinction was not lost on funeral directors who seized the opportunity provided by living quarters to distinguish themselves from their downtown competitors. "Our new funeral home," advertised James McKenna of Lowell, who moved his quarters into a remodeled Second Empire dwelling in 1933, "is not, like a purely commercial establishment, deserted at night. It is occupied just like a private residence. This is a consideration of no small importance, and one worth remembering."[171]

Some undertakers whose facilities did not include living space responded by questioning the propriety of having live persons reside on the premises. "No family living or cooking quarters are provided in any part of Friesen's large modern mortuary building," proclaimed the Friesen Funeral Home in Hutchinson, Kansas. Friesen aimed its critique at both the existence of on-site living quarters and remodeled dwellings in general. "Compare Friesen's modern funeral home," admonished a 1938 advertisement, with funeral homes of the small rooming-house type with their rambling front porches of the standard dwelling house type and so-called chapel provided by removing the partition between the old front parlor, dining-room and kitchen. Such funeral homes, housed in a small old dwelling house, invariably use the choice rooms for family living and cooking quarters adjoining or near congested mortuary service rooms. Family entertainments, cooking odors, radio, lack of privacy and many other abuses deny proper care and respect and should be prohibited by law.[172]

Others made similar jabs. Some industry experts felt that in spite of the trend toward remodeled dwellings, those in purpose-built mortuaries held a distinct advantage. "The funeral director who has a home that was built for the purpose," posited one insider, "has a talking point that is worth something, especially if his competitor has one that was only remodeled for the purpose."[173]

Efficient service, argued many funeral directors working from purpose-built mortuaries, could be rendered only in structures specifically designed to handle funerals. When the Johnsen Mortuary was opened in Las Vegas, New Mexico, in 1926, its owners noted that they could have remodeled an existing structure, "but," they explained, "we have always had it in mind to give only the best to the community. We are glad we have waited as the new and beautiful edifice now being erected will bespeak the interest we have always held in the community."[174] In 1935 C. E. Cline & Son opened its new mortuary in Frederick, Maryland, purpose-built, "not remodeled" and "especially designed," they pointed out, "for this purpose."[175] When the Plains Funeral Home opened in Lubbock, Texas, in 1943, it promised not only "the utmost in comfort and convenience" but also "the high plane of service available only when the home was designed and built for the purpose."[176] Many who erected new mortuaries rejected the claims made by those in remodeled dwellings that existing layouts and floor plans designed for daily living readily lent themselves to funeral services. "The funeral home which has been made from an old home by simply hanging a sign out in front," argued one industry expert, "has one distinct disadvantage. The so-called funeral parlors are merely two or three rooms together as much as possible, thereby making it impossible for those attending to get a view of either the minister or the floral decorations."[177]

Funeral directors who chose to remodel mansions clearly worked with what they had. They were adept at making the most of layouts that they themselves did not design. Although it was common for those in purpose-built mortuaries to refer to their establishments as funeral homes and tout the homelike quality of their facilities, those in remodeled dwellings maintained that their quarters, having once housed a family, alone were truly homelike. "We remodeled a dignified, handsome old dwelling in preference to building a new one," explained W. W. McFarland of the W. W. McFarland & Son Company Funeral Home in Warren, Ohio, "because only houses which have been lived in have a home-like atmosphere."[178] Many insisted that those in purpose-built mortuaries might have the luxury of creating the perfect layout, but former dwellings imparted their legacy and aura of hominess to the funeral directors who acquired them. This was something no newly erected mortuary could rightly claim.

The owners of the Boland Mortuary understood this. "As the Hodges Mansion," they asserted, "the house was noted for its spaces, high-ceilinged rooms and for that intangible 'homey' quality that modern builders seem unable to capture, for all their blueprints and fine airs."[179] When funeral directors operating purpose-built mortuaries made jabs at remodeled mansions, those in remodeled mansions gave it right back. This was free market capitalism at work. After all, the deathcare landscape of many cities and towns consisted of a mixture of downtown parlors, purpose-built mortuaries, and remodeled mansions. They competed with one another for business, their advertisements offering a critique of the others' products and spaces.

The significance and propriety of family living quarters as well as the merits of new construction versus remodeled dwellings were hotly debated, and what constituted a funeral home remained an open question within the industry. Consensus proved elusive, but in the end what mattered more than a structure's origin was its context. As important as even living quarters were to some, it was a residential neighborhood that garnered the support of the majority of practitioners and came closest to providing the basis for a collective definition of the funeral home. "The proper location for a funeral home," proclaimed a 1927 advertisement for the Dawson & Wikoff Funeral Home, "is a residential district."[180] The firm, having relocated just five years earlier to a residential neighborhood, may have been biased, but industry experts nationwide rallied around the idea that a funeral home relied on its residential surroundings for its character and identity as "a real, temporary home" for the bereaved family.[181] "The residence district is exactly where the funeral home is needed and desired," concluded the editor of the *American Funeral Director* in 1928. "The whole plan of the modern mortuary and the service it is designed to render," he explained, "depends on its being removed from the noise and commotion of the business district. It must be located among residences, where it can really have the appearance and atmosphere which will justify the name of funeral *home*."[182] This became a common refrain within the industry during the interwar period.

As funeral directors nationwide began to reconsider their surroundings, first in the larger cities and then in the smaller towns, many endeavored to leave the noise and congestion of the business district behind. Increased automobile usage had intensified old problems and created new ones, such as the traffic jams and parking shortages experienced by nearly every city and town in the United States. A residential address, on the other hand, offered many advantages, not the least of which was the ability to market homelike in a way that left one's downtown competitors out in the cold. At the same time, mansions themselves promised benefits of their own. A structure's elite provenance and distinguished former inhabitants lent legitimacy and respectability to an industry still struggling to shake off its past connection to the livery stable. Imposing exteriors and grand interiors fit nicely with the prevailing wisdom linking consumer desire for luxury items to sumptuous shopping spaces. Before a mansion in a residential district could be acquired or built, however, funeral directors first had to overcome the opposition of area residents, whose vision of the ideal neighborhood did not often include a funeral home.

PART TWO

CONTESTED LANDSCAPES

CHAPTER THREE

A CONSTANT REMINDER OF DEATH

The Funeral Home as a Nuisance

When Thomas Woolley's daughter learned in late 1920 that a funeral home was opening next door to her family's home on West Avenue in La Crosse, Wisconsin, she was so distraught that she became hysterical and fainted. Woolley's testimony to that effect on Tuesday, July 19, 1921, before La Crosse county circuit court judge James Wickham in the case *Cunningham v. Miller* was corroborated by several additional witnesses. Daniel Cunningham, another West Avenue resident, and several of his neighbors, including the Woolleys, were seeking a perpetual injunction that would have restrained Adelbert Miller and his wife Sophia from operating a funeral home from the Platz homestead, a circa 1885 Queen Anne mansion that the Millers had purchased the previous November (fig. 3.1).

The neighbors had already prevented the conversion of another nearby dwelling, the old Montague home, by banding together and purchasing the property when they learned that the Millers were eyeing it for a funeral home. Undeterred, the Millers tried again and eventually succeeded in moving their quarters from 320 Main Street in the heart of the downtown (fig. 3.2) to the Platz homestead, situated

FIGURE 3.1   South on West Avenue from Main Street, La Crosse, Wisconsin, *William Pryor's La Crosse by the Camera* (1894). The Platz homestead is the third house from the right in the middle of the photograph. Elsie Giles Scott's "Pasadena" is the large brick mansion on the right. With the exception of a Christian Science church at the northeast corner of West Avenue and King Street and the conversion of "Pasadena" into a YMCA, the street remained largely residential through the end of the Second World War. Murphy Library Special Collections, La Crosse Area Research Center, University of Wisconsin–La Crosse.

at 134 West Avenue between Main Street and King Street, in January 1921. So noteworthy a detail was the Woolley family's subsequent mental anguish, evinced by the daughter's hysterical fainting spell, that in its reporting of the trial, the *La Crosse Tribune and Leader-Press* made her trauma a secondary headline to the story, writing in capital letters "FAINTING OF MR. WOOLLEY'S DAUGHTER IS RELATED AGAIN."[1]

The conflict that the Millers sparked in La Crosse was hardly unique. Across the nation, funeral directors seeking to relocate from the downtown to a residential neighborhood often faced stiff resistance. In addition to injunctions sought by those who regarded an undertaking establishment on their street as a nuisance, zoning ordinances, many of which had only recently been adopted, also proved to be a formidable obstacle. There were even instances in which zoning laws came into being in response to funeral homes. Whether fighting an injunction or battling a zoning law, funeral directors were

FIGURE 3.2   Main Street, West from Fourth Street, La Crosse, Wisconsin, 1904, *Philippi Art Souvenir of La Crosse* (1904), 18. Murphy Library Special Collections, La Crosse Area Research Center, University of Wisconsin–La Crosse.

more frequently the losers than the victors, though there were notable exceptions.

Moreover, the amount and strength of resistance they encountered in any given neighborhood depended on many factors, not the least of which was the collective wealth of the area residents. Wealthier, more influential communities were more likely to take on a funeral director and win. Neighborhoods that had already seen multiple encroachments from expanding business districts were less likely to mount a successful campaign to oust an enterprising funeral director. As neighborhoods and public opinion evolved, opposition gradually lessened. During the 1950s once elite nineteenth-century residential districts, long ago having fallen out of favor among middle- and upper middle-class homeowners, continued to lose ground to newer and farther afield suburban subdivisions,[2] and conflicts between area residents and funeral directors seeking to convert old mansions gradually ceased.

CUNNINGHAM V. MILLER

During the interwar period funeral directors who, like the Millers, attempted to set up shop in a converted dwelling risked being hauled into court by their neighbors. The lawyers for the complainants in *Cunningham v. Miller* based their petition for an injunction on several claims, the first and foremost being that the neighborhood was exclusively residential in nature. In his opening statement, attorney Frank Winter argued that West Avenue was itself "the heart of the exclusive residence district in La Crosse."[3] Furthermore, locating a funeral home amid the "homes of the aristocrats" would, he claimed, have a deleterious effect on both property values and psyches.[4] "Because of funerals having been held from said place," explained Winter, pointing to the negative psychological impact of living near a mortuary, "and a consciousness that dead bodies may be or are on the Miller premises, and because of other reminders of mortality, the neighbors are discommoded and unhappy and their feelings and spirits are depressed, life for them becomes less tolerable, and their bodily resistance to disease is lessened."[5] The plaintiffs' lawyers also raised the specter of odors from disinfectants escaping to nearby premises as well as the "danger of infection and spread of disease." Their final claim asserted that the presence of a funeral home made the neighborhood "less desirable as a residence district," and as a result, property values were "accordingly depreciated."[6]

Denying the allegations of the complaint, the defense responded by arguing that the Millers conducted their business "in a lawful and legitimate way without injury to the plaintiffs or the general public."[7] The defense also reminded the court that in moving their undertaking business from Main Street to West Avenue, the Millers had violated neither state law nor any city ordinance. Attempting to allay concerns about the presence of dead bodies and large crowds of mourners in the neighborhood, their attorneys claimed that funerals were "held from the premises at infrequent intervals" and were "but little attended."[8] This is an interesting detail that prima facie sounds somewhat disingenuous, but it should be remembered that in 1920 most funerals took place at the home of the deceased. On the stand Miller himself testified that between January and July 1921, only eight funerals had been held from the funeral home, about one per month.[9] At the time of the trial, undertaking establishments, whether located downtown or in residential districts, had not yet achieved widespread acceptance as ceremonial spaces; rather, they were primarily retail spaces in which funeral arrangements were made and caskets were selected. It is not at all surprising therefore that the defense tried to capitalize on the fact that services from the funeral home were the exception.

Similarly, the defense pointed out that nearly half of all the embalmings performed by Miller occurred away from the specialized facilities offered by the funeral home. Miller testified that 45 percent of the bodies he buried were "prepared for burial at the home of the deceased," in which cases the bodies were "not brought to the funeral parlor at all."[10] In the case of deaths occurring from contagious disease, Miller reassured the court that all of the bodies were prepared for burial at the place where the death took place, either at the hospital or the home of the deceased and never at the funeral home. As late as 1920, deathbed embalmings conducted with portable equipment were not uncommon. It is true that a greater number of bodies were sent to undertaking establishments for embalming in 1920 than had been the case at the turn of the century. Still, even those remains were typically returned home for the funeral.

The defendants' boldest claim was made with respect to the character of the neighborhood in which they sought to operate their business. Rejecting the notion that the district was strictly residential, they argued that "through rapidly changing conditions West Avenue has become a commercial thoroughfare, has lost its character as a residence street, and is building up with amusement places, factories, stores, garages, and other establishments, and in recent years several churches have been built along its course and that another church is about to be built."[11] The heart of the exclusive residential district, they explained, lay many blocks to the east, out past Seventeenth Street, while West Avenue, they insisted, had already been overtaken by the commercial activity that had been moving steadily eastward from La Crosse's riverfront.

This truly was disingenuous. Funeral directors who had traded the downtown for a residential location chose neighborhoods that afforded them a quiet, noncommercial atmosphere. Those who made the move, moreover, produced advertising that contrasted their new residential addresses with the bustling, noisy, congested business districts they had left behind. In front of the judge in the case *Cunningham v. Miller*, however, the defendants made it sound as if West Avenue had been taken over by the downtown. Had the street been as they described, the Millers would likely not have chosen it in the first place. Presumably, they had to downplay the qualities that had made the neighborhood appealing to them, because those were the very same qualities that their new neighbors were seeking to preserve by preventing the operation of a funeral home. In effect, the Millers were claiming that it was impossible for them to spoil the residential character of the neighborhood because it had already been destroyed by an influx of commercial development.

Judge Wickham disagreed. In his findings of fact, he maintained that the area chosen by the Millers was indeed residential in nature, something clearly evident in the Sanborn insurance map of the street (fig. 3.3). Wickham found that one could travel half a dozen blocks eastward from West Avenue and before reaching Seventeenth Street still find oneself in the midst of

an exclusive residence district, the most valuable in said city, in which many large and expensive residences and many smaller and less expensive ones now are and have been maintained for several years last past, some of the best of which residences are located on West avenue[,] ... and no business house is located within five blocks in any direction from

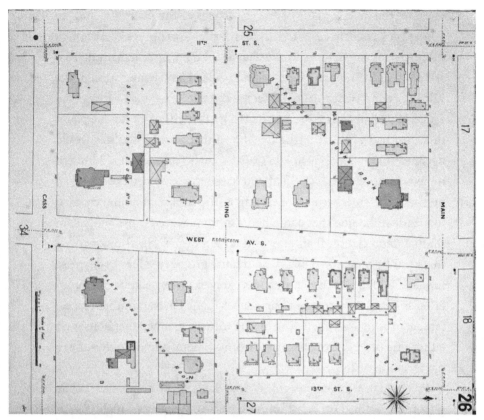

FIGURE 3.3   Plate 26 showing the Platz residence, second house on the left on West Avenue, north from King Street, La Crosse, Wisconsin, *Sanborn Fire Insurance Map from La Crosse, La Crosse County Wisconsin* (1906). Library of Congress.

the defendants' premises, except a few scattered business houses to the north, the nearest of which are a drug store and a paint shop on the west side of West avenue in the north half of the block, north of Main street.[12]

In fact, he observed that the houses owned respectively by the ten plaintiffs in the case were "all maintained in good condition," with "large sums of money . . . expended in improving and beautifying the buildings and grounds."[13] In Wickham's view, the neighborhood not only had kept its residential character intact but was also wealthy and well cared for.

Next, Wickham found that "the natural and probable result" of maintaining a funeral home in the neighborhood would be "to materially decrease the market value of the residences of the plaintiffs" and "to render such residences materially less desirable as homes."[14] Although a witness for the defense, real estate agent Sam Birmingham had asserted "that the funeral home had not caused any depreciation in the value of property near it" or impacted the sale of several nearby properties, Wickham was more persuaded by the witnesses for the plaintiffs who had testified to the likelihood that property values would decline.[15] One witness, Dr. J. L. Callahan, who on the stand admitted to being among those who had purchased the Montague property to prevent the Millers from converting it into a funeral home, claimed that a funeral home that contained a morgue would cause more substantial depreciation than one without a morgue. He also conceded that a public garage or stable "would cause property values to decrease in value" and that even a church was likely to cause neighboring properties to lose 10 percent of their value.[16] Frank Chase, another real estate agent who was called as an expert witness, claimed that houses on either side of and across the street from a funeral home would suffer a depreciation of 25 percent.

Psychological damage was likely as well, Wickham concluded. While physicians testified on behalf of both parties, Woolley's daughter's description on the witness stand of the anguish she endured was doubtless very moving. Bertha Jehlen, a neighbor from across the street, claimed that "thoughts of death had been on her mind" from the moment the Millers moved in.[17] It was only natural, Wickham reasoned, that having a funeral home within sight of one's residence would

> create in the plaintiffs and members of their families feelings of dread of contagious diseases and feelings of discomfort and dissatisfaction from the sights and noises, and in some instances from the odors incident to said business; and, by the constant reminder of death, to depress the feelings of some of the plaintiffs and members of their families, especially the women, children, and such persons who are ill or of a nervous temperament, such depressed feeling thereby impairing the comfort and happiness of all members of the family.[18]

Wickham also held that no matter how sanitary the Millers' establishment was, it would be impossible to keep their quarters "entirely free from flies," and "offensive odors arising from the use of embalming fluids and from dissected bodies" would inevitably "escape therefrom to adjoining premises." Maintaining an undertaking establishment in such an "unsuitable and improper place" had caused nearby residents both psychological and financial harm and was, Wickham declared, a nuisance.[19] The plaintiffs were therefore entitled to abatement of the nuisance, and the Millers were perpetually enjoined from operating a funeral home at 134 West Avenue.

In his verdict, Wickham did not refer to the zoning law that La Crosse had passed in April, because it had not been in effect when the Millers opened their establishment on West Avenue three months earlier. The city council had proposed a zoning ordinance as early as September 1920 before the Millers had purchased the dwelling that would become their funeral home, though it is likely that they had by that time already been thwarted in their attempt to purchase the Montague property. The ordinance would have established a residential district eight blocks by fifteen blocks wide in which "no business houses" were to be established without the consent of a majority of the residents.[20] West Avenue passed through the western end of the proposed district. An editorial titled "Helpless" that appeared in the *La Crosse Tribune and Leader-Press* on March 27, 1921, alluded to "several recent instances" in which property owners complained to the newspaper of "the purchase of sites in residence neighborhoods as locations for business establishments out of keeping with the general character of the district."[21] Although the piece did not single out particular parties by name, its author clearly had the funeral home on West Avenue in mind. After all, the plaintiffs had commenced their legal action against the Millers that very month.

One way "to forestall the intrusion," the article explained, was to purchase the targeted property, which the residents of West Avenue had already done on one occasion. However, this was expensive and generally an option only for the wealthy. For "the laboring man buying a little home" to pay "a premium for an adjoining site in order to keep it from being turned into a boiler-factory or a stable" would be impossible. "He is helpless," lamented the piece, "despite the reduction in value of his home and the vitiation of his family environment." The only way to "keep inviolate the home sections of the community and otherwise protect property-owners from the intrusion of depreciating neighbors," admonished the author, lay in "the adoption of a zoning ordinance" similar to those in effect "in most progressive cities," which "if properly worked out to suit local conditions generally prove eminently satisfactory. They are a part of the program of every modern city-plan movement."[22] Such an ordinance was passed by the La Crosse City Council in April 1921. The residential district afforded protection was slightly smaller than the zone proposed in the original draft of the ordinance, but West Avenue fell well within its borders.

On appeal, the Millers challenged the injunction of the circuit court but not La Crosse's zoning ordinance. The case was argued before the Wisconsin Supreme Court on June 6, 1922, and just over a month later a verdict was issued affirming the decision of the lower court. Writing for the majority, Justice Marvin B. Rosenberry acknowledged that there was "no zoning ordinance in the city of La Crosse or other law or regulation directly affecting the condition existing in reference to the property in question."[23] Although La Crosse's zoning ordinance had already been in effect for over a year, it could not be applied retroactively to the Millers' business, which predated the law. As a result, it had no bearing on the case. The question addressed by the court was not the validity of La Crosse's zoning ordinance; rather, the two issues at stake were whether the area in question was truly residential in nature and the soundness of the lower court's judgment that a funeral home situated in a residential district constituted a nuisance.

On the first point, the majority of justices were not persuaded by the argument made by the Millers' attorneys that the presence of several nearby churches had ruined the residential character of the district. "We think the evidence ample to sustain the finding that the locus in quo is a residential district," wrote Rosenberry, nor do we think the fact that churches have been or are about to be erected in or near the vicinity materially alters the situation. The churches are not generally or usually associated with the business district of a city. Neither is the presence of a church such a disturbing factor in the life of a community as is the presence of an undertaking and embalming establishment.[24]

Having established that 134 West Avenue was indeed located within the confines of a residential neighborhood, Rosenberry went on to consider whether "the making of post-mortems, the holding of funerals, and the removal of dead bodies to and from the premises" constituted "a nuisance when located and carried on in the residential section of a city."[25] To answer this question, he and his colleagues cited the growing body of case law from other states that spoke directly to this issue.

THE RIGHT OF THE CITIZEN

The Wisconsin Supreme Court was not the first state high court to address the legality of funeral homes in residential neighborhoods. Twelve years earlier in *Densmore v. Evergreen*, perhaps the first case of its kind nationwide, the Washington Supreme Court upheld a lower court's ruling that a funeral home operating in a residential district constituted a nuisance. Rejecting testimony that property adjacent to a funeral home would depreciate in value, the court relied exclusively on the expert opinion of the physicians who testified that a funeral home in a residential district posed a danger of infection and contagion because of "the possibility of flies passing from there to surrounding places."[26] The court also "found evidence that noxious odors, gases, especially those arising from the deodorants used in cleansing the business premises, would permeate the homes." Finally, the court held that "the conduct of the business near people would have had a depressing effect an average person's mind, would weaken his physical resistance, and would render him more susceptible to contagion and disease."[27]

In a similar case, *Saier v. Joy*, the Michigan Supreme Court in 1917 overturned the verdict of a trial court that refused to grant an injunction to the neighbors of a recently established funeral home on a residential street in Lansing. In reversing the decision and granting the injunction, the court held that "the landowners would have suffered concrete harms if a funeral home located in their midst. Their property values would have materially decreased, it was likely that noxious odors would escape the funeral home premises, and the landowners would be subject to a depressed atmosphere."[28] Any depression, moreover, was not due to an unusually high degree of squeamishness on the part of specific individuals. The court was quick to point out that it was not catering to a supersensitive minority and argued, on the contrary, that the mental health of most people would be adversely affected by the proximity of a funeral home. "We think it requires no deep research in psychology," the court explained,

> to reach the conclusion that a constant reminder of death has a depressing influence upon the normal person. . . . The constant going and coming of the hearse; . . . the not infrequent taking in and out of dead bodies; the occasional funeral with its mourners and funeral airs, held in the part of the house designed for a chapel; the unknown dead in the morgue, and the visits of relatives seeking to identify them; the thought of autopsies, of embalming; the dread, or horror, or thought, that the dead are or may be lying in the house next door, a morgue; the dread of communicable disease, not well founded, as we have seen, but nevertheless present in the mind of the normal layman—all of these are conducive to depression of the normal person; each of these is a constant reminder of mortality. These constant reminders, this depression of mind, deprive the home of that comfort and repose to which its owner is entitled.[29]

The notion that it was not merely "the exceptional individual" of "fastidious taste" or "extreme sensitiveness" who would suffer under the depressing atmosphere created by the presence of a funeral home became a hallmark of legal decisions enjoining funeral homes in residential neighborhoods.[30]

The court also held that although the funeral home business was not a nuisance per se, "the chosen location in the middle of a residential neighborhood was improper."[31] Acknowledging that undertaking was not only "lawful, but highly necessary," the court explained that it could not "overlook the right of the citizen to be protected in his home, and his right to the enjoyment there of that repose and comfort that are inherently his." Like the defendants in *Cunningham v. Miller*, W. H. Joy and his wife had argued that their business was conducted in the most sanitary and modern manner and that funerals would be "infrequent." In response, the court was careful to point out that it was not out to restrain the defendants' business but rather "its intrusion into a long-established and strictly residential district."[32] The Joys had also claimed that a large number of Michigan undertakers were operating in residential districts. The court, however, felt that this was an exaggeration and posited that in most cities undertaking establishments were located either at the edge or in the midst of the business district. Those funeral directors who had moved out of the downtown, the court observed, generally established themselves in locations in which the residential character of the district was already giving way to the advance of commerce.[33]

Both *Densmore v. Evergreen* and *Saier v. Joy* were among the precedents cited by Rosenberry, who argued that "the great weight of authority in this country" was to "the effect that the establishment and operation of an undertaking and embalming business in a residential section under such circumstances constitutes a nuisance."[34] While this may have been overstatement, as dissenting justice Franz C. Eschweiler pointed out,[35] given the relative paucity in 1922 of cases addressing funeral homes in residential neighborhoods, Rosenberry's claim was certainly true by the end of the decade. As more actions were brought against enterprising funeral directors, more injunctions were sought, and more cases were heard, state supreme courts across the nation sided with those who opposed the presence of a funeral home on their street.

THE CLEAR TREND OF THE LAW

There were many cases in which funeral home operators attempted to fight the injunctions granted by lower courts, just as the Millers and Joys had tried to do. Undertakers John R. Higgins and Harry Courtney sought unsuccessfully to appeal the verdict of the Circuit Court of Mobile, which had granted their neighbor Jacob D. Bloch an injunction preventing them from moving their business to the Leinkauf residence, which they purchased in November 1924 with every intention of converting it into a funeral home even though it stood less than ten feet from Bloch's house. Affirming the lower court's verdict, the Alabama Supreme Court held in 1925 in *Higgins v. Bloch* that the intrusion of a funeral home into "the very heart of the most popular residence part of the city" constituted a nuisance. In addition to acknowledging the "offensive odors arising from the use of disinfectants and deodorants" that are "blown to adjacent premises," the court sympathized with the neighbors who would be forced to endure the crowds who "often come to such establishments from morbid curiosity and loiter around" in the "cases of those legally executed, or who come to death by other forms of violence." Equally distressing would be the "paroxysms of grief and lamentations . . . plainly heard by those living near such establishments."[36]

There can be no doubt that in 1920 a family who suddenly found themselves living next door or across the street from a funeral home experienced genuine discomfort and emotional trauma. Undertaking parlors had for more than half a century been located downtown, far away from residential neighborhoods. The reaction of Mrs. Goodrich of Port Townsend, Washington, when a funeral home moved into an old house adjacent to hers was typical of the mental anguish and anxiety experienced by those who found themselves in her position:

> I am unable to relish my meals or sleep properly; it is on my mind continually. It has a depressing effect upon me. I don't think I am oversensitive. I have been with the dead at the time of dying, and have no

fear of spirits or anything like that; but it is very disagreeable. I have a constant fear of contagion from living in close proximity to a morgue, on account of my children and family. I have noticed a great many flies around my premises lately. I am continually fighting them in the house; we are in fear of them all the time. It suggests this morgue the moment I see a fly. I can see in the morgue. I can see from my back door the entrance there, I presume, to the basement or the cellar of the house, and upstairs I can see what goes on in the street. I can hear hysterical sobbing and the music that is played there. From my yard I can see them carrying in and out dead bodies. It spoils the enjoyment of our home. I don't care to invite guests to dine at my table. I know that a great many of my friends have the same feeling that I have in regard to it. My chief pleasure has been in caring for my garden, and I am denied that pleasure. If the morgue continues to run in close proximity to my residence, I feel that I cannot live there, and will want to move as soon as we are able.[37]

Judges took such testimony very seriously. In Mrs. Goodrich's case, the injunction she and her neighbors sought against the offending funeral director was granted and affirmed on appeal by the Washington Supreme Court.

In at least one instance, the young were singled out as being especially vulnerable to the harmful psychological effects of a nearby funeral home. In *Harris v. Sutton*, although the proposed funeral home was to be located in a residential district of Atlanta, it was "the testimony of the superintendent of the public schools of Atlanta" concerning the "deleterious effect" its presence would have on "a large public school" that prompted the lower court to grant the injunction, a ruling upheld by the Georgia Supreme Court in 1929.[38] On the other hand, when in 1926 Arthur O. Moran was prevented by his neighbor Michael W. Dillon from operating a funeral home from the Howe homestead on Grand Boulevard in Detroit, Michigan, the injunction did not even mention the threat of emotional trauma. Instead, it focused exclusively on the "material pecuniary loss" Dillon would suffer after expert witnesses testified that neighboring properties could be expected to depreciate by anywhere from 20 to 50 percent.[39] In general, however, cases were decided as was *Laughlin v. Cooney*, in which the Alabama Supreme Court considered both the psychological and pecuniary impact of a funeral home on Franklin Street in Huntsville, Alabama.

Adhering to the precedent it had set five years earlier by *Higgins v. Bloch*, the court ruled in March 1930 that although

> the business of conducting funeral parlors is a lawful business and necessary to the proper care and disposition of the dead, nevertheless the fact remains that its inherent nature is such, if located in a residential district, it will inevitably create an atmosphere detrimental to use and enjoyment of residence property, produce material annoyance and inconvenience to the occupants at adjacent dwellings, and render them physically uncomfortable, and in the absence of a strong showing of public necessity, its location in such district should not be allowed to protrude into such residential district over the protests of those who would be materially injured thereby.[40]

The justices concurred with "the learned trial judge" who had given ample weight to the claim that the value of complainants' property would be depreciated or "rendered less desirable a place of residence." At the same time, he acknowledged "that 'the lamentations and groanings' of friends and relatives of deceased persons would be of a disturbing nature" and that "the bringing or removal of dead bodies to said establishment would be either visible or audible to complainants."[41]

One issue that arose during the case was whether the presence of an apartment building or boarding house compromised a neighborhood's residential character. The property in question was the former residence of Robert Lytle. A palatial Neoclassical dwelling designed in 1902 by Huntsville architect Herbert Cowell, the structure stood at the corner of Franklin and Williams Streets, both of which the lower court recognized were "distinctively residential" and had been so "for many years—at least seventy-five years." The immediate area contained several apartment houses, "the character and nature of which is residential rather than business. The apartments are occupied by families as their homes, and they are not deprived of their residential character because they are occupied for the most part by renters rather than by owners, or because several families may be housed in each."[42] Nearby was also a boarding house that possessed "the quality of residential property more than business property," according to the trial judge. "People, as a rule," he explained, "live in boarding houses, there getting their meals and lodging, spending their time when away from their business, and seldom use them for business purposes." Both the trial court and the high court concluded that

> the fact that one or more of the residences in the neighborhood have been, in part, converted into apartments to be used as places of residence, and that one is used as a boarding house, is not such a change as to deny to the district, in which appellant proposes to establish and conduct its undertaking business and funeral parlor, the character of a strictly residential district.[43]

Although they differed in some of the particulars, similar decisions had by the 1930s coalesced into a clear "trend of the law" restraining the operation of funeral homes in residential neighborhoods.[44] Past the midcentury mark, similar rulings continued to be handed down, though by then the tide had begun to turn in favor of the residential funeral home as both public opinion and older neighborhoods evolved.

Purpose-built mortuaries in residential neighborhoods fared no better. In the early 1920s W. E. Turner maintained an undertaking parlor in the business district of El Dorado, Kansas, but owned a piece of land in the residential section of town at the corner of Pine and Washington Streets. The lot possessed a barn and a garage, which housed his motor equipment, but Turner had them taken down, and

> a building which to all outward appearance was a typical private residence of the better sort was erected[,] . . . [and] its true character was kept secret by defendants while it was being constructed; but upon completion it was revealed that it was specially designed for the business

of undertaking—an embalming workroom in the basement and a chapel for funeral services on the main floor, and for a private residence on the second floor only.[45]

Nearby residents sought an injunction that was granted by the trial court, which ruled that an undertaking establishment located at the intersection of two principal residential streets constituted a nuisance to its neighbors. Turner appealed, but the Kansas Supreme Court upheld the injunction, adding that his neighbors could not possibly "enjoy their homes in peace and quietude" while he went about his "dismal" work and that "the laughter and play of their children about their own dooryards would seem heathenish and unfeeling in such a doleful environment. Social and family gatherings in residences so placed would be a pathetic caricature of happiness and enjoyment."[46]

Almost a quarter century later in *Brown v. Arbuckle,* a California court of appeals handed down an almost identical judgment. Toward the end of December 1947, N. B. Arbuckle commenced construction of a mortuary over which there was to be "a large neon advertising sign" on Wilson Street in an area of Oildale, California, that was "primarily and substantially residential" for "a radius of several blocks."[47] An injunction was granted to his neighbor Guy W. Brown who, in addition to claiming the usual mental anguish and diminished value of his property, testified that he and his wife "used their backyard constantly in the summer as a place to eat, have picnics, lunches and parties for their friends; that the proximity of the funeral parlor, with its constant reminder of death, would have a dampening effect on this type of entertainment, and would in all probability cause their friends to refrain from visiting them." It was also alleged that Arbuckle's mortuary would "interfere with and obstruct the normal and free passage of traffic along the streets in the vicinity and adjacent to [the] plaintiff's property."[48] This was especially ironic, because among the factors compelling the earliest undertakers to venture beyond the downtown a generation earlier was a desire to be free of the traffic and congestion clogging business districts, especially as automobile use increased.

PEARSON V. BONNIE

Not every funeral director lost. Although the overwhelming opinion among judges was that a funeral home in a residential neighborhood constituted a nuisance, there were exceptions, the most notable being *Pearson v. Bonnie*, decided by the Kentucky Court of Appeals in 1925.[49] On March 5, 1924, thirty-one homeowners whose dwellings were located in the vicinity of Third and Ormsby Streets in one of Louisville's finest residential neighborhoods filed a petition for an injunction preventing the firm L. D. Pearson & Son from establishing a funeral home in the venerable Ferguson mansion, a magnificent Beaux Arts dwelling the firm had purchased in January (fig. 3.4). During the trial the judge largely dismissed the threat of contagion alleged by the plaintiffs and gave only minor weight to the possibility of either foul odors from disinfectants or sounds incidental to funeral services.

FIGURE 3.4   The Ferguson Mansion (later Pearson & Son Funeral Home), Louisville, Kentucky, ca 1912. Filson Historical Society.

At the same time, he admitted that there was no doubt in his mind that "the presence of this establishment would depress the value of neighboring property." Equally clear was the likelihood that the proximity of a funeral establishment would "have a depressing effect upon the spirit of the average person."[50] The injunction was granted, and Pearson & Son appealed.

In an uncharacteristic show of support for the funeral industry, the Kentucky Court of Appeals reversed the decision in February 1925, and the injunction was lifted.[51] In rendering its decision, the court reviewed the body of case law addressing funeral homes in residential neighborhoods and found the cases to indicate

> clearly that the courts were not satisfied, although they used in their opinions some language looking that way, to rest an injunction against an undertaking parlor solely on the grounds of depreciation in property value accompanied by mental depression due to the association of ideas, and that they all insisted on some other element being present in the case, such as a zoning ordinance or the imminent probability of odors, noise and communicable diseases coming from the property.[52]

What the court was saying in effect was that although it might look prima facie as if judges in other states had granted an injunction based on material depreciation of property values and the creation of a depressing atmosphere, in reality there was always some other factor, such as a zoning ordinance, odors, or flies. This was a stretch, but it was one interpretation of the available precedents. Writing for the majority, W. Truman Drury, commissioner for the court, concluded that because the plaintiffs failed to demonstrate either misconduct on the part of Pearson & Son or unsanitary conditions that jeopardized their health and their only real complaint was "the depreciation of the value of their property occasioned or accompanied by a sentimental repugnance to the business of appellants, the lower court erred in granting the injunction it did."[53]

THE WELL-RECOGNIZED POLICE POWER
OF THE STATE

Relief from the courts in the form of an injunction sought by unhappy persons faced with the prospect of a constant reminder of death next door was not the only means by which funeral homes were kept out of residential neighborhoods. As *Pearson v. Bonnie* pointed out, communities also turned to zoning, a relatively new regulatory tool at the disposal of municipalities around the time that undertakers began their push into residential neighborhoods. Although New York is credited with crafting in July 1916 the first comprehensive zoning ordinance in the United States, a handful of other cities had prior to that already begun to consider zoning legislation, and a few had passed ordinances that established residential districts from which certain types of industry and commerce were barred.[54] By the 1920s zoning laws were in place in many cities and towns nationwide.[55] Their purpose, explains planning historian Mel Scott, was largely to protect single-family residential areas by substituting "municipal regulation for the deed restrictions imposed by private developers." Many of these restrictions "were expiring in some residential areas and had only a few years to run in other areas," and municipalities sought to avoid the devaluation of property that would inevitably result if neighborhoods were invaded by "unwelcome flats and apartment or, worse still, by stores and small factories."[56]

Some funeral directors simply ignored zoning ordinances prohibiting them from setting up shop in residential neighborhoods and were subsequently prosecuted. In other instances funeral directors themselves were the plaintiffs, proactively challenging the validity of local zoning ordinances after being denied permits. Both situations proved to be test cases for zoning laws, the constitutionality of which judges nationwide were called upon to consider. Thus, by 1926 when the US Supreme Court handed down its landmark ruling in *Euclid v. Amber*, in which the high court upheld the validity of zoning, a handful of state supreme courts cases had already addressed the legality of primitive zoning ordinances barring funeral homes from residential districts and found such regulations to be a legitimate extension of municipal police power.[57]

In August 1919 undertakers John W. Kessler and Thomas S. Maguire of St. Paul, Minnesota, purchased the stately nineteenth-century Second Empire dwelling at 649 Summit Avenue in a section "for many years . . . held in high favor" as an exclusively residential neighborhood "distinguished for its beauty and attractiveness." They proceeded to encircle the structure with a driveway and began to "advertise the place as a funeral home. They caused a sign to that effect to be conspicuously displayed from the window facing Summit Avenue, and rearranged the interior to meet the needs of a funeral home."[58] Shortly thereafter, the two were arrested and tried in municipal court for violating the terms of Ordinance No. 5180: "No undertaking or embalming business shall be carried on and no mortuary chapel, funeral home, vault, or other house, building, structure or receptacle for the preparation of the dead for burial or for the reception, deposit, or keeping, of the dead bodies of human beings shall be established, opened, kept or maintained in any residence district in the city of St. Paul."[59] During the trial, counsel for Kessler and Maguire attacked the ordinance as unconstitutional for depriving them of the free use of their property without due process. The validity of the ordinance was upheld as a legitimate exercise of the city's police power, and the two funeral directors lost their case.[60] They subsequently appealed, and the case was heard before the Minnesota Supreme Court, which affirmed the lower court's ruling that an undertaker who "purchases and uses, as a funeral home, a dwelling house situated in a strictly residential part of a city . . . infringes upon the repose and comfort of those residing in the neighborhood, depresses their spirits and depreciates the value of their property."[61]

The Minnesota Supreme Court's ruling was based in part on the precedent set by *Osborn v. Shreveport*, in which the Louisiana Supreme Court reversed a lower court's decision to grant Roll Osborn an injunction preventing the city from enforcing Ordinance No. 27 of 1915, which declared it unlawful "to maintain or operate any undertaking shop or parlor, where bodies are embalmed, kept, or prepared for interment, except on the business streets of the city."[62] All streets not specifically named in the ordinance were considered residential. Osborn, who had migrated from Indiana with his wife, Kittie, had since 1910 been operating one of Shreveport's largest undertaking establishments on the 700 block of Texas Street, which was considered a business street even though the simple two-story wooden Queen Anne structure Osborn chose had previously served as a residence. In late August 1917 he entered into a contract to purchase the Logan mansion, a large and ornate Queen Anne structure that was designed by Shreveport's premier late nineteenth-century architect, Nathaniel Sykes Allen, and completed in 1897. Osborn had agreed to pay $18,500 for the dwelling, which was situated on Christian Street in a residential section of the city.

When the city learned that Osborn intended to convert the dwelling into a funeral home, the commissioner of public safety sent him a letter warning that he would be arrested and prosecuted for violating Ordinance No. 27 of 1915. Osborn promptly sued the city, challenging its authority to enforce the ordinance. During the ensuing trial much of the testimony focused on the question of whether noxious odors would escape from Osborn's establishment, but in the end the court was satisfied that Osborn's neighbors would not be adversely affected by his business. He was granted a preliminary injunction, which the city appealed. In considering the legal issues at stake, the Louisiana Supreme Court was "not convinced that the enactment of the ordinance was beyond the police power of the city of Shreveport."[63] The justices charged that the case seemed

> to have been presented to the district court as though the plaintiff and the city were the only parties in interest and theirs the only property rights to be considered, and none of the residents . . . given a hearing, nor were any witnesses summoned in their behalf to testify either as to the probable effect of the intrusion upon the value of their property or upon their future enjoyment of life in their homes.[64]

Although the justices acknowledged that Osborn conducted his business "after the most approved methods and with as little offense to those by whom he may be surrounded as the business will admit," they pointed out that "the business itself is a gruesome one." One could not doubt the harmful "psychological influence of being confronted, and having one's family confronted, day after day and at all hours of the day, with death, and its woeful trappings in the shape of hearses and other vehicles, carrying in and out of a neighboring building the mortal remains of some fellow being." Declaring that a funeral home in a residential neighborhood would "depreciate the value of the property as well as discommode the owners,"[65] the court annulled the injunction, and the Osborns were forced to vacate the premises.

In 1920 W. A. Brown sued the City of Los Angeles to enjoin the enforcement of what he felt was an "arbitrary and unreasonable" ordinance "restricting the location of undertaking establishments to certain zones." Ordinance No. 9695 was enacted on July 13, 1904, and prohibited undertaking establishments outside of what was designated District No. 1, which included "practically all of the business and some of the semi-business property in the central portion of the city." Brown had undertaking rooms in District No. 1, but his lease expired, and he purchased a lot 170 feet from the district's southernmost boundary upon which he planned to erect a mortuary. "He applied to the city council for an amendment to the ordinance by which the property he had purchased would be excepted," but opposition to his plans developed within the neighborhood, and his permit was denied. He went ahead with his plans and was arrested, repeatedly it seems, for violating the ordinance. Eventually he decided to sue the city, asserting that "the regulation of undertakers was not within the [city's] police power." The injunction was refused, and on appeal the California Supreme Court ruled that the ordinance fell "within the well-recognized police power of the state" and that creating a "zone in which undertaking parlors could be established was not an unreasonable exercise of legislative authority justifying court intervention."[66]

Some zoning ordinances owed their origins to mounting frustration with enterprising funeral directors who brazenly ventured into peaceful residential neighborhoods. La Crosse's zoning ordinance was clearly spawned in large part by the Millers' multiple attempts to open up a funeral home on West Avenue. Similar events unfolded elsewhere, at least in neighborhoods in which enough people of means and influence remained to mount a successful campaign. For example, there was no zoning ordinance in Tucson, Arizona, as of May 12, 1926, and all of the city's undertaking parlors "had been for many years located in what is unquestionably the business district."[67] On that date Arizona Mortuary paid $5,000 for a lot at the northeast corner of Stone Avenue and Third Street, situated in the midst of a residential neighborhood. The company subsequently applied for a building permit, which was granted, and then hired a builder and began construction of the mortuary. When Tucson residents got wind of the firm's plans, approximately fifty property owners submitted a petition to the mayor and city council to pass an ordinance restricting the location of undertaking parlors to the business district. Ordinance 600 was passed on July 6. Arizona Mortuary sued to enjoin the enforcement of the ordinance and won, but in 1928 the Arizona Supreme Court overturned the verdict and ruled that the ordinance was valid.

While the ordinance was not by any means a comprehensive zoning ordinance, it was clearly viewed by the court as a form of zoning and was referred to as such.[68] Justice Alfred C. Lockwood, who wrote the majority opinion for *Tucson v. Arizona Mortuary*, cited the authority of *Euclid v. Amber*, which he recognized as "the best general exposition of the police power on the subject of the regulation of business by zoning yet made" and quite relevant to the matter at hand. Lockwood concluded that for "ordinances dividing cities into districts on the basis of whether they are residential or business" to be declared unconstitutional, it would have to be proven that they were "clearly arbitrary and unreasonable."[69]

One of the thornier issues in *Tucson v. Arizona Mortuary* was that the ordinance appeared to have been applied retroactively.[70] After all, the firm had been granted a valid building permit, and it was only sub-sequent to this that the ordinance was passed. In response to Arizona Mortuary's allegations of a "sudden and unexplained change of the law," Lockwood argued that "up to May 12th, so far as the record shows, it had never occurred to anyone that there would be an attempt to es-tablish a mortuary outside the recognized business district. As soon as the attempt was known, proceedings were immediately initiated and carried forward to establish the restricted district."[71] What was more important, Lockwood explained, was that although Arizona Mortuary had purchased the land in question before the ordinance was adopted, the firm had been "fully advised that the ordinance was under contem-plation" before commencing construction. "Instead of awaiting the action of the council," he chided, "it apparently proceeded on the the-ory either that the ordinance would not be passed, or that, if passed, it was void." Lockwood felt that he could not justly conclude that "the or-dinance in question was so unreasonable, arbitrary, and discriminatory that it would have been unconstitutional if it had been adopted before plaintiff had commenced the erection of its building."[72]

Six years earlier the North Dakota Supreme Court Dakota had faced an almost identical situation in *Wasem v. Fargo*. Fargo did not pass a comprehensive zoning ordinance until 1925,[73] and in May 1919 B. F. Wasem purchased a site in a predominantly residential district and immediately entered into a contract for the excavation work to be done. Within days, area residents presented a petition to the city council requesting an ordinance prohibiting funeral establishments in residential areas. On May 8, 1919, the council introduced an ordi-nance barring the operation or construction of a funeral establish-ment within "those parts of the city of Fargo occupied mainly for residences." A week later the ordinance was amended to include a provision stating that no building permits would be granted for such establishments and, more importantly, that any permit previously is-sued "shall be and is hereby revoked and canceled."[74] The ordinance was then adopted and was scheduled to take effect on June 1. Mean-while, the excavation of Wasem's site continued, and on May 17

Wasem, who had attended at least one of the meetings of the city council and was well aware of neighborhood opposition to his plans, secured a building permit.

By October, Wasem's mortuary had been completed. He was arrested on October 26 for violating the terms of the ordinance. At a trial held before the police magistrate, he was convicted and fined $100. Wasem subsequently appealed, and the district court overturned the conviction. Threatened with arrest from day to day for the ongoing operation of his mortuary, Wasem sued the city in March 1920 in an attempt to have the ordinance declared void. An injunction preventing the city from enforcing the ordinance was issued, and the city appealed. While acknowledging that Fargo possessed "the power to regulate the establishment and maintenance of undertaking establishments and to prescribe the limits within which they may be operated," the North Dakota Supreme Court nonetheless held the ordinance to be invalid based on the "indefinite and uncertain territory" it covered.[75] "In determining the 'parts occupied mainly for residences,'" Justice Harrison A. Bronson asked, "what portion of the city around the locus in quo shall be included? What portion excluded? How much of a portion in extent, in length, in width, may be considered? What measure or rule stick is furnished by the ordinance, through which the undertaker may determine that his location, present or prospective, is lawful?"[76] The ordinance, in short, was unconstitutional because it failed to delineate in clear geographic terms a specific territory and chose instead to rely on a subjective and ambiguous set of qualifications.

In his dissent, Justice James Robinson accused Wasem of running "a race with the city commissioners by trying to get the establishment well under way before the passage of the ordinance." Furthermore, Robinson argued, there was no ambiguity at all as to the character of the district in which Wasem chose to build, which was clearly in "the very best residence part of the city." An undertaking establishment in such a district "is offensive and out of place," Robinson concluded. "It tends to surcharge the atmosphere with gloom and sadness, pestilential fear and forebodings [and] lessens the value of all adjacent property."

Finally, Wasem's claim to a preemptive right by virtue of winning "the race against time" and "getting the morgue well under way before the passage of the ordinance" was invalid because "under the law as it is no person can acquire any pre-emption right to conduct a business that may become a nuisance."[77]

If Fargo's 1919 ordinance was deemed to be too broad, there were other instances in which statutes born of conflict between funeral homes and area residents were far narrower in their scope, in some cases targeting a particular street. Such was the case with a series of laws passed by the city council of Baltimore, Maryland, in 1925. Baltimore had in 1923 adopted a zoning ordinance that created separate row house and cottage districts based on density, permitted only detached and semidetached dwellings in lands annexed in 1918, and barred the mixed use of land in new developments. The law was significantly amended in 1931 to create distinct districts based on land use. In between those two events, the mayor and city council of Baltimore were asked by a group of "fashionable matrons and debutantes of the smart set" to pass a law banning funeral establishments on Charles Street, one of the city's most elite neighborhoods.[78] The problem was William Cook. In the early 1920s the Baltimore undertaker, who was well known for his $75 funerals, set his sights on posh and fashionable Charles Street, "the most aristocratic and carefully guarded street in Baltimore." Lined with brownstone mansions, Charles Street was the perfect spot for an ambitious undertaker looking to branch out and attract a wealthier clientele. "The people who can't afford more than $75 for a funeral," he reasoned, "will be proud and pleased to follow me to this swell thoroughfare, and in that location I will also get the patronage of rich and prominent families that would never think of searching me out where I am now." What Cook did not anticipate was just how fierce a resistance to his plans there would be among the city's moneyed elite, specifically the women, who "called their husbands and fathers and sons and brothers and sweethearts to their aid and with their assistance they uncovered a long forgotten city ordinance that forbids the setting up any form of business at the address to which Mr. Cook planned to move his undertaking parlors."[79] Thwarted, he had no choice but to look elsewhere. Elsewhere turned out to be next door.

The neighboring parcel had once been home to the city's Lyceum Theater, recently destroyed by fire. The site was "in a different commercial zone from the mansion next door" and "had been used for commercial purposes and there was nothing to forbid its being so used again."[80] On it Cook planned to build an elaborate new mortuary "that would be a suitable monument to the enterprise behind his famous $75 funerals. It would cost in the neighborhood of $90,000 and would make all rival undertaking establishments look cheap and insignificant by comparison."[81] Thinking there was nothing that could stop him this time around, Cook underestimated "the influence his women opponents were able to bring to bear on the Baltimore city government." They asked Henry D. Harlan, former chief justice of the Maryland Supreme Court, to draft an ordinance that forbade the maintenance of an undertaking establishment on Charles Street. "Mindful of the wealth and influence of the women behind it," the city council quickly passed the bill.[82]

What is fascinating about Cook's conflict with his wealthy neighbors is that at its heart, the fight was less about smells, sounds, fear of contagion, or a depressing atmosphere than it was about class. At bridge parties and afternoon teas, the neighborhood ladies bemoaned the prospect of "having their street cluttered up with the vulgar masses to whom 'right, rich and fine funerals for $75' appeal." Cook's problem was that he catered to a broad, economically diverse clientele. It is very likely that the matrons and debutantes of Charles Street and its environs would have opposed any undertaking establishment on their street. However, Cook's reputation as a tacky salesman made the thought of having him as a neighbor especially repugnant to Baltimore's moneyed elite, at least some of whom had probably given him their patronage before he endeavored to invade their street.[83] Foiled once more, Cook continued his quest for a suitable residential site into which he could move his establishment.

Three years later in 1928, Cook finally succeeded in acquiring his mansion. Although Charles Street had ultimately eluded him, he found a place almost exactly two blocks east at the corner of St. Paul and Preston Streets, arguably just as fine an address. The 1882 brownstone and brick Chateauesque mansion he converted had been designed by Stanford White of McKim, Mead & White and had for several generations been home to the family of Ross R. Winans, an early member of the B & O Railroad's board of directors. When Cook purchased the building, the family had been leasing it to the Girls' Latin School, an elite preparatory school affiliated with Goucher College (formerly the Woman's College of Baltimore City). It is likely that the building was vacated in the early 1920s when Goucher moved from its downtown quarters ten blocks north at St. Paul and Twenty-Third Street to a newly purchased tract of land in neighboring Towson. Advertised as the "Wm. Cook Inc. Funeral Mansion," the ornate and imposing structure served as his headquarters through the 1960s.[84] It is not clear how Cook managed to get around the ladies of the smart set with their influential husbands and beaus, but the fact that an eight-story apartment house had stood across the street from the Winans house for a generation prior to Cook's acquisition of the dwelling might have led some to conclude that the street, while still home to wealthy families, was no longer worth protecting.

Together with a wide variety of incompatible land uses ranging from apartment houses to filling stations, funeral homes in residential areas had by the end of the First World War emerged as a major impetus to zoning regulations. In San Francisco, for example, the Commonwealth Club sent out a questionnaire in the spring of 1917 to the city assessor, a group of bankers, and more than 350 property owners to document the intrusions of apartment houses, garages, laundries, planing mills, stables, and undertaking parlors in residential districts.[85] The survey found that "many concrete instances clearly show the enormous cost of lack of regulation" and that over one half of the city's total property valued in excess of $300 million would to be "adversely affected for lack of a zone ordinance, such as Los Angeles, New York,

Minneapolis, and every other progressive city has already put into effect."[86]

In the midst of the myriad encroachments threatening to destabilize real estate and property values, professional planning consultants eager to be hired by cities and towns frequently raised the specter of funeral homes moving into unzoned residential neighborhoods. In late 1920 Dr. W. J. Donald, managing director of New York–based America City Consultants, went on an extensive speaking tour throughout the Northeast and Midwest to promote his company's services to municipal governments contemplating a zoning ordinance.[87] In September he spoke at the fall meeting of the Lowell, Massachusetts, chamber of commerce. "Building garages next to apartments, opening funeral homes among residences and the committing of similar crimes against the principles of modern city zoning," he warned his audience, "destroy more property values annually than is lost through fire." Zoning, he explained, also encouraged home ownership by making it "possible for citizens to own their homes in safety." More renters would buy if they felt that their investments could be protected. "In more than one city," he lamented, "skilled workmen and executives of industries continue to rent or live in rooms because there is no section of the city in which they may safely buy and build." He cited a case in which "the president of a carpenter's union in one city supported zoning because the house next door to his was to be converted into a combination apartment and funeral parlor." Such atrocities against property values and progressive planning could be avoided through the adoption of a zoning ordinance, something "no city can afford to be without."[88]

For their part, those representing undertakers prosecuted for violating zoning laws tried to exploit the fact that zoning was still new and largely unfamiliar in most communities. They attempted to punch holes in ordinances by pointing out what appeared to be inconsistencies or double standards. When in 1929 LaVerne Pelton of Neenah, Wisconsin, was charged with violating that city's zoning ordinance, the city clerk, Harry S. Zemlock, was forced to admit under cross-examination by Pelton's attorney, D. K. Allen, that the neighbors protesting the presence of a funeral home were "also near other places of business and near a railroad." He also testified that businesses were "scattered about the city in sections classified as residential."[89] At the same time, the case, which drew considerable attention in neighboring Oshkosh because of a similar conflict there, offered Neenah's city council an opportunity to revamp the law, which, the council felt, had proven inadequate in its protection of residential districts.[90]

Waukesha, Wisconsin, had experienced a similar crisis of confidence surrounding the city's zoning ordinance in 1926. When a rumor began to spread that the old James property, a large Stick Style house on the southwest corner of East Avenue and South Streets, was going to be sold to a local undertaker named Herbert Weber, area residents were, in the words of one, "up in arms and ... justly so." City engineer Hugo Eagler tried to squelch the rumor by reassuring agitated homeowners that no sale had taken place and that the property could not, in his opinion, be used for business purposes because it was zoned residential. His words did little to soothe the flap. The mere suggestion that a funeral home could disturb what was described as "one of the most desirable resident spots in the city" was enough to cause a furor. "What," one homeowner asked, "has become of the zoning system which [we] put up good money to secure?" Many in Waukesha concluded that the zoning ordinance was "to apply only to the few." Clearly, not everyone believed that the zoning law treated all areas equally. Residents became increasingly frustrated with the city council and those who were in charge of the zoning system for their perceived failure to "stop this wanton act of depreciating the value of their property" and made it clear that if civic leaders and the zoning ordinance failed to protect them, they would "bring it to the courts if necessary."[91]

While undertakers and their attorneys repeatedly attacked the validity of zoning laws and frustrated property owners lamented what appeared to be haphazard and capricious enforcement, proponents of zoning took advantage of situations in which businesses of all kinds ran afoul of zoning laws to promote and defend zoning in the local press. In 1926 when Lowell, Massachusetts, was "just beginning to get acquainted with the new zoning ordinance over which there was such a long controversy before it was enacted," William H. Saunders was denied a permit to open up a funeral home at 90 Westford Street, which was situated in "a residential district where no provision was made for business properties."[92] He appealed the decision, but his request was refused in the face of stiff opposition from Westford Street residents. Three days after Saunders's unsuccessful hearing before the board of appeals, an editorial in the *Lowell Sun* attempted to rationalize the board's decision.

Titled "Public vs. Private Rights," the piece pointed out that Lowell was witnessing "the first practical application of the zoning ordinance . . . in the refusal to allow a funeral home to be erected on Westford Street." Clearly addressed to those who found it "strange that a man cannot build as he pleases on his own land," the article explained that limits on individual property rights already existed in the form of height restrictions, and the advent of air travel would place further limitations on a homeowner's "right to control the air over his property." Additionally, property owners had to "comply with all sanitary laws provided in the building code enforced by the state."[93] Property rights, while viewed in the abstract as inviolate, were, in reality, limited by various statutes. "In recent years," the piece went on to say,

> a new form of restriction has been imposed on private rights under the so-called "Zoning Laws," one purpose of which is to prevent residential districts from invasion by business blocks or manufacturing establishments that would greatly deteriorate the property. The aim is to keep widely different classes of property in separate districts so that as a result each will enjoy an environment of its own kind. . . . Thus the rights of the individual must give way to those of the public or the district so that the homogeneity of the property in each district may be preserved.[94]

The article concluded with an acknowledgment that within the population there was "much difference of opinion as to how far the zoning principle can be carried."[95] The ordinance was indeed more flexible than many realized.

In May 1927 Saunders took his petition to the city council's committee on ordinances. In spite of lingering opposition from his neighbors, he was granted a permit four months later to convert the Second Empire dwelling on Westford into a funeral home (fig. 3.5). One factor that may have weighed significantly in Saunders's favor was the mixed character of Westford Street, especially along its north side. Although the area was principally residential, the stretch of Westford Street directly across from Saunders's property contained a number of multifamily housing units.

Some of these, such as the Gothic Revival townhouses at 99–103 Westford Street, were quite elegant (fig. 3.6). Consisting of three circa 1870s attached brick dwellings of three stories each with bayed fronts and English basements, these dwellings could hardly have been

FIGURE 3.5   90 Westford Street (formerly Saunders Funeral Home), Lowell, Massachusetts, 2010. Photograph by the author.

FIGURE 3.6   Nineteenth-century brick townhouses at 99–103 Westford Street, Lowell, Massachusetts, 2010. Photograph by the author.

thought to compromise the middle-class residential character of the neighborhood. The units at 77–95 Westford Street, however, were a different story (fig. 3.7). These modest circa 1890 two-story wooden dwellings were clearly built to house the working-class residents employed at the mills situated along Middlesex Street, a short two blocks to the north along the Middlesex Canal. A bulky turn-of-the-century four-family wooden apartment house for working-class residents stood five doors down at 128–134 Westford Street (fig. 3.8). By the time Saunders came along in the mid-1920s, the neighborhood contained a mix of middle- and working-class residents, with multifamily units and apartment houses interspersed among detached single-family homes. Zoning advocates had never attempted to hide their hostility toward apartment houses in residential districts.[96]

A handful of similar conflicts during the first half of the 1930s continued to test the effectiveness of Lowell's zoning law. The results

FIGURE 3.7 Late nineteenth-century worker housing at 79–95 Westford Street, Lowell, Massachusetts, 2010. Photograph by the author.

FIGURE 3.8 Turn-of-the-century multifamily apartment house at 128–134 Westford Street, Lowell, Massachusetts, 2010. Photograph by the author.

were mixed. Several funeral directors, including James McKenna at 757 Bridge Street and Peter Savage at 282 Pawtucket Street, succeeded in obtaining permits to convert existing dwellings into funeral homes even though both streets were zoned residential and despite, in Savage's case at least, significant neighborhood opposition. However, the ordinance prevented John Weinbeck from converting a large Queen Anne dwelling on Wilder Street in 1932 and William Mack from converting an austere Colonial Revival residence on Nesmith Street in 1934. In Mack's case, the zoning board of appeals granted the permit in February, but a group of twenty-five Nesmith Street residents filed suit in Middlesex Superior Court in March to have the board's decision reversed. In early April, Judge Joseph Walsh annulled the decision, ruling that the board of appeals was "without authority to direct the inspector of buildings to issue a permit."[97]

Mack's case pitted the zoning board of appeals against both the building inspector, William Gargan, and the planning board, led by Smith Adams. Adams, who was considered the father of Lowell's zoning ordinance, had argued that although the planning board had not been involved in the Mack case specifically, it was "invariably opposed to encroachments upon zoned residential districts by business establishments of any sort."[98] Just one year later in 1935, however, Lowell's city council voted 11 to 4 to amend the zoning ordinance "to permit funeral homes in residential districts."[99] The amendment came in part as a result of Peter Savage's request to convert the former dwelling of industrialist Everett H. Walker on Pawtucket Street into a funeral home. Area residents protested the conversion, but the zoning board of appeals granted the permit. Following the example set by property owners on Nesmith Street, Savage's neighbors sued. In October 1935 Middlesex Superior Court judge Marcus Morton upheld the board's decision, and Savage was allowed to move in.

At the same July hearing in which the board granted Savage's request, it refused to grant a permit to Mathias Laurin, who was seeking to establish a home a few blocks away at 187 Pawtucket Street. The board claimed that there were "already two such homes in that particular

neighborhood." They were referring to Archambault's at 205 Pawtucket Street and James F. O'Donnell & Sons at 166 Pawtucket Street,
both of which were housed in remodeled mansions. Although Savage's funeral home was also situated on Pawtucket Street, "the board
felt that the proposed home was sufficiently removed from any other
funeral home so as not to cause any congestion."[100] With Savage's success clearly in mind, Laurin pressed on. At a series of hearings toward
the end of July, members of Lowell's police force testified on Laurin's
behalf that "traffic in Pawtucket Street would not be congested due to
the presence of a funeral home at 187 Pawtucket Street." Laurin's attorney further reassured the board that the firm's funeral cars would
be "garaged in the rear of the premises, 300 feet from the street."[101] In
the end, the board reversed its earlier decision, and Laurin settled in
next door to Archambault and O'Donnell.

In other locales as well, funeral homes managed to find ways around
both neighborhood opposition and local zoning ordinances. In 1921
Albert and Emily Ketterlin opened a funeral home in the large and
imposing Colonial Revival dwelling at 2657 Independence Boulevard,
a residential street in Kansas City, Missouri. Their neighbors subsequently took them to court. In addition to claiming that a funeral home
in the neighborhood would "injuriously affect" both physical and
mental well-being, "destroy the comfort and repose" of area homes,
and greatly depreciate property values, the plaintiffs pointed to an ordinance prohibiting the construction or maintenance of "an undertaking establishment or morgue within one hundred feet of any building
used exclusively for residential purposes in Kansas City, Missouri."[102]

During the trial the attorney for the Ketterlins argued that the law
was void because it violated their Fourteenth Amendment rights.
They lost and appealed, but the lower court's verdict was affirmed in
1924 by the Missouri Supreme Court of Missouri in *Tureman v. Ketterlin*. Surprisingly, the high court declined the opportunity to consider
the validity of the ordinance, the constitutionality of which, they
held, was not relevant to the disposition of the case at hand. It was,
the court concluded, an instance of a private nuisance in a residential

neighborhood, rightfully enjoined based on an ample set of precedents nationwide. The Ketterlins, however, refused to budge. Whether
it was as a result of the high court's refusal to defend the ordinance,
they were eventually given an exemption and continued to run their
business from 2657 Independence Boulevard into the 1940s.

Other funeral directors were more compliant and willingly worked
within the constraints and protocol established by local zoning ordinances. Because an appeals process was built in, many felt comfortable challenging an initial refusal of permission to construct a
purpose-built mortuary or remodel an existing dwelling in an area
zoned residential. If, however, an appeal was denied, far fewer had the
stomach for a protracted legal fight, especially if neighborhood opposition was strong. Some simply chose an alternative location. For example, the firm Dawson & Wikoff of Decatur, Illinois, made three
tries before finally securing a satisfactory spot. In February 1928 the
firm sought permission from the zoning board of appeals "to erect an
elaborate funeral home on the southwest corner of West Macon and
South Edward Streets." The building was projected to cost the firm
$75,000, an enormous sum especially considering that only a month
earlier it had just put the finishing touches on the brand-new funeral
home it constructed at the corner of North College Street and West
Main Street. Having found in its new quarters "cramped conditions
and especially heavy traffic on the street in front," dismayed owners
Roy Dawson and Forrest Wikoff decided to sell the residential-style
structure to a local women's club.[103]

Shortly thereafter, Dawson and Wikoff identified the intersection
of West Macon and South Edward as a potential spot to construct
their second new mortuary in as many years, but because the area was
zoned residential, they were required "to circulate a petition among
property owners in the vicinity and get a majority of signatures to
merit a building permit."[104] In March, the board voted unanimously to
deny their request after "nineteen property owners living in the vicinity of the lot appeared in person to oppose the issuance of a permit for
the funeral home."[105] Having already stated publicly that they had "no

disposition to push their project against the will of the public," Dawson and Wikoff immediately began looking for another location rather than fight the ruling in court.[106] They chose the southwest corner of West Wood and South College Streets, an area that was, like their previous choice, zoned residential. As a result, their request for a permit was turned down by the building inspector. Not surprisingly, they petitioned the zoning board of appeals for relief, and after they obtained the consent of a majority of their neighbors, the board granted the permit.

Some undertakers, such as Roll Osborn, ended up back where they started. In 1918 when his attempt to transform the Logan mansion into a funeral home was thwarted by the Louisiana Supreme Court in *Osborn v. Shreveport*, he packed up and returned to his old quarters on Texas Street. Two years after his death in 1923, his wife and sons moved the business to nearby Marshall Street. Similarly, after losing their appeal in *Meagher v. Kessler* in 1920, Kessler & Maguire left the house it had purchased on Summit Avenue and built a new mortuary on West Seventh Street, a block away from the spot it had occupied prior to its failed move. Still others just waited for the law and the neighborhood to evolve to the point at which a funeral home would be tolerated. W. T. Vancil of Springfield, Illinois, waited twenty-five years. In May 1941 he purchased the mansion at 437 South Grand Avenue West to serve as his firm's second location. Constructed in 1906, the spacious Jacobean dwelling stood in a neighborhood that had been zoned residential since 1924. Although the city had initially granted Vancil a permit to operate a funeral home on the premises, the permit was revoked soon after the purchase was finalized. Thirty-five area homeowners "joined the city's request for an injunction on the grounds that the conduct of a funeral home would be a nuisance and seriously depreciate the value of the surrounding residence properties."[107] An injunction was issued and later upheld by the Illinois Supreme Court in 1947. Rather than selling the house, however, Vancil kept it as his family's primary residence, sans funeral home. Finally, in 1966 he acquired the requisite permits to establish a funeral home there.

A CONSIDERABLE EXPENSE

Doubtless, having their efforts thwarted cost funeral directors both time and money. Moreover, those who stood to suffer financial losses after being forced to vacate dwellings they had purchased and remodeled often found themselves in front of unsympathetic judges who were all too eager to remind them of their folly. Rulings were peppered with stern lectures scolding funeral directors who had undertaken costly renovations in full knowledge of neighborhood opposition. When Willis Crosby of Omaha, Nebraska, learned in the summer of 1920 that he had lost his appeal to have the injunction against him lifted, he was painfully reminded by Nebraska Supreme Court justice J. Aldrich Rose that when he began remodeling the "large, handsome residence" he had purchased on Wirt Street in an exclusive residential district of Omaha, he did so "in disregard of timely protest." In other words, the court explained, he knew exactly what he was getting into. "He equipped his funeral home at his peril," Rose chastised, "after he had been warned by plaintiffs of their objections."[108]

In 1932 Maurice N. Virkler and his wife of Lowville, New York, were forced by the New York Supreme Court to shut down the funeral home they had opened on Trinity Avenue "in a prestigious residential district where there were no other businesses." Virkler and his wife had "spent a substantial amount to adapt [the dwelling] to their purposes," almost $4,000. However, "even before they acquired title to their property," Justice Edmund H. Lewis explained in *Arthur v. Virkler*, "they were notified that, so far as the law would permit, the plaintiffs would resist the maintenance of an undertaking establishment on Trinity Avenue. Notwithstanding this notice and the objections filed with the village board of trustees when the defendants petitioned for a building permit, defendants chose to proceed with renovations which involved a considerable expense."[109] Lewis made sure that Virkler and his wife paid a stiff price for their blatant disregard of neighborhood opposition and concluded that they "could not recover the cost of renovations because they were on notice when they bought the property that the neighbors objected to such use."[110]

A similar situation ensued when homeowners in a "beautiful residential district" of Greenwood, Mississippi, learned in July 1938 that Alice Williams was planning to convert the Tarver residence on River Road into a funeral home. Although no zoning ordinances were involved in the case of *Williams v. Montgomery*, Williams was well aware of the impending imbroglio before she started remodeling the dwelling. Immediately after her plans became known, "protests were made by mass meetings," and notices were then sent directly to her. She ignored the protests, however, and went ahead with the planned conversion. The chancery court of Leflore County issued an injunction, which the Mississippi Supreme Court affirmed, pointing out that although the "appellants had expended a considerable sum of money in the purchase and conversion of this residence into a funeral home in excess of $25,000," they were entitled to no compensation because they had been "warned before much of the expense was incurred that stubborn resistance would be met by them in the courts if they converted the residence into a funeral home."[111]

As late as 1950, the heavy pecuniary loss suffered by a funeral director who went ahead with plans to convert an eighteen-room residential dwelling in the face of neighborhood opposition failed to sway the Connecticut Supreme Court, which ruled in *Jack v. Torrant* that

> the fact that the defendants expended a substantial amount in adapting the premises for use as such an establishment cannot avail to defeat the plaintiffs' right to an injunction, since the finding is conclusive that they were reasonably and amply warned that they had no right to use the premises for this purpose and that the plaintiffs would resist their effort to do so by every lawful means; notwithstanding, they ignored all warnings and persisted in their course.[112]

The message from numerous courts over a span of more than three decades was remarkably clear and consistent, namely that funeral directors who brazenly ventured into residential areas where they were not wanted or from which they were legally barred did so at their own financial peril.

AN ORNAMENT TO ANY NEIGHBORHOOD

During the interwar years funeral directors displayed something between cautious optimism and a delusional fantasy that their neighbors would eventually warm to their presence. After all, not everyone was opposed to the idea, as many industry leaders pointed out. In a series of editorials in the *American Funeral Director* beginning in the summer of 1920, editor Herbert S. Fassett expressed his hope that American homeowners would come to recognize the residential funeral home as an asset to the neighborhood rather than a nuisance. He understood, of course, that those funeral directors who had ventured into residential districts had not to that point received a warm welcome from their neighbors. "There has never been established in a residential district," he wrote grimly, "such an establishment, without opposition from the residents of the neighborhood."[113] At the same time, he earnestly believed that funeral directors would be able to overcome any doubt or hostility by creating establishments that were well maintained and beautiful to the eye.

"When residential districts are being selected for the establishment of the funeral director," explained Fassett in June,

> one is certain to meet with much opposition from the property owners of the immediate neighborhood. The objectors always have in mind the crude undertaking shops of a former age, forgetting that any person who will make such an advanced movement as to plant his place of business in a fine residential district would have ability and capital sufficient to make the place not only of fair comparison with the residences of the neighborhood but would strive to lead the community in the way of ornamentation and decoration that would lead the mind far away from what is usually associated with the ordinary undertaking shop.[114]

Referring to what he saw as the typical residential funeral home's attractive landscaping, neat walkways and driveways, beautiful chapels, substantial exteriors and inviting, homelike interiors, Fassett was confident that

> when these views, so pleasing and unobjectionable, are brought to the attention of the objector, and he is assured that even all of this beauty of landscape and building is to be eclipsed and excelled in the remodeling of the residence in his neighborhood, he may understand that the new place will be an advantage to every piece of property in the neighborhood.[115]

By December he seemed positively ebullient in his belief that

> funeral directors who have taken the pains and gone to the expense of erecting fine establishments for the care of the dead in residential districts are beginning to receive the thanks of their neighbors who in earlier days fought against the establishment of such enterprises. The places— one might almost say palaces in some cases—are kept in such excellent order that they are an ornament to any neighborhood.[116]

Fassett's optimism was somewhat premature, however, and one suspects that Fassett was in denial. In 1920 alone in at least three separate states, there were cases in which a funeral director was enjoined from operating a funeral home in a residential neighborhood.[117] Many more such rulings would follow.

Notwithstanding the confidence espoused by some, many experts within the industry possessed a sober awareness of the very daunting legal obstacles and financial risks funeral directors faced when venturing into hostile territory. A July 1921 article titled "Some Points of Law for the Funeral Director: Discussion of the Right of Property Owners to Enjoin the Operation of an Undertaking Business in Residential District" in the *American Funeral Director* admonished funeral directors to proceed with caution. "While the courts have consistently recognized the importance and necessity of the funeral directing business," the article explained, "they have also recognized the dislike of the average person for a residence close to where such a business is being carried on. And, by the weight of authority, the courts have restrained the establishment of funeral directing parlors in residential sections where they have been seriously objected to by surrounding property owners."[118] The article, which discussed *Saier v. Joy* and its impact on funeral directors seeking to relocate to residential districts, sought to draw a clear and honest picture of the challenges such a move entailed. "If the contemplated location is in a strictly residential district," the article warned, "some care should be exercised before an investment has been made; otherwise the funeral director may be placed in a difficult position, and possibly suffer an actual loss."[119]

Throughout the 1920s some of the industry's other publications also reported on legal decisions affecting the location of funeral homes. For example, in the July 1925 issue of *Embalmers' Monthly*, the ruling of the Alabama Supreme Court in *Higgins v. Bloch* was discussed at length in an article titled "And Again a Court Decision." After criticizing what he saw as the court's utter lack of knowledge "of the character of a modern mortuary," the author went on to conclude that funeral directors must "be on their guard, as no one can foretell what way a court may decide, and an adverse decision may be the cause of tying up a goodly sum of money."[120] Doubtless, these decisions were frequent topics of conversations at both state and national conventions. As a result, by decade's end knowledge of the legal landscape within which funeral directors had to navigate and, more specifically, the courts' proclivity to side with homeowners seeking an injunction had permeated the industry.

In spite of this, the industry's peculiar brand of cautious optimism continued throughout the interwar period, and the mostly bad news was tempered with a tendency on the part of some to exaggerate the occasional piece of good news. Industry insiders also distinguished between different types of obstacles, with nuisance litigation generating far greater optimism than either restrictive covenants or zoning ordinances. For example, at the 1930 annual meeting of the National Funeral Directors Association held in Atlanta, Georgia, a Cincinnati-based attorney and friend of the funeral industry, James R. Clark, delivered an address in which he told his audience that in the absence of a zoning ordinance, the case would be decided based on the particular circumstance and that "the courts have almost universally held that [a funeral] business is not a nuisance per se, but the nuisance must be proved by the conduct of the business."[121] This was somewhat misleading, because what the majority of courts were actually saying was that while a funeral home was not a nuisance per se, a funeral home located in a residential district was unquestionably a nuisance.[122]

A similar conclusion was reached in the 1933 publication *Legal Decisions for Funeral Directors*, which addressed the dilemma of a Wyoming funeral director who had recently relocated to a residential neighborhood. Several of his neighbors protested the move and threatened legal action, but there was "no zoning or city ordinance." In spite of many instances in which funeral directors were forced by the courts to abandon newly remodeled residential quarters, the authors were of the opinion that an injunction aimed at restraining the funeral director from entering his new premises could not be sustained and advised him to "move into the newly acquired property at once" before the town had an opportunity to pass "some ordinance or local law that would have to be considered" if he hoped to take advantage of this new location.[123] This was risky advice, but the author backed it up with several anomalous court decisions, such as *Pearson v. Bonnie*, that clearly ran contrary to the larger judicial trend granting relief to aggrieved neighbors.

The author was quick to point out, however, that the situation was very different in cities that had "adopted the modern zoning methods," adding that "the location of a business within a zone set apart by ordinance exclusively for homes, would be an unlawful location, and subject to abatement as of a nuisance *per se*."[124] The consensus within the industry was that zoning ordinances presented a far more formidable obstacle regardless of whether the ordinance was comprehensive in nature or narrower in its scope, simply delineating specific residential districts from which commercial uses were barred. "Under our present system of government," explained Clark to National Funeral Directors Association members gathered in Atlanta, practically every city of any size has some sort of an ordinance classifying and restricting the operation of certain businesses to certain localities, whether it be designated as a Zoning Ordinance or not, and if such ordinance is reasonable and treats all alike, it will be enforced and the construction and maintenance of any business in any locality prohibited in such locality by such ordinance, will not be granted.[125]

Cases in which there existed an ordinance that was not comprehensive in its scope but simply extended protection to certain residential zones were, Clark acknowledged, rarely "decided in favor of the owner of the funeral establishment."[126] Where a comprehensive zoning law existed, the prognosis for funeral directors was bleaker still. "Zoning ordinances have been almost universally upheld in the last few years and this because of the broad police power of municipalities,"[127] Clark told his listeners. Even so, by the mid-1930s zoning amendments in some locations were already being amended to allow funeral homes in residential districts, as was the case in Lowell in 1935.

ROSES, CIGARS, AND CANDY

In the meantime, funeral directors looked for strategies aimed at winning neighborhood approval and avoiding costly legal battles. For starters, to counter claims that funeral homes in residential areas were sources of contagion, funeral directors everywhere emphasized the sanitary condition in which they kept their establishments and their industry's role in promoting public health. "Standing shoulder to shoulder with public officials, doctors and nurses," proclaimed a 1923 advertisement used by multiple funeral directors in states from California to North Carolina, "thousands of American funeral directors are constantly safeguarding your health."[128] A 1931 advertisement for the Wittich Funeral Home in Muscatine, Iowa, declared "funeral directors, through scientific sterilization," to be "an important factor in the lowering of the death rate during the last 30 years."[129] This was achieved in part, explained one funeral director in 1921, through "Modern Science," which "found a way through the art of Embalming . . . for removing the peril of contagion."[130] However, it was a sanitary and sterilized preparation room, akin to "a surgeon's operating room, assuring absolute cleanliness and privacy," that held the key to preventing the spread of infectious disease.[131]

In order to demonstrate their cleanliness, embalming rooms were sometimes shown to groups of visitors. When "a party of ladies" was invited to view Kistner's Funeral Home in Waterloo, Iowa, in 1921, they were reported to have exclaimed, " 'Cleanliness is next to Godliness, and, Mr. Kistner, you surely have thought of sanitation as well as having a beautiful room in which to care for loved ones. One would think he were in an operating room of the hospital when in your Embalming room, it is so immaculately white and clean.' "[132] The first-floor room was "entirely finished in white enamel," with "an appropriate blue design worked in[to]" the floor. Facing east, the room was well lit by "a large window of stained art glass" through which "warm sunshine" entered.[133] Clearly the ladies were impressed.

Such visits were not uncommon. It was customary upon the opening of a new residential funeral home to invite the public to inspect the premises both as a means of dispelling any fears or discomfort they might have and as a way of drumming up business.[134] "Inspection of funeral homes," wrote on industry insider in 1930, "accomplishes much in breaking down the barrier which has so long existed between this profession and the public."[135] Open houses were generally well attended, if the news stories accompanying such events can be believed. Frank S. Steward of Leon, Iowa, where the total population was only 2,400, had 1,500 visitors at his formal opening in 1931.[136] When Sheboygan's Ramm Funeral Home opened its doors in May 1929, an estimated 5,000 visitors were reported to have toured the former Stick-style dwelling turned funeral home during its two-day open house.[137] Two years later the firm was still advertising that visitors were always welcome. "Inspect the facilities of our modern funeral home," the firm announced, "and see for yourself how complete and attractive it is."[138] By 1940, funeral directors from coast to coast were inviting visitors to inspect their establishments for the first ever National Funeral Home Inspection Week, which was held in May just prior to Memorial Day.[139]

Visitors were usually enticed with souvenir favors and food. The firm F. M. Evans & Wife of Walton, Indiana, served "ice cream and wafers" and distributed free outdoor thermometers, presumably with the firm's contact information, to all who called during their grand opening in November 1924.[140] "The usual plan," wrote one funeral director in 1928, "is to present roses to lady visitors, cigars to men and candy to the children."[141] Entertainment in the form of free concerts was also promised. While thousands were reported to have toured the impressive Neoclassical brick structure housing the F. C. Daehler Mortuary in Portsmouth, Ohio, as part of its grand opening in February 1925, presumably less than a quarter of them were able to squeeze into the chapel to hear a free musical recital, "which included organ, piano, and vocal selections."[142] Visitors were equally interested in the crematory that was located in the basement, which was part of the tour. Doubtless, a certain morbid curiosity played a role in bringing visitors to the funeral home, which in the 1920s was still a new and unfamiliar phenomenon. Some may have simply wanted an opportunity to tour grand dwellings that had previously belonged to wealthy and influential elites. When in July 1934 funeral director John H. Meyer of Mason City, Iowa, invited the public to inspect his quarters in a recently converted Colonial Revival dwelling built in 1909 for O. T. Denison, the town's leading brick and tile magnate, he specifically mentioned in the announcement for the open house that he had left "the home in the same condition as Mr. Denison left it" so as "to give the public an opportunity to see the home as he had planned it." Referring to the furnishings, Meyer specifically noted that "many of the original pieces [had] been retained."[143]

Funeral directors defined sanitation as more than preventing the spread of contagious disease, however. In a less literal sense it could also mean arresting the spread of decay that had begun to infect many of the older residential neighborhoods to which funeral establishments relocated. Funeral directors were eager to point out instances in which they had reclaimed and restored derelict properties that had fallen into disrepair. The dwelling at the northeast corner of Warren Avenue and Leavitt Street in Chicago, in which Otto H. Berz was attempting to set up a funeral home, was described in 1920 as having been prior to his recent remodeling "old and in a dilapidated and run down condition." The detailed description of the property is suggestive of a decomposing corpse in an advanced state of decay:

> Numberless bricks had rotten and fallen out, the gutters and eaves were in a rotten and decayed condition and the building, which had long prior thereto been painted red, had partially peeled off, and the stone coping extending from the south line of the garage on Leavitt Street to approximately the middle of the building had cracked and fallen into decay; also the front steps of the house were rotten and decayed and the hand railing was broken. The flight of stairs from the sidewalk on Warren Avenue to the doorway, which was the main entrance to the building, was rotten and decayed, and the windows were out of the building. The cornice around the entire building was hanging and rotten, and the roof leaked in many places. The vacant space on the Leavitt and Warren Avenue sides of the residence was filled with rubbish, and it was generally known as an abandoned building.[144]

Berz claimed that he had transformed the structure "formerly in a lamentable state of decadence" into "a place of beauty."[145]

A series of advertisements in the *New Castle News* during the summer months of 1934 were intended to draw attention to the fact that the Book-Leyde Mortuary in Pennsylvania had purchased and was remodeling an old dwelling at the corner of Highland and Winter Avenues that "had stood for five years . . . abandoned and neglected." In an August 1934 advertisement titled "The New Book-Leyde Funeral Home Is Taking Shape," the firm boasted that "the picture today is different. The interior of the house has been remodeled to provide proper service facilities for a Funeral Home. . . . It has been painted and redecorated inside and out. . . . An addition is now nearly completed. . . . The grounds are graded and landscaped with new side-walks to both streets."[146] Fixing up the old house was a source of great pride for its owners, who clearly hoped that their work would be celebrated by the local community rather than condemned.

When funeral directors J. E. Ryan and George Ryan of Victoria, Texas, were threatened by their next door neighbor with an injunction, they pointed out in court that they had transformed a derelict property into something beautiful. The old Mitchell home, which they leased beginning around 1940, had sat virtually abandoned for a year and a half. "It was vacant property and had been permitted by its owners to fall into a dilapidated and run-down condition," explained appeals court justice James Rankin Norvell in February 1942,

> so that the house was unsightly, badly in need of paint and repairs, and the lawn had been permitted to become ugly through lack of care. This property is adjacent to and opposite plaintiff's home and dwelling above mentioned. . . .
>
> The Mitchell property was 'renovated' and improved, the house being repaired, inside and out, and painted, sidewalks being repaired and lawn beautified, shrubbery planted and otherwise the premises were put in a first-class condition. Defendants then moved their funeral home into the new quarters and, at the time of the trial, had been operating there for a little over a month.[147]

The structure stood on South Bridge Street, just one block away from Victoria's city hall and main square. Next door was the complainant's house and next door to that a large dwelling that had been cut up into apartments. It was noted during the trial that the section of Bridge Street on which all three structures were located was very near the principal business sections of the city. In the end, Norvell refused to reverse the lower court's decision denying the injunction. Clearly the improvements that the Ryans had made to the property carried significant weight. In the eyes of the court, the area was already heavily commercialized, and a beautiful and well-kept funeral home was far better than a dilapidated vacant dwelling.

For African American funeral directors, the bar was even higher. Black entrepreneurs seeking to convert dwellings formerly owned by white families had to overcome not only the typical objections alleging contagion, flies, odors, and traffic but also racial hierarchies. When in 1930 S. W. Qualls of Memphis, Tennessee, attempted to open a funeral home in "a large stone residence" in a residential district occupied by white families, the city's building commissioner denied him the necessary permits. Qualls appealed the decision, and at a hearing before the Memphis Board of Adjustment on December 29, 1930, the board upheld the commissioner's decision and concluded that a funeral home would "be obnoxious and offensive by reason of the emission of odors and noises." The board didn't stop there, however. "The character of the neighborhood," the board stated, "is predominantly that of residence use for members of the Caucasian race." While forced to acknowledge that it could not discriminate against Qualls on the basis of either his race or the race of his clients, the board pointed out that "members of the colored race are very emotional, and that funerals of members of that race are attended by loud speaking, singing, moaning, and other sounds which would be obnoxious and offensive to persons in the immediate neighborhood, especially the persons living in the houses immediately to the east or west of the premises in question."[148] Within the context of white supremacy, African American funeral homes in predominantly white neighborhoods were perceived to produce not only the contamination with which all funeral directors were customarily charged but racial contamination as well.

In 1938 A. G. Gaston of Birmingham, Alabama, purchased a neoclassical mansion opposite Kelly Ingram Park. "A majestic colonial residence, once the home of a coal baron and later of a Postmaster,"[149] the structure had fallen on hard times during the Depression, and Gaston himself described it as being "of faded glory." At the time of the sale, it was being used as a boarding house for elderly white schoolteachers. Gaston took enormous pride in restoring the dwelling to its former state. "Gleaming white paint," he recounted in his later autobiography, "took the place of chips and peels. Carpets were laid. Nice furniture was moved in. . . . There it was, sparkling white, its Georgian columns soaring up in stateliness. I gazed at it, relishing every detail."[150]

Not everyone was pleased with Gaston's acquisition, however. While Gaston saw himself as bringing renewed vitality to an aging and run-down structure, many within Birmingham's white population looked on with suspicion and resentment toward what they perceived to be the Black invasion of a once segregated section of the city. Many were unhappy that a dwelling formerly belonging to a member of the city's white elite was now in the hands of a Black businessman. Gaston was not blind to the fact that while he saw himself as an antidote to the economic decay that had beset a once glorious piece of Birmingham, his white neighbors viewed his ownership of the building as a manifestation of the insidious social decay of integration. For that reason, he diligently "instructed his employees to keep the grounds and buildings in spotless condition, 'so it will not appear that the white people have lost the building and the Negroes are letting it go down.' "[151] In Memphis and in Birmingham, as in other parts of the United States, a funeral home in a residential neighborhood was regarded as a nuisance, but a culture of white supremacy deemed a Black funeral home in a white neighborhood an even bigger nuisance.

In addition to inviting the public to visit their funeral homes and advertising the degree to which dilapidated buildings had been reclaimed and beautified, a more proactive strategy of visiting one's neighbors to dissuade them from raising any objections was sometimes encouraged. E. M. Davis of Burr, Davis & Son, Inc., of Mount Vernon, New York, argued in 1928 "that the funeral director can accomplish much in overcoming objections by visiting nearby property owners and explaining to them why they are not justified in seeking to prohibit the location of the funeral home in the neighborhood." Others were more realistic, however, and did "not believe, on the average, that morticians would have a great deal of success in soliciting from nearby residences permission to erect a mortuary in the vicinity."[152] A similar strategy was to try to persuade one's prospective neighbors to support an amendment to the local zoning ordinance, if that was the obstacle, to allow a funeral home at the desired residential address. "A local lawyer—sympathetic with your ambitions—would be a great help," advised one expert. "If you cannot succeed in amending the ordinance," he continued, "then try to transact all your business at your present business address, but hold the religious services at your home and so word your contract as to show that the use of your home is *free* and a personal favor to the family served. Do not commercialize your residence."[153] It is difficult to imagine anyone believing that such a plan would succeed. Predictably, it failed to work for John Ullrich of Baltimore, Maryland.

Ullrich maintained a funeral parlor situated at 2008 Orleans Street in a section of Baltimore tightly packed with structures consisting of commercial space on the ground floor and apartment space above. At that location he kept "all the appliances and paraphernalia necessary for embalming and preparing the dead for burial."[154] Ullrich and his wife resided at 2200 Erdman Avenue in a large brick Jacobean structure in which no such equipment was kept. His residence, moreover, was in an area zoned for residential use. On July 15, 1945, Ullrich

at his establishment at 2008 Orleans Street ... prepared the body of Elizabeth Holle for burial, placed it in a casket, and conveyed the same to 2200 Erdman Avenue, in said city, and on the next day the said Elizabeth Holle was buried from his said residence and home on Erdman Avenue; that no charge was made for the use of the residence of the defendant and his wife, and no act or service of any kind was performed by the defendant in connection with the funeral that would not have been performed by the defendant or any other duly licensed funeral director if the said body had been kept and buried from any other private residence in Baltimore City, and that no act or service was performed at his said residence in connection with the burial of the deceased that is not customarily performed at private residences in said city and state, or that might not have been performed lawfully by any other duly licensed undertaker at this private residence.[155]

Ullrich, who was convicted of violating the city's zoning ordinance, argued that since it was lawful for Baltimoreans "not engaged in the undertaking business" to bury their dead from their homes, it should therefore be lawful for "one engaged in that business to transport a body from his place of business to the undertaker's home in a residential use district and bury it therefrom." On appeal, the Maryland Court of Appeals upheld his conviction. "We think it is preposterous," Associate Judge C. Gus Grason concluded, "to say that because citizens not engaged in the undertaking business bury their dead from their residences, that this constitutes a custom that would warrant an undertaker to use his residence in a residential use district in connection with his undertaking business."[156]

IN FULL KEEPING WITH THE SURROUNDINGS

Other funeral directors took a more nuanced approach to the notion that they should avoid commercializing their funeral homes. Rather than advocating subterfuge, some industry leaders advised funeral directors to simply pay closer attention to the outward appearance and interior arrangements of their establishments so as to ensure that they blended well with their residential surroundings, thereby minimizing opposition. Robert J. Ambruster, whose purpose-built funeral home was situated "on the outskirts of the commercial section in a multiple residential district" of St. Louis, Missouri, did just that. His elegant brick mortuary resembled "a magnificent residence, the architecture having been carried out in the Old English design." The structure was described in an article in the December 1931 edition of the *American Funeral Director*. "The entire exterior," explained the piece,

> is of native white limestone set in pure cement mortar. All exterior metal parts are of solid cast bronze, with the exception of the gutter, which is of copper. The roof is of variegated colored slate. The windows are in-swinging casements with variegated colored imported antique

glass which gives those on the inside almost perfect vision looking outward, but prevents anyone passing by from looking in.[157]

More importantly, Ambruster was careful to eschew any hint of commercialism. In addition to building a mansion-like structure that was in "full keeping with the surroundings," he "studiously avoided anything in the nature of a Neon or electric sign which might be considered by the residents of the neighborhood as a step toward commercialism." His only sign, the article pointed out, was a simple "cast bronze plate bearing the firm's name."[158]

While funeral homes housed in converted dwellings would naturally blend in with their residential neighbors, purpose-built mortuaries such as the one built by Ambruster were designed with conformity in mind. Regardless of whether one chose to convert an existing structure or build new, creating an establishment that was "pervaded by an air of comfort and hominess" was paramount to funeral directors of all kinds, at least prior to the Second World War.[159] For those venturing into residential neighborhoods, advertising the homelike quality of their establishments was a deliberate response to the numerous judges and city planning advocates who insisted that a funeral home, however homelike and wherever it was located, was a "business proposition."[160] Funeral directors, in their view, could not shed the commercialism of the business district by moving to a residential neighborhood because they inevitably carried that commercialism with them to their new location. That a great many residential funeral homes incorporated living quarters for funeral directors and their families appears to have mattered little to either zoning commissions or the courts.[161]

The obsession with homelike, in reality, predated the residential funeral home. Homelike was a quality that had been pursued by an earlier generation of downtown undertakers and figured prominently in the advertising of those who continued to operate downtown parlors during the interwar period. The homelike atmosphere of a residential address gave funeral directors a certain edge over their downtown competitors in an increasingly crowded deathcare marketplace. This thinking was aptly captured in a 1926 advertisement for the funeral home of Cahill & Sons of Hamilton, Ohio, according to which "the finest place for a funeral home is most certainly in the quiet, attractive residential district. There it most fittingly becomes a part of the background, and its homelike qualities are enhanced."[162] Not only was the firm Griesmer-Grim, another of Hamilton's funeral homes, situated in "a quiet and attractive residential district," but, they pointed out in a 1929 advertisement, their establishment also owed "much of its appeal to its charming surroundings."[163]

By the 1920s a new and improved definition of homelike had come to consist of not simply a structure's outward appearance and interior arrangements and furnishings but also its broader spatial setting, which included the oft-mentioned "quiet and attractive residential district" situated away from the congestion, noise, and commercialism of the downtown.[164] "My idea of a funeral home is an establishment where there is an atmosphere of home and sufficient room for retirement in peace and comfort. This can not be carried out in the business section of any town or city," declared J. S. Dunbar of Columbia, South Carolina, in 1926.[165] "Surely," argued a 1927 advertisement for the Dawson & Wikoff Funeral Home, "a residential district is the ideal place for a funeral home, if it is to be truly the home it should be."[166] A residential address, the key element of a revised definition of homelike, thus became the antithesis of and antidote to the commercialism with which all downtown establishments were tainted, at least according to those funeral directors who had made the move to residential neighborhoods. Highlighting a residential location formed part of a larger marketing campaign to succeed where downtown parlors had failed, namely in supplanting the home of the deceased with the funeral home as a place for holding funerals. It is no surprise that in 1920 the firm Fiss & Bills in Oshkosh, Wisconsin, took advantage of its new residential quarters in a large Italianate dwelling on Church Street to advertise "homelike surroundings and strict privacy," which, the firm argued, made its funeral home "the ideal place for the final obsequies of the departed."[167]

Even some judges believed this and expressed their appreciation for the change in atmosphere that residential funeral homes were meant to effect. In his dissent to the majority opinion in *Fraser v. Parker*, in which the South Carolina Supreme Court upheld a 1941 injunction preventing Fred Parker from moving his quarters from the business district of the town of Walterboro to a residential section of the town, Justice L. D. Lide recognized that the funeral home was "a development of modern times looking toward dignified privacy by the creation of a homelike atmosphere as contrasted with the surroundings of everyday business."[168] Lide, whose sympathies clearly lay with funeral directors such as Parker who were looking to move out of the downtown, understood that within the funeral industry a residential address had become indispensable to achieving the atmosphere of a home.[169] By Parker's time this had been the dominant paradigm within the industry for several decades.

ESSENTIALLY RESIDENTIAL IN CHARACTER

Redefining homelike in a way that made it dependent on the possession of a residential address—something downtown establishments clearly lacked—required funeral directors to engage in a kind of doublespeak. To the public the industry advertised establishments in quiet residential settings, in stark contrast to the noise and congestion of the downtown. When forced to go before a judge to fight an injunction, however, funeral directors consistently downplayed the residential quality of the neighborhoods they had chosen while simultaneously exaggerating the extent to which commerce had crept in. The Millers had employed this tactic in La Crosse when they claimed that West Avenue had "become a commercial thoroughfare" and "lost its character as a residence street."[170] Similar arguments were repeated over and over by funeral directors hoping to invalidate an injunction or a zoning ordinance by convincing judges that the quarters they sought to convert or construct were located in areas that had become de facto extensions of the downtown.

As early as 1891, the strategy was employed unsuccessfully by lawyers for the Taylor Company in New York City as a means of invalidating a restrictive covenant invoked by its next door neighbor Eliza Rowland, who was seeking to enjoin their operation. In one of the earliest instances of adaptive use of a dwelling for a funeral home, the Taylor Company converted a dwelling located at Madison Avenue and Forty-Third Street into what one individual described as a "mortuary mansion," equipped with an office, a showroom, a basement embalming room, and a chapel for the holding of funeral services for those who died "in lodgings or flats."[171] Although the structure retained the appearance of "an ordinary first-class corner dwelling house," the neighborhood itself, according to lawyers for the Taylor Company, had long since been taken over by businesses.[172]

The situation described in *Rowland v. Miller* is fascinating because the residential character of the structure itself rendered it something of a precursor to the residential funeral home, while its surroundings, which consisted of a bustling business district composed of tightly packed buildings, meant that it had more in common with the downtown parlors that were its contemporaries. The area of Madison and Forty-Third had become substantially commercialized and was, as the lawyers for the Taylor Company claimed, a business district with a few remaining residential properties left, among which was Eliza Rowland's dwelling.[173] In choosing to enforce the original restrictive covenant prohibiting any "trade or business . . . injurious or offensive to the neighboring inhabitants," the court was pointing out the simple truth that Mrs. Rowland had been there first.[174] It was not as if she had chosen to take up residence in an established business district only to turn around and complain of a neighborhood establishment that she found repugnant. A business district had grown up around her, but this did not diminish her rights.

By the 1920s lawyers for funeral directors protesting injunctions and zoning ordinances were making arguments that echoed those used by the lawyers for the Taylor Company a generation earlier, albeit in a way that stretched the truth to varying degrees. When Arthur

Moran of Detroit went to court in 1926 to fight the injunction against him, he directed most of his testimony "towards combating the plaintiff's claim that the district [was] a residential one."[175] The court disagreed. Some years earlier, Willis Crosby had argued that the eighty residents who were seeking to enjoin his undertaking business were not entitled to protection because the area in which they resided, Omaha's Kountze Place neighborhood, was "not . . . devoted exclusively to residences." Crosby claimed that business enterprises were "creeping in" and contended that the funeral home he opened up on Wirt Street in a "building . . . formerly occupied as a private residence" was "within one and one-half blocks of a garage, within two blocks of an automobile filling station, and within three blocks of a grocery." While Justice William P. Rose did not deny that business activity in the neighborhood had increased, he was of the opinion that Crosby had "invaded a district hitherto devoted exclusively to beautiful residences."[176]

The tactic was still being used in 1940 when a funeral director in McComb, Mississippi, tried to persuade a judge that he should be allowed to convert a large Neoclassical dwelling in a residential section of the city over the objections of his neighbors. According to his attorneys, the area was not residential but instead was "semi-commercial" with "bakeries, grocery stores, nurses homes, doctors clinics, apartment houses, and even another funeral home (within one and one-half blocks) already established" on the same street. The court, however, found that in the eight city blocks surrounding the property in question, there were "about 75 residences," with "2 small grocery stores and small delicatessen shop" being the only commercial places. "The area," concluded Justice Virgil A. Griffith, was "essentially residential in character," and the complainants were entitled to an injunction.[177]

The irony of funeral directors' asserting the commercial character of areas they had selected precisely for their homelike qualities was not lost on the courts. In *Ackerman v. Board of Commissioners*, the New Jersey Superior Court reversed the decision of the Town of Belleville's board of commissioners to permit a funeral home, a nonconforming use, at the corner of Union Avenue and Lloyd Place, which was zoned for single-family residences. The real estate appraiser who testified on behalf of the funeral home expressed the opinion that the "half-mile stretch of Union Avenue is doomed as a residential district; that the time is not far off when it must be zoned for business." The court disagreed, however, and pointed out that the funeral director's "intention to use his building not only for business but as his home" demonstrated "that the land is suitable for residential use in conformity with the zoning ordinance."[178] In other words, despite the claims of his expert witness to the contrary, the funeral director had "indicated that he regarded [the area] as residential by planning to establish his own home there."[179] The court had caught the funeral director in his own paradox.

ON A DIFFERENT FOOTING

If funeral directors felt that they had something to gain by exaggerating the extent to which specific residential districts had been commercialized, the actual residents felt that they had a great deal to lose by acknowledging that businesses had begun to encroach upon their neighborhood. Homeowners seeking to enjoin a funeral home assiduously avoided any suggestion that their street might be in decline or that the distance between their homes and the business district had shrunk. To concede that point in court was, they believed, to cede territory to funeral directors. If, after all, the residential character of their streets had been compromised, as many funeral directors claimed, then perhaps a judge would see no harm in allowing yet another business to take root. Homeowners needed to convince judges of the residential purity of their streets. Degraded streets would, they feared, be afforded less protection.

Casting the funeral home as a nuisance producing offensive and disturbing sights, sounds, and smells and diminishing both quality of life and property values, rather than as an instance of the downtown encroaching on a residential area, arose in part from the refusal of homeowners to acknowledge, in court at least, that the business district was spilling over its borders into the surrounding residential communities. However, this also reveals a long-standing and deep-seated antipathy to the funeral industry. In *Laughlin v. Cooney*, area homeowners argued explicitly that a funeral home would be worse for the neighborhood than some other types of business enterprise. Complainants Margaret E. Cooney and Mattie H. Fletcher claimed that their property would "be rendered less desirable a place of residence than it would as the result of making apartments and boarding houses, or other business enterprises in the immediate neighborhood."[180] In *Tureman v. Ketterlin*, the Missouri Supreme Court reached a similar conclusion, declaring in 1924 that "an undertaking establishment stands on a different footing from that of the occasional corner grocery and oil filling station which have made their appearances there. The latter may offend the aesthetic sense of those living in their proximity; the former would destroy in an essential respect the comfort and repose of their homes."[181] Clearly, the industry suffered from an image problem.

Zoning, on the other hand, tended to be more balanced in its approach. Rather than singling out a particular industry, zoning ordinances sought to protect residential areas from business and commercial activity of all kinds. Commercial activity was to be segregated from residential areas not because business was thought to be a nuisance but instead because mixed-use development was believed to lead to congestion, disorder, and unstable property values. As the Illinois Supreme Court explained in *Aurora v. Burns*, a 1925 case in which a grocery store owner prevented from building in a residential neighborhood challenged the validity of a municipal zoning ordinance,

> the exclusion of places of business from residential districts is not a declaration that such places are nuisances or that they are to be suppressed as such, but it is a part of the general plan by which the city's territory is allotted to different uses in order to prevent, or at least to reduce, the congestion, disorder and dangers which often inhere in unregulated municipal development.[182]

Even when an ordinance was born of a conflict between a funeral director and his prospective neighbors, it might not single out funeral homes. Such was the case with La Crosse's zoning law. Moreover, when funeral homes were discussed by proponents of zoning, it was in the context of a long list of land uses that threatened the repose and domestic purity of residential neighborhoods. When W. J. Donald of American City Consultants warned of "funeral parlors among residences" during his multistate tour in 1920 to preach about the dangers of unzoned municipalities, he also bemoaned "land values falling in formerly good neighborhoods owning to the coming of a butcher shop or a store, a garage or a gasoline filling station, an apartment or an industry."[183]

TWILIGHT ZONES

While funeral directors exaggerated and homeowners ignored the impact of expanding business districts on residential neighborhoods, judges nationwide weighed in and decided in most cases that the truth lay somewhere in between. Using the photographic evidence presented to them, they recorded their impressions of the older residential areas targeted by funeral directors. From judges' observations, a clear and remarkably consistent picture emerges of neighborhoods in a state of flux during the interwar and early postwar years. Although judges generally did not dispute the residential character of the neighborhoods in question, they did not consider them to be strictly residential. Rather, judges spoke repeatedly of neighborhoods that were "becoming more and more devoted to commercial and other business purposes."[184] The belief that "in all growing cities, the development of the business interests will encroach upon the residence district" seems to have been taken for granted.[185] "It is common knowledge," explained one judge in 1930, "that in our growing cities areas first occupied as residence property frequently undergo a transition and become commercial areas. Such changes are the normal result of growth."[186]

Some observers noted that older larger dwellings were falling out of favor in many places, their marketability as single-family homes becoming increasingly limited. This was pointed out when Miller was sued by his La Crosse neighbors in 1921. In response to claims that a funeral home on West Avenue was causing property values to fall, Miller's attorney argued that overall demand for dwellings the size of the Platz homestead and next-door neighbor Elsie Giles Scott's "Pasadena" had fallen in recent years. Even Scott's son Argyle was forced to admit on the stand that there was "little market for large homes."[187] In *Cunningham v. Miller*, Justice Rosenberry himself acknowledged, "It appears from the evidence that in prior years certain wealthy residents of the city of La Crosse erected very elaborate homes in this vicinity, which, by reason of death and removal from the city, had been vacated by their original owners and they are not readily salable for anything like the amount of their original cost."[188] The same argument was made decades later in 1955 at funeral director William Tripp's hearing before the zoning board of Pawtucket, Rhode Island. Applying for a permit to operate a funeral home in an area zoned residential, Tripp testified that the house was too large for continued use as a one-family dwelling, that the cost of remodeling it for use as apartments would be prohibitive, and that it had "no marketability as a one-family house."[189]

Many of the descriptions recorded in legal opinions point to the very incursions that zoning was designed to arrest. For example, it was not uncommon for apartment houses and other multifamily structures to have become part of the mix of residential dwellings. In 1925 a "two-story apartment house" was among "the encroachments of business and semibusiness, religious or social establishments or centers" considered by the Alabama Supreme Court in *Higgins v. Bloch* to have caused "the strict residential character of the locality" to be "impaired," even though the court ruled against the funeral director.[190] Alongside the "substantial homes" and "single family dwellings" of one older Detroit neighborhood targeted by a funeral director in 1926, there were also "some duplexes and some apartments." There were also references to a "few roomers" and the fact that some of houses had been rented, though most of the houses were occupied by their owners. "The particular district here involved," concluded the Michigan Supreme Court, "has retained its residential character although outside of it in some directions business has crept in and become the predominant factor."[191]

A quarter century later, the court encountered a similar mix on block 94 of Peck Street in Muskegon Heights. The area lay about a mile from the city's main business center. "Of said 12 lots in block 94," explained Justice Emerson R. Boyles, "9 are residences, 3 are vacant, 4 of said residences have apartments, 2 of them have rooms for rent to tourists. One of these homes was used by the owner for watch repair, and another in giving physiotherapy baths." Boyle's description offers an interesting snapshot of an early postwar street in the midst of transition, although the precise nature of the transition was disputed among the various stakeholders. The street itself was zoned residential, but the city council had readily voted to permit a funeral home to move in, demonstrating its opinion that the neighborhood was changing from residential to commercial. Justice Boyles disagreed. "The presence of an apartment house," he wrote, "or the rental of rooms or apartments does not change such use from being residential."[192] Perhaps Boyles and his fellow justices were more concerned with the legal rights of the current remaining residents rather than with the neighborhood's subsequent evolution or future direction, which naturally was on the minds of Muskegon Height's municipal leaders.

Judges were, of course, not blind to the fact that many of the neighborhoods they were being asked to protect had declined somewhat or were on the cusp of transitioning from residential to commercial. Still, this did not often prevent them from siding with those seeking to enjoin the operation of a funeral home. The opinion in the majority of cases was that even a neighborhood in transition was entitled to protection as long as it remained predominantly residential. The typical picture that emerges from the court documents is of a well-kept, often august neighborhood showing some signs of deterioration and possibly commercialization but still primarily residential. For example, as early as 1917 in *Saier v. Joy*, the Michigan Supreme Court heard expert testimony that the areas most likely to be targeted by undertakers

seeking to relocate from the downtown were ones in which the residential character of the district was disappearing and business was
breaking in.[193] This was the situation that the Alabama Supreme Court
was forced to consider in *Higgins v. Bloch*, in which a "long-established
residence district was being invaded by business structures, was in
course of transition from a residence to a business district." Nonetheless, the court held that the neighborhood "in effect . . . was still essentially residential in character as alleged."[194]

In 1924 the Missouri Supreme Court offered a more detailed description of a Kansas City neighborhood in the early stages of not
only change but also deterioration:

> The territory immediately surrounding it was at one time, perhaps
> twenty or twenty-five years ago, one of the most beautiful residence
> sections of Kansas City. But as a residential district it has now fallen into
> decay; no new homes are being constructed, while numerous business
> enterprises are appearing here and there. The occupation for residential
> purposes still greatly predominates over any other, however. While some
> of the fine old homes there are now occupied by tenants and show evi-
> dences of neglect, many others are occupied by owners who keep them
> in repair; and practically all are used solely as places of residence.[195]

Despite declaring the neighborhood to be a "decaying residential
district," the court could find no reason why it should be denied
protection:

> It is true that the district has entered upon a period of transition; no
> new homes are being built and business is entering here and there. Not-
> withstanding, it is still essentially residential in character. And on
> principle there can be no valid reason why its inhabitants are not enti-
> tled to the same protection in the enjoyment of their homes as that ac-
> corded home owners in residence districts generally.[196]

In cases throughout the interwar period, judges made similar observations about the changes affecting older residential neighborhoods
on the periphery of the downtown. Even when businesses had begun

to spring up, it was not unusual for judges to point to a neighborhood's remaining "costly and palatial residences." Nor did they fail to see that in many instances the encroachment of the downtown had not occurred "to such an extent as to cause [the neighborhood] to lose its primary character as a residential section of the city."[197]

As late as 1942, the Mississippi Supreme Court was willing to make a more balanced assessment of the changes affecting one of the oldest residential parts of Hattiesburg. Attorneys for the funeral directing firm Fairchild and Richard were attempting to fight an injunction by asserting that the area chosen by their clients was neither exclusively nor essentially residential in character. The attorneys pointed to the appearance three years prior of an ice manufacturing plant, a gas station seven years prior, and a grocery store, all within 1,000 feet of the dwelling Fairchild and Richard wished to convert. The court, however, rejected the claim that the relatively recent introduction of these businesses deprived the area of its residential character. The area, the court argued, "is an old residential section of Hattiesburg, and . . . the immediate vicinity of the funeral home is perhaps the oldest residential part of the City; the homes are valuable and many of the leading citizens live in the area in question." Nor should a handful of businesses deprive the neighborhood and its residents of the protection they sought:

> Thus viewing the scenes of this case, having all factors in mind, we do not think the location of an ice plant, a gas station, and a small grocery store operated in connection with the owner's home, situated as these are, within a radius of one thousand feet, with over a hundred residences therein, changes a former residential section to one not now essentially so. The transition, if such is taking place, has not reached the point where the residents are not entitled to protection.[198]

Unlike zoning advocates who tended to see neighborhoods as ruined at the first sign of commerce or multifamily housing creeping in, judges were more inclined to recognize that an incipient transformation did not immediately deprive a neighborhood of its residential character.[199]

This more nuanced approach can be seen in *Tucson v. Arizona Mortuary*. In 1928 the Arizona Supreme Court was asked to rule on the constitutionality of a law restricting the location of undertaking parlors after residents discovered that plans for one in their neighborhood had been submitted to the city. When the offending undertaker later challenged the law in court, the judge "found that the immediate vicinity of plaintiff's establishment was not strictly a residential district, but was mixed and rapidly giving way to business, and that it was a very suitable and convenient place for a mortuary" and declared the law void. When the Arizona Supreme Court weighed in two years later, however, it reversed the decision, arguing instead that "it is obvious that it would be extremely difficult, if not impossible, to find any considerable district in a growing city which was one hundred per cent either business or residential.... Even in the most exclusively aristocratic residence districts of the various cities of our country there are frequently found a few neighborhood corner groceries, drug-stores and filling stations."[200] Garages and filling stations in residential districts may have been high on the list of offenses that zoning advocates sought to remedy,[201] but in many judicial circles the presence of an occasional filling station was deemed part of the normal cycle of neighborhood growth.[202]

Descriptions of rapidly changing neighborhoods can also be found in decisions favoring funeral directors. In *Pearson v. Bonnie*, frequently cited by attorneys defending funeral directors, the Kentucky Court of Appeals concluded in 1925 that "a reasonable expansion of the business district of a growing community must be expected to encroach gradually beyond the borders of former residential property, whose owners are to suffer the resultant inconveniences or profit as an incident of residence in a city."[203] When neighbors of Wiley Henderson Luquire tried to prevent him from erecting a new mortuary in an area still home to "many residences" in Birmingham, Alabama, they were denied relief because the area was understood to be in flux. When the neighbors took their case to the Alabama Supreme Court in 1930, the court acknowledged that the "district was first built up as a residence section" during the 1880s and noted that a majority of the lots on the street in question were still occupied by residences. Nonetheless, the residential nature of the area had been compromised by the accumulation of business properties nearby, specifically "business enterprises . . . located at both ends of the block" facing the funeral home. "In recent years," the court explained, "it has been in a state of transition, becoming more and more devoted to commercial and other business purposes." The court pointed out that new construction was all for business purposes and that dwellings had been demolished to make way for new commercial structures, including a dwelling on the site of the proposed Luquire Funeral Home. The street had actually been designated as a commercial zone by Birmingham's 1926 zoning ordinance.[204] That same year in *Fentress v. Sicard*, the Arkansas Supreme Court refused to bar a funeral home from a neighborhood "in a state of transition from an exclusively residential district to a business district."[205]

As the nation neared the midcentury mark, aggrieved residents living in what one observer deemed "twilight zones," where business was "gradually crowding residences," were encountering far less sympathy from the courts. Many judges were beginning to recognize that expanding business districts were entitled to "living room."[206] As the balance from residential to commercial in many older neighborhoods tipped during the postwar years, courts once reluctant to permit residential funeral homes found it increasingly difficult to justify an injunction. "It is important to point out," noted the Louisiana Supreme Court in 1952, "that the decisions throughout the United States are uniform in holding that the proposed establishment and operation of a funeral home in an area or district which is partly commercial and partly residential or which is undergoing transition from a residential to a commercial area will not be enjoined."[207] Two years earlier in 1950 the Iowa Supreme Court had reversed a decision granting a group of Fort Dodge residents an injunction preventing Welch Laufersweiler from erecting a funeral home in their neighborhood. The proposed mortuary, the court acknowledged, was "surrounded at varying distances by residences." In fact, the area possessed "many of the older and better homes in the city." At the same time, "the main business district to the north and west," the court observed, had "expanded to within a block" of the address in question. Explaining further why it felt it was not bound by *Bevington v. Otte*, its own precedent from roughly a dozen years earlier, the court pointed out that in the earlier case "no business was located within four or five blocks of the place" and that the complainants lived much nearer to the funeral home. "In any event," the court concluded, "we are not now prepared to hold, as plaintiffs apparently would have us, that every funeral home, even when properly maintained and operated, is necessarily a nuisance merely because it is located in a residential district."[208]

The changes recorded in legal decisions affecting the location of funeral homes were part of a complex process by which the nineteenth-century residential landscape of American cities and towns was being remade just as a new residential landscape in the form of the first automobile suburbs was being created. The accounts given by judges and expert witnesses describe expanding business districts, the proliferation of apartment buildings, the demolition of some older dwellings, and the conversion of others into rooming houses and funeral homes, not to mention a general lapse in maintenance and the subsequent physical deterioration of the housing stock. What began as a gradual decline in many older neighborhoods just prior to the First World War continued through the interwar period and reached its peak during the postwar years. Already in 1914 the change was apparent to observers, at least one of whom cast the issue in terms of aging residential dwellings in close proximity to the downtown. In an article titled, "The Old House as a Social Problem," Mildred Chadsey wrote,

> Most of our cities, due to their rapid growth, have districts that are going through a transition from resident districts to factory and business districts. Rents from dwellings are decreasing, while land value is greatly increasing. The owners of many of these homes, foreseeing the opportunity to sell the land for business purposes in one year or ten years, will not repair or improve their houses, because they argue it would be a

waste to put more money in the houses that will in themselves bring no return when selling the land.[209]

However severe the problem had become by the 1920s, few, apart from funeral directors themselves, saw converting old houses into funeral homes as the solution.

In some ways, the changing neighborhoods in which residential funeral homes sprung up bore some resemblance to the "zone in transition" described by Park and Burgess in their seminal 1925 work *The City*. Although many of them, like the zone in transition, were situated at the edge of the downtown and were already "being invaded by business and light manufacture,"[210] they can hardly be compared to what Chicago School disciple Roderick D. McKenzie understood to be the transition zone in most American cities in his day. "Immediately surrounding the central business district of most cities," he wrote in the early 1920s, "is to be found a more or less disintegrated area, comprising wholesale establishments, low class hotels and apartment houses, second-hand stores, and cheap places of amusement. This region is usually inhabited by a migratory class of people, such as day laborers, immigrants, and negroes. It also tends to become the rendezvous of the vicious and criminal classes."[211] Rather, they had more in common with the "residential area" of Park and Burgess's concentric model. Within its bounds were situated either "high-class apartment buildings" or "exclusive 'restricted' districts of single family dwellings."[212] Home to economically mixed populations, with established wealthy residents predominating, these were neighborhoods on the cusp of change, not the ghettos described McKenzie.

The process by which the older residential neighborhoods targeted by funeral directors changed during the interwar years resembles the succession described by Park and Burgess in which "the tendency of each inner zone [is] to extend its area by the invasion of the next outer zone." Of course, one need exercise caution in applying the Chicago School's concentric zone model of urban growth, long criticized for its failure to accommodate a wide range of land-use patterns and landscapes that do not fit neatly into concentric rings, not to mention its racist and xenophobic undertones. Whatever theory is employed, whether it be the axial theory, the sector theory, or the theory of multiple nuclei, it is clear that within American cities and towns there have been multiple zones of transition arising from socioeconomic and demographic shifts occurring over many decades.[213] The snapshots of changing landscapes buried in countless legal decisions affecting the location of funeral homes point to not only expanding business districts but also a high degree of residential mobility as wealthy homeowners moved away to be replaced by both less affluent residents, including a large number of tenants and boarders, as well as commercial establishments.[214] Nonetheless, it should not be forgotten that in many of these declining neighborhoods, enough people of means and influence remained to mount a successful opposition to the intrusion of a funeral home onto their street. Moreover, a diagnosis of decline within any analysis, past or present, should always be problematized to acknowledge the many ways in which cultural vibrancy and strong community bonds can exist and even flourish amid deterioration of the physical fabric of a place.[215]

In other instances, the residential streets selected by enterprising funeral directors were so close to the downtown or so degraded that a successful campaign to oust the funeral home failed to materialize. In 1917, for example, when the Place Funeral Home in Los Gatos, California, moved into a circa 1891 Queen Anne mansion on the very edge of the downtown, it encountered no resistance. Similarly, despite possessing a "homelike atmosphere" and beautiful grounds, the dwelling converted into a modern funeral home by Sheboygan's A. W. Ramm was, the firm acknowledged, situated on a main business thoroughfare, and commercial structures stood directly adjacent to the house. Doubtless these locations were strategic, skillfully combining a domestic setting with an address on the periphery of the business district, thus neutralizing opposition and minimizing the chance that a viable nuisance lawsuit could be brought.

BUSINESS CREEPING IN

Notwithstanding the arguments made by zoning advocates that funeral homes together with other forms of commerce and apartment houses destabilized and blighted single-family residential districts and the claims of funeral directors themselves that they were arresting decay in aging neighborhoods, the impact of the funeral home on America's residential landscape remains ambiguous. It would be inaccurate to conclude that the residential funeral home sparked decline in older neighborhoods. The appearance of a funeral home certainly signaled that change was afoot. Ultimately the funeral home was more harbinger than catalyst. In some cases, the neighborhoods in question were perceived to be under assault from "business creeping in" even before funeral directors showed up.[216] The appearance of a funeral home, however, may have accelerated decline in neighborhoods where it had already begun to set in. Funeral directors themselves were clearly aware of the changes affecting older neighborhoods. They often sought to capitalize on the shift from residential to commercial and tended to exaggerate the shift, in court at least, while simultaneously downplaying it in advertisements promising homelike surroundings on quiet streets.

On the micro scale, converting an aging dwelling into a funeral home arrested and reversed decay in specific individual properties, especially those long neglected. Funeral directors invested huge sums to rehabilitate large dwellings whose marketability as single-family homes had diminished. Generally speaking, they maintained beautiful buildings and grounds. It could be argued—and they often did—that funeral directors were preserving the residential character of a neighborhood in transition. On the macro scale, however, the presence of a funeral home may have hastened an area's transition from residential to commercial, which was often accompanied by a gradual degradation of the neighborhood's overall housing stock. In 1928 observers in Ada, Oklahoma, tied the recent expansion of the city's business district to the appearance of the Criswell Funeral Home. "With the spontaneous growth of Ada evident at every hand," they explained in an article in the *Ada Evening News*, "the old bounds of the business district designed to care for its growing population are being torn down and expansions seen in all sections of the city." Noting the appearance of multistory brick commercial blocks, a hotel, an automobile dealership, and a garage, the article lamented how "new store fronts" were replacing "old familiar landmarks" along Twelfth Street in an area once believed to be immune to expansion from the downtown. "Helping the cause along," the article continued, was J. U. Criswell "when he erected his elaborate funeral home just east of the hotel site at a cost of $30,000."[217]

In 1930 the Arkansas Supreme Court held that the appearance of a funeral home would hasten the conversion of one Fort Smith neighborhood into a business district. In *Fentress v. Sicard*, which lifted an injunction against a funeral home in an area deemed to be in the midst of a transition from residential to commercial, the court argued that although the funeral home "would not detract from [the neighborhood's] value for residential purposes," it was more in keeping with what seemed to be the clear trajectory of a district "long since fallen into disuse" as a residential area. "The great preponderance of the testimony herein shows," the court concluded, "that the establishment of the mortuary upon the site selected would enhance the value of the surrounding property as business property."[218] When in 1930 Alabama the Supreme Court also denied relief to a group of complainants seeking an injunction against a funeral home in their Birmingham neighborhood, Justice Virgil Bouldin was of the opinion that the funeral home contributed to the shift from residential to commercial, which was already well under way. "It may be truly said," he wrote in *White v. Luquire*, "this funeral home is enlarging the business area in that block, pushing back the residence area."[219]

Another way the residential funeral home impacted its surroundings was through increased traffic, at least in some instances. In 1920 the complainants in *Beisel v. Crosby* alleged that with the opening of a funeral home in the Kountze Place section of Omaha, "the congestion in the street more than once prevented neighbors from stopping automobiles in front of their own doors."[220] Two decades later in *Smith v. Fairchild*, the Mississippi Supreme Court noted that during a funeral for a soldier at the establishment of M. G. Fairchild, "traffic blocked all streets in the area."[221] On the other hand, some were optimistic that relocating a funeral establishment from the congested business district to a semiresidential area would actually alleviate traffic problems. So concluded a New Hampshire superior court in 1945. Following a 1943 amendment to Keene's zoning ordinance permitting "undertaking establishments and funeral homes [to] be taken out of the business district and placed in the general residence district," Frank Foley left his quarters at 15 Court Street in the business district for a remodeled residence several blocks away at 49 Court Street. When one of his new neighbors challenged the amendment, a superior court judge defended the change in the law, at least in part because the judge believed that the move would relieve congestion in Keene's downtown. "Traffic conditions," the judge argued, "were congested frequently when funerals occurred at the funeral home at 15 Court Street. Such congestion will be relieved by permitting undertaking establishments and funeral homes to be conducted in a general residence district."[222]

A little over a decade later in 1956, the South Carolina Supreme Court expressed the same hope when it upheld an amendment to Charleston's zoning ordinance, allowing John McAlister to relocate from his downtown quarters at 169 Meeting Street to 150 Wentworth Street. "A major consideration in large metropolitan areas," the court explained,

> is the traffic problem. It is well known that the City of Charleston, approximately three miles long and a mile and a half wide, with a population in excess of seventy thousand, is one of the most congested municipal areas in the nation. The street on which the defendants now operate their funeral home, Meeting Street, is one of the main traffic arteries of the City. Parking is prohibited on one side of the street, and with the lack of room for expansion and other parking facilities, funeral

services at the defendants' funeral home result in severe traffic congestion. The removal from Meeting Street of the defendants' funeral home
would eliminate a major cause of traffic congestion on that street and
thereby promote the convenience and welfare of the general public.[223]

This is, of course, what funeral directors had been arguing for decades
and one of the main reasons they had fled congested downtowns in
the first place. Not everyone was as optimistic, however, and potential
traffic jams in residential neighborhoods became one of the factors considered by municipalities when presented with a request to modify existing zoning to allow a funeral home in an area from which commercial
activity was barred.[224] For example, after listening to arguments for and
against the opening of a funeral home in a residential section of Pawtucket, the city's zoning board concluded in 1955 that a funeral home
"would cause an additional traffic hazard" and denied the permit.[225]

Despite lingering concerns in many quarters, public sentiment
toward the funeral home eventually softened enough that opposition
and litigation gradually began to wane. When conflicts arose, later
judges were less willing to side with complainants than their counterparts had been a generation earlier.[226] When in 1942, for example, Win-
ifred Astle Doll of Baraboo, Wisconsin, sued funeral directors John
Scheible and Chris Dyrud for opening up a funeral home in the large
two-story Colonial Revival dwelling next door, she failed to persuade
circuit court judge Alvin C. Reis that her grievance was a legitimate
one. Disregarding the precedent set by *Cunningham v. Miller* in 1922,
Reis dismissed the $5,000 suit. "The overwhelming weight of the evi-
dence taken on a four day trial before the court," he concluded, "shows
indisputably that this funeral home is not a nuisance."[227] Defending his
action, Reis explained that he was not bound by the earlier decision,
because in his opinion modern funeral homes were not what they
were back in 1922. What had changed during the intervening decades
was not the funeral home itself but rather the spatial and cultural context within which it functioned. Not only had the older residential
neighborhoods historically targeted by funeral directors become less

residential, but a large a segment of the public had come to rely on the funeral home as an alternative to the home funeral. The residential funeral home had by midcentury gone from nuisance to necessity.

Neither neighborhood nor public opinion evolved fast enough for Adelbert and Sophia Miller. When they lost their appeal before the Wisconsin Supreme Court, they had no choice but to vacate the Platz homestead on West Avenue. Like many undertakers forced under the terms of an injunction to abandon newly remodeled residential quarters, they returned to the downtown. In May 1923 they announced the formal opening of a new funeral establishment on Pearl Street, exactly one block south of the Main Street parlors they had left behind less than three years earlier. It was advertised as the "Miller Funeral Home" even though it was situated in the heart of the business district. In addition to the main office, the facilities included "a beautifully decorated and furnished reception room, a private room for mourners, the chapel with seating accommodations for 100 persons, and rest rooms adjoining, a modern operating room, private rooms for preparing bodies for burial, stock closets, a large stock room and wardrobes."[228] For the Millers, there was no looking back. Despite their desire for residential quarters and what must have been a growing awareness that downtown funeral parlors were becoming increasingly outdated, they claimed that their new funeral home was "one of the most beautiful and up-to-date establishments of its kind in the state."[229]

As for West Avenue, in 1930 it was widened, solidifying its role as a major traffic artery and further diminishing its prestige and desirability as a residential street. By the end of the Second World War, an even bigger change had arrived. Pasadena, the palatial mansion owned by Elsie Gile Scott, whose vocal opposition to a funeral home next door had been so damning to the Millers' case, had been converted into a YMCA. It was demolished in 1969. Neither it nor the Platz homestead survived West Avenue's development into a commercial thoroughfare and the gradual destruction of its once grand residential fabric. West Avenue had gone from residential to commercial, and nobody could possibly have blamed the Millers.

CHAPTER FOUR

A HIGHER PLANE

*The Funeral Home
as a Symbolic Space*

Frank Schaffner and Asa Queen knew that the Second Empire mansion they had purchased and remodeled was far more than four walls and a roof for their funeral directing business. Situated at 360 East Center Street in Marion, Ohio, the three-story brick dwelling, with its imposing turret, stately grandeur, and spacious grounds, was once home to local tycoon Henry Barnhart, one of the founders of the Marion Steam Shovel Company. When the Schaffner-Queen Company bought the Barnhart residence in August 1927 to house its more than sixty-year-old firm, the company understood that it had acquired not just a new headquarters or merely a piece of Marion's history. While the structure was both of those, what Schaffner and Queen had purchased, they knew full well, was a symbol.

"For 62 years," proclaimed the March 1928 advertisement announcing the funeral home's grand opening, "this firm has been favorably known in the community. But in order to live we must progress. This new funeral home was created to express the spirit of progress—and to offer our clients, old and new, the finest facilities of our profession. We hope it will be a credit to our city—and to ourselves."[1] Like many funeral directors of their generation nationwide, Schaffner and Queen exchanged the bustle of the downtown for quarters in a residential district. Their new facilities possessed a long driveway that could accommodate seventy-five automobiles and an atmosphere akin to that of "a lovely old home with an air of dignity and restfulness,"[2] both of which, they hoped, would give them an advantage over their downtown competitors. The Barnhart residence offered something more, however. The structure itself, they felt, embodied progress. They were referring to advancements over the increasingly old-fashioned ways of their downtown competitors and, of course, to their progress as a firm, but they were also mindful of a bigger picture. Schaffner and Queen were offering a commentary on the state of their field, and they chose their words carefully in order to convey something about the work of funeral directors in general, not just in Marion, Ohio. For starters, funeral directing, they maintained, was not a trade or a business like others but rather a profession. It was also a profession defined by progress, not, as had often been charged, by ghoulishness or greed. The recently acquired Barnhart residence was the material expression of that progress, and an image of the remodeled dwelling featured prominently in the newspaper announcement.

Schaffner and Queen grasped the communicative power of objects. Whether it was their carriages during the nineteenth century, motorized hearses later on, lavish downtown quarters, or grand residential funeral homes, funeral directors have historically utilized a diverse body of material culture to craft messages about themselves and their work. Of course, it is true that in practical terms the funeral home provided a physical setting for the work of the funeral director. In addition to performing the mundane task of housing functions and equipment, however, mansions were also recruited to bolster the industry's claims to legitimacy and its status as a profession as opposed to a trade. Funeral directors used their buildings to solve multiple problems, both practical and complex, in much the same way that clothing is used to cover bodies as well as construct identities. Spaces are both shelter and symbol, and interwar funeral directors such as Schaffner and Queen understood this. Countless other funeral directors articulated a seemingly intuitive awareness of the different ways in which structures could be put to work. They often spoke openly about their faith in the ability of spaces to represent ideas and were not shy about assisting the public and prospective clients with visual and textual cues to ensure that the funeral home was interpreted properly. In other words, funeral directors took an active role in investing their spaces with the precise meanings they hoped those spaces would carry.

Funeral directors relied heavily on text, primarily in the form of advertisements, to guarantee that their houses and hearses were invested with the meanings required for those objects to signify the precise values and qualities that they wished to be associated with their work. Schaffner and Queen were hardly subtle in their efforts to influence the ways in which the residents of Marion viewed their funeral home. "Funeral customs," argued a 1931 advertisement for their firm, "denote the modes of thought, state of manners, and degree of civilization existing among the various races of people."[3] This had become a common refrain among funeral directors, namely that a society could be judged by its treatment of its dead. Schaffner and Queen had made it clear when they announced their opening that they considered residential funeral homes a key component of the progressive funeral customs that had emerged over the course of the previous decade. While some, especially the funeral reformers, had historically looked upon funeral customs as extravagant, unnecessary, and exploitative, Schaffner and Queen attempted to silence critics and skeptics alike by offering a different interpretation. "In this country," they claimed, "the up-to-date funeral director reflects in every detail of his service the present high state of American culture."[4] For Schaffner and Queen, the funeral home represented not simply progress within the field of professional deathcare; it also reflected the very pinnacle of civilization itself.

A DOUBLE CALAMITY

Undertakers were not yet out of the livery stable when their critics started in. Among the most well known of their antagonists was Samuel

Clemens, whom the world knew as Mark Twain. His caustic and humorous attacks on undertakers, which began during the American Civil War and spanned several decades, were unrivaled until Jessica Mitford's scathing critique of the American funeral industry appeared a little less than a century later. Clemens's quarrel with undertakers initially arose as a result of his family's dealings with Samuel C. Wright, the Carson City, Nevada, undertaker hired by Clemens's brother Orion upon the death of his beloved eight-year-old daughter, Jennie Clemens. In a piece titled "Concerning Undertakers" published on February 12, 1864, in nearby Virginia City's *Territorial Enterprise*, Clemens accused Wright of practicing a form of extortion, overcharging bereaved families when they were at their most vulnerable. "Does not this undertaker," he asked,

> take advantage of that unfortunate delicacy which prevents a man from disputing an unjust bill for services rendered in burying the dead, to extort ten-fold more than his labors are worth? I have conversed with a good many citizens on this subject, and they all say the same thing: that they know it is wrong that a man should be unmercifully fleeced under such circumstances, but, according to the solemn etiquette above referred to, he cannot help himself.[5]

There is good reason to believe that Clemens tapped into an undercurrent of antipathy, resentment, and distrust that had been steadily building toward undertakers since the antebellum period. His litany included many of the themes repeated later in the burial reform movement that emerged during the last quarter of the nineteenth century. For example, Clemens argued that the unreasonable markup on funeral goods overinflated the undertaker's profits to a disturbing degree. "This undertaker," he wrote, referring to Wright,

> charges a hundred and fifty dollars for a pine coffin that cost him twenty or thirty, and fifty dollars for a grave that did not cost him ten—and this at a time when his ghastly services are required at least seven times a week. I gather these facts from some of the best citizens of Carson, and I can publish their names at any moment if you want them. What Carson

needs is a few more undertakers—there is vacant land enough here for a thousand cemeteries.[6]

By the early twentieth century, high profit margins for undertakers at the expense of the bereaved and the extreme retail markup on burial goods had become favorite topics for reformers. A 1910 study commissioned by the City Club of Chicago found undertakers making profits of 100 to 200 percent.[7] "The honest undertaker's percentage of profits," concluded a 1910 article titled "How Undertakers Burden the Grief-Stricken" in *Pearson's Magazine*, "would make your eyes bulge; those of the unscrupulous undertaker are beyond belief."[8]

Many social critics and more than a few undertakers argued that the "coffin trust" was to blame for runaway costs. The existence of such a monopoly and subsequent price fixing among casket manufacturers was a bitterly contested topic, and an exposé in the January 4, 1913, issue of *Harper's Weekly* concluded that with 239 casket manufacturers listed in the 1910 census, it did "not look as if the sources of supply were restricted." Most of these casket makers, however, "were small, experimental companies," and "of the leading makers east of the Mississippi, the great majority," the article found, "are consolidated into one dominating concern, which exerts a nationwide influence in caskets and in the general regulation and selection of supplies."[9] That a coffin trust existed was taken as an article of faith by the general public. Some reformers believed that a greater emphasis on simplicity in funeralization would "discourage the coffin trust from manufacturing costly [caskets] and charging ten times as much as they are really worth."[10] Other reformers were less optimistic that culture would sway either manufacturers or retailers and lobbied for some kind of regulation to make funerals more affordable.[11] All agreed that high burial costs had turned dying into a luxury. "This heavy expense," argued one early twentieth-century reformer, "brings such a hardship on most of the people that [death] is really a double calamity."[12] Belief in a coffin trust did not exonerate undertakers. The 1913 *Harper's* report found that undertakers routinely made 200 to 300 percent in profits on accessories alone. "The coffin trust, the cemeteries, and the ministers play a small part in increasing the cost of dying, in comparison with the undertaker," declared *Pearson's*. Consequently, most twentieth-century crusaders for burial reform rejected the solution proposed by Clemens in 1864 that additional undertakers were needed to avoid the kind of monopoly his brother had encountered in Carson City. Within a generation of Clemens, progressive thinkers were advocating alternatives to the for-profit deathcare model, such as membership-based burial societies, as well as cremation as a less expensive option. Most reformers believed that the solution lay in fewer rather than more undertakers.

The problem, critics all agreed, was that the field of professional deathcare was too crowded. "There are too many undertakers. That is the main reason why it costs so much to die,"[13] concluded *Pearson's*. By the turn of the century as mortality rates leveled off due to improvements in medicine, many undertakers were left each month with only a handful of funerals with which to balance steadily rising operating costs. "The undertaking business is overdone," concluded one reformer in 1915. "In our country," he continued, "there are over 30,000 undertakers, and more are crowding into the business, attracted by the large profits reported. But striking an average, there is hardly a living in it, when rental and other expenses are considered, and this causes exorbitant profits to be exacted."[14] The effect of so many undertakers was to reduce the amount of business each undertaker received, hence the need to charge more per funeral. "Greater New York," explained the piece, "has 1,100 undertakers, which allots to each less than four funerals in three weeks. The average for the country is about the same."[15] To many observers, the obvious solution was simply to allow the Darwinian nature of free market capitalism to work itself out. If some undertakers lowered their rates, those unable to compete would be driven out of business, thereby thinning out the field. Why, the reformer asked, did not those undertakers left with fewer than one funeral per week "cut rates for their own good and the benefit of the public? Because," he answered, "the articles of a combine, called a 'code of ethics,' prevent them from lowering prices.

A Baltimore undertaker said: 'The undertakers of this city made the threat that if I did not stop this extensive advertising of cheap funerals, they would all go into the field against me and lower prices until they put me out of business.'"[16] In other words, underselling one's competitors was not only forsworn as unethical but was also considered a form of professional suicide, or so undertakers wanted the public to believe.

Also contributing to runaway burial costs, undertakers pointed out, was a plethora of unpaid bills, which in effect forced paying customers to subsidize delinquent customers. "We have to make up for that loss," explained one undertaker in 1910, "or we couldn't stay in business. So prices have to be high and those that do pay carry the burden of those that don't."[17] Such revelations did not generate much sympathy among the general public for undertakers. Instead, a great many viewed them as predators rather than victims of an unfair system. Far less attention was paid to the ways in which undertakers themselves struggled to make ends meet than on the ways in which they were believed to fleece the bereaved, especially the immigrant poor who, in the minds of the middle class, were already prone to overspend on funerals in order to make an extravagant display. Emotionally vulnerable people of all classes were being manipulated into spending more on funerals than they otherwise might. "Wage earners," "plain people of the day-labor class," and "the very poor," according to Congregational minister and reformer Quincy Dowd, were constrained "to desire above aught else to furnish a burial of the 'costlier' sort."[18] Undertakers were generally believed to encourage rather than discourage extravagance, a practice that drew practically universal condemnation. Even worse were widely circulated reports of undertakers swallowing up entire life insurance policies. Rather than being seen as an enterprise "conducted along modern business lines" by "men with fine sensibilities," undertaking was widely regarded as the domain of those "with the souls of delicatessen dealers."[19] Such judgments, though harsh overstatements, helped shape public opinion. "People can't go bargain hunting for coffins," lamented *Pearson's*, "and the undertaker turns their ignorance and misery into dividends. He preys upon his customer's feelings."[20]

A TRADE WHICH PREYS UPON PEOPLE
BEREAVED AND DEFENSELESS

As unpleasant as the attacks of social critics and funeral reformers were for undertakers, what was equally frustrating for them was the public's tendency to classify undertaking as a trade. By the late nineteenth century the men and women in the deathcare industry had begun to see themselves as professionals, alongside doctors, lawyers, and ministers. In addition to changes in nomenclature, with "undertaker" gradually being replaced by "mortician" or, more commonly, "funeral director," there had been attempts to professionalize the industry by forming associations, outlining a code of ethics, and setting licensing requirements. Such efforts were in large part a response to the numerous articles and exposés in the popular press that portrayed undertakers as greedy extortionists.[21] Undertakers were acutely aware of the widespread suspicion and hostility engendered by negative press and the ensuing calls for reform from consumer advocates and clergy. The earliest attempts to organize professional associations of undertakers in the 1870s and 1880s, first at the state level and then nationally, were motivated by a desire to win the respect and trust of the general public by regulating membership, elevating ethical standards, and improving quality control within the industry. Looking beyond the calls for reform, however, undertakers as a group were determined to transcend their humble origins in the livery stable and the cabinetmaker's workshop.

In contemporary parlance, the word "profession" is applied loosely to refer to virtually any kind of work or occupation. For centuries, however, it was a designation reserved exclusively for three specific vocations, namely theology, law, and medicine. Not even pedagogy was universally accepted as a profession, though some were happy to broaden the definition to include education. During the latter half of the late nineteenth century, other occupations, such as architecture, engineering, banking, and nursing, had taken steps toward professionalization by setting up membership associations and licensing bodies as a way of defining ethics, establishing universal membership criteria, and maintaining quality within the field of practice. By the turn of the century, practitioners in dozens of occupations had begun to identify and promote themselves as professionals, though some fields encountered more resistance than others in their quest for recognition as learned professions. Undertakers struggled for recognition, having long been considered a sideline to less than glamorous livery work and cabinetmaking.

With the creation of the Funeral Directors' National Association of the United States in 1882 came some recognition that undertakers were at least attempting to professionalize.[22] "If what Mr. Herbert Spencer would call the 'differentiation of occupations' is to be regarded as a concomitant and an index of advancing civilization," wrote one commentator in 1884,

> it is to be presumed that the American people will learn with unmingled complacency of the development in their midst of a new profession. For several odd centuries the professions universally recognized among civilized peoples have been the three of theology, law and medicine. True, the work of the teacher bears the characteristics of a learned profession in so marked a degree that the question has more than once been raised whether teachers also ought not to be admitted to the enjoyment of the rights and immunities accorded everywhere to lawyers, doctors and ministers; but the weight of opinion up to the present time has been that the vocation of teaching has not yet arrived at the point where it is fully entitled to be regarded as the fourth profession. That this is really the correct view of the case has now been shown very clearly in a paper read by Mr. Thomas H. Roberts at a recent meeting of the national funeral directors' association, held in Greenbaum's hall in Chicago, and in the report of the committee on funeral directors' ethics, presented on the same occasion. The subject of Mr. Roberts's paper was the Relations Existing Between the Profession and the Manufacturers; and in his discussion of these relations it became quite clear that the very liberally educated class sometimes called "undertakers" really

constitutes the fourth profession, and as such are entitled to be ranked with the members of the other learned professions. That this is really the true expression of the association long recognized as existing between doctors, undertakers, ministers and lawyers, no sane person will be inclined to deny.[23]

One detects in the tone of the observer a hint of sardonic wit and irony that undertaking, and not teaching, was assigned the honor of the fourth profession.

Others more readily granted undertaking the status and prestige of a learned profession. The courts often did so even as they denied undertakers the privilege of setting up shop wherever they pleased. In 1910 the Washington Supreme Court had no problem recognizing "the profession of morticians" but refused to recognize one practitioner's right to operate in a residential district.[24] A little over a decade later the Mississippi Supreme Court defined undertaking as a profession in terms that must have delighted many undertakers, despite the particular undertaker in question, an insolvent debtor named J. P. Meaders, having lost the case and had his funeral car repossessed by the Sayers & Scovill Company. "The business of an undertaker," declared the court, "is not the business of a merchant or trader. It would come nearer being a profession than a trade. An undertaker sells nothing except his skill in preparing dead bodies for burial and attending their interment."[25] This was an odd conclusion, considering the established role of undertakers as retail sellers of caskets and other burial goods. Regardless of such isolated instances, public opinion on whether undertaking constituted a trade or a profession was hardly settled, and references to "the undertaking trade" were common. Undertakers themselves were consistently of the opinion that their work was not afforded the respect that it deserved.

Undertakers also understood that it would take more than professional associations to gain the public's respect and trust. "Do not think," admonished Hudson Samson in his 1886 presidential address to members of the National Funeral Directors Association, "that we can get the public to receive us as professional men by simply meeting in convention and making constitutions and by-laws, by adopting a code of ethics."[26] In fact, professional associations sometimes had the opposite effect, reinforcing the image of the undertaker as extortionist and convincing an already skeptical public that funeral directors solidified their unfair advantage by banding together. Quincy Dowd warned readers in 1911 of "the stiff oppressive rules of the national and state undertakers' associations to maintain their exorbitant charges and to protect themselves in a trade that preys upon people bereaved and defenseless."[27] In spite of their efforts, undertakers continued to be viewed by many as not only a trade but also a corrupt and abusive trade. Clearly, something more was needed to improve their image.

A RESPECTED PROFESSION
HOUSED IN MANSIONS

In their seminal 1955 work *The History of American Funeral Directing*, sociologist Robert Habenstein and historian William Lamers argued that by the end of the nineteenth century, funeral directors were united by a collective "urge to bring a sense of professionalism to what had formerly been for many a mere trade or sideline."[28] They described the industry's obsession with improving the "opinion in which they were held by other occupations and by the public at large, and finally, their own self-esteem,"[29] while "building in the minds of the public a higher social estimation of the nature of their services."[30] In *The Confessions of an Undertaker*, erstwhile insider Charles Berg pointed in 1920 to the fervent desire of his former colleagues "to place their profession on that high pinnacle to which they aim."[31] A generation after organizing themselves into professional associations, however, funeral directors continued to be haunted by negative impressions and misconceptions regarding their work, a situation they openly acknowledged. "To be identified with the funeral directing business for any length of time is to become conscious of the publicity problems it confronts," admitted one West Coast funeral director in 1930.[32] "The greatest need of our profession," concluded Frederick Curtis Callaway in his 1928 work *The Art of Funeral Directing*, "is an increased public confidence."[33] Faced with the mammoth task of reshaping public opinion, funeral directors turned to what has historically been one of humankind's most persuasive tools. They turned to architecture.

To be sure, mansions provided the solution to more than one dilemma faced by early twentieth-century undertakers. Their location in residential neighborhoods beyond the borders of the increasingly congested business district offered greater quiet, a more homelike setting, and more space for parking than could ever be obtained downtown. However, such venerable dwellings in themselves, and not merely their location, promised a tantalizing fix to a problem even more pressing than parking. Their long-standing association with business and political elites would, funeral directors hoped, reinforce the notion that funeral directing was a distinguished profession, as opposed to a lowly trade. Like Schaffner and Queen, funeral directors nationwide also saw mansions as the material expression of the progress they had made as a profession, something they hoped the public would in turn recognize. Mansions, it was believed, had the power to convey respectability and legitimacy silently but far more effectively than funeral directors themselves.

As heavily laden with meaning as funeral homes are, surprisingly little attention has been paid to their communicative power. The obvious fact of square footage has largely satisfied historians of deathcare, who almost always allude to the shrinking size of domestic space—smaller single-family homes and the rise of apartment living—as a way of explaining the existence of the funeral home. Scarcely acknowledging the exodus of funeral directors from the downtown to residential districts, they have instead focused on the shift from home funeral to funeral home in a manner suggesting that size alone mattered. It is true that while funeral directors in the 1920s and 1930s were drawn by the symbolic value of a grand dwelling's illustrious provenance, they also regarded genuine domesticity and abundant square footage as an opportunity to wrest the funeral service from the home of the deceased, where it remained ensconced. Nonetheless, it would be a mistake to conclude that funeral directors chose mansions solely because they could comfortably accommodate a large number of mourners. As tempting as this purely pragmatic explanation is for historians and laypersons alike, the simplistic and spacist notion that the residential funeral home owes its existence to square footage alone ignores the symbolic qualities that made aging mansions so sought after by funeral directors. Enormous sums of money were invested to acquire and remodel them, not to mention the costs incurred as a result of drawn-out litigation when a challenge was made by prospective neighbors or the zoning board.

On the other hand, a more nuanced approach to the emergence and subsequent proliferation of residential funeral homes within the cultural landscape offers a highly instructive case study of the communicative power of objects. "Architecture," folklorist Henry Glassie astutely observed, "is one of the most useful kinds of objects."[34] Funeral homes demonstrate that architecture, like other kinds of material culture such as business attire and, closer to the case at hand, a certain class of automobile can be used by groups seeking to craft identity and achieve legitimacy. The fact that objects and spaces are used to communicate does not mean, however, that they function exactly like language. Grant McCracken has pointed out that "material culture as a means of communication works in more understated, inapparent ways than language."[35] He has argued that while material culture is "extremely limited in its expressive range" and useful only for semiotic repetition rather than innovation, objects possess a distinct advantage over language because of the inconspicuousness of their messages.[36] Because material culture communicates in a less overt and more subversive manner, it is, he argues, "able to carry meaning that could not be put more explicitly without the danger of controversy, protest, or refusal."[37] McCracken's notes how certain workplace attire, for example, is chosen to give its wearers "new credibility, presence, and authority,"[38] offering an interesting parallel to the widespread use of mansions by funeral directors to fashion a new self-image as a

legitimate professional class on par with doctors, lawyers, and ministers, three professional groups to which funeral directors habitually
compared themselves.[39] Especially relevant is his discussion of how
patina, as opposed to fashion, has been used as a marker of status. Mc-
Cracken cites the work of Lloyd Warner and Paul Lunt, who concluded in their classic work *Yankee City* (1941–1959) that one of the
ways individuals and families validate their claims to upper-class status is by moving into houses whose "distinguished lineage" has been
well established by previous generations of inhabitants.[40]

The widespread preference within the funeral industry for vintage
dwellings, at least in part because of their past association with illustrious families, strongly suggests that the accumulated patina of past
generations was worth more to funeral directors than architectural
fashion. A great many funeral directors saw virtue in an older structure
because they believed that visible and demonstrable age or, better yet,
status as a recognizable community landmark would infuse their work
with dignity and respectability. On the other hand, those who opted for
purpose-built facilities, especially beginning in the 1940s when architectural modernism began to exert its influence over mortuary design,
clearly were more swayed by fashion. Of course, virtually every funeral
director, regardless of whether in a remodeled dwelling or a purpose-
built mortuary, described their quarters as modern. It is hard to imagine
that those who chose Victorian houses considered them to be modern
architecturally in either their style or their form; surely they did not.
Funeral directors in residential quarters of whatever type used the
term "modern" primarily to distinguish their new facilities from downtown undertaking parlors, which they stigmatized as old-fashioned, the
very antithesis of modern. A "modern" funeral home promised modern
deathcare amenities, such as state-of-the-art embalming facilities, slumber rooms, a spacious and well-equipped chapel, a private family room,
and a well-lit and efficiently arranged showroom, but did not, however,
guarantee a contemporary or fashionable look.

Funeral directors themselves were unlikely to have articulated the
choice between a purpose-built mortuary and a remodeled mansion

as a choice between fashion and patina. Less likely still would have been a discussion of the theoretical distinctions between material culture and language. There is no evidence that funeral directors intuitively recognized a distinction that would only be drawn by later generations of theorists, even as they took advantage of the communicative power of objects. Whether people consciously turn to material culture out of a belief that objects can more safely communicate messages that are likely to stir controversy with words likely varies from group to group and individual to individual. Funeral directors spoke explicitly to one another in the pages of their industry publications about the meanings they believed mansions carried by virtue of their age, size, beauty, and past associations with a community's civic and business leaders. What they did not specifically articulate, however, was a conviction that houses were more effective than words at conveying certain messages. Such theoretical musings in 1920 would have been unusual and would have predated by more than a generation the scholarly work of anthropologists and ethnographers, whose theories of the expressive power of objects didn't emerge until the 1970s and later.[41] Nonetheless, funeral directors were certainly astute when it came to using material culture to communicate and remarkably articulate about what they hoped it would say to a public that viewed the funeral industry with skepticism and a distaste often verging on hostility.

For example, funeral cars and casket coaches, vehicles that within the industry were generally referred to as "rolling stock," were believed to convey success, dignity, respectability, leadership, and progress. "Looking the Part" was the title of a 1920 advertisement for the Lorraine by the Motor Hearse Corporation of America, whose profits depended on funeral directors' willingness to embrace the communicative power of objects (fig. 4.1):

"Nothing succeeds like success" is an old saying, but a true one. The world passes judgment at a glance.

Ownership of the beautiful Lorraine bespeaks success. It is the mark of merit. "Looks may not make the man," but the growth of your bank

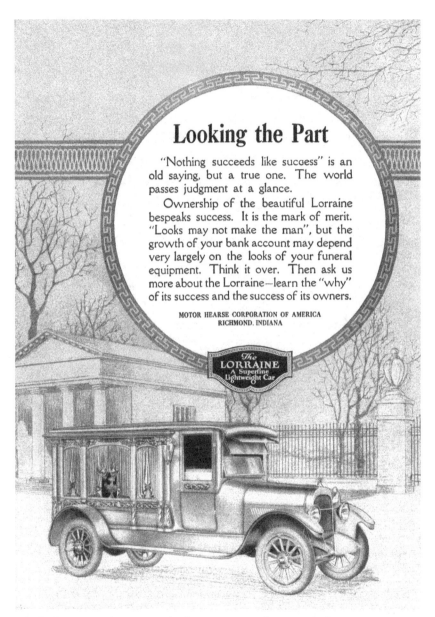

Looking the Part

"Nothing succeeds like success" is an old saying, but a true one. The world passes judgment at a glance.

Ownership of the beautiful Lorraine bespeaks success. It is the mark of merit. "Looks may not make the man", but the growth of your bank account may depend very largely on the looks of your funeral equipment. Think it over. Then ask us more about the Lorraine—learn the "why" of its success and the success of its owners.

MOTOR HEARSE CORPORATION OF AMERICA
RICHMOND. INDIANA

The LORRAINE
A Superfine Lightweight Car

FIGURE 4.1   Advertisement for the Motor Hearse Corporation of America, Richmond, Indiana, 1920. *American Funeral Director.*

account may depend very largely on the looks of your funeral equipment. Think it over. Then ask us more about the Lorraine—learn the "why" of its success and the success of its owners."[42]

"What do people think of you . . . and what does your rolling stock say?" asked a 1930 advertisement for the Sayers & Scovill Company. "Like every progressive funeral director," posited the advertisement, "you know that quality look, in a Casket Coach, means quality service, in people's minds." Theirs, they promised, was a "Casket Coach that speaks so well of its owner."[43] Promises such as those made by the Sayers & Scovill Company, offering not just quality but also a product's ability to express specific qualities, by the 1920s had become a key element of modern consumer culture. Their advertisements consistently demonstrated what was quickly becoming a revered dogma within the world of commerce, namely that the key to selling goods lay in appealing to psychology and understanding consumers' desires, dreams, hopes, fears and, most importantly, the qualities and attributes that they coveted, how they wanted to be seen by those around them, from successful to sexy. The Sayers & Scovill marketing strategy reflects more, however, than a mere passive reliance on and respect for the symbolic role played by material goods; the firm actively invested goods with a set of meanings based on an insightful reading of its target market's distinct psychology. "*Equipment* Tells Your Story!" was the title of a 1930 advertisement for the Riverside, "the Aristocratic Town Car Hearse." Skillfully linking its product with the very qualities most prized by funeral directors, the ad spoke directly to the firm's highest aspirations. "Rolling stock that stamps you as progressive, alert, able and willing to serve," the ad counseled, "is the only kind you can really afford to own." The Riverside, promised Sayers & Scovill, "proclaims you a leader in your Profession."[44]

The advertisements crafted by hearse manufacturers for the pages of the *American Funeral Director* and other funeral industry publications doubtless highlighted the communicative power of material goods, because funeral directors themselves made no secret of their reliance on material objects as symbols. In fact, the role of the funeral home itself as a means of branding—and not just for individual firms but for the industry as a whole—was well known to hearse manufacturers. A 1926 Sayers & Scovill advertisement featuring Joseph A. Vitt of the Cincinnati firm Vitt & Stermer discussed the importance of a modern funeral home to a funeral director's public image. As Vitt explained in the ad,

> The funeral director is judged by his establishment. . . . So, when you are thinking of the advance in the funeral directing profession, remember the importance of the funeral home. From a rarity a few years back it has become almost a necessity today. And I consider the welcome which funeral directors have given to the funeral home a tribute to the professional standards of today. I believe that the funeral home, as much as any other one thing, has advanced the funeral director in the estimation of the public.[45]

Such a sentiment was based on the shared conviction that the funeral home's material setting and mansions in residential neighborhoods in particular inspired confidence and trust, just as dark and dreary undertaking parlors in dusty, noisy, congested business districts had bred mistrust. "One of the reasons why the undertaker of other days found the public somewhat unappreciative of his services," argued Vitt, "was the fact that his place of business was not very prepossessing."[46] At the same time, eliminating lingering misconceptions and prejudices was an ongoing struggle for the funeral industry, one in which the residential funeral home was believed to play a key role. "A properly equipped and attractively furnished home is an asset which inspires public confidence, and such confidence means a great deal to the funeral director," pointed out one Atlanta-based funeral director in 1930.[47] The idea that the funeral home was more than just a physical structure housing one's business and equipment and could also be a powerful symbol of professionalism and progress as well as a public relations tool had by the 1920s taken hold of the funeral industry. In addition to concerns over parking, increased congestion downtown, and a renewed emphasis on homelike conditions, this was one of the factors driving funeral directors out of the downtown in search of new quarters in the form of old mansions.

That funeral directors believed in the symbolic power of space was repeatedly demonstrated in the ways they themselves wrote and spoke to one another about their funeral homes. "No other single factor," wrote one industry expert in 1931, "so clearly denotes the strides forward made by the funeral directing profession as the beautiful and efficient type of funeral homes now found throughout the country."[48] With so many abandoning their downtown quarters for residential locations, space became a frequent topic within industry publications such as the *American Funeral Director*. Throughout the 1920s and 1930s it was common for several different recently opened establishments to be featured each month in lengthy articles often accompanied by photographs showing both exterior and interior views. "During the last several years it has been [our] privilege," wrote a spokesperson for the *Embalmers' Monthly* in 1921, "to print articles descriptive of a number of funeral homes—stepping stones in the profession which mark its progress to a degree which can be presented in no more visible way."[49]

Such pieces shed light on not only how the funeral industry viewed space but also the specific messages that mansions were believed to communicate through their grandeur and distinguished provenance. Old and often revered dwellings afforded funeral directors an opportunity to capitalize on the accumulated patina and prestige of past owners. The respect afforded a dwelling's former inhabitants would, they imagined, be imputed to its new owners. When Forest E. Klute of the Richmond, Indiana, firm Klute & Son's was interviewed in the September 1930 issue of the *American Funeral Director*, his story doubtless struck a familiar chord with readers. Once he had made up his mind to leave the downtown, he recounted, he set out "to acquire a stately old residence that had always been occupied by some old and prominent family."[50]

Four years after the Indianapolis firm Hisey & Titus moved into "an exclusive 'old families' residence district," a 1921 article in the

American Funeral Director mentioned both the tangible and intangible qualities of the space that had lured its owners from their previous location in the business district. "The choice of this substantial old two-story brick house was a very 'happy' one," explained the article, "not only for physical but for spiritual reasons: the floor plan made the rooms admirably adapted to the practical needs of a funeral home; and the new business could not help but take on some of the dignity and 'atmosphere' given the place by former tenants and to reflect the character of the neighborhood."[51] The dwelling had been the home of John Wocher, a prominent and respected Indianapolis businessman and former president of the Franklin Fire Insurance Company. Wocher's position and dignity, it was believed, infused the house even after his departure. "One need only glance at the house or at a photographic reproduction of it to know that it 'comes from an old family,' so to say," the article boasted. Not just the house itself but the entire neighborhood lent the firm an air of respectability; nearby dwellings continued to be occupied by illustrious inhabitants, all of whom contributed to the overall prestige that Hisey & Titus hoped would rub off on the firm. Directly across the street from Hisey & Titus, for example, was the home of Vice President Thomas R. Marshall's "most intimate friend," while "hardly three blocks away" were the homes of "a late U. S. consul to London, a president of the United States and an attorney general." By moving into to such an old and established neighborhood, Hisey & Titus had "put the whole profession on a higher plane."[52]

Equating mansions with the elevation of funeral directing to the status of a profession, at least in the minds of funeral directors themselves, quickly became a recurring theme in discussions of space whether addressed to customers or colleagues. It was, after all, relatively easy and natural for funeral directors to cast the decision to move into a mansion beyond the confines of the downtown as progress, especially when one considered the industry's early roots. "In a few short years," boasted the Cincinnati College of Embalming in 1926, "an appreciable percentage of the profession has lifted itself literally from the livery stable to the plane of a respected profession housed in mansions."[53] Mansions symbolized the distance that funeral directing had traveled, both physically and professionally, from the downtown livery stable and the cabinetmaker's workshop. "The funeral director who has a high grade establishment is and should be proud of it," counseled one industry expert in 1930.[54] The rise of the residential funeral home did more than simply alter funeral directors' perceptions of themselves, however. It was widely held by funeral directors that a dramatic change of scenery had the ability to alter the public's perception of their work and remove many of the old prejudices and misconceptions that belonged to an earlier period, the dark ages, back when undertaking was regarded as a trade. The old critique, it was believed, was no longer relevant because funeral directing itself had entered a new era, of which mansions were the most visible symbol.

A well-coordinated, space-centered public relations program included both open houses and advertising. "A handsome, well-equipped funeral home," pointed out one industry expert in 1926, "is one of the best means of publicity which any funeral director can possess. It is concrete evidence of his desire and ability to render the best of service; it denotes *progressiveness*. In consequence, every attempt should be made to bring the public to the funeral home—and *bring the home to the public*, by means of advertising."[55] Inviting the public to view the funeral home was not only a way to advertise one's business, in other words, nor did opening the funeral home's doors to curious visitors end with victory over those opposed to its presence on a particular residential street. Because of the funeral home's importance as a symbol of progress and professional advancement, advertisements picturing the funeral home and frequent open houses shouldered the additional task of educating the public about the state of the field and introducing them to what had become a new industry standard.

THE PRIDE OF THE NEGRO COMMUNITY

Residential funeral homes arguably played an even more important role for African American funeral directors, for whom a stately well-kept establishment represented not merely respectability and the progress made by funeral directors as a profession but also the elevation of the race amid the deprivations and humiliations of Jim Crow. It was only natural that Black funeral establishments reflected the status and economic power of their owners, who constituted an elite class within the larger African American community.[56] Their wealth and prominence stemmed from their virtual monopoly over funerals within the Black community. By the mid-1940s, the nation's roughly 3,000 Black funeral directors constituted "nearly one-tenth of all undertakers in America," observed the prominent Swedish sociologist Gunnar Myrdal in 1944. "In the South," he concluded, "they have an almost complete monopoly on Negro funerals, as whites would not want to touch the corpses. In the North their competitive position is almost as strong. They never handle white funerals. Since, in addition, Negroes are likely to spend relatively much on funerals, the funeral homes represent one of the most solid and flourishing Negro businesses."[57] Allan Morrison, writing for *Negro Digest* in 1945, put the number of Black funeral directors slightly lower but reached a similar conclusion. "The nation's 2,175 Negro morticians," he wrote, "form a privileged caste in the American business world. Since few whites care to compete for the business of burying Negro dead, the Negro funeral homes enjoy a virtual monopoly in their field. . . . Negro morticians have therefore welcomed the refusal of white operators to handle black bodies. This kind of discrimination means more money."[58] The financial success and prosperity derived from their monopoly over Black burials was a source of pride for Black funeral directors. They "share the general ideologies of race pride," observed sociologists St. Claire Drake and Horace Cayton in 1945.[59] As a result, their funeral homes stood as symbols of Black pride, prosperity, and progress. Black funeral homes also symbolized the crossing of the color line, both economically and spatially.

As early as 1908 when Nashville's Andrew N. Johnson moved his business into the historic Porter Mansion, his funeral home was already being cast as a symbol of racial progress and a blow to deeply rooted cultural texts demanding deference and subservience. The two-story, free-standing, antebellum brick dwelling on 422 Cedar Street was once home to a prominent white family, and most residents of Nashville, reported the Black-owned *Nashville Globe*, never dreamed that the structure, "one of the most valuable pieces of property[,] . . . at any time would become the possession of a Negro." Johnson himself was well aware of the magnitude of his purchase. "In other days," he proclaimed in the advertisement announcing the formal opening, "fortunate and favored were the Negroes who were allowed to gaze on the splendors of festal occasions in that mansion and it was never contemplated that its walls would echo their tread except in an attitude of servility."[60] With his acquisition of the revered structure, Johnson had struck a blow to the nation's racial hierarchy, and many other Black funeral directors would follow in his footsteps.

A. G. Gaston's 1938 purchase and rehabilitation of a previously white-owned Birmingham mansion renewed African American interest in Kelly Ingram Park, the segregated outdoor space across the street from which Blacks had historically been barred.[61] Although the cost to acquire the building strained Gaston's limited resources, he "locked his mind on owning that particular building and refused to let the idea go," recounted his biographers, Carol Jenkins and Elizabeth Gardner Hines. "Maybe," they imagined, "it was the notion of a black man owning the biggest home facing Ingram Park—where blacks were still forbidden to gather for recreation, and through which they had until only recently been forbidden even to walk."[62] With rehabilitation of the structure under way, Gaston's business partner, Abraham Lincoln Smith, saw the grand mansion as a symbol of their success as entrepreneurs, "a 'show-place' for all they had achieved."[63] Gaston's vision, however, was broader. He later described his new funeral home as the "pride of the Negro community,"[64] and he understood that among both Black and white residents of Birmingham, the structure was a symbol of not only the recent advances made by the funeral profession but African American progress as well.[65]

The funeral home almost certainly possessed additional significance for Birmingham's Black residents. Less than a generation earlier in 1905, the United Daughters of the Confederacy had erected the Confederate Soldiers and Sailors Monument, a commemorative obelisk that stood in Birmingham's Linn Park. Between 1895 and 1920 similar Confederate memorials were erected in cities and towns throughout the South. Ostensibly intended to honor the Confederate war dead, the memorials were understood by both Black and white residents to communicate a racial hierarchy. In 1931 W.E.B. DuBois wrote that such monuments should be inscribed "sacred to the memory of those who fought to Perpetuate Human Slavery."[66] DuBois recognized the real meaning behind the many monuments and statues that had been erected throughout the South. They were meant to intimidate the Black community and constituted part of the landscape of white supremacy, which Black funeral directors throughout the South sought to subvert by acquiring mansions previously owned and occupied by white elites. The mansion acquired by A. G. Gaston in 1938 stood only blocks away from the city's Confederate memorial.[67] His purchase can be read as Gaston's response on behalf of the Black community to both the monument and the racial hierarchy that it was meant to convey by imprinting an alternative cultural text of racial equality onto the landscape.

PICKLES VS. CAVIAR

Some funeral directors recognized a potential downside to housing their business in a grand and imposing structure, whether a remodeled mansion or a purpose-built, residential-style mortuary. Beyond the threat of a protracted battle with one's neighbors or with the municipality over zoning, there were concerns that even though mansions were intended to serve as symbols of legitimacy and progress, they might inadvertently hint at businesses catering solely to a wealthy clientele. Funeral directors acknowledged that their luxurious spaces risked scaring off a whole body of potential customers who might conclude that they couldn't possibly afford the services of such a fine establishment. Mansions might give the wrong impression or send mixed signals.

One cannot help but wonder why an industry whose reputation had been chronically tarnished by accusations of greed, price manipulation, and exploitation would have chosen such grand quarters at all when more modest spaces might have gone further to reform their public image. The truth is that funeral directors genuinely believed their own rhetoric. Just as they convinced themselves that an attractive, well-kept mortuary could win them the approval of wary neighbors, even as tales of funeral directors being hauled into court circulated at their state and national conventions and filled the pages of their industry publications, they also believed that the beauty and illustrious heritage of vintage dwellings would silence their critics. Funeral directors believed that the positive associations possessed by mansions could crowd out negative stereotypes. Quite simply, they believed in the power of rebranding even as controversy continued to roil the waters around them.

Certainly funeral directors believed in the power of advertising and its ability to control the messages conveyed by material objects. Their absolute faith in advertising is amply demonstrated by an article that appeared in the July 1931 edition of the *American Funeral Director*. Titled "Pickles vs. Caviar," the article addressed one of the quandaries posed by luxurious spaces, namely how one could attract the business of the classes without alienating the masses. Although the article was written about the J. J. Mottell Mortuary, a purpose-built mission-style mortuary in Long Beach, California, its message was relevant to any funeral director who was contemplating a move—or had already relocated—from the business district to larger, grander, more opulent quarters, which could be obtained either by building new or remodeling the old. Mottell, who wrote the article himself, began by recounting an anecdote that had been used at a recent associational meeting of funeral directors.

In the story a middle-class man went out in search of caviar. The first establishment he found was a "delicatessen store of rather shabby aspect," which he quickly passed by "without even slackening his pace. In such a place," the story went, "he might hope to purchase a pickle, but of course they wouldn't stock caviar." Next, he came upon a "lavish establishment with modernistic windows and huge limousines standing in front," but this too the man passed by, for it struck him as "quite too expensive for his average means." Finally, he found his store, "not very fancy looking, yet trim and clean in appearance." The man's wealthier friends, the anecdote concluded, would likely have found the store "beneath notice," while "in the eyes of his laundress or stenographer it might have appeared a trifle beyond reach." For him, however, it was just right, and he got his caviar.[68]

Mottell took issue with the anecdote's main message, namely that a middle-of-the-road establishment, neither too shabby nor too lavish, is best. "I am not at all sure that I agree," Mottell confessed, "with the gloomy picture which this story sets before anyone contemplating a new funeral establishment." A few years earlier Mottell had moved into his new Long Beach establishment, "with pride in our bearing, but with numerous twinges of trepidation over the fate of our middle-class patronage. The establishment," he explained, "was a great deal finer than any Long Beach had ever before looked upon; indeed it was probably a lot more pretentious than most residents of moderate-sized cities had witnessed." The new structure was, he boasted, "a thing of beauty, an impressive and imposing affair." The firm was confident that its market share among the wealthier class would increase, and it did. At the same time, they worried that the "vastly larger group of people with average incomes" would be intimidated by the mortuary's "new splendor," and in this too their suspicions were confirmed. Within two years, although the firm's gross revenues rose, the number of cases it was handling per year began to fall off. "The plain truth," Mottell explained, "was that we were getting more of the de luxe business and less of the lower and middle classes."[69]

Mottell eventually hired a consultant who suggested some immediate changes to his merchandising methods, but that was only the beginning. The real solution lay beyond the funeral home itself. "As you know," Mottell reminded readers, "while ten per cent of the population can be attracted simply by impressive quarters, at least seventy per cent of the remaining population should be and can be won over through persistent, plain spoken, *intelligent advertising*."[70] The advertising campaign created by a professional firm hired by Mottell emphasized not merely the quality of his service or the "many extra refinements and comforts" included in the price but also that all of his prices were marked in plain figures. "Everything is included in the one plainly marked charge," explained one advertisement, "making it far easier for every family to select an appropriate service within their means."[71] Mottell's advertisements conveyed the simple fact that in spite of the firm's lavish and imposing quarters, they were there to serve any family regardless of their means. Mottell gradually saw an increase in the volume of small cases his firm was handling alongside "a flattering number of expensive ones."[72] He had succeeded in attracting both the masses and the classes. "We know now, through our own experiences," he concluded, "that a funeral director can erect the finest establishment his means will allow and still obtain the bulk of middle-class patronage necessary to financial success."[73]

The message was clear. One need not worry that a grand setting would discourage the middle class, provided that good advertising was used to prevent the public from misreading the funeral home. Funeral directors such as Mottell believed that advertisements were indispensable if the mansions they built or remodeled were going to get their messages across properly. Any campaign to communicate with the public about the nature of their work and the services they offered therefore had to be multifaceted, combining pictorial representations of the funeral home with carefully worded text. Funeral directors were uncomfortable allowing the public to interpret symbols without some guidance. In other words, they did not leave the weighty task of branding themselves to objects alone. Material culture in the form of structures, hearses, and attire worked with printed pieces, large and small, which served as interpretive aids. Regular advertisements along with lengthy newspaper articles, usually paid for by the funeral home whenever a new funeral home opened or an existing funeral home was updated or redecorated, combined images with narratives and descriptions that were crucial to investing the material world of professional deathcare with the precise meanings that funeral directors hoped would take root in the public's consciousness.

Advertising, McCracken points out, often functions in this way. Its purpose is to join the material object shown, a luxurious-looking mortuary in Mottell's case, with a particular concept or quality, such as universal affordability. "Verbal material," he writes, "serves chiefly as a kind of prompt which instructs the viewer/reader in the salient properties that are supposed to be expressed by the visual part of the advertisement."[74] The text helps the reader decode the message. Funeral home advertisements used a variety of textual cues to send different messages. Some, such as those of David Webb and Sons, sought to convey that large grand structures and luxurious hearses were symbols of professionalism, respectability, and progress (fig. 4.2); others,

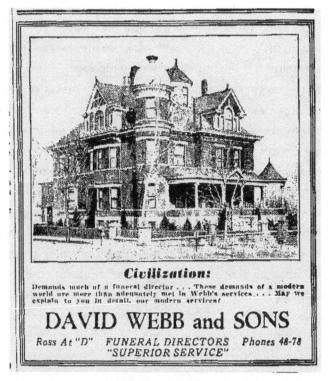

FIGURE 4.2   Advertisement for the David Webb and Sons Funeral Directors, Hamilton, Ohio, 1936. *Hamilton Daily News Journal,* May 11, 1936, 9. Cox Ohio Publishing.

such as the ones used by Mottell, often paired images of the funeral home with a discussion of pricing or such phrases as "within the means of all" in order to emphasize affordability, lest the funeral home's grandeur be misconstrued as a marker of unattainable luxury. These funeral homes were luxury within reach, a democratized luxury, which was one of the defining properties of twentieth-century consumer culture and a hook used by merchants of all kinds.

It is safe to assume that semiotic concerns caused funeral directors far fewer sleepless nights than lingering negative stereotypes or legal battles over the ability to locate in the neighborhoods of their choosing. Some advertisements seemed to court calamity by playing up the connection between mansions and wealthy elites. "Why, It Looks Like Some Wealthy Man's Country Home!" exclaimed the heading of one suggested advertisement discussed in the June 1926 edition of the *American Funeral Director*.[75] "That is what a visitor to our mortuary recently said. And she spoke truthfully, for that was the effect for which we strove," concluded the ad, which many within the industry would have shunned as sending the wrong message.

While not every funeral director chose such provocative advertisements or publicly embraced the image of wealth and privilege evoked by mansions, those who chose mansions, whether old or new, found themselves with a powerful and complex symbol that stood for luxury and professional advancement alike. Far from seeing this as a liability, they capitalized on the ability of mansions to communicate, silently but unmistakably, the controversial message that luxury in deathcare mattered. After all, funeral directors understood that the public was constantly exposed to the gospel of luxury consumption and was accustomed to shopping in opulent settings, namely department stores with their grand and lavish interiors. The prevailing wisdom on commercial spaces, merchandising, and consumer behavior saw a sumptuous setting as a stimulus to spending. Such thinking encouraged funeral directors, who were, of course, engaged in selling, to put mansions to work to serve another of their ends, one that ranked at least as high as the desire to elevate their profession.

PART THREE

A DELICATE BALANCE

CHAPTER FIVE

LUXURIOUS SIMPLICITY

The Funeral Home
as a Retail Space

A nyone who has ever paid for a funeral understands that funeral homes are sites where money, often large sums of it, changes hands. Jessica Mitford knew it and said so in such a humorous and caustic way that her 1963 exposé *The American Way of Death* became an instant best seller. Others, both before her and since, have leveled similar accusations against America's deathcare industry. In addressing exorbitant burial costs and the commodification of death, however, critics have referred to the funeral home more as an institution than a space. As a retail space, the funeral home has had a complicated and little understood history. Although the idea of space within the funeral home for selling burial goods was accepted by the general public, it was regarded with ambivalence by the funeral industry itself, whose comfort with modern ideas about merchandising and salesmanship arose gradually and not altogether smoothly.

This ambivalence is reflected in the diversity of funeral home layouts and marketing strategies from the middle half of the twentieth century. Some owners felt that too prominent a space for merchandising or too great an emphasis on goods undermined the professional status they had long coveted. Other funeral directors perceived a direct relationship between their success as businessmen and the funeral home's overall luxuriousness. This latter group emphasized modern methods of lighting and arranging their casket display rooms. The majority of funeral directors were torn between these two factions so that even as the funeral home assumed its place as an established and recognizable feature of the consumer landscape, the physical space of the funeral home became the battleground in the debate over merchandising and whether the funeral director could be both a professional man and a merchant.

As middle-class expenditures on consumer goods increased during the first quarter of the twentieth century, funeral directors took their cues from merchants nationwide, who were collaborating with advertisers to democratize luxury. At the same time, the space of the funeral home reflected the industry's awareness of new aesthetic trends toward simplicity in home decor as well as its preoccupation with the constant critique coming from the funeral reformers, whose calls for less extravagant burials were difficult to ignore. To ease anxiety over luxury consumption and neutralize the funeral reform movement's scathing critique of their industry, funeral directors once again turned to the larger world of retail, which had attempted to resolve the tension between extravagance and indulgence, on one hand, and simplicity and restraint, on the other, by blending the two. The resulting hybrid, branded as "luxurious simplicity," co-opted simplicity from the critics of consumerism and put it to work to sell luxury. Ever attuned to innovations within retail culture, the nation's funeral directors caught on quickly, and their awareness of this new trend can be read in the different ways they furnished and advertised their funeral homes.

LIFE WOULD BE A DULL AFFAIR

From the very moment that the earliest residential funeral homes began to appear in the older neighborhoods of American cities and towns around the time of the First World War, they housed the retail functions that had previously been located downtown. Prior to the rise of the residential funeral home, in fact, the showroom was argu-ably the downtown undertaking parlor's chief component. As late as 1928 when David Webb of Hamilton, Ohio, remodeled his down-town parlor, nearly three-quarters of the town's funerals were still be-ing held at home despite the availability of other options, including a few residential funeral homes that had begun to compete with the older downtown establishments. Webb's newly renovated service rooms, like the chapel spaces in other establishments, whether down-town or residential, were underutilized. His display room, on the other hand, was quite popular, and the publicity announcing his re-opening suggests that it was the biggest draw for families. "Aside from the funeral home feature of the new Webb establishment, there is an exceptionally attractive display room, where those articles so neces-sary to the conduct of the business are artistically arranged and can be judged upon their merits and by comparison. This feature of the Webb establishment is one that will be much appreciated."[1] In pro-moting his display room, Webb went so far as to hype the fact that he carried an exact duplicate of the silver bronze casket "in which Ru-dolph Valentino, the movie star, was buried."[2]

With professional deathcare's shift from business district to resi-dential district, consumers adapted very quickly to a situation in which they no longer had to go downtown in order to pick out a cas-ket and burial garments. Generally speaking, the residential funeral home was accepted as a retail space before it took hold as a ceremo-nial space. A not unusual scenario of the 1920s and 1930s was for a bereaved family member to visit the funeral home to select a casket—with the body typically being brought to the funeral home for embalming—only to have the memorial itself at the home of the de-ceased, as had long been the custom. As the industry struggled to wrest the memorial service from the family home, many understood that in the eyes of the public the funeral home was primarily a retail establish-ment.[3] Some might argue that acceptance of the funeral home's retail function was less a matter of choice than a function of where the ma-jority of caskets were being sold. Some downtown establishments persisted for those who preferred that option but were increasingly outnumbered. What is more likely to have constrained consumer choice in some cases was ethnicity, race, or a preference for a specific funeral director regardless of the address.

Part of the residential funeral home's success as a retail space was certainly its location. Beginning in the 1920s, funeral directors who had relocated to residential neighborhoods were advertising that they were close enough to the downtown—where many churches and hospitals were situated—to be convenient but far enough away to be free from noise and congestion. Within the context of a burgeoning automobility, funeral directors clearly saw an advantage to locations that offered ample parking. During a time when parking and traffic problems were intensifying in city and town centers as automobile usage rose, residential funeral homes confidently boasted to their patrons of their ample parking facilities.[4] Already in 1928, the Bender Funeral Home in Gettysburg, Pennsylvania, for example, possessed in "a large yard behind the funeral home . . . parking space for thirty or more automobiles."[5] Funeral directors were among the earliest merchants to recognize that the automobility in particular portended a future in which retailing moved beyond the confines of the downtown. Regardless of whether they saw their choice of location as prophetic, the rapid proliferation of residential funeral homes during the interwar years foreshadowed the postwar period's decentralization of commerce and retail, a key element of twentieth-century consumer culture.[6]

Savvy funeral directors certainly envisioned themselves within the broader context of a rapidly expanding culture of mass consumption. They perceived a direct correlation between "the public's habits in the purchase of funeral requirements" and its "general buying demands." It was widely held that the demand for better-quality funeral goods was "in keeping with the trend of the American consumer's demand in other lines."[7] In other words, the industry repeatedly pointed to rising consumer demand not just for high-end burial goods but also luxury goods of all kinds. "More than one-third of the total national income of the people of the United States is spent for luxuries," wrote one funeral director in 1931, "for jewelry, perfumery and cosmetics, candy, entertainment, joy rides, sporting goods, tobacco and the rest. But life would be a dull affair stript [sic] of its luxuries."[8] Often this argument was made in response to criticism that the general public spent too much on funerals, to which the funeral industry responded, "Do our people, to-day, go into our stores and shops and purchase cheap merchandise? Do the men buy plain serviceable clothing and shoes? Do our ladies ignore the style in vogue in their purchase of seasonable wear? How then can you expect a public to retrench on an expenditure for that which occurs so seldom as a funeral in the average family?"[9] A little over a quarter century later in *The History of American Funeral Directing*, industry insiders Robert Habenstein and William Lamers used the same reasoning, claiming that the "general upgrading of consumer demands—for furniture, automobiles, housing, dress, and the like—has carried with it to some degree a demand for more expensive funerals."[10]

Such observations helped funeral directors rationalize "merchandising upward," the deliberate phasing out of cheaper, lower-end funeral goods in favor of new, more expensive products, effectively limiting consumer choice to more costly items. This practice was widely defended within the industry, and funeral directors understood that they were corralling consumers toward more expensive purchases by narrowing their options. While advising funeral directors to offer a "range [of merchandise] adequate to our community requirements," Albert Kates, editor of the *American Funeral Director*, also maintained that display rooms should contain a "narrow choice in low-grade merchandise," "wider choice in medium and good quality groups," and "enough top-grade goods to provide free choice and give fair play to the client's own standard of taste and expenditure."[11] Funeral directors assumed that given the right circumstances, customers naturally and voluntarily gravitated toward high-end burial goods.

With such merchandising strategies in mind, funeral directors defended regular upgrades to their product lines by claiming that they were simply responding to "the desire of the American people for better goods."[12] The freedom to choose luxury was, in their view, inviolate. "It is public demand," the industry argued, "that has created the many improvements in funeral service in the past few years. It is only reasonable that the standards of burial equipment and service should keep pace with the standard of living."[13] In 1926 one funeral director, summarizing his industry's faith in consumer demand, succinctly explained:

> The general dilemma of the funeral director is that he must give better service, better goods and the use of more elaborate and luxurious establishments and equipment and at the same time keep prices down. In essence this dilemma bears a striking resemblance to the dilemma of all Americans. We want the advantage of constantly rising standards of living, we want to keep up with the Joneses, we want more comfort, more luxury, more amusement, we want to escape the hardships and the labors of our parents and even of our early lives, and yet we complain about the price demanded of us.[14]

Another made the case more bluntly:

> Demand is made up of wants and wishes, wants being limited to the necessities of subsistence and wishes accounting for everything else going to make up the market for the complex business and industrial organism constituted by this country. If you say that we may go beyond our wants and indulge our wishes in the matters of shelter, clothing, food, heating, travel, amusements and newspapers, but that we must limit ourselves rigidly to minimum wants in the matter of caring for our dead, why not go the whole distance and limit burial to a corpse and a hole in the ground?[15]

Stifling what was seen as legitimate consumer demand for costly, high-quality burial goods was, funeral directors argued, inconsistent with American industrial capitalism and the consumerism needed to make it work as an economic engine and wealth-generating mechanism. So palpable was the potency and prevalence of consumer demand that even some funeral reformers were forced to acknowledge that the tendency toward extravagant funerals arose from a growing demand for luxury goods in general.[16] When the Metropolitan Life Insurance Company completed its groundbreaking 1928 report on rising burial costs, *Funeral Costs: What They Average; Are They Too High? Can They Be Reduced?*, it concluded that "the demand for more elaborate and expensive caskets and funeral services has accompanied the general demand for more expensive goods of all kinds."[17]

BUYERS ARE BUYERS

If a key article of faith within the world of retail merchandising was that consumer demand for luxury items naturally rose in direct proportion to a society's standard of living, then an important corollary was that a merchant or industry could stimulate demand if it wasn't increasing quickly enough.[18] "The public is ready to be educated to high grade funeral merchandise. Progressive funeral directors have demonstrated that it can be done," declared one funeral director at the beginning of the Great Depression.[19] "It is possible," explained another, "for every man to gradually lead his people to use better things, and as they become more and more prosperous they should buy better funeral furnishings just as they buy better merchandise for the home."[20] One way to do this was through print media and advertising. "Booklets are also distributed; a description of the establishment or funeral home . . . serving to educate the lay mind with reference to the highly specialized service offered, and to particularly foster a local demand for a higher and more satisfactory type of funeral goods," explained former funeral director Charles Berg in his 1920 work *The Confessions of an Undertaker.*[21] Another tool used to awaken desire was the physical space of the funeral home itself.

Consequently, in the vehicles they used, the goods they sold, and the spaces in which those goods were sold, funeral directors consciously cultivated an aesthetic that was rooted in a carefully crafted image of comfort, beauty, and luxury. The emphasis on luxury was apparent in white and Black funeral homes alike. "Colored undertakers," wrote Allan Morrison in *Negro Digest* in 1947, "have grown steadily along with the general industry of which they are a part. They resort to expensive advertising to sell their services to the public. . . . They build elaborate funeral homes and acquire fleets of long, luxurious limousines. They hustle for trade."[22] Throughout the industry, funeral directors created opulent spaces that were seen as a key tool in the stimulation of desire. They were not shy, moreover, about drawing attention to the luxuriousness of their quarters.

Establishments boasted of tapestries, paintings, silk carpets, velvet drapes, carved tables and chests, and damask-covered chairs along with paneled walls, beamed ceilings, and ornate staircases (fig. 5.1). Luxuriousness in the funeral home consisted of a combination of furnishings and finishes alongside architectural ornaments, which funeral directors who opted for remodeled dwellings were careful to preserve intact. For example, in 1926 when the Ford & Douglas Funeral Home established itself in the substantial dwelling of a former doctor in Gastonia, North Carolina, the story that ran in the *Gastonia Daily Gazette* offered an especially effusive description of both the sumptuousness of the new quarters and the merchandise on offer:

> A handsome staircase in the spacious hallway on the ground floor leads upward to the second story, where there are four display rooms. These are elegantly appointed throughout, with well-chosen draperies and wall papers. Here are shown everything which is needed in time of bereavement, including caskets ranging from those of moderate cost to the more luxurious and imposing ones. Among the handsomest of these is one of cedar wood covered with imported grey broadcloth, containing an inner casket of solid copper. The linings and fittings of the caskets are most luxurious.[23]

An article in the *American Funeral Director* also emphasized the opulent setting. "The structure, which has been remodeled to house the Ford & Douglas establishment, was formerly known as the Sloan residence and was one of the show places of Gastonia. Its imposing exterior and generous proportions made it admirably suited for a mortuary, and the decorators have made the most of its luxuriously finished in-

FIGURE 5.1 First floor looking from stair hall to southeast room, Egelhof-Casper Funeral Home (Fannie Stout House, ca. 1891), Dubuque, Iowa, after 1933. Library of Congress.

terior."[24] Likewise, the proprietors of Klute & Son's Funeral Home in Richmond, Indiana, boasted of their facility's opulent interior and original features. "The interior woodwork is of cherry and oak, with oak floors. Especially notable is the open stairway in the reception hall, hand carved out of solid cherry wood and widely known as the most beautiful piece of woodwork of the kind in the region."[25]

Similar descriptions of residential funeral homes appeared in industry publications and in newspaper articles accompanying the opening of new establishments. When in 1926 Cincinnati's Corken Funeral Home was featured in the *American Funeral Director*, the article described an interior rich in period detail and original woodwork. Housed in a massive late nineteenth-century Queen Anne dwelling, the establishment possessed an interior that blended "the richly beautiful without a trace of the somber or the ornate. The walls are papered in embossed gray with gold bordering, contrasting with ivory woodwork and old rose draperies. On a highly polished hardwood floor is spread a silk oriental rug in old rose, and a mahogany shelf holds a removable glass over a rich onyx fireplace."[26] While phrases such as "luxuriously appointed," "lavishly furnished," and "showplace" were common, some establishments, including the Ralph James Balbirnie Funeral Mansion in Muskegon, Michigan, and the William Cook Funeral Mansion in Baltimore, Maryland, boldly advertised with their very names that it was not a modest dwelling that housed them. The majority simply let imposing exteriors and elaborate interiors speak for themselves.

This was true of purpose-built, residential-style structures as well. When the Wichmann Funeral Home was completed in Appleton, Wisconsin, in 1931, the local paper reported that the "large service room . . . resembles a room one might expect to find in an English mansion. The room is luxuriously furnished with old English furniture, and at the extreme right is a large fireplace constructed of white Bedord [*sic*] stone."[27] No less than those who opted for converted mansions, those who chose to invest in a purpose-built mortuary placed their emphasis on luxury, opulence, and Old World grandeur.

Within the industry as a whole, it was an article of faith that a sumptuous space was needed.

Luxuriousness generally trumped style. Residential funeral homes consisted of a wide range of styles from Federal, Greek Revival, and Gothic to Italianate, Queen Anne, Colonial Revival, Beaux Arts, Neoclassical, and Craftsman. Whether converted dwellings or purpose-built, what the majority of these structures had in common was that they were mansions. While those who constructed new mortuaries favored Colonial architecture, the style of the dwelling was less an issue for advocates of purpose-built mortuaries than was their conviction that structures not specifically designed with the needs of the funeral director in mind were less efficient. Funeral directors who chose converted mansions countered by pointing to Old World craftsmanship and their spaces' distinguished provenance.

While luxuriousness was emphasized by funeral directors housed in both converted dwellings and purpose-built mortuaries, it was only the former who could rely on their past associations with the wealthy elites who had once resided there. For example, the year-old funeral home Klute & Son's was described in 1930 as "a spacious mansion which was built a few years ago by one of the oldest and most prominent families of the community. It occupies a 60 by 160 foot lot . . . in the center of the residential district. Built of brick and stone, it is massive and impressive with its plate and stained glass windows."[28] Converted mansions lent the funeral industry an aspect of luxury, elegance, and class, which funeral directors readily embraced. By the 1920s and 1930s, funeral homes operated as retail spaces within a context in which opulent settings were widely understood to foster desire for expensive goods and encourage extravagance. It was no accident that an explosion of lavish funeral establishments occurred during an era in which the persuasive power of a luxurious retail space was taken for granted by merchants of all kinds.

Space, after all, was persuasive. As new kinds of retail spaces emerged during the final decades of the nineteenth century and the first decade of the twentieth century, they were understood to play a major role in the creation of desire. As grand department stores gradually replaced the disorganized and dowdy dry goods emporia of the nineteenth century, faith in the power of these retail palaces to sell goods rose sharply. Opulent well-lit interiors adorned with stained glass and mosaics in particular, such as the Tiffany dome of the Marshall Field's department store in Chicago, were seen as a powerful stimulus to spending (fig. 5.2). Gary Cross shows how "department stores imparted an aura of luxury to shopping."[29] Cross cites fellow historian William Leach to argue that "the turn-of-the-century department store and its elegant and colorful displays democratized desire, encouraging a taste for luxury and tempting consumers to buy finer goods."[30] Funeral directors repeatedly demonstrated how well versed they were in this aspect of retail culture. Speaking of the need for quality physical space, one industry leader declared, "Undoubtedly good establishments and good service bring the demand for better merchandise. That is evident everywhere."[31]

It was not unusual for funeral directors to compare their establishments to department stores while also drawing comparisons between themselves and other purveyors of luxury items, such as "the automobile dealer, the furrier, the clothing merchant."[32] Speaking to his colleagues about their casket display rooms, one funeral director pointed out that "the funeral director's display room is very similar to the window and counter displays in the up-to-date retail store—the department store, for example."[33] Another, discussing how merchandise was arranged within his display room, explained that "in entering the display room, the customer will see our line of metallic caskets first, and it is our custom to group our metals together, and then a grouping of better wood caskets, and the cheaper grades in the background. I think that such a rule would prevail in the display of most any kind of merchandise, whether in a department store or otherwise."[34] Often the comparison was made in the midst of debates over whether caskets should display price tags showing the entire cost of the service. Many funeral directors, explained one industry leader,

FIGURE 5.2   Detail of the 1907 Tiffany favrile glass dome in the atrium of the Marshall Field & Company flagship department store (now Macy's), Chicago, Illinois, 2012. Photograph by the author.

are now marking the caskets and other merchandise in their display rooms in plain figures so that the buyer may know at a glance exactly what everything will cost him—the same as if he were buying in a retail store. Those who follow out this policy maintain that it is the only businesslike procedure—that it is favored by the public—that it creates confidence in the fact that the same prices apply to all. They state that the public has the same buying desires whether purchasing radios, shoes, groceries or funeral merchandise.[35]

Frank Fairchild of Fairchild Sons in Brooklyn, New York, believed that his display room was not so unlike the display rooms of other merchants:

> The goods in the Fairchild display room have been marked in plain figures for years, and like other "merchants," we have taken a pride in making the "figures" as reasonable as we could. . . . The public (and that includes you and me) are and have been trained for years to buy all our supplies of merchandise from stocks of plainly priced goods. Now why, when we are required to enter a funeral director's display room to buy merchandise, should we not expect to find the same condition? . . . Do not you and I enjoy "browsing" in the other fellow's display room—furniture, for instance, and looking over his price—before we buy?[36]

Creating effective display rooms meant emulating the department store in other ways as well, such as in the lighting and layout, how merchandise was arranged, and the type of display cases used. An attractive arrangement, it was believed, was crucial to successful sales. "I find that an attractive showroom promotes the sale of better caskets," declared funeral director Frank Stewart of Leon, Iowa.[37] "It is evident," explained another funeral director, "that any discussion of selling is closely interwoven with the matter of showroom arrangement, for the successful sale implies a satisfied client, and the client can best be satisfied through a combination of a compelling sales appeal and a good showroom arrangement."[38] Especially important was good lighting, and funeral homes took their cue from other retail settings (fig. 5.3).

FIGURE 5.3   An example of a well-arranged and well-lit casket display room, 1931.
Courtesy of Kates-Boylston Publications.

One funeral director explained how in "the retail store it is a vital factor in making possible the proper display of merchandise. In funeral home construction illumination is a very important consideration."[39] He went on to say that

> as a merchant displays his goods to the best advantage to cut down sales resistance, so should the funeral director have his showroom well lighted to show the caskets to the best advantage. . . . More and more are business and professional men coming to appreciate the importance of proper illumination. . . . The effectiveness of casket displays in the showroom is greatly enhanced through modern lighting effects. . . . Good illumination brings out the beauty of the wood or the splendid finish on the metal casket. It shows the interior of the casket to the best advantage, which is frequently a factor in its purchase. . . . Many caskets made of both metal and wood have a very high luster. If a direct light is thrown on this type of casket there may be reflections which detract from its beauty. For this reason the lighting should be indirect. In this type of illumination the light is redirected from the ceiling to the caskets

in a well diffused light free from glare. .... The caskets stand out and are shown in detail. Even the folds of silk are plainly seen. The finish and color appear to the best advantage. All these little details are important and make the selection of a casket easier.[40]

Many funeral directors sought to innovate by installing indirect lighting systems or "cleverly constructed electric lighting," while others employed the "newest style of racks" for displaying merchandise.[41]

The enthusiasm shown by some funeral directors for the merchandising and display strategies employed by department stores might have arisen from the perception that women were far more likely than men to shop for burial goods. While many funeral directors spoke of selling in connection with "bereaved families" and naturally had experience dealing with widowers looking to choose caskets and burial garments for their deceased wives, it was not uncommon for funeral directors to argue that a disproportionate number of visitors to their showrooms were women.[42] These may have been wives, but they could also have been daughters, daughters-in-law, granddaughters, and even nieces. Whatever the case, Harry Allen of Peru, Indiana, claimed that "women select 75 per cent of the caskets we sell. Women appreciate good designing and are becoming expert judges of material."[43] Others drew broader inferences:

> The statistics of every line of business tell us that the women folks do most of the buying of the world. The interiors of caskets, silks and satins, are things with which the women folks are more familiar than the men folks. It has seemed to us, therefore, advisable to carefully select such things as appeal to the women folks and about which we can talk understandingly to them.[44]

Whether funeral directors sought to emulate retail environments in which women were thought to be the principal shoppers, they set out to create luxurious, attractive, well-lit display rooms because they were convinced that their success depended on it. While not all funeral directors saw themselves as pioneers, many believed that they were

changing the way in which burial goods were sold and sought to transform their sector of the retail world by taking their cues from department stores and other merchants. "After all," asked one funeral director,
"is funeral merchandise so vastly different from other merchandise
that the same principles of selling do not apply? Absolutely not.
Proper display of funeral merchandise creates sales in just the same
way that the display of any other articles does."[45]

Like department stores, funeral homes also strove to create a homelike atmosphere akin to that of a "finely appointed private residence of
the better class."[46] The funeral industry was by no means unique in its
attempt to furnish shoppers with "homelike comforts" in addition to
luxuriousness.[47] First-generation department stores, posits historian
Susan Benson, modeled their stores "along two complementary
lines: as a home and as a downtown club." She cites the example of
Hortense Odlum, president of Bonwit Teller during the 1920s and
1930s, who strove to make customers feel at home in her stores: " 'I
tried to have the policy of the store reflect as nearly as nearly as it was
possible in the commercial world, those standards of comfort and
grace which are apparent in a lovely home.' "[48] An important component of a truly homelike environment was privacy, one of the residential funeral home's primary features and most assiduously advertised
attributes.

Privacy mattered, especially in the casket display room. Using advertisements, funeral directors sought to assure prospective patrons
that they would be able to select the casket of their choice within their
means, "without any embarrassment" and "at their own leisure and
with none but the members of their own family as observers."[49] This
was a well-known concept within the world of retail in which the more
elite department stores also sought to protect customers from the gaze
of strangers.[50] In many funeral homes the bereaved were promised
not simply privacy but freedom of choice. For those funeral directors
who argued that the family should enter the display room and make
their selection unaccompanied by any funeral home staff, the display
room was used to advance the notion that the funeral home was an

environment free from high-pressure sales tactics. In this idealized shopping space, a highly romanticized version of the consumer was imagined to exercise his or her own will, free from the salesman's influence. Even though families were clearly choosing from a limited range of high-grade merchandise, the casket display room was often used to symbolize the fiction of personal freedom and autonomy within the marketplace.

Not only were casket display rooms believed to be similar to other types of display rooms, but customer behavior was also thought to be more or less the same. Albert Kates made the case that those

> funeral directors who plainly mark the prices on the caskets in their show-rooms—and there is a growing number—work on the theory that the *public* is the *public*—that *buyers* are *buyers*—whether they are purchasing dresses, automobiles or funeral merchandise; that the same buying psychology holds good in any case; that when the buyer sees prices on the various items of merchandise handled, she feels more free to select as her taste and pocketbook dictate.[51]

Kates went on to credit merchandising giants Marshall Field and John Wannamaker with the "one-price system" and argued that price haggling and bargaining survived in only "the cheapest of stores. . . . Why," he asked, "shouldn't the funeral industry borrow from the book of other lines of business?"[52] Moreover, a basic element of "buying psychology," whether in the context of the department store or the funeral home, was that it could be influenced by the spatial setting in which purchases were made. Within the funeral industry it was largely taken for granted that a luxurious establishment in combination with a prominent, well-lit, and efficiently arranged display room would increase profits.

RICHNESS WITH SIMPLICITY

Not everyone within the industry agreed. Some tried to temper the emphasis on luxury, while others were uncomfortable with the whole idea of merchandising and salesmanship. For starters, even those who created luxurious spaces for their customers were cognizant of the funeral reformers' ever-present critique of costly, extravagant funerals and their ongoing calls for simplicity. This critique predated the appearance of the residential funeral home, with nineteenth-century reformers condemning the luxury and ostentation of "the ordinary fashionable funeral" as vulgar and undignified.[53] Dignity and simplicity went hand in hand. In short, what was simple was dignified and vice versa. In the lexicon of the American funeral reform movement, to be simple also meant being understated, modest, and restrained. Late nineteenth-century critics had frequently lashed out against "the foolish extravagance of the ordinary funeral" and left no room for compromise when it came to their Spartan vision of simplicity:

> The Duke of Westminster has shown excellent sense in becoming a member of a funeral reform association, and by permitting his deceased son to be buried in a plain pine coffin instead of the usual expensive casket. . . . We all know that the departed rest as well under the green sod as under roofs of polished granite,—as well in a winding sheet as in a metallic casket hermetically sealed,—but because the latter admit of a greater outlay of money we employ them.[54]

Others within the movement called for doing away with expensive hardwood and metal caskets and having "burials directly within the soil."[55]

Some reformers envisioned committing the body of the deceased in a "simple winding sheet to mother earth, without coffin or casket or any such thing. If this seems unbefitting (not inhuman nor yet unnatural), then put it in a light coffin of soft wood or wicker work, or wood pulp or other perishable material, such would offer the least resistance to decomposition, while sufficiently strong for purposes of transportation."[56] Funeral reformers were not alone in their rejection of luxury. Calls for a return to simplicity sometimes came from within the funeral industry itself. When the newly constructed Aubuchon Funeral Home, a simple brick structure of modest size and appearance, opened in Fitchburg, Massachusetts, in 1927, the accompanying publicity assured prospective patrons that "no effort was made to establish a pretentious, lavishly furnished establishment." The owners pointed out that their funeral home, "while beautiful," was "practical and moderate in cost."[57]

Most funeral directors sought a more nuanced approach. As funeral reformers continued to equate dignity with an austere simplicity, many within the funeral industry responded by tweaking this formula and redefining what could qualify as simple. By no means should simplicity be confused with "bare necessities," experts argued.[58] Sumptuous funeral homes and burial goods could, they argued, also possess simplicity and dignity. Funeral directors eventually developed a kind of doublespeak that emphasized simplicity even as their spaces promoted luxury. They used oddly paradoxical phrases such as "richness with simplicity" to describe their establishments.[59] Luxurious, elaborate, and ostentatious goods and settings were said to possess what was termed "quiet dignity."[60] The notion of a simplicity that could accommodate richness was a significant departure from the simplicity championed by the funeral reform movement.

At times the industry's attempt to reconcile richness and simplicity produced strange, somewhat tortured results. For example, when Gettysburg's Bender Funeral Home opened in 1928, its publicity claimed it combined "features of the elaborate, tempered by quiet, stately dignity; strictly modern without being flashy or gaudy."[61] The schizophrenic advertisements of the Emrick Funeral Home in Portsmouth, Ohio, are also quite revealing. Housed in a substantial brick mansion, the firm boasted in May 1933, "our chapel is the last word in pretentious appearance and appointments. Our rolling equipment is luxurious."[62] By October of that same year, however, the firm had switched to an entirely different message:

> True grief never seeks a showy display. Rather does it demand beauty and simplicity. Here, in the subdued quiet of our beautiful funeral home, hearts that are bowed in grief because of the visit of the Death Angel, will find a solace and comfort that not only reveals their genuine devotion, but an environment that aids greatly in softening their grief

and sorrow. Surrounding Emrick conducted funeral services is an atmosphere of real beauty—all tending to soften [undecipherable] most hallowed of memories."[63]

Likewise, in 1933 when James McKenna opened the McKenna Funeral Home in Lowell, Massachusetts, he described the large Second Empire dwelling as "elaborate" while insisting in the same newspaper article that "I have planned and arranged my new home so that due honor may he paid to departed ones by friends and relatives in an atmosphere of reverence and simplicity."[64]

The funeral reform movement's ongoing critique was only one of the reasons that funeral directors felt compelled to work simplicity into their establishments and the advertisements promoting them. Simplicity in home furnishings was in vogue. Criticizing the previous generation's "craze for something 'fancy'" and parlor suites heavily "ornamented with carving and moulding," a new generation of tastemakers was cultivating "a feeling for the value of simplicity, sincerity, and restraint."[65] As early as the late nineteenth century, a rejection of the ornate in favor of a more rustic simplicity had begun to dominate a new aesthetics that touched everything from clothing and hats to furniture and housing.[66] Excessive ornamentation had become a sure sign of bad taste. In *The Decoration of Houses*, Edith Wharton condemned "the indiscriminate amassing of 'ornaments.' Decorators," she argued, "know how much the simplicity and dignity of a good room are diminished by crowding it with useless trifles."[67] It was most likely in response to such ideas that owners of purpose-built mortuaries opted for the "stately Colonial," whose "classic simplicity of design," they argued, "gives just that atmosphere of dignity and calm which should hang about every mortuary."[68] Furnishings in the Colonial style, moreover, were thought to introduce a note of tasteful simplicity inside the funeral home and the private home. "The word, 'Colonial,' is almost synonymous with simplicity, beauty, refinement and dignity," asserted Mary Harrod Northend in her 1921 work *The Art of Home Decoration*.[69]

Funeral directors who remodeled Victorian dwellings were no less attentive to the prevailing trends in home furnishings and sought to create rich-looking interiors that tempered formality and opulence with simplicity and restraint. Many funeral directors turned to wicker to achieve this balanced effect. By 1920 the use of wicker in domestic settings was no longer limited to the piazza or sunroom.[70] "The appropriateness of wicker furniture for porch, sun-parlor, summer bungalow, or yacht is obvious. Gradually, however," noted one wicker advocate in 1917, "it has been making its way into other parts of the house."[71] That same year one observer claimed that wicker was being used "in five out of every ten living-rooms."[72] Wicker was widely seen as lending a room comfort and informality and was easily combined with other pieces. "It is excellently made, attractive, comfort yielding, and durable," argued one home decor expert in 1916, "being at the same time adaptable to many different settings. It is the one modern material that combines easily with antiques and particularly with those early American pieces that are so popular to-day."[73]

The danger, of course, was that wicker would be too informal. "It should be remembered," admonished Amy Wolfe in her 1924 work *Interior Decoration for the Small Home*, "that it is of a distinctly informal type. No room in which it is used could be very stiff and dignified" (fig. 5.4). Stiff, perhaps not, but every funeral director wanted rooms that were dignified. She noted, on the other hand, that wicker furniture was "very cheerful," a much sought-after quality by funeral directors at least in theory, lest the older charges of gloominess gain renewed currency.[74] More importantly, funeral directors had to be careful not to go too far in the direction of simplicity in their choice of furnishings or risk inadvertently creating a setting in which a plain and inexpensive casket would appear at home. The proper balance between luxuriousness and simplicity and between extravagance and restraint was not easy to achieve and was a challenge with which retailers of all kinds wrestled and could trace its roots to the tension between extravagance and restraint at the heart of modern consumer culture.

FIGURE 5.4   "A charming cottage living room in which wicker furniture predominates."
From Amy L. Rolfe, *Interior Decoration for the Small Home* (New York: Macmillan, 1924), 106.

The paradox at play within the funeral home mirrored tensions within the complex consumer culture that flourished beyond its four walls. The funeral home was, after all, part of the larger retail landscape, which encouraged excess while simultaneously preaching simplicity.[75] "On one hand," explains historian Sarah Elvins, "advertisers and manufacturers encouraged Americans to give in to the hedonism of luxury goods and conspicuous consumption; on the other, a simultaneous emphasis on control and personal efficiency underscored their messages."[76] Embedded within the world of advertising and retailing, with its trappings of democratized luxury, ran a deep countercurrent that cherished frugality and restraint and considered fashion and luxury to be corrupting influences.[77] One solution to this tension was to blend decadent luxury with virtuous simplicity.

That simplicity and luxuriousness could be made to coexist was a concept that had already taken root in the broad aesthetic revolution that defined early modernism.[78] While previous eras had seen the production of high-end, elegant items that blended richness with simplicity, what modernism did more than any previous aesthetic trend was to sever the tie between opulence and ornament while solidifying the bond between luxury and simplicity. While the funeral home's unique blend of luxurious simplicity owed its origins primarily to the larger retail universe of which it was a part, retail culture itself was evolving within a cultural context in which the gap between luxury and simplicity was shrinking under the influence of early modernism.

Modernism redefined the conversation around simplicity and restraint by casting ornament rather than luxuriousness as the chief antagonist to dignity. Modernism also transformed simplicity into a commodity in itself and an expensive one at that. While the funeral industry did not invent the concept of luxurious simplicity or even popularize it more than other sectors, such as clothing and automobiles, the funeral home and its advertisements represent a key synthesis within American consumer culture, namely the union of decadent richness and virtuous restraint. Within the historiography of consumer culture and theories of consumer behavior, however, the tension between these two polar opposites is often understood to have been resolved when the middle class rejected simplicity in favor of luxury, thus launching mass consumerism in its modern form.

In *The Romantic Ethic and the Spirit of Modern Consumerism*, for example, Colin Campbell argues that the spread of Romanticism among the bourgeoisie produced new patterns of luxury consumption during the nineteenth century and also during the twentieth century with the emergence of new romanticisms, namely Jazz Age decadence and beatnik and hippie bohemianism. At the outset, Campbell posits that Romanticism and the accompanying desire for novelty overcame middle-class anxiety over spending and luxury. The former displaces the latter, unleashing new consumer forces in the process.[79] Similarly, in David Shi's *The Simple Life: Plain Living and High Thinking*, the dynamic between luxury and simplicity is also one of displacement. Shi argues that the expansion of consumerism during the 1920s represented a repudiation of the ideal of simplicity.[80] The standard thesis has been that because simplicity and luxury were opposing forces, for one to triumph, the other had to be vanquished. For luxury to be in the ascendancy, simplicity had to be in decline.

The proliferation of luxury goods and services and extravagant spending habits among the middle class did not, however, mean the death of simplicity as a virtue to be extolled and pursued. Together with the larger world of consumer goods and advertising, the funeral home debuted a new simplicity that had shed its anticonsumption bias. Within both the aesthetic framework of early modernism and the universe of retail culture, luxury was wed to simplicity in much the same way it had once been wed to ornament, and this marriage helped birth modern consumer culture. Rather than being displaced, simplicity and restraint were absorbed, co-opted, recast, and assimilated within a rebranded luxuriousness, the dynamic being more syncretic and synthetic. As a result, what was once seen as a vice was redeemed by its union with a traditional virtue. By midcentury, luxurious simplicity had become a key element of American consumer culture and was being evoked in advertising campaigns to sell everything from clothing and cars to caskets. This proved to be a winning combination that worked to release inhibitions and ease traditional anxiety over luxury consumption.

NEITHER WHOLLY A PROFESSIONAL MAN NOR WHOLLY A MERCHANT

In addition to striking the proper balance between luxuriousness and simplicity, funeral directors faced an even greater challenge that hit much closer to home. If some felt a certain amount of ambivalence toward their luxurious appointments, many also had serious misgivings about the impact of merchandising on the funeral home and their directors' claim to professional status, which the residential funeral home was supposed to bolster. Too large or prominent a showroom, many felt, would result in an overly commercial atmosphere, and this was one of the reasons why funeral directors had begun to abandon the downtown business districts in the first place. Many believed that an overemphasis on merchandising not only threatened the homelike quality of the funeral home but also compromised the professional status they had fought so hard to achieve.

"For years," explained Albert Kates in 1931, "the funeral director has been handicapped by the belief that it was 'unprofessional' to 'sell' merchandise. He felt that merchandising was not for men of his calling—that it was demeaning."[81] This attitude lingered for decades, with one funeral director arguing in 1947 that "service in our field is far more important than merchandise, and accounts for from 70 to 80 per cent of what the public pays for[;] . . . merchandise only comprises a small portion of what the funeral director sells."[82] Some industry leaders charged that all too often a result of this prejudice was that

> the funeral director in planning his establishment, concentrates on making it beautiful and providing all sorts of conveniences in the way of slumber rooms, etc., but neglects to give the proper amount of attention to the arrangement of the show room. This tendency can perhaps be attributed to the fact that the funeral director is often inclined to think more in terms of his profession than his *business*.[83]

Some believed that the problem lay in attempting to convert an existing dwelling. Harry Samson of Pittsburgh argued in 1926 that "a large number of the establishments erected recently have been remodeled residences and in these it has proven very difficult to work out ideal display rooms. It has not only proven difficult, but I think there has been a reluctance to give it the thought and study it requires and a greater amount of attention has been given to the chapel and slumber rooms." He also acknowledged, however, that "there are very few open minded funeral directors who claim that they have absolutely solved the question of display rooms."[84] In some funeral homes, another funeral director complained, the "show rooms (if they have any) are carelessly laid out."[85]

While some funeral directors had poorly arranged showrooms and others devoted enormous attention and resources to the development of their display spaces by employing "modern" ideas about merchandising, there were at the far extreme a group of funeral directors who saw no place for a showroom within their establishments at all and relied on casket manufacturers' showrooms. According to one funeral director, writing in 1931,

> There is now and probably will be a wide difference of opinion about the manufacturers' show rooms. Many funeral directors favor them and some feel that if the manufacturers were to discontinue the show rooms today, it would be the best thing that ever happened for the funeral directors. But the point remains that manufacturers' show rooms are an established fact, and are likely to remain so for a time at least.[86]

Manufacturers' showrooms were common enough during the 1930s that funeral directors who had their own display rooms advertised them as an "additional convenience for the patrons," which, they pointed out, "saves relatives from making an extra trip to a public display room."[87] However, by the 1950s they had all but disappeared. "Caskets . . . are now predominantly selected from the display rooms of the funeral director," explained Habenstein and Lamers in 1955.[88]

During the interwar years the issue of whether the funeral home could or should successfully accommodate both sales and service was hotly contested. Widespread disagreement over display rooms reflects what was often a contentious debate within the industry over the identity of the funeral director. One funeral director expressed the conflict this way:

> If the funeral director will get over the idea that he is purely a professional man, and will consider himself as a business man as well—and think in terms of business—it will help him greatly to put his establishment on a firmer basis. After all, unlike such professional men as the doctor, the lawyer and the teacher, the funeral director has something *additional to service* to sell. He sells *merchandise*. He sells caskets, grave vaults, funeral garments and other articles, and largely upon his ability to sell these articles, depends his profit.[89]

While some tried to downplay their role as salesmen, arguing that they were professional men and belonged in the same class as doctors, lawyers, and ministers, others warned that "there exists a definite danger, rather than any hope of gain, in this effort to garb ourselves in the raiment of other professions."[90] This controversy and its eventual resolution left their imprint on the American funeral home.

"The funeral director," concluded one astute practitioner in 1930, "is in one respect different from many retailers in other types of business. He is neither wholly a professional man nor wholly a merchant. He is, or should be, something of both."[91] Many funeral homes possessed layouts that reflected this uneasy balance. One solution was simply to relegate the showroom to an out-of-the-way spot within the funeral home. Although it probably had more to do with keeping gloomy reminders of death out of sight than with any hostility toward merchandising per se, it is interesting nonetheless that when explaining the location of the display room in the substantial and opulent mansion that housed Fred G. Marshall Sons Funeral Home in Detroit, a 1921 article in the *American Funeral Director* noted rather meekly how the "show room, always a dreaded feature, is in the basement."[92] Even those who embraced the merchandising side of their work generally believed that display rooms should be "out of the way so that visitors and others will not come into contact with them unless the occasion requires."[93]

In reality, attractive and well-lit display rooms were frequently situated in less visible locations, such as basements and upper stories. For example, although the display room of Peoria's Winzeler Funeral Home was located at "the top of the staircase, on the second floor," it was "artistically arranged and the lighting effect soft and restful."[94] Similarly, in the grand Federal mansion that housed the Lanoue Mortuary in Warren, Rhode Island, caskets of various types covering a wide price range were "attractively arranged" in a series of rooms reached by means of the structure's "Colonial stairway," which furnished "a very attractive approach to the five display rooms on the second floor."[95] Lowell's James McKenna displayed a greater awareness than some of his peers that his funeral home need accommodate his dual role as a professional man and a merchant. At the same time, he hinted at what he believed the heart of the funeral home to be:

> It now is recognized that a funeral director is not merely a business man but that he is a professional one as well. There are preliminary angles, such for instance, as the providing of caskets that must be considered as business propositions. But the part of the work that may be considered as a profession involves many of the details that must be attended to and here, the funeral director is considered as not only the adviser but the friend of those left behind. All these matters have been considered in the equipment of the new home, for first, one finds an excellent display room where a large variety and style of caskets may be seen; then, on the main floor is the real funeral home which is made up of large adequate rooms tastefully furnished and in keeping with the needs which they serve.[96]

Some funeral directors, such as DeWitt Morrow, who managed the John S. Orr Funeral Home in Youngstown, Ohio, appeared somewhat defensive about placing their showrooms on the second floor and were quick to point out that it was more a function of spatial limitations than any bias against merchandising: "Our show room is located on the second floor, for the only reason it gives us the first floor to be used for other purposes. It is one large room, forty by fifty feet, with an arched ceiling; lighting is all indirect; entire floor carpeted."[97]

Irrespective of the specific location, most funeral directors were careful and deliberate about maintaining a strict separation between the retail and ritual functions of the funeral home, even while attempting to keep them both on equal footing. Several funeral homes in different parts of the United States used identical advertisements to communicate this setup to prospective patrons. "Distinct and separate from each other by ideal arrangements are private mortuary chapel and casket display room. Yet they are convenient to each other and in their appointments they reflect that quiet elegance so desirable to the atmosphere of the modern mortuary."[98] Naturally, purpose-built

funeral homes had even greater flexibility in planning their arrangements. For example, the Ruppe Mortuary in Los Angeles, completed
in 1928, was "designed with the idea in mind of separating those sections of the mortuary meant for service to the public and the other
activities incidental to the work of the establishment. This plan is carried out by setting aside the ground floor for chapel purposes."[99] The
second floor contained "a large show room, 77 feet long by 22 feet
wide" with a "section partitioned off for the bronzes." Some, however,
managed to balance sales and service without shifting the showroom
to the second floor:

> An even balance between the funeral service and business department
> is found in the new quarters of the Hudson Funeral Home at 1800 An-
> gier Ave., Durham, N.C., into which the organization moved just one
> year ago this month. As will be noticed . . . , the left half is used exclu-
> sively for service, while the right half, with the exception of the prepa-
> ration room in the right rear center, is devoted to business functions. . . .
> A wide porch extends over about two-thirds of the front of the building
> from which there are two entrances, one to the reception room and the
> other directly to the chapel. The reception room opens into the busi-
> ness office and the casket display room may be entered directly from
> the office in addition to the hallway delivery entrance.[100]

The same concern shaped the plans of architect Harvey Clarkson,
who was asked by the *American Funeral Director* in 1947 to craft a set
of schematic drawings for a purpose-built mortuary. He specifically
designed the modernist structure "to provide a complete separation
of funeral services from the other elements in the business."[101]

Funeral directors were, of course, careful to separate the public
spaces of the funeral home from private spaces such as the preparation
room and the family's living quarters, a distinction that still matters.[102]
However, the tension within the public sphere of the funeral home between retail and ritual can be read in the interiors of American funeral
homes and the various spatial strategies employed to make room for
both. While some funeral directors rejected retailing altogether, far

more attempted to fulfill their desire for professional status while simultaneously fostering good merchandising practices. Within the rapidly expanding consumer landscape, the residential funeral home reflected the tension between the noncommercial atmosphere demanded by the professional man and the spatial needs of a successful merchant, for whom a large, prominent, attractive, luxurious, and well-lit display room constituted a powerful and persuasive selling tool. Striking the proper balance between these two competing demands was not easy. Just as it had made room for both luxury and simplicity, the funeral home found a way to accommodate both sales and ceremony, which turned out to be a key component of their strategy to dislodge the home funeral.

CHAPTER SIX

FROM HOME FUNERAL TO FUNERAL HOME

The Funeral Home as a Ritual Space

C onstantine "Gus" Stratis belonged to the greatest generation. He lived through the Great Depression and fought valiantly for his country in the Second World War. Though born in the 1920s to Greek-speaking immigrants from Eastern Thrace, he was fiercely patriotic in a way that second-generation Americans of his era were apt to be when they grew up. Fluent in Greek, he spoke English with a heavy Boston accent that belied his lineage and allowed him to blend in. Politically liberal and a staunch Democrat, Stratis was at the same time socially conservative; though warm, he was also traditional, stern, and patriarchal, a hybrid of a classic Greek father and a typical postwar American family man. He was as proud of his service in the US Marine Corps as he was of his Greek roots. The medals he earned were framed alongside photographs of his parents taken before they left Constantinople at the turn of the century. The American flag flew from the front porch of his nineteenth-century Greek Revival home in Everett, Massachusetts, through whose open windows on summer days passersby were as likely to hear the sound of tinny Greek 78 rpm records playing on his turntable, as they were Big Band classics.

When Gus died in July 2001, his wife Olympia—"Olly" to her friends—and their four grown children decided that he would be waked from their home. Their decision, nontraditional for the twenty-first century and hypertraditional at the same time, raised more than a few eyebrows. In the end, the funeral director consented to their unorthodox wishes, and Gus's body was delivered to the funeral home for embalming, after which he was returned to the family's home in Everett. If their lives hadn't already been turned upside down by his sudden death, readying their house for a home funeral brought a host of new disruptions. Downstairs rooms were emptied of their furniture, and folding chairs were brought in. Dozens of stands for the flower arrangements crowded both living room and dining room. Doors had to be removed from their hinges so that the casket could pass through. A steady stream of mourners shuffled in and out to pay their final respects. However, when the Greek Orthodox priest arrived to conduct the brief ceremony normally held at the funeral home prior to the body's removal to the church for the last rites, the modest dwelling was unable to accommodate everyone present. The immediate family and close relatives gathered indoors, while the vast majority of guests remained outdoors in the side yard and driveway, listening to the ceremony through open windows.

Although a home funeral in 2001 seemed strange to their family and friends, the Stratis family chose to follow a custom that was once commonplace throughout the United States. As late as the 1930s, funerals held at the home of the deceased were the norm, much to the dismay of the nation's funeral directors. It's not as if there was a shortage of alternatives. By the 1920s practically every city and town in America had one or more residential funeral homes with well-equipped chapels and service rooms, not to mention downtown funeral parlors, which had been offering chapel space in some form since at least the turn of the century. While it is difficult to assess the frequency with which funeral homes and chapels were used for services during the first third of the twentieth century, anecdotal evidence and period observations by industry insiders suggest that prior to the mid-1930s, the number was indeed quite small throughout most of the United States.

It is generally accepted within the historiography of American deathcare that the majority of funerals were held at home until roughly the middle of the twentieth century, by which time downtown funeral parlors were decidedly out of fashion and residential funeral homes had been established in virtually every city and town from one end of the nation to the other.[1] Although its impact was not felt immediately, there is no doubt that the rise of the residential funeral home contributed to the demise of the home funeral. Precisely how the residential funeral home supplanted the family home as the setting of choice for funerals is a complicated story, however. A growing emphasis on convenience within American consumer culture and on relaxed informality in the arrangement of domestic space during the middle decades of the twentieth century caused many families to rethink the home funeral and the resultant disruption, not to mention the gloom it brought into the home. Nonetheless, the shift from home funeral to funeral home was the result of a combination of factors and occurred gradually. A cultural shift of this magnitude was the result of millions of individual family decisions, most if not all of which were made during a period marked by significant emotional trauma. For later generations, holding the funeral at the funeral home had become a matter of custom. For the generation that collectively effected the shift from home funeral to funeral home, however, their individual decisions broke with the established norm. At present there is a dearth of archived sources shedding light on the matter. Consequently, the reasons underlying individual and family decisions concerning the location of funerals remain something of a mystery. The way in which this change unfolded across the landscapes of ethnicity, race, class, and geography certainly merits further study.

What this means is that in seeking to explain the shift from home funeral to funeral home, historians must acknowledge this missing piece when turning to broad cultural narratives, such as the privatization of the family and the medicalization of death and dying, lest they inadvertently fall into the trap of determinism. On one hand, it is true that individuals do not make decisions within a cultural vacuum but instead by engaging with historically and culturally specific discourses. Nonetheless, what motivates consumers is not so easily pinned down, especially when choices run counter to conventional wisdom. One could easily speculate that consumers were simply persuaded by an aggressive and persistent advertising campaign promoting the use of the funeral home for funeral services at no extra cost. Of course, understanding the strategies used to promote the funeral home as a setting for the funeral service does not necessarily reveal why consumers eventually took the bait. Advertisements are not in and of themselves evidence of consumer rationale. Rather, they are evidence of the discourse with which consumers engage.

Deathcare historians have chimed in, positing particular changes to domestic space as an explanation for the shift from home funeral to funeral home. Physical changes of one form or another to living quarters most certainly played a role in dislodging the funeral from the family home but not as much as changes in the way the home was perceived. Moreover, deathcare historians with little or no grasp of ordinary buildings and landscapes have been far too preoccupied with square footage and the amount of space within the home while neglecting its arrangement. In reality, funeral directors, who were increasingly eager to undermine public confidence in the home funeral, crafted advertisements that raised concerns about both square footage and privacy. With great subtlety they delivered a message to the public that the relaxed informality and openness so celebrated by interwar housing reformers, architects, builders, and decorators actually deprived families of privacy during home funerals. Funeral directors skillfully identified what they believed to be modern housing's secret

Achilles' heel and used it to their advantage to promote the funeral home as a ceremonial space.

Together with caskets and burial garments, space, convenience, comfort, and privacy were commodified and marketed, helping the residential funeral home succeed where the downtown parlor had failed. However, the battle was not won overnight. Public acceptance of the funeral home as a setting for the funerals of their loved ones lagged behind the industry's abandonment of the downtown in favor of residential neighborhoods by more than a decade. In other words, as funeral directors began relocating their operations from the downtown to residential quarters, the majority of consumers—across the spectrum nationally as well as locally within individual cities and towns—were initially reluctant to follow and viewed the funeral home solely as a retail space while holding steadfastly to the tradition of the home funeral. Moreover, one cannot fully grasp what motivated funeral directors to promote the use of the funeral home for services, the strategies they used, or what might have led consumers to break with the past without first taking a close look at what was once a common practice.

THESE LITTLE DETAILS

There is no doubt that the precise manner in which individuals and families experience the loss of a loved one has changed over time. So too has the manner in which the house itself experiences death. Death's impact on domestic space has changed dramatically since the early decades of the twentieth century, a period in which home funerals were the norm. Despite being standard practice, however, a home funeral was a complicated affair. For starters, furniture often had to be moved and folding chairs had to be brought in, and space had to be set aside in a front room for flowers and, more importantly, the catafalque or bier for the casket (fig. 6.1). Before any of this took place, the body of the deceased had to be prepared for burial, and as late as the 1920s this too often took place at home.

FIGURE 6.1   "Mrs. S. Nesselhauf in casket covered with flowers," Oxford, Ohio, 1915. Photograph by Frank R. Snyder. Miami University Libraries.

The practice of embalming the body of the deceased at home began with the spread of arterial embalming during the last quarter of the nineteenth century and continued up to the turn of the century, after which it steadily declined as professional undertakers began to equip their downtown quarters with specialized embalming facilities. Home embalming lingered on, however, through the first decades of the twentieth century. As late as 1921, a funeral director working in La Crosse, Wisconsin, noted that 45 percent of the bodies he embalmed were prepared at the home of the deceased.[2] There is also some evidence that the practice persisted in the eastern states after it had been abandoned elsewhere. "In the East," observed one California funeral director in 1926, "it is the general custom to move the bodies home after they are prepared, or to prepare them in the house and leave them."[3]

Moreover, rural areas throughout the United States held on to the practice longer than cities and towns. For example, in a 1928 piece written by Esther Weerts for the *American Funeral Director* describing her work as a "lady assistant" in a rural community in Illinois, she wrote as if embalming and funeral services only ever took place at the home of the deceased.[4] In 1948 when Jack Pence began working as a funeral director in the village of McGaheysville, Virginia, just outside of Harrisonburg, a quarter of that rural community's funerals were conducted from the home. "Many people," he recalled in 1984, "also still insisted that the undertaker come to the house to embalm the body rather than taking the body back to the funeral home for preparation."[5] Similarly, William Lee Shannon, a funeral director from Shelbyville, Kentucky, located about halfway between Louisville and Lexington, noted in 2007 that as recently as the middle of the twentieth century, he was still performing home embalmings. "When I first started in the business back in the 1940s, even in the 1950s," he recalled, "we were still doing preparations in the homes. We would go in, take our daybed, and all the equipment we needed to do embalming. We did the work in their parlor, bedroom, or wherever it needed to be done. Quite often the family helped us do different things." Shannon also added that it was not unusual to "put the deceased's body back in bed" immediately after embalming until the arrival of the casket a day or two later.[6]

Bedrooms were not the only option for the remains, however. It was not uncommon for the embalmed body to be moved to a front room while the family waited for the casket to arrive. Recalling an earlier generation's practices, deathcare historians Robert Habenstein and William Lamers pointed out in 1955 that in rural areas and small towns, "the deceased was moved from the bedroom to the parlor, to be viewed even before a casket was obtained."[7] Although Habenstein and Lamers did not specifically name the piece of furniture upon which the remains rested, industry expert Curtis Frederick Callaway noted in 1928 that prior to casketing, the embalmed body sometimes rested "on the couch with floral offerings arranged about."[8]

Home embalmings were still common enough in 1920 that Charles Berg commented on them in his exposé *The Confessions of an Undertaker*, noting that the body should be in a room "that will permit of being closed, and where the family will not have to pass in and out," and also that it was the family's responsibility to have "underclothing, hose, towels, basins, water, etc. ready and accessible" in anticipation of the undertaker's arrival.[9] After the body was washed in bed and the orifices plugged, the deceased was typically placed on a portable folding couch brought by the undertaker to the home.[10] Home embalming required undertakers to transport a wide assortment of other tools as well, including bottles of embalming fluid, disinfectants, moisturizing creams, syringes, pumps, rubber sheets and gloves, aprons, drip pans, and cooling boards.[11] Additionally, many undertakers found it helpful to have a female assistant present. "If the body be that of a lady," explained Berg, "this duty is generally performed by the nurse or the undertaker's lady assistant. . . . The presence of a lady in the death chamber at this time lends a touch of refinement and gives the family the satisfaction of knowing that the body of their dead is being prepared by kind and sympathetic hands."[12] While family members might assist with the washing of the body, the work of embalming was usually carried out by one or more undertakers in strict privacy, without family members present.[13]

It is not surprising that home embalming, which was a messy affair requiring an array of portable specialized equipment, was abandoned long before the public was ready to relinquish the custom of the home funeral. This shift was at least partially driven, Habenstein and Lamers point out, by the widespread desire on the part of funeral directors nationwide to perform the work of embalming "in more functional surroundings."[14] What is surprising, however, is that sending the body of a loved one to the funeral home to be embalmed in its well-equipped facilities did not guarantee that the body would remain there for the funeral service. In other words, while the majority of families were persuaded that the funeral home was more suitable than their homes for the work of embalming, this did not mean that they viewed the funeral home as a more suitable setting than their homes for the funeral service. Charles Paquelet of Massillon, Ohio, understood this and advertised accordingly. "There is no added expense," he assured the public in a 1929 advertisement, "for the moving of the body of your loved one from your home to my preparatory rooms where all preparations for the burial are made after which you can have your choice of holding the service in our funeral parlors or at your own home."[15]

Even when a death took place in a hospital and the body was subsequently sent to the funeral home for embalming, the deceased was often returned home for the funeral. "In our larger cities," observed Berg in 1920, "it is no uncommon procedure to remove the body to the undertaker's for its care. In many instances, after the body has been prepared and placed in the casket, it is returned to the home for the funeral service."[16] Habenstein and Lamers noted that "when death occurred in a hospital or other place outside of the home the family was most insistent upon bringing [the body] to the house as soon as possible."[17] Nonetheless, some historians of American deathways have pointed to the increased medicalization of death and the shift from home deaths to hospital deaths during the beginning decades of the twentieth century to explain the shift from home funeral to funeral home.[18] The qualitative data makes it clear, however, that the dramatic rise in the number of hospital deaths did not by itself wrest the funeral service from the home of the deceased. As Berg noted, the body customarily proceeded from the hospital to the funeral home for embalming and then home for the funeral.

Bodies embalmed at the funeral home or downtown parlor were dressed and casketed there after family members had paid a visit to select a burial receptacle. Even those who chose to have the bodies of their loved ones prepared at home had to visit the funeral home or be brought by the funeral director to the casket manufacturer's showroom in order to pick out a casket, which would then be delivered to the home while the dressed body lay in state in either a bedroom or the parlor. Upon arriving at the home with either the casket or the casketed remains, a responsible funeral director made a mental inventory of the house—its size, furnishings, and general arrangement—in order to begin planning for the funeral service. "As the casket is brought into the home," admonished Callaway, "we should study the best means of exit. Some homes afford a real problem in the passing out with the body and frequently it is necessary to use a rear or side door or to pass through a window. This should all be planned early enough to avoid confusion and delay at the moment when all eyes are upon the director."[19] Planning for a funeral service in the home required a funeral director to "take into account the general room arrangement," but also "the location and size of porches, the width and condition of steps leading up to the front of the home, and many other little details that will be important . . . To leave these little details until the very last minute may bring criticism from the family, and may finally disrupt all plans made up to that time."[20] Steps and porches, Callaway recognized, were especially troublesome (fig. 6.2):

> The matter of the steps will seem of little importance to many, but the director must take into account the fact that six men, plus the weight of the casket and body of the deceased, will rest upon these steps at one

FIGURE 6.2   "Body of Dago Frank being carried to hearse," New York, New York, 1914. The photo shows the funeral of "Dago Frank" Cirofici, a New York City gangster convicted of murder and executed at Sing Sing prison in Ossining, New York, on April 13, 1914. Library of Congress.

time as the casket is borne from the home, and it is important that these should not be asked to risk their lives upon the unsafe steps we find in many homes.[21]

Navigating a new and unfamiliar domestic setup with each funeral they were called upon to handle posed a real challenge to funeral directors. Doubtless, it must have been a source of ongoing frustration and puzzlement to those whose chapels and service rooms remained largely underutilized and generally ignored by the public as families continued to request services from the home in spite of the inconvenience to both themselves and funeral directors.

Chief among the considerations for a home service was the placement of the casket and the remains. "The casket," noted a 1921 etiquette book, "is placed on a draped stand at one end of the drawing-room, such flowers as are being used placed on and around it" (fig. 6.3).[22] According to Callaway, placement of the casket was at the funeral direc-

FIGURE 6.3   "Funeral or wake in the home," Davenport, Iowa, ca. 1915–1916. Photograph by J. B. Hostetler. Note the placement of the casket by the mantel. Davenport Public Library and the Upper Mississippi Digital Image Archive.

tor's discretion. "It is best," he argued, "to arrange the casket across a corner or in front of a mantel, with the thought in mind of a place to arrange flowers to the best advantage. Then the casket should be so set that friends approaching will come directly to the side of the casket rather than approach either end."[23] While bodies prepared at the funeral home returned to the home already casketed, bodies prepared at home were not always casketed before the arrival of mourners and the start of the funeral service. Practices varied, and there were instances in which the body of the deceased rested on a couch in the parlor and was casketed only after the funeral service had ended and mourners had exited. "In a number of communities," Callaway observed, "we find the custom of leaving the body on the couch until after the close of the home funeral is growing. After the service is concluded the friends retire and the family take their leave. The body is then placed in the casket, the casket closed, and the interment is private." He noted that many funeral directors objected to this custom because they felt that casketing the body at the close of the service was disruptive and took up too much time. "We doubt if very much more time is necessary," he countered, "and we must all admit that it is a beautiful custom."[24]

FUNERAL DIRECTORS ARE NOT AUTOCRATS

Just as there was no set formula for the location of the remains during a home funeral, there were several different options for seating the immediate family. By far the weight of opinion rested with those who felt that the family should be in a separate room, out of sight but within earshot. "The more favored usage in seating the family," counseled Berg, "is to place them within hearing, but not in sight. This relieves them of the strain of trying to appear composed in view of curious eyes."[25] Others agreed. "If the service is to be held at the house," stated a 1905 treatise on funeral customs by Joseph N. Greene, "let arrangements be so made that the bereaved may occupy a room apart from the people."[26]

Etiquette manuals spanning the last quarter of the nineteenth century through the 1920s routinely instructed the family to be seated in a separate room during the funeral service, away from the casketed remains of their loved one. "The corpse is usually exposed in the drawing-room," counseled Eliza Bisbee Duffey's *The Ladies' and Gentlemen's Etiquette* in 1877, "while the family are assembled in another apartment."[27] More than a generation later, in 1913 the same position was taken by Helen L. Roberts, who claimed that it was "invariably more dignified and considerate for the immediate members of the deceased's family not to appear in the room" in which the services were to be conducted.[28] Many believed that the family should be seated in an adjoining room. "It is becoming customary," observed one authority on manners and etiquette in 1881, "to reserve a room of the house adjoining that in which the services are held for the exclusive use of the near relatives and members of the family during the services. Then the clergyman takes his position at the door between the two rooms while conducting the services."[29] Others agreed that the casket be placed in the drawing room but recommended that the family "assemble in a room near, but not adjoining."[30] Some suggested that "those whose loss and grief are a poignant source of suffering should gather in a room in the rear, or across the hall from the scene of the ceremony, and from that distance hearken to and follow the religious rites."[31]

Still others argued that the family should not be seated on the ground floor at all but rather upstairs. "At a house funeral," opined one such advice giver in 1898, "the family remains up-stairs, and is not seen. The remains are in the drawing-room, where they are usually seen by those who attend the funeral. The clergyman stands where his voice can be heard."[32] Perhaps one reason to seat the immediate family upstairs was that setting aside an entire room where they could sit in isolation wasted precious ground-floor space that could be used to accommodate mourners. This appears to have been the rationale behind the advice of Margaret E. Sangster in her 1904 work *Good Manners for All Occasions*:

In the ordinary house the immediate family and closest friends are seated in a room upstairs. The body, almost hidden by heaps of flowers, lies in state, in the drawing-room, and there, seated in camp chairs in crowded ranks, the friends and acquaintances of the dead await the beginning of the services. The overflow of these friendly people is seated in the dining room, or on the stairs, the halls being crowded with men, who stand.[33]

By the 1920s some advice givers, such as Anna Steese Richardson and Emily Post, had decided that any of these locations were appropriate for the immediate family during a home funeral. "The nearest relatives," wrote Post in 1923, "may stay apart in an adjoining room or even on the upper floor where they can hear the service but remain in unseen seclusion."[34] Some maintained that in the end it was up to the family to decide where they would sit during the funeral service. "At a house funeral," concluded *Vogue's Book of Etiquette* in 1925, "it depends upon their wishes. Some families do not come down-stairs at all; some sit in a room apart; some join with the few friends they have asked to the simple service and have no special reserved place beyond the chairs arranged for them in whatever room is chosen."[35] Some families ultimately disregarded mainstream etiquette and chose to sit near the casketed remains of their loved one during the funeral service. At least some authorities, including some clergy, saw this as a valid option. "It is appropriate," counseled Reverend William C. De-Witt, dean of the Western Theological Seminary in Chicago, "but not always expedient, that [the family] should be in the room with the body."[36] Similarly, manners expert Lillian Eichler recommended that "a row of seats should be reserved near the casket for the immediate family, one being set aside for the clergyman who is to officiate."[37] Clearly, there were choices. Precisely what room the immediate family was to occupy, however, depended on not only who was giving the advice but also the family's wishes and the layout of the house itself. One of the challenges was that while the advice remained largely the same, house layouts changed.

Industry experts also recognized that a sensitive and responsible funeral director could not simply dictate to the family where they should sit. Rather, their placement during the service would be determined through consultation. Callaway understood that the funeral director's role was to respect the family's wishes, not impose his own will, and that in the end there was a degree of unpredictability about the whole business. "No funeral director," he argued, "can afford to assume that the family will sit just where he asks them to sit. Funeral directors are not autocrats." In Callaway's view, the funeral director's role was about dispensing advice rather than giving orders. "The funeral director may," he wrote,

> advise the family that it is customary for the family to occupy a certain place; but when he has offered advise [sic] and all the information at his command, it then remains for him to be instructed by the family as to where they would prefer to be, and it becomes his own humble duty to see that this family are as comfortable as possible in just the position and location they select for themselves. The director might plan to have the family in a certain place and arrange accordingly, only to find, at the last minute, that they rebel against such arrangement.[38]

Like narrow or rickety porch steps, the notion that the family could decide at the very last minute to alter the seating plan must have brought an added element of stress to the task of conducting a home funeral.

Equally vexing to funeral directors was the task of traveling to and from the home of the deceased. Multiple trips in an automobile cost time and money and made it more difficult to maintain their equipment. As cost accounting grew in importance within the industry and more accurate methods of calculating one's overhead began to include the hidden costs of doing business, trips to and from the home were looked upon as an unnecessary and expensive burden. At the same time, funeral directors had to balance concerns about cost with the family's wishes. "There is no doubt," explained one industry expert in 1931, but that using equipment of various kinds on our own premises prevents much loss and abuse through handling of this equipment to and from other locations. I have purposely not mentioned the time element, as I consider that we are servants of the public and that their preference should prevail first in the matter of deciding where the services should be held, . . . rather than his own preference simply because it might be easier for him.[39]

For the nation's funeral directors, funeral services from their premises meant not just greater savings and efficiency but also greater control over the funeral and a strategic advantage in the showroom. For example, a family might be inclined to purchase a more expensive casket if it was going to be displayed in the funeral home's luxuriously furnished service room rather than in their own more modest living room. Funeral directors understood that the setting mattered. Nonetheless, the tantalizing vision of reduced overhead and increased profits remained frustratingly out of reach for the nation's funeral directors. As late as the 1930s, the majority of funerals throughout the United States were still being held at the home of the deceased, despite the availability of well-appointed alternatives and the counsel of funeral directors who were, after all, not autocrats.

INFREQUENT INTERVALS

Investing in a comfortable and homelike service room or a spacious and beautiful chapel did not guarantee that a funeral director would be free from having to make house calls. For example, in 1924 the Griesmer-Grim Company of Hamilton, Ohio, spent "a large sum of money, well in the thousands," converting a large, ornate Queen Anne mansion into a "magnificent funeral home" complete with a chapel possessing "all the appurtenances of an auditorium." Several years later, however, nearly three-quarters of the town's funerals were still being held at home.[40] By the late 1920s, residents of Hamilton could choose from a handful of alternatives to a home funeral besides Griesmer-Grim's "light and airy" chapel. Cahill & Sons also operated a residential funeral home a few blocks away, and David Webb offered comfortable service rooms from his downtown funeral parlor, remodeled in 1928 to reflect "the atmosphere of a real home." Still, in 1931 barely a quarter of Hamilton's funerals were conducted from downtown parlors such as Webb's or the residential funeral homes that had emerged during the prior decade. Webb was astute enough to see the handwriting on the wall and by November 1931 had relocated his business to the remodeled Sohngen mansion, long known as "one of the fine old homes of Hamilton,"[41] but in spite of the investments made by Webb and his colleagues, shifting their operations from the downtown to residential district did not immediately inspire the residents of Hamilton to change their customs.

The same was largely true elsewhere. Historian James Farrell's exploration of the changing patterns of deathcare in Vermillion County, Illinois, noted that even in the county seat of Danville, most funerals in 1920 took place at home despite the availability of alternatives.[42] During the interwar period, funeral homes competed with the home of the deceased as well as churches and cemetery chapels. Many funeral directors were lucky to have barely one funeral per week conducted from their premises, the rest being performed elsewhere, a fact they readily pointed out when they found themselves hauled into court by neighbors opposed to the presence of a funeral home on their street. In response to accusations that a funeral home constituted a nuisance because it served as a constant reminder of death to area residents, funeral directors countered that they could hardly be accused of disturbing their neighbors when so few funerals were conducted from the funeral home compared with the number of funerals held in private residences.

"Funerals," testified Adelbert Miller before the Wisconsin Supreme Court in 1922, "are held from the premises at infrequent intervals and are but little attended."[43] When he was first called upon the previous July to defend his right to operate from a residential district in La Crosse, he claimed that since opening his doors in January 1921, he had conducted only eight funerals from the funeral home so detested by his neighbors.[44] While a figure of less than two funerals per month may suggest that Miller was strategically downplaying the number held from his premises in order to persuade the court of the minimal impact his business would have on the neighborhood, there is nothing odd or unusual about such an estimate in 1921. In 1927 lawyers for a funeral director in Amarillo, Texas, made a similar argument while defending their client from charges that his establishment constituted a public nuisance. "Only small funerals attended by comparatively few people are and will be held in said place," they assured the court, with "all large and more numerously attended funerals being held in churches and at the homes of deceased persons."[45]

By the early 1930s, on the other hand, some industry insiders were quick to point out a steady increase in the number of ceremonies being held in funeral homes, a development they regarded as a growing trend nationwide. A 1931 survey undertaken by the *American Funeral Director* estimated that where funeral directors maintained "high grade mortuaries," from 55 to 90 percent of all funerals were held at the funeral home.[46] This number seems high for 1931 in light of conflicting observations made elsewhere, but it was not the most outrageous claim to be made. W. W. McFarland of Warren, Ohio, boasted in 1931 that approximately 90 percent of the funerals he was hired to arrange were conducted from his premises, an estimate that seems impossibly high for Ohio in 1931.[47] In a similar report issued that same year, Arthur Mackey of Greenville, South Carolina, estimated that since relocating to a "modern mortuary" four years earlier, he had conducted twenty funerals from his quarters to every one conducted from the home of the deceased, which comes out to more than 95 percent.[48]

Julius Emmert of Lawrence, Massachusetts, could not hope to compete with such numbers. Acknowledging that residents of New England were "somewhat more conservative than in many other sections of the country," he claimed a percentage that seems inflated nonetheless.[49] He reported that after remodeling his funeral home in 1927, the funerals conducted from his quarters rose dramatically from 10 percent to 60 percent in just four years, an incredible claim considering that in nearby Lowell, less than 40 percent of all funerals in 1931 were being held at the city's residential funeral homes and downtown parlors.[50] One suspects that within the pages of industry publications, funeral directors were apt to inflate the number of funerals conducted from their premises, just as they were inclined to minimize the number before judges. By the early 1930s, the percentage of funerals being held from the funeral home likely hovered around 40 percent for most of the nation. Much higher than that is difficult to imagine, the hyperbole of some funeral directors notwithstanding. The timing of the shift from home funeral to funeral home was roughly the same for Americans, irrespective of race. Concerning Black Americans, Suzanne Smith has argued that by midcentury "the wake was usually held at the local black funeral home."[51] As late as 1954, Amy Vanderbilt was answering questions about funeral etiquette in her advice column as if services from the funeral home were a relatively recent development.[52]

Much likely depended on location, and in more rural areas claims of funeral homes hosting infrequent and sparsely attended funerals continued into the 1930s and 1940s. W. F. Otte of Clarinda, Iowa, estimated in 1937 that he conducted no more than two or three funerals per year from his funeral home, the majority being held at "the homes of deceased persons or their relatives or from churches."[53] This figure may seem small except that in 1937, Clarinda's population was less than 5,000. Walterboro, South Carolina, was even smaller, with a population in 1941 of approximately 3,300 when circuit court judge G. B. Greene commented on the number of funerals being held from Fred Parker's funeral home. "There has been nothing about the operation of this undertaking establishment," he wrote,

> that would differentiate it from the ordinary undertaking establishment in its operations; that the defendant is now conducting approximately one hundred and twenty (120) funerals a year, that is, an average of one about every three days, and that though comparatively few of these funerals are held from this particular location, nevertheless, all of the

embalming and preparation of the bodies is done at this particular house; that bodies are kept there for varying periods; that in nearly every instance the members of the family come to this establishment for the purpose of making arrangements, buying coffins and caskets.[54]

In other words, of the 120 funerals Parker conducted annually, "comparatively few" of them were held at his funeral home. Greene's observations confirm what was certainly true for rural districts and generally throughout the United States, namely that as late as 1940, the funeral home was a place where bodies were sent to be embalmed and where caskets were selected but not necessarily where funerals were held. Although by 1940 home funerals were on the decline nationwide and the balance had finally tipped in favor of the funeral home as a setting for funeral services, the public in places large and small had been slow to give up what was a cherished custom. The one exception was California.

UPWARDS OF FIFTY THOUSAND STRANGERS

While statistical or other quantitative data charting the frequency with which funeral homes were used for services are scarce for specific decades or geographic locations,[55] anecdotal evidence and observations by industry insiders suggest that Californians were far quicker to adopt the funeral home for funeral services than their fellow citizens in other parts of the United States. It appears that by the 1920s the majority of funerals in California were being held at a funeral home or mortuary. Already in 1910, a southern California funeral director boasted at the National Funeral Directors Association's annual convention that 90 percent of all funerals in his part of the country were conducted from funeral homes and downtown parlors.[56] L. R. Comer, a funeral director based in Long Beach, California, noted in 1926 that virtually all of the cases he handled included a service held at his establishment. He stated that "99 per cent of our work is done from first to last in our own workrooms, concluding

with the funeral in our chapel," which, he suggested, "might be interesting to some eastern mortician."[57] Although it is possible that Comer exaggerated his numbers, he gave no indication that there was anything
exceptional about the fact that so large a percentage of the funerals he
handled were conducted from his premises.[58] On the contrary, he made
a point to contrast his practice with that of his colleagues in the East,
not with his fellow funeral directors in California.

Comer believed that one of the factors driving so many residents of
Long Beach to forgo a home funeral was the type of housing prevalent
in his community. "Most people," he observed, "live in bungalows and
small apartments, and when a death occurs the mortician is called in
at once to take charge of everything until after the funeral. The practice is looked on with favor here by the authorities, and is encouraged
by apartment house owners."[59] In Comer's case, the perception mattered more than reality. While bungalows were common, apartment
houses were less common in Los Angeles, of which Long Beach was a
part, than in the rest of the country. "The freestanding, single-family
house," explains historian Richard Longstreth,

> dominated the landscape of Los Angeles as it did no other American
> metropolis, continuing a pattern established well before 1900. . . . By
> 1930, single-family residences comprised 93 percent of the city's resi-
> dential buildings, almost twice that in Chicago and surpassing those
> found in Philadelphia and Washington. Well under half as many fami-
> lies lived in apartment buildings as in houses despite the substantial
> increase in multiple-unit construction during the 1920s. At the decade's
> end, single-family houses stood on more than 60 percent of all occu-
> pied lots within the city limits.[60]

To Comer, however, the actual number of apartment dwellers in Long
Beach was as irrelevant as the actual size of the average bungalow. He
and other funeral directors were engaged in creating an illusion. Over
and over again their advertisements posited a scarcity of domestic
space as the problem to which the funeral home was the solution. What
mattered was not whether the people of Long Beach lived in apart-

ments or bungalows but rather the way in which they viewed their living quarters when it came time to plan the funeral of a loved one.

Comer's explanation was very likely based at least in part on the testimony of his customers. Industry insiders in other parts of the country made similar claims. "Now that the housing problem has become so acute," observed the *Casket and Sunnyside* in 1925 about housing trends in cities and towns in New York, "large numbers of people have gone into small apartments or tiny bungalows or other restricted living quarters, which make the holding of a funeral a difficult matter." For bereaved families in New York, however, living in small quarters was apparently not cause enough to abandon the practice of the home funeral. "A comparatively small number of these people," the article lamented, "are acquainted with the conveniences and availability of the funeral home. Even yet many people think of it as a place from which the stranger and the friendless only are taken to their last resting places."[61] Clearly, size was not the only thing that mattered.

What separated residents of Long Beach and other parts of California from most Americans was transience. Comer saw a connection between newcomers in his city and the frequency with which his quarters were chosen for funerals. "While Long Beach is now a large city and constantly growing," he explained, "much of our business is with the non-resident, or the family which has not yet decided to make Long Beach its home. There are always upwards of fifty thousand strangers in Long Beach."[62] Newness, transience, and mobility characterized a much larger segment of California's population during the interwar era than was true in other parts of the United States. The population of Los Angeles, for example, increased fivefold between 1900 and 1910, and as Richard Longstreth points out, "the more than tenfold rise within the county limits during the first three decades of the twentieth century was by far the greatest rate of increase in any major metropolitan area of the United States at that time."[63] It is little wonder that such rapid growth transformed California into an incubator for novel ideas and practices of all kinds, including new burial practices. Connecting California's unique population with the demise of the home funeral in that part of the country, James Farrell describes how "funeral directors in California capitalized on their transient population to draw most funerals into funeral homes."[64] Industry insiders understood that demographics mattered. Whether they were explaining the prevalence of home funerals or their demise, funeral directors were quick to point out that living conditions alone were not responsible for determining where funerals were held. Just as Long Beach had its many strangers and nonresidents, deep roots and strong family ties in other parts of the United States kept the funeral firmly rooted in the home of the deceased, no matter how cramped.

It is tempting to assume that Comer and those like him who singled out small apartments and bungalows as being incompatible with home funerals were alluding exclusively to the size of the dwelling. Funeral directors were, of course, not blind to the possibility that the size of a family's living quarters might influence their willingness to consider services at the funeral home. On the contrary, they often tried to convince families that their living quarters were too small. Nonetheless, references to bungalows in particular should not be interpreted as an allusion to size alone. Bungalows were problematic for funeral directors because they possessed floor plans that were more open with fewer ground-floor partitions than their late nineteenth-century and turn-of-the-century predecessors. Such plans posed a challenge to the traditional practice of placing the casketed remains in one room and the family in another. Moreover, many bungalows lacked an entrance hall, a common feature of older houses (fig. 6.4). The main entrance often opened into a large living room, and without the benefit of a hallway to serve as a buffer, mourners poured directly into the room in which the remains were placed.[65] Mourner after mourner arriving in this potentially disruptive and unceremonious manner no doubt made for a disorderly home funeral.

J. Ed. Phillips of Glendale, California, recognized that the spatial challenges posed by bungalows went beyond size. Like so many funeral directors, he adhered to the practice of seating the immediate family apart from the other mourners. "Those who have just lost a

Gordon-Van Tine Home No. 557

A Handsome Two-Story Bungalow

For Prices on This Home See First Page.

Read Pages 9 and 10 for Full Description of Materials.

IF a bungalow is a favorite with you, but you feel that you need the space afforded by the two-story house, this plan offers a happy solution. Our architects succeeded remarkably well in keeping the characteristics of the one and giving the added advantages of the other.

The substantial lines of the porch, the wide cornice, and the exposed rafter ends all unite to make this a distinctive home. The outside walls are covered with Clear Red Cedar shingles, another pleasing feature. These extend to the grade line, helping to further the low broad effect sought after in the bungalow. The hooded dormers add dignity to the exterior, and room and light to the house sized attic.

The wide porch along the whole front is roomy. The living room is large, light and airy and connected with the dining room by a wide cased opening, making the entire front of this home practically one large room, receiving light and air from every direction. A hall opens from the back of the living room.

The room opening off the left of this hall will make either a very cool and quiet ground floor bed room, not far from the bath at the head of the stairs, or a mighty fine den or library. The closet to the right of the stairway can be used with this room, or as a coat closet, near to the living room.

The kitchen, besides opening from the dining room, is also easy of access to the other rooms, because of its connection with the lower hall. The built-in kitchen case, design "D", must

First Floor Plan

Second Floor Plan

meet with your absolute approval, since its location is ideal. See the colored insert for illustration of this handsome and convenient case. In fact, the entire kitchen arrangement is such as will make work easy and pleasureable, and at the same time leave the room always orderly and attractive.

Not an unnecessary step will be taken in getting supplies from the basement or refrigerator, and the putting away of winter stores will not result in an untidy kitchen, for the grade door at the walk level prevents this. The basement extends under the entire house. It is well lighted, as we furnish four cellar sash, as well as stairs, girders and girder posts.

On the second floor are two large well lighted chambers, a bath and an attic. The attic gives splendid storage space, without the necessity of climbing a second flight of stairs. The bath is unusually large. The linen case which we supply is shown in the colored section.

All in all this is a plan for a home that is comfortable, economical and attractive. From those who have lived in it, we learn that the longer they have called it "home" the more they have to say in its favor.

PAINT—Unless otherwise instructed, we will furnish brown shingle stain for wall shingles and white trim.

For Plumbing, Heating, Lighting for this Home, See Last Pages of Book

FIGURE 6.4 "A Handsome Two-Story Bungalow," Gordon-Van Tine Homes No. 557. Such a design, with its living and dining room connected by "a wide cased opening, making the entire front of this home practically one large room," and the absence of an entrance hall, would have been a daunting setting to funeral directors accustomed to older, more formal plans. The front steps only added to their woes. *Gordon-Van Tine Homes* (1923), 76.

friend or relative," he reasoned, "shrink from the gaze of the curious." The problem, he found, was that many houses didn't afford such a separation. "The impossibility of shutting off any part of the average California house," he explained in 1926, "has made it necessary to keep the bodies at the funeral home."[66] Thus, the issue was less the lack of square footage than the lack of privacy. This was to become a recurring theme in funeral home advertisements, namely that the funeral home offered not only more room but also greater privacy during the service for the immediate family than their own living quarters.

Such statements do not in themselves explain the demise of the home funeral. They shed light only on the features of some houses that made home funerals challenging from the funeral director's point of view and also highlight the features of the funeral home that funeral directors believed most appealed to the public. In addition, such statements do not constitute evidence of what ultimately appealed to the public or what actually inspired bereaved individuals and families to make the switch. More importantly, buried within statements made by industry insiders and funeral home advertisements was a tacit critique of "modern" housing. Together with the vintage dwellings funeral directors chose to remodel, the ways in which those spaces were promoted to the public offered an alternative vision to the cult of openness and informality that sacrificed privacy and was the antithesis of Victorian living. Quite apart from its size, modern housing of the interwar period embodied a set of ideals that were prized by housing reformers and largely embraced by the public but made home funerals impractical and inconvenient for families and funeral directors alike. Funeral directors were not shy about pointing this out.

THE AVERAGE MODERN HOME

Advertisements alone neither drive nor explain consumer behavior. They reveal what sellers believe will sell. On one hand, it is true that the American public, first in California and then gradually in other parts of the country, made the switch from home funeral to funeral home. It is also true that the funeral home as a setting for funeral services was aggressively marketed during the interwar period. It would be easy, then, to conclude that funeral directors successfully sold the funeral homes to consumers and that their advertising campaigns worked. On the other hand, the advertising campaigns that doubtless helped to promote and popularize the funeral home were multifaceted. It is therefore difficult to pinpoint with any certainty the precise components and strategies that worked. What resonated with and motivated the public to make the switch is not at all obvious at first glance.

The uncertain impact of advertising on consumer behavior lies somewhere in the misty territory of persuasion. Funeral directors knew this territory well, operated comfortably within its borders, and spoke its language fluently. Precisely who was listening remains unclear, but the message itself was unmistakable. Funeral home advertisements nationwide sought to persuade the public that, for starters, their living quarters were too small to accommodate a home funeral. "But few homes today are of a size to receive comfortably the number of family friends who sincerely desire to indicate their respect and sympathy," claimed the Griesmer-Grim Company in a 1928 article discussing the firm's long history in Hamilton, Ohio, and the rise of the residential funeral home nationwide.[67] One of its competitors, William F. Cahill, agreed. "Style of houses being built nowadays," he noted in 1929, "make it almost impossible to keep a body properly for three days. And then, too, houses now are too small for services to be held there."[68] Large crowds of mourners, funeral directors insisted, simply couldn't be comfortable in such cramped quarters. "In private homes," one funeral director lamented, "the relatives are often crowded into upstairs and hear nothing of the services," whereas "the regular funeral home," argued a 1928 advertisement for Dumm's Colonial Funeral Home in Emporia, Kansas, "can handle the crowd better than a private home."[69] Others pointed to "cities where the smallness of apartments" made the funeral home a necessity.[70] "In this day and age of cramped living quarters," proclaimed a 1930 advertisement for the Joyce Funeral Home in Madison, Wisconsin, "a funeral home is often an imperative necessity."[71]

A 1928 advertisement run by the Fiss & Bills Funeral Home in Osh-kosh, Wisconsin, summarized the funeral industry's "Goldilocks" approach to the question of where to hold the last rites: "The growth of cities, the development of apartments, the use of elevators, the passing of the large house, have effected changes in funeral customs. The average modern home is now too small for services, the church too large. So the modern funeral home has become a community necessity."[72] Such advertisements were intended to convince people that the funeral home was a much better choice than their own living quarters, which were inadequate and ill-suited to the task of accommodating a funeral service. There can be little doubt that these arguments slowly crept into the public's consciousness.

Of course, if size mattered to the public during the interwar years, it hadn't before. Prior to the 1920s there was little connection between the size of one's house and the location of one's funeral, even though not every nineteenth- and early twentieth-century family lived in a palatial Queen Anne (figs. 6.5, 6.6). Nineteenth-century dwellings, like their interwar successors, consisted of a broad spectrum spanning small and modest at one end and large and grand at the other (fig. 6.7). There is surprisingly little evidence that houses got smaller after the First World War, notwithstanding the claims by some historians of American vernacular architecture. "In most new houses of the early twentieth century," writes Gwendolyn Wright in *Building the Dream: A Social History of Housing in America*, "square footage was dramatically reduced to compensate for the increased expenses of plumbing, heating, and other technological improvements."[73] Similarly, in *The American Family Home, 1800–1960*, Clifford Clark discusses "the substantial reduction of house size" and refers repeatedly to "smaller size" when describing houses built during the first decades of the twentieth century.[74] Such unscientific oversimplifications belie not only the modest living quarters for many working-class and lower

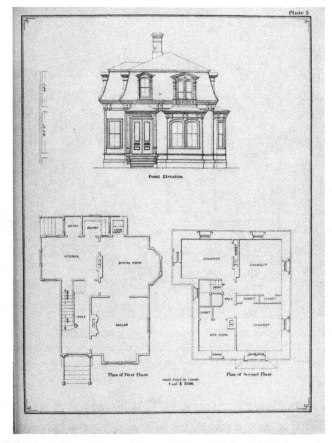

FIGURE 6.5   A "French Cottage" from an 1871 A. J. Bicknell & Co. pattern book. Small, modest one-and-a-half-story nineteenth-century cottages, in this case with a mansard roof, were numerous, and surviving examples, such as the dwellings pictured in fig. 6.6, can be found in older residential neighborhoods throughout the northeastern part of the United States. *Supplement to Bicknell's Village Builder Containing Eighteen Modern Designs for Country and Suburban Homes of Moderate Cost* (New York: A. J. Bicknell & Co., 1871), plate 5.

middle-class Americans during the nineteenth century but also the popularity during the early twentieth century of housing types such as the commodious four-square and large multistory Colonial Revivals, which differed in outward appearance and ornamentation from their Victorian predecessors but not necessarily in square footage.[75]

What changed for interwar families was not the size of their living quarters but rather the perception that private dwellings were no longer

FIGURE 6.6   A group of ca. 1870 French cottages on Amory Street in the Jamaica Plain section of Boston, Massachusetts, 2013. Out of the seven along that stretch of road, five are shown here. Another five sit across the street. Photograph by the author.

suitable for holding funeral services. This altered way of seeing was no doubt fueled at least in part by the barrage of funeral home advertisements disseminating this particular cultural text. Funeral directors such as Frank Bishop of Nevada, Iowa, charged that the average private residence was "not large or well enough arranged" for an efficient, orderly funeral service.[76] While the diversity of living quarters during the interwar period is reflected in neither the persistent claims by funeral directors nor the erroneous assumptions of a later generation of architectural historians that houses had shrunk, the notion that modern houses were not adequately arranged to accommodate a home funeral comes closer to hitting the mark.

For example, fewer partitions and the blending of public spaces within modern dwellings of the early twentieth century meant less formality and less privacy, two ingredients deemed essential to a proper funeral. In many houses, especially bungalows, living and din-

FIGURE 6.7   A page from the 1913 edition of the *Sears Modern Homes* catalog showing actual houses built using the company's plans. The houses represent a wide variety of styles, forms, and sizes ranging from small and modest bungalows to larger and more elaborate dwellings in the Colonial Revival and Queen Anne styles. *Sears Modern Homes* (1913).

ing rooms were combined into one large space, which lent itself to more relaxed and less formal living but not necessarily to a funeral service in which the immediate family of the deceased was expected to sit in seclusion.[77] Funeral directors in California were already hinting at this dilemma because of the popularity of bungalows in that part of the country. Ironically, deathcare historians have instead made much of the alleged disappearance of the parlor as a key factor in the demise of the home funeral. "By the early twentieth century," posits Gary Laderman, "changing tastes in home design, new practical considerations in planning domestic space—especially in urban settings— and shifting attitudes about family life led to the disappearance of the parlor." As a result of this change, he concludes, "the available suitable space for the dead in the home" was reduced, in effect pushing the funeral out of the home and into the funeral home.[78] Likewise, in discussing the shift from home funeral to funeral home, James Farrell has asserted that as funeral directors were beginning to build funeral parlors, "the domestic parlor was becoming an anachronism."[79]

Such statements miss the point, however. Not only were stiff, formal parlors replaced by stiff, formal living rooms in many houses, but the disappearance of the partition between parlors and other adjoining spaces likely presented a far greater challenge for families and funeral directors.[80] When, for example, the entrance hall fell as a casualty in the war waged under the banner of simplicity by housing reformers and builders alike against Victorian formality, the home was deprived of an intermediate space in which mourners could enter from the street before proceeding to view the remains.[81] While the improved flow brought about by the absence of an entrance hall produced a more relaxed atmosphere, this did not make for a smoother home funeral, which relied on separation, rather than flow, between spaces. Simplicity as well as smallness proved challenging to funeral directors forced to make house calls. On the other hand, both the vintage dwellings selected by funeral directors and the purpose-built, residential-style mortuaries they built were almost certain to possess entrance halls, which lent the proceedings an air of formality and allowed for greater privacy, order, and decorum (fig. 6.8).

As one of the major tenets of the burial reform movement, simplicity had already proven to be a persistent thorn in the side of funeral directors. By the second decade of the twentieth century, simplicity's impact on domestic space had doubtless begun to leave funeral directors accustomed to more formally arranged living quarters feeling frustrated and disoriented. As a result, their advertisements frequently portrayed home funerals as a recipe for confusion and disorder and offered the funeral home as an alternative. "The modern funeral home," explained a 1932 advertisement for Hudson-Keith in Ada, Oklahoma, "is designed to provide a place where the bereaved family can perform all the duties of this trying period with privacy and dignity, and without the inevitable confusion of a residence visited by death. Our establishment is arranged and equipped to combine comfort and convenience for those who mourn."[82] Another funeral director

FIGURE 6.8   Entrance hall, Keeney and Basford Funeral Home (Trail Mansion, ca. 1854), Frederick, Maryland, 2012. Photograph by the author.

declared, "Even in a large family home, confusion [was] inevitable."[83] Others argued that services from the funeral home enabled "the bereaved family to perform the duties of this trying period with the minimum of distraction and annoyance."[84]

Some of those annoyances included "moving furniture, carrying in of chairs and otherwise disarranging [the house] for a purpose for which it was not designed."[85] Habenstein and Lamers recalled how home funerals had often necessitated the removal of doors from hinges and, in some cases, door trim in order to move the casket in and out.[86] Funeral directors wrote about such things as if they added to the bereaved family's burden, but they themselves doubtless experienced stress and strain as a result of having to work under less than optimal conditions in houses of more recent vintage. Funeral directors were not alone in their belief that home funerals were inconvenient.

As early as 1914, Reverend William C. DeWitt came out against the home funeral in his advice book for pastors, *Decently and In Order*. Of course, his solution was neither funeral home nor undertaker's parlor. "In most cases," he claimed, "a 'home funeral' is far more inconvenient to the family than one from the church. For, in the first place, it requires a house-cleaning before the service and throws the home into a prolonged distraction, opens it to the curious as well as to the friends, and in many cases prohibits the attendance of some who cannot find place in the house."[87] Still, it was funeral directors who took the lead when it came to pointing out the inconvenience of home funerals in order to promote the use of their facilities. The funeral home, they argued, offered unparalleled convenience, homelike comfort, and privacy to families during their time of greatest need. Together with the promise of additional space for mourners, these benefits figured prominently in the campaign to popularize the funeral home. A 1936 article announcing the opening of the Wrenn-Yeatts Funeral Home in Danville, Virginia, exemplifies the way in which spaciousness and privacy worked together to promote the use of the funeral home. Its owners noted that spaciousness of the converted dwelling, "one of the oldest in North Danville," facilitated the conversion of "the large lower floor to provide an interior where funeral services could be held surrounded by a home atmosphere. The whole lower floor," they continued, "has been arranged so that two large parlors can be thrown en-suite into the equally large hall where funeral services can be plainly heard by all and with quarters provided especially for the members of the bereaved family."[88]

Arguing that the funeral home alone was able to protect the immediate family "from the curious gaze of others in attendance" was a tactic used by funeral directors everywhere to encourage the use of their quarters.[89] By sacrificing privacy to openness and informality, modern dwellings had lost some of their ability to shield family members during funeral services. Conversely, the vintage dwellings remodeled by funeral directors preserved an older and mostly discredited housing ideal that valued formality, strict separation, and the compartmentalization of domestic spaces. Nonetheless, it was left to funeral directors to make the case that such spaces were better suited for funeral services than were private homes, and their advertisements brought this point home with unmistakably clarity. "People often decline the use of our funeral home," explained a 1930 advertisement for Caldwell & Crain in Rushville, Indiana, "because they prefer the privacy of their own homes. As a matter of fact, the bereaved family is much better protected from intrusion in a well managed Funeral Home than it could be in its own residence."[90] Those in residential locations understood that they were competing less with their colleagues who had chosen to remain downtown than they were with the family home. If parking had been the key to selling the funeral home as a retail space, privacy helped sell the funeral home as a ritual space.

Naturally, slumber rooms and private family rooms became major selling points, and funeral directors assiduously advertised these spaces. "When the slumber room is made use of," noted a 1925 advertisement for the Dawson & Wikoff Funeral Home in Decatur, Illinois, "one is assured of absolute and uninterrupted privacy. There can be no disturbing entrances or exits of any kind. Another tremendous advantage of the funeral home over the private residence."[91] For the next two decades funeral directors continued to market privacy as a chief feature of the "modern" funeral home, and specialized spaces set apart for the immediate family's exclusive use featured prominently in advertisements. In addition to pledging "complete privacy of the family during services in the chapel," a 1937 advertisement for the Simpson Funeral Home in Charleston, West Virginia, promised "separation by appropriate curtain effects of casket and audience immediately after the services; separate rooms for the family; all vehicles housed in the rear for utmost privacy." Such features, they explained, were "but a few of the advantages our modern Funeral Home enables us to offer."[92]

Funeral directors assured family members that they were free to opt for a home funeral for their loved one but that the use of the funeral home for services came free of charge. "There is no extra charge," promised the New Orleans firm P. J. McMahon & Sons in a 1932 advertisement, "for use of our luxurious funeral home, nor for any of the additional comforting features which have made this firm known for its beautiful services for almost half a century."[93] Funeral directors were unapologetic in opining that the funeral home was by far the better choice. "The decision to use our parlor for services," counseled a 1926 advertisement for the Gregory Funeral Home in Carroll, Iowa, "rather than attempt makeshift arrangements in the residence is always a satisfactory one. The funeral parlor offers facilities and comforts that could not be arranged for in the private home."[94] Nonetheless, the choice of location belonged to the family alone, just as it was up to the family to decide where the casket would be placed or where they would sit during a home funeral, even when their decisions ran counter to the funeral director's wishes. "We do not," pointed out a 1928 advertisement for Dumm's Colonial Funeral Home in Emporia, Kansas, "try to force [the funeral home] upon a family, but it is offered without charge to all."[95] W. T. Nicholson, who operated a funeral home in Statesville, North Carolina, went so far as to concede in 1928 that while the funeral home was "eminently desirable" in many cases, "in other cases it would not, perhaps, be as suitable as the private residence."[96]

While funeral directors of the interwar period understood that it was important not to bully families into using the funeral home, subtle pressure tactics were frequently used. For the next two decades funeral directors continued to send mixed signals. They paid lip service to the family's wishes and consumer choice while simultaneously denigrating the home of the deceased as the wrong choice. By the 1940s, funeral directors were able to claim not only that the home of the deceased offered inferior facilities, comfort, and privacy but also that home funerals were outdated. For example, a 1940 advertisement for the Gordon-Shaidnagle-Hollinger Funeral Home in Massillon, Ohio, reminded families that although services from the home of the deceased could be arranged if so desired, services from the funeral home were becoming increasingly common. "It's for you to decide," promised the advertisement, "but we recommend the funeral home. Services, of course, may be conducted from the residence, if desired. But the use of our attractive, modern funeral home is becoming more and more the accepted thing, and we suggest that, in time of need, it be given serious consideration."[97] There was, of course, nothing unusual about this kind of psychological manipulation in the world of advertising. How effective it was in swaying public opinion is nonetheless difficult to assess.

A LASTING IMPRESSION

It is impossible to pinpoint with any precision what motivated the first generation of funeral home users to make the switch, but the demise of the home funeral reveals a shift in the way people thought about their homes. Specifically, this suggests that the home had become space in which death was no longer welcome. Although, as period observers pointed out, dying at the hospital did not guarantee that one's funeral would take place at the funeral home, the steady increase in hospital deaths during the interwar period constitutes further evidence that the home itself was changing. While the relationship between hospital deaths and the demise of the home funeral is not one of causation, they were both part of the same trend toward banishing death from the home.

It is true that by the 1930s more than a quarter of deaths took place in hospitals, and by 1940 the number had risen to one-third.[98] Naturally, the experience of dying in a hospital varied according to one's socioeconomic status. Wealthier patients in private hospitals were much more likely to be surrounded by family members and loved ones, but even there one was not guaranteed a good death. Emily Abel points out in her study of hospital deaths during the interwar period that those who died in large wards in public facilities were "especially likely to die alone. The many dying patients relegated to chronic care facilities and almshouses frequently lacked even the most rudimentary medical attention." Even in private hospitals, she writes, "various forces led both medical and nursing staff to limit personal involvement with terminal patients and discourage their contact with family members."[99] What this suggests is that those who died in hospitals were not guaranteed a good death, and this was especially true for the working class, the poor, immigrants, and people of color. It is possible that what mattered most about the increasing medicalization of death and the steady rise in the number of hospital deaths was not that the distance between the body and the family home but that hospital deaths were considered bad deaths, especially if the deceased died alone. An extravagant burial from an elaborate funeral home might have appealed to family members whose loved one had been deprived of a good death. Then again, a home funeral in familiar surroundings might also have eased the pain of a bad death. In the end, it is challenging to make the case that an increase in the number of hospital deaths and the shift from home funeral to funeral home were directly connected even though both developments occurred during roughly the same period.

Nonetheless, Thomas Lynch, both funeral director and poet, makes an admirable attempt to connect the dots in *The Undertaking: Life Studies from the Dismal Trade*. "Elders," he explains, "grew aged and sickly not upstairs in their own beds, but in a series of institutional venues: rest homes, nursing homes, hospital wards, sanatoria. Which is where they died: the chance, in 1960, of dying in your own bed: less than one in ten."[100] In addition to dying away from one's bed, other changes were afoot. Lynch artfully connects the advent of modern plumbing with the demise of the home funeral:

> Just about the time we were bringing the making of water and the movement of bowels into the house, we were pushing the birthing and marriage and sickness and dying out. . . . And just as bringing the crapper indoors made feces an embarrassment, pushing the dead and dying out has made

death one.... Make it go away, disappear. Push the button, pull the chain, get on with life.[101]

While a sharpened focus on sanitation was busy reshaping domestic space by bringing in new rooms, such as bathrooms, and transforming others, such as kitchens, the public spaces of the home were being stripped of the formal rituals—baptisms, weddings, and funerals—that had previously had a place there. Lynch's playful cynicism aside, his observations ring true; sanitized private spaces and less formal public spaces were part of the same idealized vision of the home that dominated the first half of the twentieth century.

This is not to suggest that the home funeral itself was ever the target of sanitary crusaders. Although the shift away from the home funeral and deathbed embalming occurred amid a renewed emphasis on domestic sanitation, neither practice was considered unsanitary.[102] On the contrary, even as the deathbed gave way to the funeral director's preparation room, it was not because funeral reformers had crusaded against home embalming. For funeral reformers, concerns about sanitation meant questioning the impact on public health of large cemeteries and, as historian Stephen Prothero points out, becoming ardent advocates of cremation as a more sanitary method of final disposition.[103] When reformers turned their attention to the home funeral, their critique focused on cost rather than contamination.[104]

If biological contamination never emerged as a challenge to the home funeral, however, emotional contamination was becoming a growing concern. Beginning around the First World War, critics and reformers charged that the gloominess of most home funerals prolonged the family's grief. A 1917 article titled "The Unseemliness of Funerals" in *Literary Digest* described one man's dread at the thought of his mother's funeral taking place at home. Little did he know that his dying mother and sister had made alternative arrangements. "I came home with my blood freezing," he recalled, "as I thought of the crape on the door, a coffin in the front room.... That was because I didn't know how far ahead of that age of barbarism my mother and [sister] Nora had planned. . . . The evening that my mother died her body was taken to a chapel."[105] Even those who were not yet ready to endorse an alternative to the home funeral understood the importance of having the house put back in order so that no trace of the funeral greeted the family upon their return from the cemetery or the church.[106]

Even as home funerals remained the norm in most parts of the country, Americans questioned the funeral's impact on the home. Despite being severely critical of the funeral industry overall, the influential survey on burial costs in the United States undertaken by the Metropolitan Life Insurance Company between 1926 and 1928 suggested that funeral services were better managed in the establishment of a professional. When the option of holding funeral services in either a mortuary chapel or a parlor was chosen, the survey pointed out, "everything is done to relieve the bereaved family of annoying details and to remove from the home the gruesome aspect of the old-fashioned funeral."[107] Funeral directors themselves were making the very same argument. "Much of the grimness of the old fashioned funeral services," claimed a 1931 advertisement for the Walter C. Oehler Home for Funerals in Des Plaines, Illinois, "has been relieved through our care to make such occasions more bearable by providing appropriate surroundings."[108] In this instance at least, funeral reformers and funeral directors found common ground.

During the 1920s commentators also argued that the children were especially vulnerable to trauma as a result of being exposed to a home funeral. While those who raised this concern were not necessarily advocates of services from the funeral home, they did argue that children should be kept "away from places of mourning as far as possible."[109] Ever attuned to patterns of behavior and public opinion that could be useful in marketing the funeral home and its goods and services, funeral directors doubtless picked up on this idea and used it to their advantage. Naturally they took the argument further, reasoning that the surest way to avoid exposing one's children to the trauma of death was to hold the service at the funeral home. "It is particularly desirable to use the mortuary," advised one industry expert in 1931, "when there are children in the family. Children's minds are very impressionable, and the presence of death in the home—the grim tragedy of it—may make a lasting impression on the child-mind." The funeral home, on the other hand, allowed the family to avoid "impressions that might be made on childish minds that would continue through life to create a horror of death."[110]

Funeral directors had to tread carefully, however. They were reluctant to run advertisements that drew too much attention to the gloom that a funeral brought to a private residence because such a notion would mean that the funeral home was, by extension, a gloomy place, a conclusion they vigorously discouraged. Funeral homes, they argued, were cheerful, bright, and homelike, especially when contrasted to their downtown predecessors. Some even argued that recent changes to funeral customs made for a less gloomy affair than had been the case previously. "Only in the last generation," claimed a 1933 advertisement for the John R. Loutzenhiser Home for Funerals in Greenville, Pennsylvania, "has the gloom which pictured the end of everything been replaced with a beauty emblematic of a new life."[111] Looking back on more than a half century of funeral customs, Habenstein and Lamers viewed the demise of the home funeral and the growing popularity of the funeral home within the context of the gradual elimination of gloom from the funeral itself. "The new 'aesthetic' of death," they argued in 1955,

> has today reached its culmination in the popular demand for funeral homes, once rather plain, functional, and gloomy, but now beautiful and well appointed edifices with nothing or very little to suggest the funeral about them. . . . It is the essence of modern funeral service to put the burial of the dead in a context of things pleasant and beautiful, and to consider the comfort of the bereaved.[112]

At the same time, increasing demand for funeral homes did not mean that the funeral home was viewed in a positive light. The public embrace of the funeral home for services was cool and ambivalent.

There is little evidence that the public shared the industry's rosy view of the funeral home. Funerals were thought to taint private homes and funeral homes alike. It was precisely because consumers rejected the industry's picture of a gloom-free funeral that they eventually let go of the home funeral. If gloom was inevitable, in other words, better for it to be pushed out of the home and into the funeral home. It is no surprise that stereotypes of dismal, gloomy funeral homes abounded in the popular imagination and in popular culture for much of the twentieth century. The gradual shift from home funeral to funeral home unfolded amid a consensus that it was better to keep one's home free from unpleasantness and leave the dismal necessities to the funeral home.

THE NEW WAY

It would be tempting to conclude that the rise of the residential funeral home singlehandedly brought about the demise of the home funeral. It is true that the frequency with which professional death-care facilities were selected for services did not increase until after funeral directors had begun to abandon their downtown quarters in favor of residential neighborhoods. On the other hand, home funerals remained commonplace throughout the interwar period in most parts of the United States despite the proliferation of residential funeral homes after 1920. Whatever the impact of the residential funeral home on the overall incidence of home funerals, its effect was gradual rather than immediate. As an innovation, the residential funeral home altered the deathcare marketplace by providing consumers with a new and more attractive alternative to both home services and the downtown undertaking parlor, which in its heyday had never managed to draw more than a scant share of services away from private residences.

Funeral directors caught on very quickly. As the decades passed, their experiences led them to draw their own conclusions about what had killed the home funeral. With great candor and pride, they attributed the disappearance of the home funeral to the appearance of the residential funeral home. Looking back in 1940 on his twenty years as a funeral director in Muscatine, Iowa, N. W. Meyers recalled that when he made the bold decision to move his business to a new residential location at the corner of Seventh and Walnut Streets in 1920, "the idea of conducting services in a home other than that of the family was unheard of." At that time, "the era of the old fashioned funeral parlor was almost ended," he explained, referring to old-style downtown undertaking parlors. "At first," Meyers reflected, "people were slow to realize the advantages of the new way ... [but] today all funeral directors have funeral homes."[113] Despite the simplicity of Meyers's narrative, it is certainly more than coincidental that the shift from home funeral to funeral home followed the shift from downtown to residence district. Still, it is safer to think of the residential funeral home as an alternative to the home funeral, one that took some getting used to, rather than a catalyst of some kind. Whether the shift would have occurred had funeral directors remained downtown is not a particularly useful inquiry.

Examining exactly what made the residential funeral home attractive as an alternative to the deeply rooted custom of the home funeral is a more fruitful endeavor. Whether the funeral home actually offered more space than one's home depended, of course, on one's home. Some dwellings, especially older dwellings, offered as much privacy as the funeral home, though many modern dwellings of the interwar period doubtless would have left bereaved families feeling exposed during funeral services. In such dwellings funeral directors must have felt frustrated. For their part, they certainly tried to convince families that they would feel cramped and compromised were they to stick to the custom of the home funeral. When selling the idea of services at the funeral home, funeral directors emphasized privacy and convenience as much as square footage, and one can assume that various advertising campaigns resonated with different families depending on their particular circumstances. Furthermore, while downtown funeral parlors continued to boast homelike quarters long after the first residential funeral homes had begun to alter the landscape of professional deathcare, it is not at all surprising that a space that looked and felt like a private dwelling, albeit a wealthy one, situated among other dwellings, with ample parking for large groups of mourners, was an easier sell.

That funeral directors appear to have swayed the public does not mean that their assumptions about domestic space—or those made by deathcare historians, for that matter—should be considered valid architectural history. Funeral directors understood that in the realm of advertising, perception mattered far more than reality. They reasoned that if families could be persuaded that their dwellings were too small, then perhaps they would consider switching to services at the funeral home. Statements about shrinking living quarters were all the more credible because funeral directors were not alone in making that claim. Other observers were making the same argument. "The model home of a generation and more ago was a spacious object," declared a 1919 article in *Literary Digest*. "But the model home," the article continued, "is dwindling in size, along with families. The cost of maintenance, in the matter of servants, lights, fuel, and furniture, not to speak of the cost of building materials, is too burdensome to encourage the building of large houses. It has become necessary to make smaller houses. When something had to be sacrificed, everybody agreed on the parlor."[114] Here, it would be wise to separate the history of houses from the changing discourse on housing.

Whether they are traced to interwar funeral directors and the housing reformers who were their contemporaries or present-day historians, claims about shrinking living quarters reveal more about the interwar discourse surrounding domesticity and the cultural landscape than the actual cultural landscape itself. They offer insight into the historically and culturally specific ways particular communities think about housing but say precious little about actual houses. It is best to exercise caution when confronted with generalizations about a given housing stock that do not have actual surveys and quantitative data to back them up. Moreover, the simplistic notion that either smaller houses or the imaginary shift from parlor to living room killed the home funeral ignores not only the complex nature of each family's decision but also the diversity of interwar dwellings. The absence of reliable historical data on consumer choice within the deathcare marketplace means that the shift from home funeral to funeral home cannot be conclusively tied to any one particular change in domestic architecture. In spite of spurious claims made by deathcare historians, the shift provides no proof of a sea change in the physical properties of domestic space, though it does point to changes in the social construction of domestic space. In other words, it's not about what happened to houses but about what happened to the people living in them.

Neither did the shift from home funeral to funeral home signal a sea change in public opinion concerning funeral directors or their establishments. That the funeral home had been popularized as a setting for services did not mean that either funeral homes or their owners were popular. The Metropolitan Life Insurance Company's widely distributed 1928 survey of rising burial costs leveled the familiar accusations of "extortion and overselling" and concluded that true reform would come only with fewer funeral establishments.[115] Widespread use of the funeral home did not spell an end to the campaign of vitriol waged by reformers and critics against the funeral industry. On the contrary, the press found numerous opportunities to fire barrage after "editorial barrage" against funeral directors over the next several decades.[116]

Likewise, funeral homes continued to be viewed by many neighborhoods as a nuisance and by judges as a "constant reminder of death" well into the 1950s. By the 1960s, 1970s, and 1980s, American cinema was capturing the uneasy undercurrents of disgust, disdain, and dread with which the public viewed the funeral home, even though a home funeral would by then have been considered eccentric if not bizarre. To the delight of funeral directors everywhere, burial customs eventually changed, although negative stereotypes lingered

and continued to haunt the industry throughout most of the twentieth century. Whatever ambivalence remained in people's minds, however, the collective decision to relinquish the once cherished custom
of the home funeral and embrace the residential funeral home as a
ceremonial space solidified for generations to come its iconic place
within the American cultural landscape.

BUILD ME NO STATELY MANSIONS

Within the ever-changing cultural landscape of the United States, the residential funeral home has consistently carved out a middle ground for itself. The funeral home has occupied a liminal space between contrasting landscapes and opposing ideas: commercial versus residential, luxuriousness versus simplicity, and retail versus ritual. Moreover, the funeral home has done so consciously and deliberately, exploiting dichotomies and paradoxes in an attempt to assuage critics and satisfy consumers while also resolving tensions and debates within the industry itself. What the residential funeral home has less successfully navigated is the territory of public opinion, as the ambiguity of its spatial setting has been matched by the public's own ambivalence. Funeral homes and their owners have for generations been situated on the border between being utilized and being reviled.

Public discomfort with the funeral home has always covered a broad spectrum of reactions, ranging from fear of contagion and being reminded of one's mortality to lowered property values and questions of taste. For much of the twentieth century, the industry's response wavered somewhere between a tin ear and the desire to counter negative stereotypes. During the interwar period funeral directors took refuge in conformity and maintained an unshakable faith that by blending in with their residential surroundings, they would neutralize opposition, a strategy that produced, at best, mixed results.[1] By midcentury the spread of architectural modernism saw the industry's adherence to a strictly domestic model become more relaxed, although a more broadly construed conformity continued to inform decisions about mortuary architecture planned for residential and suburban settings. In 1947 at the annual meeting of the Ohio Funeral Directors Association, a group of funeral directors met with a group of professionals from "the fields of architecture, city planning, interior decorating, landscaping, lighting and air conditioning" to discuss "the Funeral Home of Tomorrow." Remodeled mansions, though still numerous, were no longer the dominant trend for new funeral homes. "Above all," the participants concluded, the funeral home "will be an individual expression of the proprietor's personal taste and purposes, rather than a stereotyped pattern for all funeral homes. In every respect it will be unobjectionable from any esthetic viewpoint—a desirable 'neighbor' which conforms to the general character of the community in which it is located."[2] As had been the case with earlier generations of funeral directors, their midcentury counterparts continued to convince themselves that attractive, unobtrusive establishments would win over the public. The messages conveyed by their spaces were, as always, far more difficult to control.

Even as more streamlined and less ornate purpose-built mortuaries began to challenge the hegemony of converted mansions, the emphasis on luxury continued unabated, inspiring a new generation of critics. Notwithstanding attempts to brand the funeral home as a purveyor of "luxurious simplicity" in order to attract the business of both the caviar and the pickle crowd while simultaneously silencing their critics, paeans to simplicity fell on deaf ears. Statements about "quiet dignity" were unable to compete with the powerful image of opulence presented by the material setting the industry had chosen for itself. Mansions, it turned out, were more effective public speakers than funeral directors had anticipated. Outspoken critics listened in turn to what funeral homes were saying, and their takeaway was not flattering. If anything, the funeral home fueled the critique that professional deathcare was a soulless business driven by greed at the expense of the bereaved and was seen by many as an exploitative industry's sinister accomplice. This was the risk funeral directors had taken.

While the luxuriousness of the average funeral home certainly raised questions of affordability, many also found the grandeur and opulence of the funeral home distasteful and unappealing. In a 1947 editorial titled "Build Me No Stately Mansions," one critic took issue with what had become the commonplace setting of the typical American funeral.[3] He noted how in every American city, there was "somewhere off in a cool green lawn, protected by noble trees and clipped hedges, an imposing palace dedicated to final ritual over the lifeless flesh. It seems an odd way of arranging matters," he reasoned, "and I would just as soon have no part of it." He humorously asked his surviving loved ones that upon his demise his remains "be not removed to a mortuary that looks like the castle of some medieval king. . . . It is enough," he argued, "that in life one should give obeisance to the kings and the owners of medieval towers, without in the end paying them the homage of resting briefly in their kind of cold and useless luxury." It was not that he felt such luxury was beyond his family's ability to pay. Far poorer families, he imagined, scrimped and saved in order to keep up payments to their burial societies so they would "have a chance to enter an earthly mansion before proceeding to others presumably reserved for them elsewhere."[4]

The chief reason he bemoaned the industry's emphasis on opulence was that it encouraged funerals that belied one's station in life, his own included. "Such simple pleasures should not be denied those who want them," he reasoned,

> but the idea strikes a chill along my personal spinal column. Having become accustomed to the ramshackle, or never-find-time-to-fix-that-roof, type of dwelling, I can only look with horror upon being introduced to kingly elegance when I am beyond doing anything about it. I can feel comfortable in a room cluttered with toys and well ventilated

because of cracked window panes, but one adorned with marble fire-
places, tapestry on the walls and brocade wherever there's space for it
makes me look for the quickest exit.[5]

Acknowledging that the poor were free to make their own choices
about their final disposition, he nonetheless maintained "that there is
nothing elevated or appropriate about consigning the remains to housing infinitely more ritzy than the subject had been able to afford while
living." Beyond this was his obvious discomfort with imposing exteriors and pretentious interiors. It is clear that he did not find "establishments that look like manorial estates" either simple or homelike.[6]

Another vocal critic of the funeral industry, Leroy Bowman, challenged the notion that funeral homes were beautiful, cheerful, and
homelike in *The American Funeral: A Study in Guilt, Extravagance, and
Sublimity*, written in 1959, four years before Jessica Mitford's scathing
and better-known exposé of the funeral industry, *The American Way
of Death*. Bowman noted how common it was for funeral homes to be
"garish" and "over-elaborate" and argued that at least some of the public who used funeral homes came away with impressions that differed
significantly from the images put forward by their owners. "The funeral parlor," he observed, "provides for some the satisfaction of en-
tertaining in a spacious room; for others, however, the strangeness of
its surroundings is depressing. For a very considerable number the
place and the proceedings seem pretentious. . . . Some complain that
the atmosphere is not that of home or church, but is charged with
commercialism."[7] Homelike, it seems, was a tough sell after all.

As newer mortuaries became more innovative and minimalist, the
resulting atmosphere became even less homelike, at least according to
some observers. "The funeral homes of the 1950s," recalled sociologist Hugh Dalziel Duncan a decade later,

> do not stress "hominess." They are built around the chapel, modern in
> every particular, air-conditioned throughout with the latest develop-
> ment in livery equipment (limousines), luxuriously appointed rooms,
> beautifully landscaped grounds where everything moves smoothly

with a reserved elegance. . . . The architecture of funeral homes varies widely from "Early Colonial" to "modern." But, whatever the style, the building must be imposing, accessible to transportation, highly public, and kept in good order.[8]

Such an observation could also have been made about any newly constructed suburban department store or midcentury retail space possessed of what Richard Longstreth has called "great unadorned bulk."[9] As the larger retail landscape changed, funeral homes changed with it. Still, remodeled mansions remained prominent both within the landscape and in the popular conception of what constituted a funeral home.

The deathcare industry itself changed as well. By the closing decades of the twentieth century, multinational funeral conglomerates were moving in and taking over, and independent funeral homes felt the crunch. For consumers conditioned by decades of negative stereotypes, it took an even greater monster in the form of corporate giants such as Service Corporation International and the Loewen Group to play Goliath to the small family-run funeral home's David, a theme picked up by the immensely popular HBO series *Six Feet Under* (2001–2005). For at least some consumers, the "old-school" funeral home in an ancient and venerable mansion came to symbolize the virtues of the locally owned business as an antidote to faceless corporate chains. It didn't hurt that Victorian architecture itself underwent a perceptual shift from garish to vintage. Many twenty-first-century funeral directors, especially those with deep roots at a particular location, now use their historic structures to construct an identity and image that has less to do with luxury and grandeur than it does with patina, pedigree, and community presence. Whatever the message, many historical commissions have begun to applaud the positive contributions made by funeral directors to the preservation of the built environment. Today, sites that were once regarded as nuisances by their neighbors bear historic plaques and are listed on the National Register of Historic Places.

More recently, the pandemic has focused our attention on the funeral industry and funeral directors, who became frontline workers and were called upon to handle the body count, while the funeral home became the longed-for space we never knew we loved when grieving survivors were suddenly barred from the funerals and memorials of loved ones because of lockdowns. Virtual Zoom funerals had to suffice, a horrifying prospect for some while raising new questions for others about whether an in-person memorial is necessary at all.[10] In the long shadow of the pandemic, the conversation around the need for brick-and-mortar spaces isn't going away. Whether our society will continue to value an in-person modality—from work and school to shopping and sacred rituals—and the myriad spaces that accommodate these activities is not at all clear, and the funeral home is on the front line of a changing discourse surrounding both in-person retail and in-person ritual.

Just as retail establishments will be unable and unwilling to pay premium rents in downtown shopping districts and suburban malls to allow customers the privilege of browsing merchandise only to turn around and make their purchases online, it is unlikely that funeral directors will be able to continue the costly upkeep of nineteenth-century mansions as a gathering space for families if they consistently choose the less expensive burial goods associated with green burials. The wooden and wicker containers used in green burials cost a fraction of the price of a traditional casket, and vaults aren't typically used for these biodegradable vessels, eliminating another line item. The impact of green burials on the funeral industry remains unclear, however. A century ago, cremation was widely feared to be the end of the industry, which endured. Nonetheless, if both cremation and green burials become the dominant trend, it is likely that funeral directors will see a significant reduction in their profits.[11] It remains to be seen what this would mean for their brick-and-mortar establishments.

The residential funeral home continues to take on new meanings and will have to weather new threats as well. Even as new purpose-built mortuaries march across suburban and exurban landscapes, a

preference for virtual services and a growing demand for green burials promise to undercut the industry's spatial needs and profit margins. While the funeral home is no longer reviled as it was for decades,
it now stands at the threshold of irrelevancy. It will be a great irony
and an even greater tragedy if, in spite of its newly won status as a beloved icon of small, local free enterprise and historic preservation, the
residential funeral home in a stately mansion is in the end seen simply
as an anachronism.

NOTES

INTRODUCTION. THE OTHER PRESERVATION

1. Carter and Cromley, *Invitation to Vernacular Architecture*, 59–60.
2. Amid the chorus of detractors, there was a minority who found a kind of beauty in America's Victorian houses, Edward Hopper being among its more prominent members. In his 1928 essay on fellow painter Charles Burchfield, Hopper wrote, "Our native architecture with its hideous beauty, its fantastic roofs, pseudo-Gothic, French-Mansard, Colonial, mongrel or what not, with eye-searing color or delicate harmonies of faded paint, shouldering one another along interminable streets that taper off into swamps or dumps heaps—these appear again and again as they should in any honest delineation of the American scene." Quoted in Levin, *Edward Hopper*, 279–80.
3. The connection between adaptive use and funeral homes received only the briefest of nods in the seminal preservationist manifesto *With Heritage So Rich* (1966): "Houses remaining on their original sites have been converted to new uses; where, in their transformation to apartments, schools, clubs, funeral homes or offices, the exteriors, and sometimes a number of the interior features, have remained unchanged" (p. 50). While William Murtagh's classic work *Keeping Time* (1988) devotes a chapter to adaptive use, it focuses more on methodology than history and says nothing about funeral homes.

    More recent works, such as Norman Tyler's *Historic Preservation* (1994) and Max Page and Randall Mason's *Giving Preservation a History* (2003), explore the self-conscious preservation activities of governments and nonprofits, and while they acknowledge the contributions made by adaptive use, they fail to mention funeral homes. Finally, Stewart Brand's *How Buildings Learn* (1994) combines a primer on preservation methods and advice on how to produce more enduring and adaptable buildings with a survey of the most and least enduring and adaptable types of buildings and the particular features, processes, and outside (largely economic) forces that make them adaptable. Not really a history of adaptive use, his study makes a fascinating argument about change within the realm of vernacular architecture as an evolutionary process guided by natural selection. Just as it is a species' ability to adapt that allows it to survive, the key to a building's survival is its adaptability. Brand's brief foray into historical analysis cites the 1964 rehab of Ghirardelli Square in San Francisco as "the prototype for adaptive-use commercial projects all over the world." The 1964 project was for Brand a watershed moment, after which, he claims, "adaptive-use took off as the mainstream of preservationist activity" (p. 104). This may be the case, but it ignores almost half a century of adaptive use by funeral directors.

4. Johnson and Franza, "An Unheralded Preservation Influence," 33.

5. Barr, "Funeral Homes."

6. For this reason, it is difficult to determine precisely how many funeral homes are now or have been housed in remodeled mansions.

7. Excellent treatments include works by industry insiders such as Robert Habenstein and William Lamers's *The History of American Funeral Directing* (1955) and Vanderlyn Pine's *Caretaker of the Dead: The American Funeral Director* (1975). Both provide comprehensive (though biased) histories of the industry but are more useful as road maps to the industry's collective consciousness, how it has viewed itself and how it wished to be viewed. James Farrell's pioneering work *Inventing the American Way of Death, 1830–1920* (1980) offers a detailed snapshot of the industry on the eve of the shift from downtown mortuary to residential funeral home, while Ronald Smith's *The Death Care Industries in the United States* (1996) does the same for the deathcare economy of the late twentieth century. Smith's attention to the funeral home is limited to a discussion of consolidation and the acquisition of independent funeral homes by large corporations and national chains. Two location-based treatments are Robert Wells's *Facing the 'King of Terrors': Death and Society in an American Community, 1750–1990* (2000), which tracks the evolution of the funeral industry in Schenectady, New York, over the course of two centuries, and William Montell's *Tales from Kentucky Funeral Homes* (2009), which gives voice to African American funeral directors across Kentucky. Despite its title, Gary Laderman's *Rest in Peace: A Cultural History of Death and the Funeral Home in Twentieth-Century America* (2003) treats the funeral home primarily as an institution rather than a space. Nonetheless, Laderman offers an interesting analysis of how the industry has dealt with popular critiques, the funeral reform movement, and government attempts to regulate funeral practices. Finally, Suzanne Smith's exploration of the African American way of death in *To Serve the Living* (2010) acknowledges the funeral home as a physical space but focuses exclusively on the role played by Black-owned funeral homes in the civil rights movement. Two additional works are worth mentioning. Prothero, *Purified by Fire*, looks exclusively at the practice of cremation and its emergence as an alternative to interment but pays little attention to the crematories themselves and none to the funeral home. Likewise, Sloane, *Is the Cemetery Dead?*, analyzes the present critique of traditional chemical-laden interment and manicured lawns of the cemetery and the emergence of more environmentally friendly burial practices.

8. The best-known critique of the industry and the one with which Gary Laderman is preoccupied is Jessica Mitford's *The American Way of Death* (1963), which changed the way Americans viewed what was already a maligned industry. Both

Mitford's best-selling work and an earlier assault by Leroy Bowman, *The American Funeral: A Study in Guilt, Extravagance, and Sublimity* (1959), mix history with an exposé of industry practices. Both offer insight into the controversies that have historically dogged funeral directors. One thing that stands out in the historiography of American deathcare is that even well-researched and well-written histories take sides in the debate over the economics of funeralization and funeral reform. While social critics such as Mitford and Bowman have criticized what they saw as the commodification of death along with manipulative and unethical practices within the industry, others have felt compelled to come to the industry's defense. The history of American deathcare is hotly contested and highly charged, with unbiased analysis frequently replaced by either critique or apology. There are exceptions, such as Wells's *Facing the 'King of Terrors'* and Farrell's *Inventing the American Way of Death*, while Laderman is shamelessly profuneral. He doesn't attempt to hide his disdain for Mitford, whose bitter indictment of the industry followed a century of criticism within the popular press.

9. Farrell, *Inventing the American Way of Death, 1830–1920*, 10.
10. Laderman, *Rest in Peace*, 18.
11. I am referring to an increase in the number of deaths taking place in hospitals during the interwar period. See Abel, "In the Last Stages of Irremediable Disease."
12. Farrell, *Inventing the American Way of Death*, 175.
13. Laderman, *Rest in Peace*, 5.
14. Bowman, *The American Funeral*, 113–14.
15. Habenstein and Lamers, *The History of American Funeral Directing*, 569–70.
16. For a better understanding of how domestic space was changing during the early decades of the twentieth century, I look to previous studies within the field of vernacular architecture. Gwendolyn Wright and Clifford Clark have both written extensively about modern housing ideals during the first quarter of the twentieth century, housing ideals that were ultimately rejected by funeral directors. In *Moralism and the Model Home* (1980) and *Building the Dream* (1981), Wright explores how simplicity and informality emerged as key components of the new domestic vision articulated by architects, builders, and critics during the first quarter of the twentieth century, an idea that is echoed in monographs such as Clay Lancaster's "The American Bungalow." Similarly, Clark's *The American Family Home, 1800–1960* (1986) traces the development of middle-class suburban housing and single-family detached dwellings and sheds light on the developments that shaped the new structures that predominated on the eve of the shift from home funeral to funeral home.
17. Ames, *Death in the Dining Room & Other Tales of Victorian Culture*, 7–43.
18. Consumers accepted the residential funeral home as a retail space from the moment it appeared.
19. Grier, *Culture & Comfort*, 52.
20. See Smith, *To Serve the Living*, 82–83.
21. McCracken, *Culture and Consumption*, 77.
22. McCracken, 79.

23. This phrase has been used in funeral home advertising for at least half a century if not longer. I first encountered it on a matchbook cover produced by the Sampson Hall Funeral Home (now the Sampson-Hickey-Grenier Funeral & Cremation Service) in Brockton, Massachusetts. The cover has the phrase above an artist's rendering of the funeral home.

24. Twenty years of scholarship on the rise of American consumer culture provide a set of interpretive tools to help decipher funeral home advertisements along with valuable insight into the retail context within which funeral directors chose mansions. Works such as William Leach's *Land of Desire* (1993), Gary Cross's *An All Consuming Century* (2000), and Lizabeth Cohen's *A Consumer's Republic* (2003) explore the spread of mass consumption and democratized luxury over the course of the twentieth century.

25. For further reading on Gilded Age public parlors, lounges, and commercial spaces, see Benson, *Counter Cultures*; Schlereth, *Victorian America*; Leach, *Land of Desire*; Groth, *Living Downtown*; Cross, *An All Consuming Century*; Whitaker, *Service and Style*; Sandoval-Strausz, *Hotel*; Fenske, *The Skyscraper and the City*; and Howard, *From Main Street to Mall*.

26. This was the phrase used repeatedly by judges in their formal written opinions.

CHAPTER 1. DEATH DOWNTOWN

1. "Klaehn & Melching Have Moved into Their Elegant New Undertaking Parlors on Washington Boulevard East," *Fort Wayne Daily News*, June 21, 1913, 5.

2. "Finest and Best Equipped Undertaking Establishment in the Middle West," *Fort Wayne Journal-Gazette*, June 22, 1913, 30.

3. "Klaehn & Melching," 5.

4. "Klaehn & Melching," 5.

5. "J. C. Peltier: Oldest and Most Prominent Undertaking and Embalming Concern in the State," *Fort Wayne Journal-Gazette*, March 18, 1908, 12.

6. As late as the 1880s, there were still instances in which undertaking continued as a sideline to other lines of business. In 1887, for example, W. H. Mague operated a large livery stable on Chestnut Street in West Newton, Massachusetts. His two-story edifice, measuring 40 × 140 feet, was able to accommodate "sixty horses and a large number of vehicles." He employed ten grooms, furnished "teams and stylish turnouts of all kinds and for all occasions," and ran hacks "to and from all trains arriving at the West Newton and Auburndale stations." Horses were boarded at his stable by the day, week, or month. In addition, Mague also conducted "the business of general undertaker and funeral director." See *Leading Manufacturers and Merchants of Eastern Massachusetts: Historical and Descriptive Review of the Industrial Enterprises of Bristol, Plymouth, Norfolk, and Middlesex Counties* (New York: International Publishing Company, 1887), 236, http://www .archive.org/details/leadingmanufactu00newy. For further reading on undertaking as a sideline to cabinetmaking and the livery stable, see Berg, *The Confessions of an Undertaker*; Farrell, *Inventing the American Way of Death, 1830–1920*; Haben-

stein and Lamers, *The History of American Funeral Directing*; Laderman, *The Sacred Remains*; and Wells, *Facing the 'King of Terrors.'*

7. "Many undertakers," noted one observer in 1920, "or funeral directors, as those in the field prefer to be known, conduct furniture stores in connection with their establishments, this being true principally in the smaller communities. In the small towns and villages the amount of work to be done by the funeral director is limited, so that furniture is handled as a logical side-line." See *Crain's Market Data Book and Directory of Class, Trade, and Technical Publications* (Chicago: G. D. Crain, Jr., 1920), 195.

8. Habenstein and Lamers, *History of American Funeral Directing*, 394.

9. *Westcott v. Middleton*, 11 A. 490 (N.J. 1887); and "Can't Stand the Coffins: Mr. Westcott of Camden Complains of an Undertaker's Shop," *New York Times*, December 10, 1887, 1.

10. *Rowland v. Miller*, 15 N.Y.S. 701 (N.Y. Misc. 1891).

11. *Rowland v. Miller*, 1891.

12. *Rowland v. Miller*, 1891.

13. *Rowland v. Miller*, 1891.

14. *Rowland v. Miller*, 34 N.E. 765 (N.Y. 1893). The real problem was the presence on the premises of dead bodies. In the end, McAdam upheld the ruling of the lower court judge, who stipulated that the Taylor Company could sell coffins and use its chapel for legitimate worship but was enjoined from operating a morgue, performing autopsies, preparing dead bodies, and conducting funeral services at which the deceased was present.

15. *Rowland v. Miller*, 1893.

16. *Rowland v. Miller*, 1893.

17. *Rowland v. Miller*, 1893.

18. *Rowland v. Miller*, 1893.

19. "Finney Undertaking Parlors," *Oakland Tribune*, January 20, 1906, 17.

20. "City Has Modern Funeral Home," *Capital Times*, February 28, 1923, 10.

21. "A Model Undertaking Establishment," *Kansas City Star*, November 15, 1904, 2.

22. Richings, *Evidence of Progress among Colored People*, 488–89.

23. Pipkin, *The Story of a Rising Race*, 177.

24. "Jordan Marsh & Co.," *Boston Globe*, March 21, 1899, 7.

25. "Brevities," *The Argus*, May 8, 1884, 1.

26. "Howard Wolf's New Undertaking Rooms," *Democratic Standard*, September 1, 1905, 5.

27. "Display Room and Chapel," *Lock Haven Express*, August 13, 1909, 4.

28. "City In General," *Fort Wayne Daily Gazette*, July 3, 1879, 4.

29. "Dust to Dust. The Requirements of the Dead—The Mode of Burial in Civilized and Uncivilized Countries," *Fort Wayne Gazette*, March 18, 1883, 6.

30. "A Leading Undertaking Establishment," *Oxnard Courier*, December 12, 1913, 6.

31. "Late Undertaking: Many Changes Have Been Made in the Business," *Portsmouth Daily Herald*, April 16, 1906, 3.

32. "Late Undertaking," 3.

33. "New Undertaking Rooms," *Saint Albans Daily Messenger*, October 8, 1892, 6.

34. "The Sheeted Dead: There Are Styles in Coffins and Caskets as There Are in Hats; An Undertaker Has to Keep Pace with the Times as Well as the Customer; A Visit to a Fashionable Establishment, Metal and Rosewood Caskets Compared," *Fort Wayne Gazette*, July 13, 1883, 10.

35. "Greeks Hold Funeral," *Portsmouth Times*, July 1, 1911, 8.

36. "A Model Establishment: Trueman & Woodrow's New Undertaking Parlors," *Evening Times*, May 28, 1887, 3.

37. "A Model Establishment, 3."

38. There is widespread agreement among historians of American deathways that the shift from home funeral to funeral home took place sometime between 1925 and midcentury. A church funeral, moreover, did not preclude a viewing at the home of the deceased. See Bowman, *The American Funeral*, 17; Farrell, *Inventing the American Way of Death*, 172, 209; Habenstein and Lamers, *History of American Funeral Directing*, 570; Laderman, *Rest in Peace*, 19, 24; Pine, *Caretaker of the Dead*, 17–18; and Wells, *Facing the 'King of Terrors,'* 261–262, 273.

39. Berg, *Confessions*, 40.

40. "New Undertaking Parlors," *San Francisco Bulletin*, March 16, 1889, 7.

41. *Indianapolis of To-Day* (Indianapolis: Consolidated Illustrating Company, 1896), 207.

42. "An Elegant Outfit," *New Castle News*, October 5, 1898, 2.

43. "New Parlors in Boise," *Idaho Statesman*, November 5, 1906, 4, http://www.newspaerarchive.com.

44. "Build Burial Chapel: Two Undertaking Firms Rear Structure New for This City," *Omaha World Herald*, February 3, 1907, 1.

45. Richings, *Evidence of Progress*, 269–70.

46. "Colored Director's Fine Establishment in Gary, Indiana," *American Funeral Director*, 49, no. 4 (1926): 56. Historian Suzanne Smith points out that Black undertakers "regularly rented out rooms in their funeral homes to secret societies and fraternal orders for meetings and social events." However, she also points out instances in which Black undertaking parlors housed illicit activities such as gambling and bootlegging that formed the core of an underground economy. See Smith, Smith, *To Serve the Living*, 90, 95.

47. "The New Home of the Murray-Smith Co.," *Grand Rapids Furniture Record*, 29, no. 7 (1914): 56.

48. *Indianapolis of To-Day*, 150.

49. Richings, *Evidence of Progress*, 269–70.

50. "Malloy Remodeling: When Completed Will Be a Modern and Sanitary Establishment," *Galveston Daily News*, April 10, 1910, 15.

51. "Dillon & Smith's Nice Undertaking Parlors," *Cleburne Morning Review*, November 24, 1912, 3.

52. *Manufacturing and Mercantile Resources of Indianapolis, Indiana: A Review of Its Manufacturing, Mercantile & General Business Interests, Advantageous Location, to Which Is Added a Historical and Statistical Sketch of Its Rise and Progress* (1883), 593.

53. *Quarter-Century's Progress of New Jersey's Leading Manufacturing Centres* (New York: International Publishing Company, 1887), 150.

54. "Fine Building Being Erected," *Evening Times*, May 27, 1911, 7.

55. "Hileman & Gindt's New Undertaking Establishment," *Waterloo Evening Courier*, January 20, 1913, 11.

56. "Finest and Best Equipped," 30.

57. "Wilder to Build Chapel Here: Undertaker to Make Improvements in Undertaking Parlors on 25th Avenue," *Daily Herald*, December 10, 1913, 2.

58. *Marion Daily Star*, March 20, 1915, 2.

59. An 1896 article on current undertaking practices in the *Springfield Sunday Republican* declared that the "embalming and laying out require much skill. Both are generally done at the house where the person dies." See "The Work of the Undertaker. Styles of Burying Now in Vogue," *Springfield Sunday Republican*, November 8, 1896, 8. According to Charles Berg, deathbed embalming was still practiced as late as 1920. "When the body is to be prepared at the residence of the deceased, a room should be selected that will permit of being closed, and where the family will not have to pass in and out." See Berg, *Confessions*, 64.

60. "Modern Establishment Is the One Now Conducted by Undertaker Harrington," *Kalamazoo Gazette*, August 5, 1900, 8.

61. "Fine Building Being Erected," 7.

62. "Malloy Remodeling," 15.

63. "Finest and Best Equipped," 30.

64. "Build Burial Chapel," 1.

65. "Finney Undertaking Parlors," 17.

66. "Finest and Best Equipped," 30.

67. "City Has Modern Funeral Home," 10.

68. "Formal Opening of Decatur's New Funeral Home," *Decatur Sunday Review*, November 16, 1924, 10.

69. "A Real Funeral Home with Efficient Services in Every Respect," *Decatur Review*, November 12, 1924, 11.

70. Merze M. Seeburgher, "Pretty Nursery for Children's Funerals," *American Funeral Director*, 44, no. 5 (1921): 245.

71. *Indianapolis Star*, September 3, 1908, 10.

72. "Formal Opening of Decatur's New Funeral Home," 9.

73. "Build Burial Chapel," 1.

74. "City Has Modern Funeral Home," 10.

75. "Funeral Homes" (Advertisement), *Pacific Coast Undertaker* 7, no. 1 (1921): 29.

76. "Beffel Undertaking Establishment Opens: New Building on Sixth St. Is Conveniently Arranged and Artistic," *Racine Journal-News*, December 6, 1913, 5.

77. "New Firm Is Well Equipped," *Evening News*, July 29, 1907, 4.

78. "New Parlors in Boise," 4.

79. "Formal Opening of Decatur's New Funeral Home," 9.

80. "Deaths," *Trenton Evening Times*, July 20, 1909, 3.

81. "Home and Foreign Gossip," *Indian Journal*, November 21, 1878, 3.

82. "A Fine Testimonial: Dedication of the Bigelow Chapel at the Newton Cemetery," *Boston Daily Globe*, September 27, 1885, 5.

83. *Weekly Telegraph*, March 11, 1896, 12.

84. "New Chapel at Vale Cemetery," *Park and Cemetery and Landscape Gardening*, 33, no. (1923): 43.

85. Stephen Prothero points out that while "independent crematories dominated into the 1890s," the cemetery crematory eventually "emerged as the dominant American model." See Prothero, *Purified by Fire*, 118–19.

86. "The Cremation Idea," *Carroll Sentinel*, July 7, 1892, 1. Prothero puts the number at twenty-five in 1900. See Prothero, *Purified by Fire*, 127.

87. Cobb, *A Quarter Century of Cremation in North America*, 32–33.

88. Cobb, 35.

89. Similar conflicts erupted elsewhere. In Detroit, the Michigan Cremation Association attempted to erect a crematorium shortly after its founding in 1885, but "progress was interfered with through various obstacles. The land first selected had to be relinquished on account of opposition from surrounding property owners, and another location substituted." See Cobb, *Quarter Century of Cremation*, 36, 41.

90. Cobb, *Quarter Century of Cremation*, 36.

91. Cobb, 36–37.

92. Prothero, *Purified by Fire*, 114–15.

93. Cobb, *Quarter Century of Cremation*, 37–38.

94. Prothero puts the cremation rate at 1 percent by the early 1920s, and by the early 1930s it had reached 2 percent. See Prothero, *Purified by Fire*, 128.

95. Prothero, *Purified by Fire*, 132–42.

96. "Build Burial Chapel," 1.

97. "Missing Links," *Mountain Democrat*, January 17, 1890, 3. See also "Odds and Ends," *Logansport Pharos*, December 9, 1890, 3.

98. *Indianapolis of To-Day*, 207.

99. "The Funeral of Dr. M. Perl Is Largely Attended by Prominent Citizens," *Galveston Daily News*, January 3, 1895, 3.

100. "Mortuary Chapels," *Sacramento Daily Record-Union*, October 21, 1885, 2.

101. "Funeral Bills Reduced," *Altoona Herald*, November 16, 1916, 4.

102. It is important to point out that prior to the 1930s, the number of Americans dying in hospitals was relatively small, with most people dying at home. During the early decades of the twentieth century, private hospitals routinely refused terminal cases. Even public hospitals often discharged dying patients to almshouses and chronic care facilities. Hospital architect Edward F. Stevens wrote in 1918 that the "people are realizing that the hospital is built to benefit humanity and not to afford a place in which to die." Stevens, *The American Hospital of the Twentieth Century*, 1. See also Abel, "In the Last Stages of Irremediable Disease," 33, 44.

103. "Modern Funeral Home of Getz & Cahill," *Fort Wayne Journal-Gazette*, June 30, 1920, 10.

104. "Modern Funeral Home of Getz & Cahill, 10."

105. "Modern Funeral Home of Getz & Cahill, 10."

106. In 1893, the Indianapolis firm Flanner & Buchanan moved from the downtown into a two-and-a-half-story brick house in an area at the edge of the downtown. It was very likely the first in the state to operate a funeral establishment from a converted residential dwelling. The firm remained in that location for twenty years before returning to the downtown with the construction of a new purpose-built mortuary.

107. "Hisey & Titus Establish 'Funeral Home' as a New Institution for Indianapolis," *Indianapolis Star*, May 17, 1916, 6.

108. For further reading on the appearance and makeup of American business districts, see Longstreth, *The Buildings of Main Street*.

109. Longstreth, 13.

110. Longstreth, 15.

111. Relph, *The Modern Urban Landscape*, 81–82.

112. "Quietness and Solitude," *Daily Northwestern*, January 22, 1923, 7.

113. "Krohn and Ernser, Inc., to Open New Funeral Establishment," *Wisconsin Rapids Daily Tribune*, April 25, 1928, 7.

CHAPTER 2. A NEW DEPARTURE

1. "New McDonough Funeral Home Is Opened by Morticians to Public Inspection," *Lowell Sun*, October 11, 1923, 4.

2. "New McDonough Funeral Home Is Opened," 5.

3. "Residential Funeral Parlors Are in Vogue," *American Funeral Director* 44, no. 6 (1921): 269.

4. "In relatively recent years," noted the owners of the Griesmer-Grim Funeral Home in Hamilton, Ohio, in 1928, "the Funeral Home has become an inseparable fixture of the business of the mortician. This dates from a period about the time of the World War. At least this is a practical approximation of the period of the time when the Funeral Home was to be found nowhere save, possibly, in the largest cities." See "Funeral Home Becomes Adjunct to Mortician, Says Griesmer-Grim Co.," *Hamilton Daily News*, February 18, 1928, 11.

5. "Hisey & Titus Establish 'Funeral Home' as a New Institution for Indianapolis," *Indianapolis Star*, May 17, 1916, 6.

6. *Pictorial and Biographical Memoirs of Elkhart and St. Joseph Counties Indiana* (Chicago: Goodspeed Brothers, 1893), 53.

7. "An Innovation for Elkhart," *Elkhart Daily Review*, June 18, 1909, 1.

8. "Beautiful Funeral Parlors Established by Thomas B. Mooney," *Catholic Journal*, September 14, 1906, 15.

9. Morgues and Undertakers' Establishments, Location of, Chicago, IL (Ord. November 4, 1912). Los Angeles had a similar ordinance by 1904, limiting the location of undertaking establishments to the business sections of the city. Restrictions concerning the proximity of residential dwellings were not specifically included, however. See Ordinance No. 9695, enacted July 13, 1904. Cited in *Brown v. Los Angeles*, 192 P. 716 (Cal. 1920).

10. *Saier v. Joy*, 164 N.W. 507 (Mich. 1917).

11. *Osborn v. Shreveport*, 79 So. 542 (La. 1918).

12. "Review of Court Case Involving Right to Locate Mortuary in Residence District," *American Funeral Director* 51, no. 7 (1928), 39.

13. "Modern Funeral Home Elaborate Example," *American Funeral Director* 43, no. 2 (1920): 70.

14. Allen P. Child, "Proposed Building Zones in Portland, Ore.," *American Funeral Director* 43, no. 2 (1920): 83.

15. "Modern Funeral Homes," *American Funeral Director* 43, no. 2 (1920): 54.

16. Callaway, *The Art of Funeral Directing*, 194–95.

17. "Albert Buenneke," *Oelwein Register*, October 29, 1921, 2.

18. "A. F. Koller Furniture and Undertaking," *News-Comet* (East Berlin, PA), October 30, 1931, 8.

19. Deathcare historians Robert Habenstein and William Lamers noted in 1955 that "at mid-20th century, about one-fifth of all funeral establishments are combination operations, and these, it should be noted, are more likely to be found in the rural and small town areas of the country." Habenstein and Lamers, *History of American Funeral Directing*, 469.

20. "The Johnson & Wilkins Home Provides All Possible Service—Beautiful Place on Delaware Avenue," *American Funeral Director* 44, no. 12 (1921): 630.

21. "The Johnson & Wilkins Home Provides All Possible Service."

22. "Opens New Funeral Home in Convenient Location," *Lowell Sun*, April 16, 1929, 3.

23. "New Undertaking Firm for San Jose," *Evening News*, June 1, 1910, 4.

24. Wilber M. Krieger, "The Funeral Industry To-Day," *American Funeral Director* 53, no. 6 (1930): 41.

25. "Modern Idea in Undertaking Establishments," *American Funeral Director* 43, no. 12 (1920): 435.

26. "Funeral Industry To-Day," 41.

27. Warfield Webb, "Modern Funeral Service in Highest Form," *American Funeral Director* 43, no. 9 (1920): 418.

28. "Modern Idea in Undertaking Establishments," 435.

29. "Modern Funeral Service," 418.

30. "Opening of Ford & Douglas New Funeral Home This Week," *Gastonia Daily Gazette*, May 26, 1926, 6.

31. Callaway, *Art of Funeral Directing*, 189.

32. Frayser Hinton, "Progress in Funeral Directing," *American Funeral Director* 49, no. 2 (1926): 54.

33. "Residential Funeral Parlors Are in Vogue," 269.

34. Rising property values in central business districts meant higher rents for funeral directors leasing space in downtown buildings. There can be no doubt that in addition to the desire to escape noise and congestion, economic incentives were part of the equation as more and more undertakers sought quarters beyond the confines of the old downtown. See John T. Bartlett, "Considering Mortuary History in Greater Kansas City, Mo., and Kansas," *American Funeral Director* 49, no. 1 (1926): 44.

35. Habenstein and Lamers, *History of American Funeral Directing*, 394.

36. Berg, *The Confessions of an Undertaker*, 39.

37. "Beautiful Funeral Home in the North-West," *American Funeral Director* 44, no. 2 (1921): 69.

38. "Beautiful Funeral Home in the North-West," 69.

39. "The Ideal Funeral Home," *American Funeral Director* 43, no. 8 (1920): 369.

40. "The Ideal Funeral Home," 369.

41. "Hisey & Titus," 6.

42. *Indianapolis Star*, September 3, 1908, 10; and "City Has Modern Funeral Home," *Capital Times*, February 28, 1923, 10.

43. "The Griesmer-Grim Company," *Hamilton Evening Journal*, September 11, 1924, 20.

44. "Accommodations," *Sheboygan Press*, October 7, 1933, 6.

45. "Most Suitable," *Hamilton Evening Journal*, September 9,1929, 5.

46. "Funeral Home," *Logansport, Indiana, Pharos-Tribune*, December 5, 1925, 6.

47. "Announcing the Opening of Ehlers New Funeral Home," *Dunkirk Evening Observer*, July 10, 1930, 10.

48. "Firm Has Best of Facilities: Funeral Home on East Center Street is Ideally Located," *Star, Marion, Ohio*, June 6, 1931, 9.

49. "Modern Funeral Service," 418.

50. "Modern Funeral Service, 418."

51. Warfield Webb, "Funeral Home in Historic Kentucky Mansion," *American Funeral Director* 44, no. 3 (1921): 128.

52. See Relph, *The Modern Urban Landscape*, 81–82; Longstreth, *City Center to Regional Mall*, 13–20.

53. "Roberts-Blue to Have New Home," *Emporia Gazette*, April 26, 1938, 1.

54. "Announcing the Opening of the Daehler Funeral Home," *Portsmouth Daily Times*, February 3, 1925, 8.

55. "You Are Cordially Invited to Visit the New Home of the Thorpe J. Gordon Funeral Service," *Jefferson City Post-Tribune*, August 18, 1938, 10.

56. See "Dawson & Tanner Undertaking Firm Entering into Eighth Year of Business in Jefferson City," *Daily Capital News and Post-Tribune*, December 13, 1931, 3-B; and "Wrenn-Yeatts Open Modern Funeral Home on North Side," *Bee, Danville, Va.*, March 7, 1936, 4.

57. By 1909, motorized hearses were, according to one source, used by roughly half a dozen undertakers in the United States. See "Taxicabs for Funerals," *Commercial Vehicle* 4, no. 6 (1909): 152.

58. "Says Chapel Idea is Unsympathetic and Cold," *American Funeral Director* 44, no. 7 (1921): 354.

59. "Says Chapel Idea is Unsympathetic and Cold, " 354.

60. "Says Chapel Idea is Unsympathetic and Cold," 354.

61. Drake and Cayton, *Black Metropolis*, 456–57.

62. For more information on the James Bailey House/M. Marshall Blake Funeral Home, see Adams and Rocheleau, *Harlem Lost and Found*, 62–66; Christopher Gray, "Streetscapes/150th Street and St. Nicholas Place: 1888 Mansion Built by

the Bailey of Barnum & Bailey; It's a Spectacularly Intact, but Unoccupied, Victorian Showplace," *New York Times*, April 8, 2001, RE5; and Adams, "Mulattos, Mammies and Maids."

63. Drake and Cayton, *Black Metropolis*, 457.

64. Allan Morrison, "Monopoly in Death," *Negro Digest* 5, no. 3 (1947): 57–58.

65. His earlier attempt in 1930 to open up a full-fledged funeral home was thwarted by his neighbors. On his second try he eliminated both the chapel and the embalming room, thus eliminating any possible nuisance. See *Qualls v. Memphis*, 15 Tenn. App. 575 (Tenn. App. 1932) and *Memphis v. Qualls*, 64 S. W. 2d 548 (Tenn. App. 1933).

66. "Death Is Big Business," *Ebony* 8, no. 5 (1953): 17.

67. "You and Your Friends Are Most Cordially Invited," *Nashville Globe*, December 25, 1908, 5.

68. Smith, *To Serve the Living*, 90.

69. "Most Cordially Invited," 5.

70. Smith, *To Serve the Living*, 114, 204, 207.

71. Dowd, *The Negro in American Life*, 35–36.

72. Dowd, 33.

73. "Modern Funeral Service," 418.

74. "Modern Funeral Service," 418.

75. "Beauty an Important Consideration in Planning a Funeral Home," *American Funeral Director* 51, no. 1 (1928): 46.

76. *Modesto Evening News*, March 11, 1922, 12.

77. "Getting the Public to Visit Your Mortuary," *American Funeral Director* 53, no. 12 (1930): 35.

78. "A New Angle on Zoning," *American Funeral Director* 51, no. 1 (1928): 35.

79. Elmo Scott Watson, "Men's Styles throughout the Ages," *Fayette County Leader*, March 22, 1928, 2.

80. Walter A. Dyer, "The Passing of the Parlor Suite," *Art World* 2, no. 9 (1917): 565.

81. "Modernizing Old Residence into a Funeral Home," *American Funeral Director* 44, no. 10 (1921): 498–99.

82. "Ford Undertaking Co. Leases Sloan Home," *Gastonia Daily Gazette*, March 6, 1926, 1.

83. "Ideal Funeral Home," 369.

84. "Modern Funeral Service," 418.

85. Jack Wooten, "Finds Residence District Best for Funeral Home," *American Funeral Director* 49, no. 4 (1926): 38.

86. *Goodrich v. Starrett*, 184 P. 220 (Wash. 1919).

87. "New Heinrichs Funeral Home at 712 East High Street Is Now Complete," *Daily Capital News and Post-Tribune*, January 24, 1932, 8-A.

88. "Morticians in New Quarters. Loudermilk-Sparkman Co. Take Over Former Belo Mansion," *Dallas Morning News*, June 27, 1926, 1.

89. The firm spent the equivalent of over $420,000 in 2023 dollars.

90. "New Ramm Funeral Home to Have Formal Opening Two Days," *Sheboygan Press*, May 17, 1929, 6.
91. "Trail Mansion to Be Left Intact Despite Many Modern Improvements," *Frederick Post*, July 14, 1939, 9.
92. "McDonough Funeral Home," 4–5.
93. "Robert H. Kroos Announces the Opening of His Beautiful New Building," *Sheboygan Press*, February 12, 1925, 9.
94. "Formal Opening Robert H. Kroos Funeral Home," *Sheboygan Press*, February 12, 1925, 11.
95. "New Malloy Funeral Home Now Open," *Galveston Daily News*, August 17, 1930, 11.
96. Callaway, *Art of Funeral Directing*," 194.
97. Callaway, 189.
98. "A modest sign," Callaway counseled, "should indicate the firm's name and the business." See Callaway, *Art of Funeral Directing*, 191.
99. Webb, "Funeral Home in Historic Kentucky Mansion," 128.
100. "Ford & Douglas New Funeral Home," 6.
101. Callaway, *Art of Funeral Directing*, 190.
102. "The Johnson & Wilkins Home," 631.
103. "Invite Public to New Funeral Home Saturday," *Gettysburg Times*, September 6, 1928, 1.
104. "Ford & Douglas New Funeral Home," 6.
105. "New Baker Mortuary Has Informal Opening Tomorrow," *Wisconsin Rapids Daily Tribune*, September 23, 1927, 5.
106. "McDonough Funeral Home," 5.
107. "Grand Formal Re-opening," 5. By the 1920s this system of displaying caskets was largely obsolete. See Callaway, *Art of Funeral Directing*, 192.
108. "The Modern Riemann Funeral Home in Gulfport, Miss." *American Funeral Director* 51, no. 2 (1928): 41.
109. "From Mansion to Mortuary," *American Funeral Director* 53, no. 9 (1930): 44.
110. "Ford & Douglas New Funeral Home," 7.
111. Webb, "Funeral Home in Historic Kentucky Mansion," 129.
112. "Regardless," *Newark Advocate*," January 21, 1957, 2.
113. "Modern Idea in Undertaking Establishments," *American Funeral Director* 43, no. 12 (1920): 435.
114. Callaway, *Art of Funeral Directing*, 191.
115. Berg, *Confessions*, 40
116. "Funeral Home Planning," *American Funeral Director* 54, no. 12 (1931): 43.
117. "New Funeral Home," 1.
118. "Chapel Idea Is Unsympathetic," 355.
119. "Ramm Funeral Home," 6.
120. "Modern Funeral Service in Highest Form," 419.
121. "The Handsome Boland Mortuary—One of the 'Show Places' of Peoria," *American Funeral Director* 49, no. 10 (1926): 32.

328   Notes to Pages 100–111

122. "Beauty an Important Consideration," 47–48.
123. "McDonough Funeral Home," 5.
124. "McDonough Funeral Home," 5.
125. "One Will Find," *Lowell Sun*, September 12, 1925, 3.
126. "An Uncommon Combination," *Lowell Sun*, November 20, 1925, 3.
127. *Cambridge City Tribune*, September 10, 1925, 1.
128. "The Highest Degree," *Sheboygan Press*, June 12, 1925, 10.
129. "Nowhere Else," *Mansfield News*, November 26, 1926, 5.
130. "Mansion to Mortuary," 43.
131. "A Mortuary for the 50 to 100 Case Operator," *American Funeral Director* 64, no. 8 (1941): 24.
132. "Modern Funeral Service," 419.
133. "Handsome Boland Mortuary," 31–32.
134. Wooten, "Residence District Best," 38.
135. M. J. Phillips, "Being Sympathetic Won a Fine Business for J. Ed. Phillips, Glendale, Cal.," *American Funeral Director* 49, no. 1 (1926): 33.
136. "Chapel Idea Is Unsympathetic," 355.
137. "Handsome New Corken Funeral Home Opened in Cincinnati," *American Funeral Director* 49, no. 10 (1926): 40.
138. Phillips, "Being Sympathetic," 33.
139. "Malloy Funeral Home," 11.
140. "Taking the Gloom out of the Funeral Home," *American Funeral Director* 49, no. 12 (1926): 40.
141. Harold F. Ashe, "W. B. Coon's New Funeral Home," *American Funeral Director* 49, no. 4 (1926): 55.
142. Phillips, "Being Sympathetic," 33.
143. Callaway, *Art of Funeral Directing*, 190–91.
144. Callaway, 211.
145. "Ford & Douglas New Funeral Home," 6.
146. Guest rooms were not absent from downtown funeral parlors. The purpose-built Moran Funeral Home, which opened in 1924 in downtown Decatur, Illinois, included "two spare bed rooms . . . for the use of out-of-town mourners who do not wish to go to a hotel, preferring to be in the same house with their dead." See "Formal Opening of Decatur's New Funeral Home," *Decatur Sunday Review*, November 16, 1924, 10.
147. Berg, *Confessions*, 41.
148. "Hisey & Titus," 6.
149. "The Johnson & Wilkins Home," 630–31.
150. "McDonough Funeral Home," 5.
151. "The Things That Are Desired," *Lowell Sun*, August 21, 1925, 3.
152. Callaway, *Art of Funeral Directing*, 190.
153. "Mansion to Mortuary," 44.
154. "Remodeled Residence Now a Beautiful and Well-Maintained Funeral Home," *American Funeral Director* 51, no. 9 (1928): 42.

155. "New Baker Mortuary," 5.

156. *Cambridge City Tribune*, 1.

157. Callaway, *Art of Funeral Directing*, 190.

158. "Right in the Heart of Things," *American Funeral Director* 54, no. 5 (1931): 45.

159. "McDonough Funeral Home," 5.

160. "Sumrall-O'Quinn Funeral Home Retains Atmosphere Suggestive of Real Home," *Laurel Leader-Call*, June 3, 1935, 6.

161. The Daehler Mortuary in Portsmouth, Ohio, included "a most modern crematory" on-site when it opened in 1925. See "Announcing the Opening of the Daehler Funeral Home," *Portsmouth Daily Times*, February 3, 1925, 8. When the plans for the elaborate Nichols Mortuary in Bozeman, Montana, were announced in August 1937, the notice mentioned both a crematory and a mausoleum. See "Plan New Mortuary and Crematory for Bozeman Location," *Helena Daily Independent*, August 21, 1937, 6.

162. Callaway, *Art of Funeral Directing*, 195–96.

163. "McDonough Funeral Home," 5.

164. "We Offer Our Services in Times of Sorrow," *Racine (Wis.) Journal-News*, March 11, 1922, 74.

165. "Barlow Undertaking Establishment Moves into New Quarters," *Charleston Daily Mail*, November 12, 1933, 6.

166. "McDonough Funeral Home," 5.

167. "New Funeral Home," 1.

168. "Modern Idea," 436.

169. "What Is a Funeral Home?," *American Funeral Director* 53, no. 8 (1930): 44.

170. Callaway, *Art of Funeral Directing*, 199, 205.

171. "Occupied," *Lowell Sun*, March 28, 1933, 3. Virtually identical ads were run throughout the 1930s by several other funeral directors in Pennsylvania and New York.

172. "Another Step Forward to Higher American Standards Bring New Low Funeral Prices," *Hutchinson, Kansas, News-Herald*, October 16, 1938, 3.

173. *American Funeral Director* 49, no. 3 (1926): 47.

174. "Rome Was Not Built in a Day," *Las Vegas Daily Optic*, August 14, 1926, 6.

175. "The Need for a Modern Funeral Home," *Frederick Post*, November 19, 1935, 8.

176. "Beauty Becomes Even Greater When it Serves a Genuine Need . . . ," *Lubbock Avalanche-Journal*, March 14, 1943, 3.

177. *American Funeral Director* 49, no. 11 (1926): 74.

178. "What the Funeral Home Has to Offer," *American Funeral Director* 54, no. 4 (1931): 44.

179. "Handsome Boland Mortuary," 31.

180. "Dawson & Wikoff Funeral Home," *Decatur Herald*, July 31, 1927, 14.

181. "Homelike Comforts," *Decatur Daily Review*, March 19, 1925, 9.

182. "New Angle on Zoning," 35.

CHAPTER 3. A CONSTANT REMINDER OF DEATH

1. "Fight over Funeral Home Comes to End in Circuit Court," *La Crosse Tribune and Leader-Press*, July 20, 1921, 1.
2. There were exceptions, of course. During the 1950s a notable countertrend was taking place in the neighborhood of Brooklyn Heights in New York City. See Osman, *The Invention of Brownstone Brooklyn*. For further reading on interwar suburban developments, see Gowans, *The Comfortable House*, 16–20.
3. "Attack Made in Court on Miller House," *La Crosse Tribune and Leader-Press*, July 19, 1921, 6.
4. "Attack Made in Court on Miller House," 6. One such home was "the palatial residence 'Pasadena,' owned by Mrs. Elsie Giles Scott," who lived next door. In the "immediate vicinity" were "other handsome and costly residences."
5. *Cunningham v. Miller*, 189 N.W. 531 (Wisc. 1922).
6. *Cunningham v. Miller*.
7. *Cunningham v. Miller*.
8. *Cunningham v. Miller*.
9. "Attack Made in Court on Miller House," 6.
10. "Attack Made in Court on Miller House," 6. The circuit court judge also noted that "dissections and autopsies are made in about five per cent of the cases handled." See *Cunningham v. Miller*.
11. *Cunningham v. Miller*.
12. *Cunningham v. Miller*.
13. *Cunningham v. Miller*.
14. *Cunningham v. Miller*.
15. "Fight over Funeral Home," 1.
16. "Attack Made in Court on Miller House," 6.
17. "Attack Made in Court on Miller House," 6.
18. *Cunningham v. Miller*.
19. *Cunningham v. Miller*.
20. "Council Ends Lengthy Fight Friday Night," *La Crosse Tribune and Leader-Press*, September 11, 1920, 6.
21. "Helpless," *La Crosse Tribune and Leader-Press*, March 27, 1921, 3.
22. "Helpless," 3.
23. *Cunningham v. Miller*.
24. *Cunningham v. Miller*.
25. *Cunningham v. Miller*.
26. Although New Jersey's Court of Chancery had ruled almost a quarter century earlier in *Westcott v. Middleton*, a case extensively cited by undertakers challenging injunctions, that "the business of an undertaker is not a nuisance *per se*," the case did not address residential funeral homes. In the majority opinion for *Evergreen v. Densmore*, Justice J. Chadwick pointed out that the Westcott decision was of little use to proprietors of residential funeral homes because Middleton's establishment had been located downtown: "There, so far as the decision indicates, the

undertaking establishment was in the most populous section of the city. We may assume that it was not in a residence section, for the lower floor of the building occupied by the complainant was given over to business purposes, the upper floors only being occupied for residence purposes; and further, the establishment had been carried on without complaint for eleven years." See *Densmore v. Evergreen*, 112 Pac. 255 (Wash. 1910); and *Westcott v. Middleton*, 11 A. 490 (N. J. Ch. 1887).

27. *Densmore v. Evergreen.*

28. *Saier v. Joy*, 164 N.W. 507 (Mich. 1917).

29. *Saier v. Joy.*

30. *Cunningham v. Miller*; and *Higgins v. Bloch*, 104 So. 429 (Ala. 1925).

31. *Saier v. Joy.*

32. *Saier v. Joy.*

33. *Saier v. Joy.* The Louisiana Supreme Court told one undertaker making a similar claim in 1918 that that it was "not convinced that undertaking establishments, with morgues attached, were located in other cities in strictly residential districts." See *Osborn v. Shreveport*, 79 So. 542 (La. 1918).

34. *Cunningham v. Miller.*

35. Eschweiler argued that of the seven cases cited by the majority "as supporting the conclusion that the establishment and operation of an undertaking and embalming business in a residential district under such circumstances as here disclosed constitutes a nuisance," only two of them involved anything like the business described in the case at hand. Of the others, one each addressed "the erection of a hospital for the treatment of cancer," "the establishment of a gas works," and "the maintaining of dead bodies in an overground family tomb adjacent to plaintiff's residence," while another addressed "the proposed erection of an insane asylum;" and yet another addressed "the deposit of refuse from a starch factory polluting a river to the injury of a lower riparian owner." See *Cunningham v. Miller.*

36. *Higgins v. Bloch.*

37. *Goodrich v. Starrett*, 184 P. 220 (Wash. 1919).

38. *Harris v. Sutton*, 148 S.E. 403 (Ga. 1929).

39. *Dillon v. Moran*, 211 N.W. 67 (Mich. 1926).

40. *Laughlin v. Cooney*, 126 So. 864 (Ala. 1930).

41. *Laughlin v. Cooney.*

42. *Laughlin v. Cooney.*

43. *Laughlin v. Cooney.*

44. In at least one instance, the likelihood that "the conducting of funerals on their premises would cause traffic congestion in the adjoining streets" was one of the deciding factors weighing against the funeral home. See *Bevington v. Otte*, 273 N.W. 98 (Iowa Sup. 1937). A decade and a half later in Michigan, a similar concern was expressed by a group of Muskegon Heights residents, who argued that "the large crowds at the home and the coming and going of mourners will cause traffic and parking congestion so as to prevent the plaintiffs' free ingress and egress to their respective properties." The Michigan Supreme Court found the argument unconvincing but granted the injunction on other grounds. "There is

no probative value in any testimony," the court declared, "to show that a parking problem or traffic congestion will necessarily arise." See *Rockenbach v. Apostle*, 47 N.W.2d 636 (Mich. 1951). See also *Bragg v. Ives*, 140 S.E. 656 (Va. 1927); *Street v. Marshall*, 291 S.W. 494 (Mo. 1927); *Jordan v. Nesmith*, 269 P. 1096 (Okla. 1928); *Hatcher v. Hitchcock*, 281 P. 869 (Kan. 1929); *Haan v. Heath*, 296 P. 816 (Wash. 1931); *Lewis v. Mayor and City Council of Baltimore*, 164 A. 220 (Md. 1933); *Weinmann v. Miles*, 4 P.2d 437 (Kan.1931); *Arthur v. Virkler*, 258 N.Y.S. 886 (N.Y. Misc. 1932); *Albright v. Crim*, 185 N.E. 304 (Ind. App. 1933); *Fink v. Smith*, 36 P.2d 976 (Kan. 1934); *McGowan v. May*, 196 S.E. 705 (Ga. 1938 Ga); *Williams v. Montgomery*, 186 So. 302 (Miss. 1939); *Clutter v. Blankenship*, 144 S.W.2d 119 (Mo. 1940); *Davis v. Holmes*, 198 So. 25 (Miss. 1940); *Kundinger v. Bagnasco*, 298 N.W. 386 (Mich. 1941); *Smith v. Fairchild*, 10 So.2d 172 (Miss. 1942); *Fraser v. Parker*, 21 S.E.2d 577 (S.C. 1942); *Reiser v. Osborn*, 53 N.E.2d 545 (Ind. App. 1944); *Ullrich v. Maryland*, 46 A.2d 637 (Md. 1946); *Springfield v. Vancil*, 76 N.E.2d 471 (Ill. 1947); *Cassel v. Mayor and City Council of Baltimore*, 73 A.2d 486 (Md. 1950); *Jack v. Torrant; The Zoning Commission of the Town of Litchfield v. Torrant*, 71 A.2d 705 (Conn. 1950); *Rockenbach v. Apostle; Veal v. Leimkuehler*, 249 S.W.2d 491 (Mo. App. 1952); *Leffen v. Hurlburt-Glover Mortuary*, 257 S.W.2d 609 (Mo. 1953); *Mahoney v. Chicago*, 137 N.E.2d 37 (Ill. 1956); *Tripp v. Zoning Board of Review of the City of Pawtucket*, 123 A.2d. 144 (R.I. 1956); and *Whittle v. Board of Zoning Appeals of Baltimore County*, 125 A.2d. 41 (Md. 1956).

45. *Leland v. Turner*, 230 P. 1061 (Kan. 1924).

46. *Leland v. Turner.*

47. *Brown v. Arbuckle*, 198 P.2d 550 (Cal. App. 1948).

48. *Brown v. Arbuckle.*

49. During the 1930s many judges began citing Cooley on torts, which stated, "By what appears to be the weight of modern authority, . . . it is held that the location of such a business in a residential district is sufficiently objectionable to make it a nuisance. Thus it has been stated: The inherent nature of an undertaking establishment 'is such that, if located in a residential district, it will inevitably create an atmosphere detrimental to the use and enjoyment of residence property, produce material annoyance and inconvenience to the occupants of adjacent dwellings, and render them physically uncomfortable, and in the absence of a strong showing of public necessity, its location in such a district should not be permitted over the protests of those who would be materially injured thereby.'" See Cooley, *A Treatise on the Law of Torts, or, The Wrongs Which Arise Independently of Contract*, 180.

50. *Pearson v. Bonnie*, 272 S. W. 375 (Ky. 1925).

51. Although *Pearson v. Bonnie* was the most well-known decision refusing to enjoin a residential funeral home, there were others, such as *Meldhal v. Holberg*, 214 N. W. 802 (N. D. 1927), and *McCord v. Bond*, 165 S. E. 590 (Ga. 1932).

52. *Pearson v. Bonnie.*

53. *Pearson v. Bonnie.*

54. Berkeley, California, for example, had a primitive type of zoning regulation in place by March 1916. See Scott, *The San Francisco Bay Area*, 165.

55. "Between 1907 and 1917 over 100 towns undertook 'comprehensive planning'—half the 50 largest cities, 13 per cent of all with populations over 10,000." See Hancock, "Planners in the Changing American City, 1900–1940." By 1922, seventy-eight cities in the United States had adopted zoning regulations, and 75 percent of American cities with populations over 100,000 were zoned, with the smaller cities and towns far outnumbering the larger cities in zoning activity. See Mary T. Voorhees, "Zoning Activity in the United States," *Engineering News-Record*, 89, no. 13 (September 28, 1922): 519.

56. Scott, *San Francisco Bay Area*, 165. For further reading, see Scott, *American City Planning since 1890*.

57. *Euclid v. Amber*, 272 U. S. 365 (1926). See also *Osborn v. Shreveport*; *Brown v. Los Angeles*, 192 P. 716 (Cal. 1920); and *St. Paul v. Kessler*, 178 N. W. 171 (Minn. 1920). In other cases that dealt with ordinances of questionable validity, including *Tureman v. Ketterlin*, 263 S. W. 202 (Mo. 1924), and *Leland v. Turner*, the courts remained silent on the issue of their constitutionality. About these and other rulings on the validity of zoning, *Euclid v. Amber* stated, "The decisions of the state courts are numerous and conflicting; but those which broadly sustain the power greatly outnumber those which deny altogether or narrowly limit it; and it is very apparent that there is a constantly increasing tendency in the direction of the broader view."

58. *Meagher v. Kessler*, 179 N. W. 732 (Minn. 1920).

59. *St. Paul v. Kessler*.

60. *St. Paul v. Kessler*.

61. *Meagher v. Kessler*.

62. *Osborn v. Shreveport*. As early as 1912, Shreveport had amended its charter in order to authorize the city council to "prohibit and prevent" various businesses deemed offensive. Act 220 of 1912 stated that "all establishments where any nauseous or unwholesome business may be carried on shall be restricted to certain limits within the city, to be determined by the city council."

63. *Osborn v. Shreveport*.

64. *Osborn v. Shreveport*.

65. *Osborn v. Shreveport*.

66. *Brown v. Los Angeles*.

67. *Tucson v. Arizona Mortuary*, 272 P. 923 (Ariz. 1928).

68. Tucson didn't adopt a comprehensive zoning ordinance until 1930. See Sonnichsen, *Tucson*, 281.

69. *Tucson v. Arizona Mortuary*.

70. A similar situation unfolded in Amarillo, Texas, in 1926. Amarillo did not pass a comprehensive zoning ordinance until 1931. However, following the conversion of a dwelling in one of the city's best residential sections an ordinance was passed, which the undertaker was subsequently accused of violating. The Texas Court of Appeals argued that the business could be legally enjoined on the basis of the threat of contagion and its deleterious effect on the mental health of nearby homeowners. See *Blackburn v. Bishop*, 299 S. W. 264 (Tex. App. 1927); and Siegan, *Land Use without Zoning*, 73.

71. *Tucson v. Arizona Mortuary.*

72. *Tucson v. Arizona Mortuary.*

73. Hubbard and Hubbard, *Our Cities, To-Day and To-Morrow,* 357.

74. *Wasem v. Fargo,* 190 N. W. 546 (N. D. 1922).

75. *Wasem v. Fargo.*

76. *Wasem v. Fargo.*

77. *Wasem v. Fargo.*

78. "Baltimore Society and Those '$75.00 Funerals,'" *Post Standard,* February 7, 1926, 68.

79. "Baltimore Society and Those '$75.00 Funerals,'" 68.

80. "Baltimore Society and Those '$75.00 Funerals,'" 68.

81. "Baltimore Society and Those '$75.00 Funerals,'" 68.

82. "Baltimore Society and Those '$75.00 Funerals,'" 68.

83. It was written of Cook that "in newspaper advertisements and in other ways he extolled the excellence of his undertaking service with almost the glowing enthusiasm of a circus press agent." "Baltimore Society and Those '$75.00 Funerals,'" 68.

84. In 1940 Cook purchased the Garrett-Jacobs Mansion, located seven blocks away at 11 Mount Vernon Place. A colossal dwelling, it had grown through a series of enlargements as neighboring properties were acquired over a period of many decades beginning in 1853 and continuing through 1915. Baltimore's zoning ordinance prevented Cook from converting the opulent forty-room structure into a funeral home, and he sold it the following year to Boumi Temple, a Shriners organization. By the 1950s it was threatened with demolition.

85. Scott, *Bay Area,* 166.

86. *Transactions of the Commonwealth Club* 11 (January 1917): 638, in Scott, *Bay Area,* 166.

87. Stops included Madison, Wisconsin; Sandusky, Ohio; Kingston, New York; and Lowell, Massachusetts.

88. "Talks on City Planning," *Lowell Sun,* September 19, 1920, 7.

89. "Ask Injunction to Prevent Operation of Funeral Home," *Daily Northwestern,* June 6, 1929, 17.

90. "Alderman Urges Full Revision of City Ordinances," *Appleton Post-Crescent,* February 12, 1929, 4.

91. "Zoning Law Is Again Basis for Argument," *Waukesha Daily Freeman,* April 13, 1926, 1.

92. "Public vs. Private Rights," *Lowell Sun,* September 20, 1926, 10. Lowell had passed a temporary zoning law in 1922, which was followed by a permanent ordinance in 1926.

93. "Public vs. Private Rights," 10.

94. "Public vs. Private Rights," 10.

95. "Public vs. Private Rights," 10.

96. See Scott, *American City Planning,* 74–75, 152, 162, 192; and "Advantages of Zoning Told," 1.

97. "Mack Loses Fight for New Funeral Home," *Lowell Sun*, April 9, 1934, 9.

98. "Planning Board against Petition," *Lowell Sun*, March 1, 1934, 6.

99. "Council to Amend Zoning Ordinances," *Lowell Sun*, May 22, 1935, 1.

100. "Arena Permit Turned Down," *Lowell Sun*, July 10, 1935, 6.

101. "Allows Funeral Home Application," *Lowell Sun*, July 27, 1935, 2.

102. *Tureman v. Ketterlin*.

103. "Undertakers Will Pass a Petition," *Decatur Herald*, February 16, 1928, 4.

104. "End Tangle on Building Plans," *Decatur Herald*, February 13, 1928, 2.

105. "Zoning Board Denies Funeral Firm Permission to Build at Corner of Macon and Edward," *Decatur Herald*, March 3, 1928, 3.

106. "Zoning Board Meets Tonight," *Decatur Herald*, March 2, 1928, 2.

107. *Springfield v. Vancil*.

108. *Beisel v. Crosby*, 178 N. W. 272 (Neb. 1920).

109. *Arthur v. Virkler*.

110. *Arthur v. Virkler*.

111. *Williams v. Montgomery*, 186 So. 302 (Miss. 1939).

112. *Jack v. Torrant*; and *The Zoning Commission of the Town of Litchfield v. Torrant*.

113. Herbert S. Fassett, "Funeral Homes in Residential Districts," *American Funeral Director* 43, no. 6 (1920): 258.

114. Fassett, 257.

115. Fassett, 257.

116. Fassett, 257.

117. See *Beisel v. Crosby*; *Brown v. Los Angeles*; and *Meagher v. Kessler*.

118. "Some Points of Law for the Funeral Director: Discussion of the Right of Property Owners to Enjoin the Operation of an Undertaking Business in Residential District," *American Funeral Director* 44, no. 7 (1921): 345.

119. "Some Points of Law," 345.

120. "And Again a Court Decision," *Embalmers' Monthly* 38, no. 7 (1925): 23.

121. James R. Clark, "Decisions Affecting the Location of Mortuaries," *American Funeral Director* 53, no. 12 (1930): 45–46.

122. Cooley, *Law of Torts*, 180.

123. *Legal Decisions for Funeral Directors* (New York: The Casket and Sunnyside, The Casket, Inc., 1933), 29, 30.

124. *Legal Decisions for Funeral Directors*, 31.

125. "Location of Mortuaries," 46.

126. "Location of Mortuaries," 46.

127. "Location of Mortuaries," 48.

128. "Roland's Funeral Directors," *Adams County Free Press*," July 28, 1923, 1. The ad—which also ran in Beatrice, Nebraska; Covina, California; Roswell, New Mexico; and Statesville, North Carolina, to name a few—was reproduced by permission of the Cincinnati Coffin Company from a copyrighted message that appeared in *Saturday Evening Post* on December 17, 1921.

129. "The Public's Guardian," *Muscatine Journal and News-Tribune*, July 8, 1931, 6.

130. "When the Shades Are Drawn," *Daily Northwestern*, July 27, 1920, 10.

131. "What 'Superior Service' Means, No. 5," *Linton Daily Citizen*, June 28, 1926, 4.

132. "Cleanliness Is Next to Godliness," *Evening Courier and Reporter*," July 23, 1921, 13.

133. "Cleanliness Is Next to Godliness," 13.

134. Following his firm's first open house in February 1931, funeral director Mark A. Pierce of Los Angeles, California, wrote in an article in the *American Funeral Director* that "naturally, it is too early to trace any definite new patronage to our visitations, but the freely expressed praises voiced by all the visitors give rise to the hope that this activity will confer a direct benefit upon future business." See Mark A. Pierce, "Visitations: They Open the Door of Your Funeral Home to the Public and Remove the Mystery from It," *American Funeral Director* 54, no. 3 (1931): 41.

135. "Getting the Public to Visit Your Mortuary," *American Funeral Director* 53, no. 12 (1930): 35.

136. "Serving a Small Town in a Big Way," *American Funeral Director* 54, no. 7 (1931): 35.

137. "Thousands of Visitors at Modern Ramm Funeral Home," *Sheboygan Press*, May 21, 1929, 6.

138. "Ramm Funeral Home," *Sheboygan Press*, May 26, 1931, 10.

139. Mary Morris, "Woman to Woman," *Van Wert Times-Bulletin*, May 24, 1940, 5.

140. "F. M. Evans & Wife," *Logansport Morning Press*, November 26, 1924, 4.

141. "Interesting Ideas on Conducting Formal Opening of a Mortuary," *American Funeral Director* 51, no. 1 (1928): 48.

142. "Thousands Inspect New Daehler Funeral Home," *Portsmouth Daily Times*, February 5, 1925, 4.

143. "Meyer Funeral Home Opening Is Set for Friday," *Mason City Globe-Gazette*, July 19, 1934, 5.

144. C. Alden, "Is Funeral Director's Business a Nuisance?," *American Funeral Director*, 43, no. 2 (1920): 92.

145. Alden, 92.

146. "The New Book-Leyde Funeral Home Is Taking Shape," *New Castle News*, August 6, 1934, 2.

147. *O'Connor v. Ryan*, 159 S. W. 2d 531 (Tex. App. 1942).

148. *Qualls v. Memphis*, 15 Tenn. App. 575 (Tenn. App. 1932).

149. Gaston, *Green Power*, 74.

150. Gaston, 74. See also Jenkins and Hines, *Black Titan*, 113–14.

151. Gaston, *Green Power*, 126.

152. "Locating Mortuaries in Residential Districts—How Objections from Neighbors are Overcome," *American Funeral Director* 51, no. 6 (1928): 76.

153. *Legal Decisions*, 26.

154. *Ullrich v. Maryland*.

155. *Ullrich v. Maryland*.

156. *Ullrich v. Maryland*. Similar practices were rejected in *Street v. Marshall; Bevington v. Otte*; and *Momeier v. McAlister*, 27 S. E. 2d 504 (S. C. 1943).

157. "Winning Neighborhood Consent and Approval," *American Funeral Director* 54, no. 12 (1931): 34.
158. "Winning Neighborhood Consent and Approval," 34.
159. "Invite Public to New Funeral Home Saturday," *Gettysburg Times*, September 6, 1928, 1.
160. *St. Paul v. Kessler.*
161. On this issue, the Kansas Supreme Court held in 1924 that "it is immaterial that the owner of the business intends to reside in the upper stories of the building." See *Leland v. Turner.*
162. "Just the Right Place!," *Hamilton Evening Journal*, September 25, 1926, 2.
163. "Most Suitable," *Hamilton Evening Journal*, September 9, 1929, 5.
164. "Most Suitable," 5.
165. "Finds Residence District Best for Funeral Home," *American Funeral Director* 49, no. 4 (1926): 38.
166. "Surely," *Decatur Review*, March 31, 1927, 8.
167. "A Funeral Home," *Daily Northwestern*, December 23, 1920, 8.
168. *Fraser v. Parker*, 21 S. E. 2d 577 (S. C. 1942).
169. Lide observed that funeral homes "are of course to be found in a great many towns and cities, of the State, and sometimes, as in this case, buildings formerly used only as residences are now devoted to this purpose, frequently being improved and the surroundings beautified." See *Fraser v. Parker.*
170. *Cunningham v. Miller.*
171. "Note and Comment," *Sunday Herald*, June 28, 1891, 4.
172. *Rowland v. Miller*, 34 N.E. 765 (N.Y. 1893).
173. Rowland's dwelling had been erected sometime after 1865 when Madison Avenue was still a relatively new street. The area experienced rapid change, however, beginning with the completion of the Grand Central Depot one block east on Vanderbilt Avenue in 1871. Twenty years later, the residential character of Rowland's street had been largely destroyed. In 1885 the area between Forty-Second Street and Forty-Fourth Street, bound by Grand Central Depot (Vanderbilt Avenue) in the east and Fifth Avenue in the west, contained four hotels, three banks, three churches with several others nearby, a florist, a carriage repository, and a vacant lot comprising an entire block (later home to the Biltmore Hotel). A large car shed for the Grand Central Depot was situated two blocks north at the corner of Madison Avenue and Forty-Fifth Street. On Rowland's block alone stood the Holy Trinity Episcopal Church (demolished by 1897) and the Hotel Wellington (replaced by the Hotel Manhattan in 1897).
174. *Rowland v. Miller*, 15 N.Y.S. 701 (N.Y. Misc. 1891).
175. *Dillon v. Moran.*
176. *Beisel v. Crosby.*
177. *Davis v. Holmes.* See also *Hatcher v. Hitchcock; Laughlin v. Cooney; Weinmann v. Miles;* and *Fink v. Smith.*
178. *Ackerman v. Board of Commissioners*, 62 A. 2d 476 (N. J. 1948).

179. A. L. H. Street, "Pointers on Mortuary Law," *American Funeral Director* 73, no. 2 (1950): 74.

180. *Laughlin v. Cooney.*

181. *Tureman v. Ketterlin.*

182. *Aurora v. Burns,* 149 N. E. 784 (Ill. 1925). This was one of a handful of cases quoted extensively in *Euclid v. Amber.*

183. "Advantages of Zoning Told," *Kingston Daily Freeman,* December 11, 1920, 1.

184. *White v. Luquire,* 129 So. 84 (Ala. 1930).

185. *Meldahl v. Holberg.*

186. *White v. Luquire.*

187. "Attack," 6. By 1944 "Pasadena" had been converted into a YMCA. The structure was demolished in 1969.

188. *Cunningham v. Miller.*

189. *Tripp v. Pawtucket.*

190. *Higgins v. Bloch.* See also *Laughlin v. Cooney.*

191. *Dillon v. Moran.*

192. *Rockenbach v. Apostle.*

193. *Saier v. Joy.*

194. *White v. Luquire.* In *White v. Luquire,* decided by the Alabama Supreme Court in 1930, the court cited its ruling in *Higgins v. Bloch* from five years earlier.

195. *Tureman v. Ketterlin.*

196. *Tureman v. Ketterlin.*

197. *Bultman v. New Orleans,* 140 So. 503 (La. 1932). The injunction in this case was sought by the funeral director attempting to prevent the city from enforcing its zoning law, and the court left behind a vivid description of the street in question: "Business has encroached somewhat upon this section of St. Charles Avenue, although not to such an extent as to cause it to lose its primary character as a residential section of the city. There are still costly residences in the neighborhood, which are occupied as residences. In fact, St. Charles Avenue is reputed to be the principal residential street in the city, in that it has more costly and palatial residences on it than any other street therein, although, it may be said, the lower part of the avenue, for some blocks, is being given over to business."

198. *Smith v. Fairchild.*

199. See also *Beisel v. Crosby; Leland v. Turner; Laughlin v. Cooney; Davis v. Holmes; Rockenbach v. Apostle;* and *Whittle v. Baltimore County.*

200. *Tucson v. Arizona Mortuary.*

201. "Advantages of Zoning Told," 1.

202. See also *Whittle v. Board of Zoning Appeals of Baltimore County.* There were, of course, exceptions. See *Leary v. Adams,* 147 So. 391 (Ala. 1933); and *Bortz v. Troth,* 59 A. 2d 93 (Pa. 1948).

203. *Pearson v. Bonnie.*

204. *White v. Luquire.*

205. The court pointed to the "many places of business—drug stores, fillings stations, pressing parlors and grocery stores" that had already become established in the neighborhood. See *Fentress v. Sicard*, 25 S. W. 2d 18 (Ark. 1930).
206. A. L. H. Street, "A Notable Funeral Home Location Decision," *American Funeral Director* 64, no. 10 (1941): 49.
207. *Frederick v. Brown Funeral Homes*, 62 S. 2d 100 (La. 1952).
208. *Dawson v. Laufersweiler*, 43 N. W. 2d 726 (Iowa Sup. 1950).
209. Mildred Chadsey, "The Old House as a Social Problem," *Annals of the American Academy* 25, no. 1 (1914): 87.
210. Park, Burgess, and McKenzie, *The City*, 50.
211. McKenzie, "The Neighborhood," 149.
212. Park, Burgess and McKenzie, *The City*, 50.
213. See Berger, *The City*, 131–39; and Fellmann, Getis, and Getis, *Human Geography*, 392–93.
214. Excellent residential mobility studies touching on the interwar years include Chudacoff, *Mobile Americans*; and Cutler and Gillette, *The Divided Metropolis*.
215. For example, James Borchert's study of alley landscapes in Washington, D.C., reminds us that what are deemed slums by reformers and municipal leaders can be home to vibrant communities with strong communal bonds. Because "alley folk did much of their living outside regardless of the weather and thus the alley street itself became a communal living space," outside observers, "expecting the worst from alley dwellers, no doubt found their negative expectations fulfilled by what they perceived as dangerous and unwholesome commotion." See Borchert, "Alley Landscapes of Washington," 281. For further reading, see Borchert, *Alley Life in Washington*.
216. *Beisel v. Crosby*.
217. "Business Section Expands; Suburban Areas in Demand," *Ada Evening News*, September 2, 1928, 6.
218. *Fentress v. Sicard*.
219. *White v. Luquire*.
220. *Beisel v. Crosby*.
221. *Smith v. Fairchild*.
222. *Scott v. Davis*, 45 A. 2d 654 (N. H. 1946). The New Hampshire Supreme Court struck down the amendment in 1946, but on a subsequent appeal Foley prevailed and continued to operate from his new quarters at 49 Court Street, where his firm is still located.
223. *Momeier v. McAlister*, 99 S. E. 2d 177 (S. C. 1957). See also *Awtry and Lowndes v. Atlanta*, 50 S. E. 2d 868 (Ga. 1948).
224. This was not always the case, however. In 1958 the Georgia Supreme Court reversed a lower court's decision upholding a variance to a funeral home because in granting the variance, "the matter of the traffic problem was not considered by the Board in its award, nor as a basis for its award of a variance." See *Mobley v. Thomasville*, 104 S. E. 2d 586 (Ga. 1958).
225. *Tripp v. Pawtucket*. See also *Mahoney v. Chicago*.

226. See *Moss v. Burke & Trotti*, 3 So. 2d 281 (La. 1941); *O'Connor v. Ryan; Dawson v. Laufersweiler; Frederick v. Brown; Momeier v. McAlister; Cianciarulo v. Tarro*, 168 A.2d 719 (R. I. 1961); and *Bauman v. Piser*, 180 N. E. 2d 705 (Ill. App. 1962).
227. "Decision Given by Court Is in Favor of Funeral Home," *Sheboygan Press*, January 26, 1942, 5.
228. "Miller Funeral Home Is Opened on Pearl Street," *La Crosse Tribune and Leader-Press*, May 16, 1923, 6.
229. "Miller Funeral Home Is Opened on Pearl Street," 6.

CHAPTER 4. A HIGHER PLANE

1. "Announcement," *Marion Star*, March 1, 1928, 7.
2. "Announcement," 7.
3. "Culture Gaged by Funeral Customs," *Marion Star*, October 31, 1931, 13.
4. "Culture Gaged by Funeral Customs," 13.
5. Mark Twain, "Concerning Undertakers," *Territorial Enterprise*, February 12, 1864.
6. Twain.
7. "The High Cost of Dying," *American Magazine* 70, no. 7 (1910): 427.
8. Lewis Edwin Theiss, "How Undertakers Burden the Grief-Stricken," *Pearson's Magazine* 24, no. 9 (1910): 358.
9. Arthur B. Reeve, "The High Cost of Dying: How the Expensive Funeral East up the Insurance Policy," *Harper's Weekly* 57 (January 4, 1913): 15. "Probably nothing short of a legislative inquiry," argued *Pearson's*, "could settle the question of whether or not there is a 'coffin trust' of national scope. Manufacturing conditions vary so throughout the country, and so many concerns are engaged in making funeral supplies that there probably is none. That there are local 'combinations in restraint of trade' there can be no doubt whatever. Throughout the East, for instance, the casket trade is dominated by the National Casket Company, with its 24 branch houses. 'Even the coal barons,' says one investigator, 'are not more autocratic in fixing prices than is the National Casket Company.'" Theiss, "How Undertakers Burden the Grief-Stricken," 357.
10. "Heartaches That Could Be Avoided," *Ogden Standard*, December 8, 1913, 4.
11. Some reformers advocated treating burial as a public utility. "Burial," wrote one reformer, "should be made a municipal service for all persons alike. This is the prevalent practice in cantons of Switzerland." Quincy L. Dowd, "The Undertaker's Bill," *The Independent* 73 (June 13, 1912): 1323.
12. "Heartaches That Could Be Avoided," 4.
13. Theiss, "How Undertakers Burden the Grief-Stricken," 360.
14. "The High Cost of Dying," *Lutheran Witness* 34 (November 2, 1915): 341.
15. "The High Cost of Dying," 341.
16. "The High Cost of Dying," 341.
17. Theiss, "How Undertakers Burden the Grief-Stricken," 359.
18. Dowd, "Undertaker's Bill," 1321.

19. Theiss, "How Undertakers Burden the Grief-Stricken," 362. "In numberless cases," bemoaned Dowd, "widows are thrown into debt and obliged to eke out payments for funeral charges at the cost of their children's food." He witnessed a Greek funeral in Salt Lake City in which a "day laborer had been killed at one of the big stamp mills. He was [a] member in an insurance sodality with a $300 policy. A friend in the burial party," he recounted, "told me that this whole sum would be spent on the funeral." Dowd, "Undertaker's Bill," 1321.

20. Theiss, "How Undertakers Burden the Grief-Stricken," 358.

21. Deathcare historians Robert Habenstein and William Lamers single out the public health and burial reform movements as a key impetus prompting efforts to professionalize the funeral industry during the late nineteenth century. For further reading, see Habenstein and Lamers, *History of American Funeral Directing*, 446–57.

22. Later the National Funeral Directors Association.

23. "Current Affairs," *Index: An Independent Journal of Liberal Education*, no. 34 (October 11, 1884): 4.

24. *Densmore v. Evergreen*, 112 Pac. 255 (Wash. 1910).

25. *Sayers & Scovill Co. v. Doak*, 89 So. 917 (Miss. 1921).

26. Habenstein and Lamers, *History of American Funeral Directing*, 473.

27. Quincy L. Dowd, "High Cost of Modern Funerals," *The Advance* 61 (April 27, 1911): 14.

28. Habenstein and Lamers, *History of American Funeral Directing*, 467.

29. Habenstein and Lamers, 501.

30. Habenstein and Lamers, 591.

31. Berg, *The Confessions of an Undertaker*, 92.

32. "Price Advertising." *American Funeral Director* 53, no. 8 (1930): 39.

33. Callaway, *The Art of Funeral Directing*, 234.

34. Glassie, "Eighteenth-Century Cultural Process in Delaware Valley Folk Building," 396.

35. McCracken, *Culture and Consumption*, 68.

36. McCracken, 69.

37. McCracken, 69.

38. McCracken, 97.

39. Habenstein and Lamers, *History of American Funeral Directing*, 593–94; and Berg, *Confessions*, 91.

40. McCracken, *Culture and Consumption*, 41–43; and Warner and Lunt, *The Social Life of a Modern Community*, 107–8.

41. Grant McCracken argued in 1988 for the likelihood that "a critical eye to the ethnographic literature" would reveal "instances in which material culture undertakes expressive tasks that language does not or cannot perform." McCracken, *Culture and Consumption*, 68. See, for example, Forge, "Learning to See in New Guinea," 269–91.

42. Motor Hearse Corporation of America, "Looking the Part," advertisement, *American Funeral Director* 43, no. 2 (1920): 12.

43. Sayers & Scovill Company, "What do—people think of You?," advertisement, *American Funeral Director* 53, no. 2 (1930): 6.
44. Sayers & Scoville Company, "*Equipment* Tells Your Story!," advertisement, *American Funeral Director* 53, no. 8 (1930): 23.
45. Sayers & Scovill Company, "The funeral home . . . a tribute to the professional standards of today," advertisement, *American Funeral Director*, 49, no. 5 (1926): 14–15.
46. Sayers & Scovill Company, "The funeral home . . . a tribute," 14.
47. "Getting the Public to Visit Your Mortuary," *American Funeral Director* 53, no. 12 (1930): 35.
48. "Services from the Funeral Home," *American Funeral Director* 54, no. 5 (1931): 33.
49. "Progress in the Profession," *Racine Journal-News*, December 20, 1921, 5.
50. "From Mansion to Mortuary," *American Funeral Director* 53, no. 9 (1930): 43.
51. "Funeral Home in Favor in Exclusive Section," *American Funeral Director* 44, no. 2 (1921): 60.
52. "Funeral Home in Favor in Exclusive Section," 60.
53. Cincinnati College of Embalming, advertisement, *American Funeral Director* 49, no. 6 (1926): 22.
54. "Getting the Public to Visit Your Mortuary," 35.
55. "Attracting Visitors to the Funeral Home," *American Funeral Director* 49, no. 6 (1926): 28.
56. Lincoln and Mamiya, *The Black Church in the African-American Experience*, 246; and Smith, *To Serve the Living*, 46–78. "Undertakers," observed *Ebony* magazine in 1953, "are often among the wealthiest and most influential men in Negro society." "Death Is Big Business," *Ebony* 8, no. 5 (1953): 17.
57. Myrdal, *An American Dilemma*, 309–10. By the mid-1940s Robert R. Reed of Atlanta, editor of the *Colored Mortician*, also put the number of Black funeral directors at 3,000. Guzman, Foster, and Hughes, *Negro Year Book*, 195.
58. Allan Morrison, "Monopoly in Death," *Negro Digest* 5, no. 3 (1947): 56.
59. Drake and Cayton, *Black Metropolis*, 457.
60. "You And Your Friends Are Most Cordially Invited to Attend Our Grand Formal Re-opening On Friday, January 1, 1909," *Nashville Globe*, December 25, 1908, 5.
61. Jenkins and Hines, *Black Titan*, 125–26.
62. Jenkins and Hines, 113–14.
63. Jenkins and Hines, 117.
64. Gaston, *Green Power*, 76.
65. Black funeral homes were not immune from the mob violence that destroyed Black-owned homes and businesses during racist rampages. For example, the Tulsa race massacre of 1921 saw a white mob set fire to Jackson's funeral parlor at 600 Archer Street. In 1963 the House of Wills in Cleveland, Ohio, received two bomb threats stemming from racial tensions that nearly erupted into a full-scale race riot, and such attacks were not uncommon. During the struggle for civil rights, Black funeral homes were often targeted because of the political, financial, and logistical support given to activists by Black funeral directors. See Madigan, *The*

Burning, 196; "Cleveland Rape, Shooting Push Whites, Negroes to the Brink of Race Riots," *Jet* 24, no. 7 (1963): 54; and Smith, *To Serve the Living*, 118–20.

66. W.E.B. Du Bois, "The Perfect Vacation," *The Crisis* 40, no. 8 (1931): 279.
67. In 2020 authorities in Birmingham dismantled and removed the monument.
68. "Pickles vs. Caviar," *American Funeral Director* 54, no. 7 (1931): 31.
69. "Pickles vs. Caviar," 32.
70. "Pickles vs. Caviar," 60.
71. "Pickles vs. Caviar," 32.
72. "Pickles vs. Caviar," 60.
73. "Pickles vs. Caviar," 32, 60.
74. McCracken, *Culture & Consumption*, 79.
75. "Special Advertising Service for Funeral Directors," *American Funeral Director* 49, no. 6 (1926): 59.

CHAPTER 5. LUXURIOUS SIMPLICITY

1. "Webb Funeral Home to Be Open to Inspection on Saturday," *Hamilton Evening Journal*, April 27, 1928, 16.
2. "David Webb and Sons Complete Remodeling of Modern Funeral Home," *Hamilton Daily News*, April 27, 1928, 13.
3. "Interesting Features Included in Layout of New Bremerton Funeral Home," *American Funeral Director* 51, no. 5 (1928): 37.
4. Cohen, "From Town Center to Shopping Center," 1052; and Longstreth, *City Center to Regional Mall*, 3–13 and 96–101.
5. "Invite Public to New Funeral Home Saturday," *Gettysburg Times*, September 6, 1928, 1.
6. Longstreth, *City Center to Regional Mall*; Cohen, "From Town Center to Shopping Center."
7. C. H. Logan, "Let the Public Have the Opportunity to Choose Quality," *American Funeral Director* 51, no. 10 (1928): 65.
8. Burlingame, "Selling an Appropriate Service," *American Funeral Director* 54, no. 8 (1931): 43.
9. Berg, *Confessions*, 99–100.
10. Habenstein and Lamers, *History of American Funeral Directing*, 549.
11. Albert Kates, "Prices and Profits," *American Funeral Director*, 54, no. 3 (1931): 37.
12. John Byrne, "The Funeral Director's Problems: Text of Interesting Address Delivered at Illinois Booster Meeting," *American Funeral Director*, 49, no. 5 (1926): 53.
13. "Special Advertising for Funeral Directors," *American Funeral Director*, 51, no. 1 (1928): 61.
14. Byrne, "The Funeral Director's Problems," 52.
15. "The Press Fires Another Editorial Barrage," *American Funeral Director*, 59, no. 12 (1936): 32.
16. Ironically, both critics and apologists of the funeral industry had been making this argument since the late nineteenth century. In 1882 one funeral director wrote

344   Notes to Pages 237–246

that "the growing wealth and prosperity of our country has caused people to demand something more in accordance with their surroundings." See Charles Benjamin, "Essay," *The Casket* 7, no. 2 (1882): 2.

17. Gebhart, *Funeral Costs*, 222.

18. Logan, "Let the Public Have the Opportunity," 65.

19. Albert Kates, "This Industry Is Not Depression Proof," *American Funeral Director*
54, no. 1 (1931): 35.

20. Callaway, *Art of Funeral Directing*, 193.

21. Berg, *Confessions*, 88.

22. Allan Morrison, "Monopoly in Death," *Negro Digest* 5, no. 3 (1947): 57.

23. "Opening of Ford & Douglas New Funeral Home This Week," *Gastonia Daily Gazette*, May 26, 1926, 7.

24. "Ford & Douglas Open New Mortuary," *American Funeral Director* 49, no. 7
(1926): 44.

25. "From Mansion to Mortuary," *American Funeral Director* 53, no. 9 (1930): 44.

26. "Handsome New Corken Funeral Home Opened in Cincinnati," *American Funeral Director* 49, no. 10 (1926): 40.

27. "Hoeppner Company Built Wichmann's New Funeral Home," *Appleton Post-
Crescent*, 19 March 1931, 18.

28. "From Mansion to Mortuary," 43.

29. Cross, *All-Consuming Century*, 32.

30. Leach, *Land of Desire*, 29. See also Benson, *Counter Cultures*, 83; Sheumaker and
Wajda, *Material Life in America*, 145–46.

31. Callaway, *Art of Funeral Directing*, 218.

32. George Algoe et al., "Let's Do a Better Selling Job," *American Funeral Director* 54,
no. 8 (1931): 35–36.

33. "Your Display Room and the Merchandising Problems Revolving around It,"
American Funeral Director 49, no. 12 (1926): 31.

34. "Your Display Room," 32–33.

35. "Price Tags in the Showroom," *American Funeral Director* 54, no. 2 (1931): 39.

36. "Price Tags in the Showroom," 41.

37. Algoe, "Better Selling Job," 37.

38. Algoe, 37.

39. G. W. Fergason, "Effective Funeral Home Lighting," *American Funeral Director* 54,
no. 5 (1931): 37.

41. "E. L. Cummins Builds Modern Funeral Home," *Titusville Herald*, November 2,
1933, 8; and "Funeral Home Credit to City," *Sheboygan Press*, February 12, 1925, 9.

42. Mark Pierce, "Selling in the Show Room," *American Funeral Director* 54, no. 9
(1931): 31.

43. "Funeral Directors See Increasing Demand for Quality Interiors," *American Funeral Director* 51, no. 4 (1928): 54.

44. "Allowing the Public a Selection of Interiors," *American Funeral Director* 51, no. 12
(1928): 55.

45. "Your Display Room," 31.

46. "One Will Find," *Lowell Sun*, September 12, 1925, 3.

47. "Homelike Comforts," *Decatur Daily Review*, March 19, 1925, 29.

48. Benson, *Counter Cultures*, 83.

49. "Griesmer-Grim Co. Offers Fitting Appointments at the Time of Sorrow," *Hamilton Daily News*, September 17, 1927, 12; and "Heitger Funeral Home Has Served Massillon 73 Years," *Evening Independent*, July 20, 1942, 9.

50. Whitaker, *Service and Style*, 36.

51. Albert Kates, "Buying Habits and Price Marking," *American Funeral Director* 54, no. 2 (1931): 37.

52. Kates, 38.

53. Howarth, *Death and Dying*, 241; and "Concrete Sorrow," *Oakland Daily Evening Tribune*, March 22, 1890, 1.

54. "Burial Reform," *Lowell Sun*, August 15, 1891, 1; and "Funeral Reform," *Waukesha Freeman*, March 13, 1884, 4.

55. "Funeral Reform," *Syracuse Standard*, December 10, 1892, 1.

56. "About Burials," *North Adams Transcript*, February 4, 1897, 4.

57. "New Aubuchon Funeral Home Will Be Open for Inspection on Sunday and Memorial Day," *Fitchburg Sentinel*, May 25, 1927, 1.

58. Logan, "Let the Public Have the Opportunity," 65.

59. "Corken Funeral Home," 39.

60. "Quiet Dignity," *Daily Mail* (Hagerstown, MD), October 4, 1930, 2. Whether funeral directors borrowed this phrase from the world of advertising is unclear, but the phrase itself had currency apart from the funeral industry. During the first quarter of the twentieth century, it was used to sell everything from shoes and flatware to furniture and houses.

61. "Invite Public to New Funeral Home Saturday," *Gettysburg Times*, September 6, 1928, 1.

62. "Magnificent Equipment! Modern Management!," *Portsmouth Times*, May 20, 1933, 2.

63. "Beautiful in Its Simplicity," *Portsmouth Times*, October 21, 1933, 2.

64. "In New Funeral Home," *Lowell Sun*, January 10, 1933, 2.

65. Walter A. Dyer, "The Passing of the Parlor Suite," *Art World*, 2, no. 9 (1917), 565–66.

66. Leach, *Land of Desire*, 34–35.

67. Wharton, *The Decoration of Houses*, 185.

68. "Colonial Architecture Featured in Kentucky Funeral Home," *American Funeral Director* 51, no. 5 (1928): 51.

69. Northend, *The Art of Home Decoration*, 33.

70. Much earlier during the Victorian era, wicker furniture had been commonly used as accent pieces in the lavishly furnished and eclectic parlors of wealthy and prominent individuals throughout the United States. See *Artistic Houses: Being a Series of Interior Views of a Number of the Most Beautiful and Celebrated Homes in the United States* (New York: B. Blom, 1883).

71. Walter A. Dyer, "A Justification of Wicker," *Art World* 2, no. 4 (1917): 83.

72. Wright, *Interior Decoration for Modern Needs*, 121.

73. James Collier Marshall, "Why Not Wicker?," *Garden Magazine* 23, no. 3 (1916): 130.

74. Amy L. Rolfe, *Interior Decoration for the Small Home* (New York: Macmillan, 1924), 105–6.

75. See Cross, *All Consuming Century*, 111–19.

76. Elvins, *Sales & Celebrations*, 111.

77. Leach, *Land of Desire*, 34–35 and 202–10; Voorsanger and Howart, *Art and the Empire City*, 259–61; Sheumaker and Wajda, *Material Life in America*, 101.

78. Raizman, *History of Modern Design*, 103–10.

79. Campbell, *The Romantic Ethic and the Spirit of Modern Consumerism*, 206.

80. Shi, *The Simple Life*, 219.

81. Albert Kates, "Sell Satisfaction, Not Just Merchandise," *American Funeral Director* 54, no. 6 (1931): 33.

82. "Chain Operation in the Funeral Field," *American Funeral Director* 69, no. 3 (1947): 51.

83. "Your Display Room," 31.

84. "Your Display Room," 32.

85. "Your Show Room," *American Funeral Director*, 49, no. 11 (1926): 34.

86. "Favor Price Marking in Manufacturers Showrooms," *American Funeral Director* 54, no. 2 (1931): 48.

87. "Heitger Funeral Home," 9.

88. Habenstein and Lamers, *History of American Funeral Directing*, 568.

89. Albert Kates, "What Do You Know About Your Business?," *American Funeral Director*, 49, no. 11 (1926), 33.

90. Mark Pierce, "Why We Advertise Price," *American Funeral Director* 53, no. 9 (1930): 35.

91. "Advertising Merchandise," *American Funeral Director* 53, no. 9 (1930): 54.

92. Ruth Campbell, "Says Chapel Idea Is Unsympathetic and Cold," *American Funeral Director* 44, no. 7 (1921): 355.

93. "Your Display Room," 32.

94. "Colonial Architecture Featured in New Winzeler Establishment," *American Funeral Director* 49, no. 12 (1926): 44.

95. "A Funeral Home with a Pleasingly Rural Atmosphere," *American Funeral Director* 53, no. 8 (1930): 43.

96. "In New Funeral Home," 2.

97. "Your Display Room," 32.

98. "Prominent in Lancaster's Business and Professional Life," *Lancaster Daily Eagle*, January 19, 1927, 6; "Frank J. McAllister 'Funeral Director,'" *McKean County Miner*, April 11, 1929, 11; and "Hohenschuh Mortuary," *Oxford Leader*, March 6, 1930, 7.

99. "Efficiency and Comfort of Patrons Well Provided for in New Los Angeles Mortuary," *American Funeral Director*, 51, no. 6 (1928): 35.

100. "A Well Balanced Funeral Home," *American Funeral Director* 69, no. 12 (1947): 52.
101. "Design for a De Luxe Funeral Home," *American Funeral Director* 69, no. 6 (1947): 52.
102. Selket, "Bring Home the Dead."

CHAPTER 6. FROM HOME FUNERAL TO FUNERAL HOME

1. Historians generally place the period of transition from home funeral to funeral home within the second quarter of the twentieth century and agree that by the middle of the century, the shift was complete. For more, see Bowman, *The American Funeral*, 17; Farrell, *Inventing the American Way of Death*, 172, 209–11; Habenstein and Lamers, *History of American Funeral Directing*, 570; Laderman, *Rest in Peace*, 24; Smith, *To Serve the Living*, 84; Pine, *Caretaker of the Dead*, 17–18; and Wells, *Facing the 'King of Terrors,'* 261–62, 273.
2. "Attack Made in Court on Miller House," *La Crosse Tribune and Leader-Press*, July 19, 1921, 6.
3. M. J. Phillips, "Being Sympathetic Won a Fine Business for J. Ed. Phillips, Glendale, Cal.," *American Funeral Director* 49, no. 1 (1926): 33.
4. Esther C. Weerts, "The Lady Assistant's Important Place in the Sun," *American Funeral Director* 51, no. 8 (1928): 50.
5. Margie Shetterly, "A Century of Service—Kyger and Pence Funeral Home," *Daily News-Record*, August 13, 1984, 9.
6. Montell, *Tales from Kentucky Funeral Homes*, 18.
7. Habenstein and Lamers, *History of American Funeral Directing*, 395.
8. Callaway, *The Art of Funeral Directing*, 60.
9. Berg, *The Confessions of an Undertaker*, 64–65.
10. Berg, 51. It was not unusual, however, for the deceased to be embalmed in his or her bed. See Howard S. Eckels and Charles A. Genung, *The Eckels-Genung Method and Practical Embalmer: A Practical and Comprehensive Treatise on Embalming Together with a Complete Description of the Anatomy and Circulation of the Human Body* (Philadelphia: H.S. Eckels & Co., 1906), 76.
11. See Habenstein and Lamers, *History of American Funeral Directing*, 396–97.
12. Berg, *Confessions*, 52, 65.
13. Berg, 49. Habenstein and Lamers point out that during the nineteenth century when embalming was still a strange and largely misunderstood science, "it was sometimes necessary to permit a close friend or male member of the family to watch the process" especially "if the family raised the mutilation objection strenuously," referring to the widespread misconception that embalming required the removal of the internal organs. Habenstein and Lamers, *History of American Funeral Directing*, 398.
14. Habenstein and Lamers, 394.
15. "Charles Paquelet, Jr. Announces the Opening of His Funeral Home," *Evening Independent*, July 18, 1929, 3.
16. Berg, *Confessions*, 40.

17. Habenstein and Lamers, *History of American Funeral Directing*, 394.

18. In his discussion of burial practices in Vermilion County, Illinois, James Farrell connects the rise in hospital deaths with the demise of the home funeral. "By 1920," he writes, "the internal developments which eventually led to the widespread use of funeral homes had begun. Changes in the place of death due mainly to specialized medical practice influenced funeral procedures. . . . In the 1880s less than one in fifty people died in hospitals, but by 1920 almost one in seven Vermilion County deaths occurred in a hospital. . . . When people died in institutions, the undertaker often brought the body in his ambulance from the hospital to his undertaking parlours, where he prepared it for burial before taking it to the house. Eventually people decided that the last trip home was superfluous, and they began to plan funerals from funeral homes." See Farrell, *Inventing the American Way of Death*, 210.

19. Callaway, *The Art of Funeral Directing*, 57.

20. Callaway, 32–33.

21. Callaway, 32–33.

22. Eichler, *Book of Etiquette*, 95.

23. Callaway, *The Art of Funeral Directing*, 57.

24. Callaway, 187.

25. Berg, *Confessions*, 72.

26. Joseph N. Greene, *The Funeral: Its Conduct and Proprieties* (Cincinnati: Jennings and Graham, 1905), 76.

27. Eliza Bisbee Duffey, *The Ladies' and Gentlemen's Etiquette* (Philadelphia: Porter and Coates, 1877), 219.

28. Helen L. Roberts, *Putnam's Handbook of Etiquette: A Cyclopaedia of Social Usage, Giving Manners and Customs of the Twentieth Century* (New York: Putnam, 1913), 496.

29. John H. Young, *Our Deportment, or the Manners, Conduct and Dress of the Most Refined Society* (Detroit: F. B. Dickerson & Co., 1881), 291.

30. George Arthur Gaskell, *Gaskell's Compendium of Forms* (Chicago: Fairbanks, Palmer & Co., 1881), 443–44.

31. Roberts, *Handbook of Etiquette*, 496.

32. *Etiquette for Americans, by A Woman of Fashion* (Chicago: Herbert S. Stone & Co., 1898), 127.

33. Margaret E. Sangster, *Good Manners for All Occasions: A Practical Manual* (New York: Louis Klopsch, 1904), 211.

34. Emily Post, *Etiquette: In Society, in Business, in Politics and at Home* (New York: Funk & Wagnalls, 1923), 396. See also Anna S. Richardson, *Standard Etiquette* (New York: Harper & Brothers, 1925), 205.

35. *Vogue's Book of Etiquette: Present-Day Customs of Social Intercourse with the Rules for Their Correct Observance* (New York: Conde Nast Publications, 1925), 534.

36. William C. DeWitt, *Decently and In Order: Pastoral Suggestions in Matters Official and Personal* (Milwaukee: Young Churchman Co., 1914), 164.

37. Eichler, *Book of Etiquette*, 95.

38. Callaway, *The Art of Funeral Directing*, 33–34.
39. "Services from the Funeral Home," *American Funeral Director* 54, no. 5 (1931): 33.
40. Hamilton's funerals conducted from funeral homes did not approach 50 percent until the mid-1930s but jumped from 48 percent in 1936 to 73 percent in 1941. These figures are based on my own data, compiled using obituaries and death notices to determine the location of funerals during the month of May at five-year intervals beginning in 1911 and continuing through 1941. Although this method is by no means precise, the data are consistent with observations made at various points during the same period by industry insiders.
41. "Webb Funeral Home Finished," *Hamilton Daily News*, November 13, 1931, 3.
42. Danville's population in 1920 was just under 34,000, which made it comparable in size to Hamilton, Ohio, whose population in 1920 was just under 40,000.
43. *Cunningham v. Miller*, 189 N.W. 531 (Wisc. 1922).
44. "Attack," 6.
45. *Blackburn v. Bishop*, 299 S. W. 264 (Tex. App. 1927).
46. "Services from the Funeral Home," 33.
47. W. W. McFarland, "What the Funeral Home Has to Offer," *American Funeral Director* 54, no. 4 (1931): 44.
48. "Services from the Funeral Home," 34.
49. "Services from the Funeral Home," 34.
50. This figure is based on data collected employing a method identical to that used for Hamilton, Ohio.
51. Smith asserts that during the 1910s and 1920s African American wakes were typically held at the home of the deceased. See Smith, *To Serve the Living*, 84.
52. "Increasingly, too," she wrote in her column on etiquette, "funerals are held in funeral homes rather than in private residences." See Amy Vanderbilt, "Few Americans Go into Actual Mourning," *Syracuse Herald-Journal*, October 29, 1954, 30.
53. *Bevington v. Otte*, 273 N.W. 98 (Iowa Sup. 1937).
54. *Fraser v. Parker*, 21 S. E. 2d 577 (S. C. 1942).
55. In 1926 R. L. Seezholtz of Canton, Ohio, provided the following information to the *American Funeral Director*: "For convenience, we have divided our funeral services into three classes; our records indicate that about 80 percent of our clients' services are conducted from the family home, 8 percent are held from churches and the remaining 12 percent from our own home." Such data are rare. See R. L. Seezholtz, "Differences of Opinions as to the Desirability of Music at Funerals," *American Funeral Director* 49, no. 1 (1926): 28.
56. Farrell, *Inventing the American Way of Death*, 174.
57. M. T. Harding, "Pacific Coast Mortuary of Remarkable Beauty and Efficiency," *American Funeral Director* 49, no. 2 (1926): 47–48.
58. Even 75 percent of funerals being conducted from funeral homes in 1926 would have been far greater than in other parts of the United States, where less than a quarter of services were held at funeral homes.
59. Harding, "Pacific Coast Mortuary," 48.

60. Longstreth, *City Center to Regional Mall*, 9–10.

61. "Popularizing the Funeral Home," *Casket and Sunnyside*, March 1, 1925.

62. Harding, "Pacific Coast Mortuary," 47.

63. Longstreth, *City Center to Regional Mall*, 6.

64. Farrell, *Inventing the American Way of Death*, 174. According to Gary Laderman, California led the nation in the adoption of progressive burial practices. "Without a doubt," he writes, "Californians were exposed to 'progressive' alterations in funeral traditions earlier than most of the country." Laderman, *Rest in Peace*, 146.

65. For more on the role of the entrance hall, see Ames, *Death in the Dining Room & Other Tales of Victorian Culture*, 7–43.

66. Phillips, "Being Sympathetic Won a Fine Business," 33.

67. "Funeral Home Becomes Adjunct to Mortician, Says Griesmer-Grim Co.," *Hamilton Daily News*, February 18, 1928, 11.

68. "New Funeral Home Merits High Praise," *Hamilton Daily News*, July 26, 1929, 10.

69. "What the Funeral Home Has to Offer," 45; and "Dumm's Colonial Funeral Home," *Emporia Daily Gazette*, September 27, 1928, 2.

70. "We Offer Our Services in Time of Sorrow," *Racine Journal-News*, March 11, 1922, 75.

71. "When Wanted," *Capital Times*, September 28, 1930, 2.

72. "Changes Take Place before You Know It," *Daily Northwestern*, November 26, 1928, 15. This particular advertisement was used by funeral directors nationwide. The identical ad ran, for example, in the *San Antonio Express* on November 19, 1928.

73. Wright, *Building the Dream*, 171.

74. Clark, *The American Family Home, 1800–1960*, 162–63, 168.

75. When one examines "the full range of dwelling types" in the United States during the nineteenth and early twentieth centuries, a more varied picture emerges. This is precisely the view taken in 1989 by John Jakle, Robert Bastian, and Douglas Meyer in *Common Houses in America's Small Towns*. Their conclusions, based on extensive surveys of extant dwellings in twenty sample towns rather than on mere speculation or reliance on plan books, reveals a variety of common house types ranging from modest to large. Size variability, they found, often depended on different rates of prosperity between regions. There was little evidence of a dramatic change in size between periods. See Jakle et al., *Common Houses in America's Small Towns*, 2, 202.

76. "Render Service of Distinction, Bishop Funeral Home in Nevada Meet Requirements of Each Case," *Ames Daily Tribune Times*, September 15, 1934, 6.

77. Wright, *Building the Dream*, 166, 171; Clark, *The American Family Home*, 146, 162–67, 173; and Schlereth, *Victorian America*, 93, 123.

78. Laderman, *Rest in Peace*, 5.

79. Farrell, *Inventing the American Way of Death*, 175.

80. Historian Gary Cross correctly points out that twentieth-century living rooms differed far less from nineteen-century parlors than has been previously imagined. He argues that they "remained private museums, much as they had been in Victorian times." See Cross, *An All-Consuming Century*, 47.

81. "The Bungalow," wrote architect Henry L. Wilson in 1910, "is a radical departure from the older styles of cottage, not only in outward appearance, but in inside arrangement. The straight, cold entrance hall and the stiff, prim, usually darkened parlor have no place in it. Entrance is usually into a large living room— the room where the family gathers, and in which the visitor feels at once the warm, homelike hospitality." Wilson, *The Bungalow Book*. See also Wright, *Building the Dream*, 172; Clark, *The American Family Home*, 132, 163; and Gowans, *The Comfortable House*, 28.

82. "Convenience and Comfort," *Ada Evening News*, November 6, 1932, 8.

83. "What the Funeral Home Has to Offer," 44.

84. "Why a Funeral Home," *Morning Herald* (Hagerstown, Maryland), April 23, 1931, 4.

85. "What the Funeral Home Has to Offer," 45.

86. Habenstein and Lamers, *History of American Funeral Directing*, 406.

87. DeWitt, *Decently and in Order*, 163.

88. "Wrenn-Yeatts Open Modern Funeral Home on North Side," *The Bee*, March 7, 1936, 4.

89. "Free," *Wisconsin Rapids Daily Tribune*, June 20, 1932, 2.

90. "Seeking Privacy," *Rushville Republican*, April 21, 1930, 4.

91. "Inviolate Privacy," *Decatur Daily Review*, July 9, 1925, 10.

92. "Announcing the Opening Saturday and Sunday of the Newly Remodeled and Enlarged Simpson Funeral Home," *Charleston Gazette*, July 10, 1937, 9.

93. "How to Choose a Funeral Director," *Times-Picayune*, October 18, 1932, 2.

94. "The Decision," *Carroll Times*, August 12, 1926, 4.

95. "Dumm's Colonial Funeral Home," 2.

96. *Statesville Landmark*, March 19, 1928, 8.

97. "It's for You to Decide," *Evening Independent*, February 19, 1940, 3.

98. Abel, "In the Last Stages of Irremediable Disease," 55.

99. Abel, 49, 56.

100. Lynch, *The Undertaking*, 36.

101. Lynch, 36–37.

102. Laderman, *Rest in Peace*, 16–17; and Clark, *The American Family Home*, 155–57.

103. Prothero, *Purified by Fire*, 50–51.

104. Laderman, *Rest in Peace*, 5, 31–33, 53–59.

105. "The Unseemliness of Funerals," *Literary Digest* 54 (April 21, 1917): 1170.

106. "Present Day Funeral Customs Only Serve to Make Grief More Heavy," *Des Moines News*, March 28, 1914, 5.

107. "Metropolitan Burial Survey Summary Report Made Public by Gebhart," *American Funeral Director* 51, no. 2 (1928): 38.

108. "Appropriate Settings," *Daily Herald*, October 2, 1931, 8.

109. "Mothers and Their Children, Dispel the Gloom," *Altoona Mirror*, March 12, 1926, 6; and *San Antonio Express*, March 19, 1926, 17.

110. "Services from the Funeral Home," 34.

111. "Modern Funeral Service Is Better Than at Any Previous Time," *Record-Argus,* January 18, 1933, 2.

112. Habenstein and Lamers, *History of American Funeral Directing,* 550.

113. "Do You Know . . . ," *Muscatine Journal and News Tribune,* May 31, 1940, 146.

114. "Changed Manners Are Reflected in the Passing of the Parlor," *Literary Digest* 62 (July 19, 1919): 40.

115. "Metropolitan Burial Survey," 61, 66.

116. "The Press Fires Another Editorial Barrage," *American Funeral Director* 59, no. 12 (1936): 29.

CONCLUSION. BUILD ME NO STATELY MANSIONS

1. "Winning Neighborhood Consent and Approval," *American Funeral Director* 54, no. 12 (1931): 34.

2. "The Funeral Home of Tomorrow," *American Funeral Director* 69, no. 7 (1947): 49.

3. George F. Weaks, "Build Me No Stately Mansions," *Chicago Heights Star,* February 21, 1947, 14.

4. Weaks, 14.

5. Weaks, 14.

6. Weaks, 14.

7. Bowman, *The American Funeral,* 17.

8. Dalziel, *Culture and Democracy,* 149.

9. Longstreth, *City Center to Regional Mall,* 251.

10. See Jeremy Smith, "In Praise of the Zoom Funeral," *Slate,* August 4, 2020, https://slate.com/technology/2020/08/praise-of-zoom-funeral.html; Abby Ohlheiser, "The Lonely Reality of Zoom Funerals," MIT Technology Review, April 13, 2020, https://www.technologyreview.com/2020/04/13/999348/covid-19-grief-zoom-funerals/; and Andie MacNeil et al., "Exploring the Use of Virtual Funerals during the Covid-19 Pandemic: A Scoping Review," *Omega—Journal of Death and Dying* (2021), https://journals.sagepub.com/doi/epub/10.1177/00302228211045288.

11. See "The Future of the Funeral Industry: Moving Past Traditional Funeral and Burial Services," Research for Life, https://www.researchforlife.org/blog/the-future-of-the-funeral-industry/; "Guide to Green Burial—A Natural Approach to Funerals," Lincoln Heritage Funeral Advantage, https://www.lhlic.com/consumer-resources/green-burial/; and Kate Wight, "Average Cost of a Natural (Green) Burial: A Price Breakdown," Cake, January 17, 2023, https://www.joincake.com/blog/natural-burial-cost/#natural.

BIBLIOGRAPHY

Abel, Emily K. "In the Last Stages of Irremediable Disease." *Bulletin of the History of Medicine* 85, no. 1 (Spring 2011): 29–56.

Adams, Michael Henry. "Mulattos, Mammies and Maids: Accessing 'The Help.'" *Huffington Post,* August 15, 2011. http://www.huffingtonpost.com/michael -henry-adams/mulattos-mammies-and-maid_b_926813.html.

Adams, Michael Henry, and Paul Rocheleau. *Harlem Lost and Found: An Architectural and Social History, 1765–1915.* New York: Monacelli, 2002.

Andrzejewski, Anna Vemer. *Building Power: Architecture and Surveillance in Victorian America.* Knoxville: University of Tennessee Press, 2008.

Ames, Kenneth L. *Death in the Dining Room and Other Tales of Victorian Culture.* Philadelphia: Temple University Press, 1992.

Ames, Kenneth L. "Meaning in Artifacts: Hall Furnishings in Victorian America." In *Common Places: Readings in American Vernacular Architecture,* ed. Dell Upton and John M. Vlach, 243–44. Athens: University of Georgia Press, 1986.

Archer, John. *Architecture and Suburbia: From English Villa to American Dream House, 1690–2000.* Minneapolis: University of Minnesota Press, 2005.

Ball, Edward. *The Sweet Hell Inside: The Rise of an Elite Black Family in the Segregated South.* New York: HarperCollins, 2001.

Barr, Christine Ann. "Funeral Homes: History and Preservation." Master's thesis, School of the Art Institute of Chicago, 2006.

Barthel, Diane. *Historic Preservation: Collective Memory and Historical Identity.* New Brunswick, NJ: Rutgers University Press, 1996.

Baxandall, Rosalyn, and Elizabeth Ewen. *Picture Windows: How the Suburbs Happened.* New York: Basic Books, 2000.

Beckson, Karl, and Arthur Ganz. *Literary Terms: A Dictionary.* 3rd ed. New York: Farrar, Straus and Giroux, 1991.

Benson, Susan. *Counter Cultures: Saleswomen, Managers, and Customers in American Department Stores, 1890–1940.* Urbana: University of Illinois Press, 1987.

Berg, Charles W. *The Confessions of an Undertaker.* Wichita, KS: McCormick-Armstrong, 1920.

Berger, Alan S. *The City: Urban Communities and Their Problems*. Dubuque, IA: W. C. Brown Publishers, 1978.

Borchert, James. "Alley Landscapes of Washington." In *Common Places: Readings in American Vernacular Architecture*, ed. Dell Upton and John Michael Vlach, 281–291. Athens: University of Georgia Press, 1986.

Borchert, James. *Alley Life in Washington: Family, Community, Religion and Folklife in the City, 1850–1970*. Urbana: University of Illinois Press, 1980.

Bowman, LeRoy. *The American Funeral: A Study in Guilt, Extravagance, and Sublimity*. Westport, CT: Greenwood, 1959.

Brand, Stewart. *How Buildings Learn: What Happens after They're Built*. New York: Viking, 1994.

Bryant, Clifton, ed. *Handbook of Death and Dying*. 2 vols. Thousand Oaks, CA: Sage Publications, 2003.

Callaway, Curtis Frederick. *The Art of Funeral Directing; a Practical Manual on Modern Funeral Directing Methods*. Chicago: Undertakers' Supply Co., 1928.

Campbell, Colin. *The Romantic Ethic and the Spirit of Modern Consumerism*. Oxford, UK: B. Blackwell, 1987.

Carter, Thomas, and Elizabeth Collins Cromley. *Invitation to Vernacular Architecture: A Guide to the Study of Ordinary Buildings and Landscapes*. Knoxville: University of Tennessee Press, 2005.

Cassell, Dana, et al., eds. *The Encyclopedia of Death and Dying*. New York: Facts on File, 2005.

Charmaz, Kathy. *The Social Reality of Death: Death in Contemporary America*. Reading, MA: Addison-Wesley, 1980.

Chudacoff, Howard D. *Mobile Americans: Residential and Social Mobility in Omaha, 1880–1920*. Oxford: Oxford University Press, 1972.

Clark, Clifford E. *The American Family Home, 1800–1960*. Chapel Hill: University of North Carolina Press, 1986.

Cobb, John Storer. *A Quarter Century of Cremation in North America*. Boston: Knight and Millet, 1901.

Cohen, Lizabeth. *A Consumer's Republic: The Politics of Mass Consumption in Postwar America*. New York: Knopf, 2003.

Cohen, Lizabeth. "From Town Center to Shopping Center: The Reconfiguration of Community Marketplaces in Postwar America." *American Historical Review* 101, no. 4 (1996): 1050–81.

Cooley, Thomas McIntyre. *A Treatise on the Law of Torts, or, The Wrongs Which Arise Independently of Contract*. 4th ed. Chicago: Callaghan & Co., 1932.

Cross, Gary. *An All-Consuming Century: Why Commercialism Won in Modern America*. New York: Columbia University Press, 2000.

Curl, James Stevens. *A Celebration of Death: An Introduction to Some of the Buildings, Monuments, and Settings of Funerary Architecture in the Western European Tradition*. New York: Scribner, 1980.

Curl, James Stevens. *The Victorian Celebration of Death*. London: David & Charles, 1972.

Cutler, William W., III, and Howard Gillette Jr., eds. *The Divided Metropolis: Social and Spatial Dimensions of Philadelphia, 1800–1975*. Westport, CT: Greenwood Press, 1980.

Dalziel, Hugh. *Culture and Democracy: The Struggle for Form in Society and Architecture in Chicago and the Middle West during the Life and Times of Louis H. Sullivan*. Totowa, NJ: Bedminster Press, 1965.

Davis, Timothy. "The Miracle Mile Revisited: Recycling, Renovation, and Simulation along the Commercial Strip." In *Perspectives in Vernacular Architecture VII: Exploring Everyday Landscapes*, 93–114. Annapolis: Vernacular Architecture Forum, 1997.

DeWitt, Wm. C. *Decently and In Order: Pastoral Suggestions in Matters Official and Personal*. Milwaukee: Young Churchman Co., 1914.

Dowd, Jerome. *The Negro in American Life*. New York: Century, 1926.

Drake, St. Claire, and Horace R. Cayton. *Black Metropolis: A Study of Negro Life in a Northern City*. New York: Harcourt, Brace, 1945.

Eichler, Lillian. *Book of Etiquette*, Vol. 1. Oyster Bay, NY: Nelson Doubleday, 1921.

Elvins, Sarah. *Sales & Celebrations: Retailing & Regional Identity in Western New York State, 1920–1940*. Athens: Ohio University Press, 2004.

Farrell, James J. *Inventing the American Way of Death, 1830–1920*. Philadelphia: Temple University Press, 1980.

Faust, Drew Gilpin. *This Republic of Suffering: Death and the American Civil War*. New York: Knopf, 2008.

Fellmann, Jerome Donald, Arthur Getis, and Judith Getis. *Human Geography: Landscapes of Human Activities*. 5th ed. Dubuque, IA: W. C. Brown and Benchmark, 1997.

Fenske, Gail. *The Skyscraper and the City: The Woolworth Building and the Making of Modern New York*. Chicago: University of Chicago Press, 2008.

Forge, Anthony. "Learning to See in New Guinea." In *Socialization: The Approach from Social Anthropology*, ed. Phillip Mayer, 269–91. London: Tavistock, 1970.

Fox, Richard Wightman, and T. J. Jackson Lears, eds. *The Culture of Consumption: Critical Essays in American History, 1880–1980*. New York: Pantheon, 1983.

Gaston, A. G. *Green Power: The Successful Way of A. G. Gaston*. Birmingham: Southern University Press, 1968.

Gebhart, John. *Funeral Costs: What They Average; Are They Too High? Can They Be Reduced?* New York: Putnam, 1928.

Gilbert, Sandra M. *Death's Door: Modern Dying and the Ways We Grieve*. New York: Norton, 2006.

Glassie, Henry. "Eighteenth-Century Cultural Process in Delaware Valley Folk Building." In *Common Places: Readings in American Vernacular Architecture*, ed. Dell Upton and John M. Vlach, 394–425. Athens: University of Georgia Press, 1986.

Glassie, Henry. *Folk Housing in Middle Virginia: A Structural Analysis of Historic Artifacts*. Knoxville: University of Tennessee Press, 1975

Gowans, Alan. *The Comfortable House: North American Suburban Architecture, 1890–1930*. Cambridge: MIT Press, 1986.

Grier, Katherine C. *Culture & Comfort: Parlor Making and Middle-Class Identity, 1850–1930*. Washington, DC: Smithsonian Institution Press, 1997.

Grier, Katherine C. *Culture and Comfort: People, Parlors and Upholstery, 1850–1910*. Amherst: University of Massachusetts Press and the Margaret Woodbury Strong Museum, 1989.

Groth, Paul. *Living Downtown: The History of Residential Hotels in the United States*. Berkeley: University of California Press, 1994.

Guzman, Jessie Parkhurst, Vera Chandler Foster, and William Hardin Hughes. *Negro Year Book: A Review of Events Affecting Negro Life, 1941–1946*. Tuskegee, AL: Department of Records and Research, Tuskegee Institute, 1947.

Habenstein, Robert W., and William M. Lamers. *The History of American Funeral Directing*. Milwaukee: Bulfin Printers, 1955.

Hancock, John L. "Planners in the Changing American City, 1900–1940." In *American Urban History: An Interpretive Reader with Commentaries*, 3rd ed., ed. Alexander B. Calloway Jr., 515–33. Oxford: Oxford University Press, 1982.

Hayward, Mary Ellen. *Baltimore's Alley Houses: Homes for Working People since the 1780s*. Baltimore: Johns Hopkins University Press, 2008.

Heath, Kingston Wm. *The Patina of Place: The Cultural Weathering of a New England Industrial Landscape*. Knoxville: University of Tennessee Press, 2001.

Heathcote, Edwin. *Cinema Builders*. Chichester, West Sussex, UK: Wiley-Academy, 2001.

The History of American Funeral Directing. VHS. Directed by Bill Rock. 1995.

Howarth, Glennys. *Death & Dying: A Sociological Introduction*. Cambridge, UK: Polity, 2007.

Howarth, Glennys. *Last Rites: The Work of the Modern Funeral Director*. Amityville, NY: Baywood Publishing, 1996.

Howarth, Glennys, and Oliver Leaman, eds. *Encyclopedia of Death and Dying*. London: Routledge, 2001.

Hubka, Thomas. *Big House, Little House, Back House, Barn: The Connected Farm Buildings of New England*. Hanover, NH: University Press of New England, 1984.

Hubka, Thomas. *Houses without Names: Architectural Nomenclature and the Classification of America's Common Houses*. Knoxville: University of Tennessee Press, 2013.

Hubbard, Theodora Kimball, and Henry Vincent Hubbard. *Our Cities, To-Day and To-Morrow: A Survey of Planning and Zoning Progress in the United States*. Cambridge, MA: Harvard University Press, 1929.

Hunt, Angela. *Doesn't She Look Natural?* Carol Stream, IL: Tyndale, 2007.

Huntington, Richard, and Peter Metcalf. *Celebrations of Death: The Anthropology of Mortuary Ritual*. Cambridge: Cambridge University Press, 1979.

Isenberg, Nancy, and Andrew Burstein, eds. *Mortal Remains: Death in Early America*. Philadelphia: University of Pennsylvania Press, 2003.

Isenstadt, Sandy. *The Modern American House: Spaciousness and Middle-Class Identity*. Cambridge: Cambridge University Press, 2006.

Jakle, John, et al. *Common Houses in America's Small Towns: The Atlantic Seaboard to the Mississippi Valley*. Athens: University of Georgia Press, 1989.

Jalland, Pat. *Death in the Victorian Family*. Oxford: Oxford University Press, 1996.

Jenkins, Carol, and Elizabeth Gardner Hines. *Black Titan: A. G. Gaston and the Making of a Black American Millionaire*. New York: One World, 2004.

Jennings, Jan, and Herbert Gottfried. *American Vernacular Interior Architecture, 1870–1940*. New York: Van Nostrand Reinhold, 1988.

Johnson, Ronald W., and Mary E. Franza. "An Unheralded Preservation Influence: The American Funeral Industry." *Cultural Resource Management* 2 (2001): 33–36.

Kastenbaum, Robert, ed. *Macmillan Encyclopedia of Death and Dying*. 2 vols. New York: Macmillan Reference USA, 2003.

Kearl, Michael C. *Endings: A Sociology of Death and Dying*. Oxford: Oxford University Press, 1989.

Kubler, George. *The Shape of Time: Remarks on the History of Things*. New Haven, CT: Yale University Press, 1962.

Laderman, Gary. *Rest in Peace: A Cultural History of Death and the Funeral Home in Twentieth-Century America*. Oxford: Oxford University Press, 2005.

Laderman, Gary. *The Sacred Remains: American Attitudes toward Death, 1799–1883*. New Haven, CT: Yale University Press, 1996.

Lancaster, Clay. "The American Bungalow." *Art Bulletin* 40 (September 1958): 239–53.

Leach, William. *Land of Desire: Merchants, Power, and the Rise of a New American Culture*. New York: Vintage, 1993.

Levin, Gail. *Edward Hopper: An Intimate Biography*. Berkeley: University of California Press, 1998.

Lincoln, C. Eric, and Lawrence H. Mamiya. *The Black Church in the African-American Experience*. Durham, NC: Duke University Press, 1990.

Longstreth, Richard. *The Buildings of Main Street: A Guide to American Commercial Architecture*. Washington, DC: Preservation Press, 1987.

Longstreth, Richard. *City Center to Regional Mall: Architecture, the Automobile, and Retailing in Los Angeles, 1920–1950*. Cambridge, MA: MIT Press, 1998.

Lynch, Thomas. *The Undertaking: Life Studies from the Dismal Trade*. New York: Norton, 1997.

Madigan, Tim. *The Burning: Massacre, Destruction, and the Tulsa Race Riot of 1921*. New York: Thomas Dunne Books/St. Martin's, 2001.

Matson, Tim. *Round-Trip to Deadsville: A Year in the Funeral Underground*. White River Junction, VT: Chelsea Green, 2000.

McAlester, Virginia, and A. Lee McAlester. *A Field Guide to American Houses*. New York: Knopf, 1992.

McCall, Walter M. P. *American Funeral Vehicles 1880–2003: An Illustrated History*. Hudson, WI: Iconografix, 2003.

McCracken, Grant D. *Culture and Consumption: New Approaches to the Symbolic Character of Consumer Goods and Activities*. Bloomington: Indiana University Press, 1988.

McCracken, Grant D. *Culture and Consumption II: Markets, Meaning, and Brand Management*. Bloomington: Indiana University Press, 2005.

Melnick, Ross, and Andrea Fuchs. *Cinema Treasures: A New Look at Classic Movie Theaters.* St. Paul, MN: MBI Publishing, 2001.

Menager, Arlin. *Embalming Is Not a Sport.* Bloomington, IN: 1st Book Library, 2001.

Mitford, Jessica. *The American Way of Death.* New York: Simon and Schuster, 1963.

Mitford, Jessica. *The American Way of Death Revisited.* New York: Knopf, 1998.

Moller, David Wendell. *Confronting Death: Values, Institutions, and Human Mortality.* Oxford: Oxford University Press, 1996.

Montell, William Lynwood. *Tales from Kentucky Funeral Homes.* Lexington: University Press of Kentucky, 2009.

Morrison, Craig. *Theaters.* New York: Norton, 2005.

Murtagh, William J. *Keeping Time: The History and Theory of Preservation in America.* Pittstown, NJ: Main Street Press, 1988.

Myrdal, Gunnar. *An American Dilemma: The Negro Problem and Modern Democracy.* New York: Harper & Brothers, 1944.

Norberg-Shulz, Christian. *Intentions in Architecture.* Cambridge, MA: MIT Press, 1965.

Northend, Mary Harrod. *The Art of Home Decoration.* New York: Dodd, Mead, 1921.

Osman, Suleiman. *The Invention of Brownstone Brooklyn: Gentrification and the Search for Authenticity in Postwar New York.* Oxford: Oxford University Press, 2011.

Page, Max, and Randall Mason. *Giving Preservation a History: Histories of Historic Preservation in the United States.* New York: Routledge, 2003.

Park, Robert E., Ernest W. Burgess, and Roderick D. McKenzie. *The City.* Chicago: University of Chicago Press, 1925.

Pine, Vanderlyn R. *Caretaker of the Dead: The American Funeral Director.* New York: Irvington, 1975.

Pipkin, James Jefferson. *The Story of a Rising Race: The Negro in Revelation, in History, and in Citizenship.* St. Louis: N. D. Thompson Publishing, 1902.

Prothero, Stephen. *Purified by Fire: A History of Cremation in America.* Berkeley: University of California Press, 2002.

Rains, Albert, and Laurance G. Henderson. *With Heritage So Rich.* New York: Random House, 1966.

Raizman, David. *History of Modern Design.* 2nd ed. Upper Saddle River, NJ: Pearson Prentice Hall, 2011.

Ramsland, Katherine M. *Cemetery Stories: Haunted Graveyards, Embalming Secrets, and the Life of a Corpse after Death.* New York: HarperCollins, 2001.

Reiff, Daniel D. *Houses from Books: Treatises, Pattern Books, and Catalogues in American Architecture, 1738–1950.* University Park: Pennsylvania State University Press, 2000.

Relph, Edward. *The Modern Urban Landscape.* Baltimore: Johns Hopkins University Press, 1987.

Richings, G. F. *Evidence of Progress among Colored People.* Philadelphia: Geo. S. Ferguson Co., 1903.

Roach, Mary. *Stiff: The Curious Lives of Human Cadavers.* New York: Norton, 2004.

Rosenow, Michael K. *Death and Dying in the Working Class, 1865–1920.* Urbana: University of Illinois Press, 2015.

Sandoval-Strausz, A. K. *Hotel: An American History*. New Haven, CT: Yale University Press, 2007.

Schechter, Harold. *The Whole Death Catalog: A Lively Guide to the Bitter End*. New York: Ballantine Books, 2009.

Schlereth, Thomas J. *Material Culture: A Research Guide*. Lawrence: University of Kansas Press, 1985.

Schlereth, Thomas J. *Victorian America: Transformations in Everyday Life, 1876–1915*. New York: HarperCollins, 1991.

Scott, Mel. *American City Planning since 1890: A History Commemorating the 50th Anniversary of the American Institute of Planners*. Berkeley: University of California Press, 1969.

Scott, Mel. *The San Francisco Bay Area: A Metropolis in Perspective*. 2nd ed. Berkeley: University of California Press, 1985.

Seeman, Erik R. *Death in the New World: Cross Cultural Encounters, 1492–1800*. Philadelphia: University of Pennsylvania Press, 2010.

Selket, Kyro. "Bring Home the Dead: Purity and Filth in Contemporary Funeral Homes." In *Dirt: New Geographies of Cleanliness and Contamination*, ed. Ben Campin and Rosie Cox, 49–59. London: I. B. Tauris, 2007.

Sheumaker, Helen, and Shirley Teresa Wajda. *Material Life in America: Understanding Everyday Life*. Santa Barbara, CA: ABC-CLIO, 2008.

Shi, David. *The Simple Life: Plain Living and High Thinking*. Oxford: Oxford University Press, 1985.

Siegan, Bernard H. *Land Use without Zoning*. Lexington, MA: Lexington Books, 1972.

Smeins, Linda E. *Building an American Identity: Pattern Book Homes and Communities, 1870–1900*. Walnut Creek, CA: AltaMira, 1999.

Smith, Ronald G. E. *The Death Care Industries in the United States*. Jefferson, NC: McFarland, 1996.

Smith, Suzanne E. *To Serve the Living: Funeral Directors and the African American Way of Death*. Cambridge, MA: Harvard University Press, 2010.

Sonnichsen, C. L. *Tucson: The Life and Times of an American City*. Norman: University of Oklahoma Press, 1982.

Stannard, David E., ed. *Death in America*. Philadelphia: University of Pennsylvania Press, 1975.

Stevens, Edward Fletcher. *The American Hospital of the Twentieth Century: A Treatise on the Development of Medical Institutions, Both in Europe and in America, Since the Beginning of the Present Century*. New York: Architectural Record, 1918.

Stipe, Robert T. *A Richer Heritage: Historic Preservation in the Twenty-First Century*. Chapel Hill: University of North Carolina, 2003.

Strange, Julie-Marie. *Death, Grief and Poverty in Britain, 1870–1914*. Cambridge: Cambridge University Press, 2005.

Tilley, Christopher, ed. *Reading Material Culture: Structuralism, Hermeneutics, and Post-Structuralism*. London: Basil Blackwell, 1990.

Tyler, Norman. *Historic Preservation: An Introduction to Its History, Principles, and Practice*. New York: Norton, 1994.

Upton, Dell. *Another City: Urban Life and Urban Spaces in the New American Republic.* New Haven, CT: Yale University Press, 2008.

Upton, Dell. *Architecture in the United States.* New York: Oxford University Press, 1998.

Upton, Dell. "Vernacular Domestic Architecture in Eighteenth-Century Virginia." In *Common Places: Readings in American Vernacular Architecture,* ed. Dell Upton and John M. Vlach, 315–35. Athens: University of Georgia Press, 1986.

Vernez Moudon, Anne. *Built for Change: Neighborhood Architecture in San Francisco.* Cambridge, MA: MIT Press, 1986.

Voorsanger, Catherine Hoover, and John K. Howart, eds. *Art and the Empire City: New York, 1825–1861.* New York: Metropolitan Museum of Art, 2000.

Warner, Lloyd W., and Paul S. Lunt. *The Social Life of a Modern Community.* New Haven, CT: Yale University Press, 1941.

Warner, Sam Bass, Jr. *Streetcar Suburbs: The Process of Growth in Boston, 1870–1900.* 2nd ed. Cambridge, MA: Harvard University Press, 1978.

Weiss, Marc A. *The Rise of the Community Builders: The American Real Estate Industry and Urban Land Planning.* New York: Columbia University Press, 1987.

Wells, Robert V. *Facing the 'King of Terrors': Death and Society in an American Community, 1750–1990.* Cambridge: Cambridge University Press, 1999.

Wharton, Edith. *The Decoration of Houses.* New York: Scribner, 1897.

Whitaker, Jan. *Service and Style: How the American Department Store Fashioned the Middle Class.* New York: St. Martin's, 2006.

Williamson, Jefferson. *The American Hotel: An Anecdotal History.* New York: Knopf, 1930.

Wilson, Henry L. *The Bungalow Book.* 5th ed. Mineola, NY: Dover, 2006.

Wright, Agnes Foster. *Interior Decoration for Modern Needs.* New York: Frederick A. Stokes, 1917.

Wright, Gwendolyn. *Building the Dream: A Social History of Housing in America.* New York: Pantheon, 1981.

Wright, Gwendolyn. *Moralism and the Model Home: Domestic Architecture and Cultural Conflict in Chicago.* Chicago: University of Chicago Press, 1980.

INDEX

Page numbers in *italic* refer to illustrations.